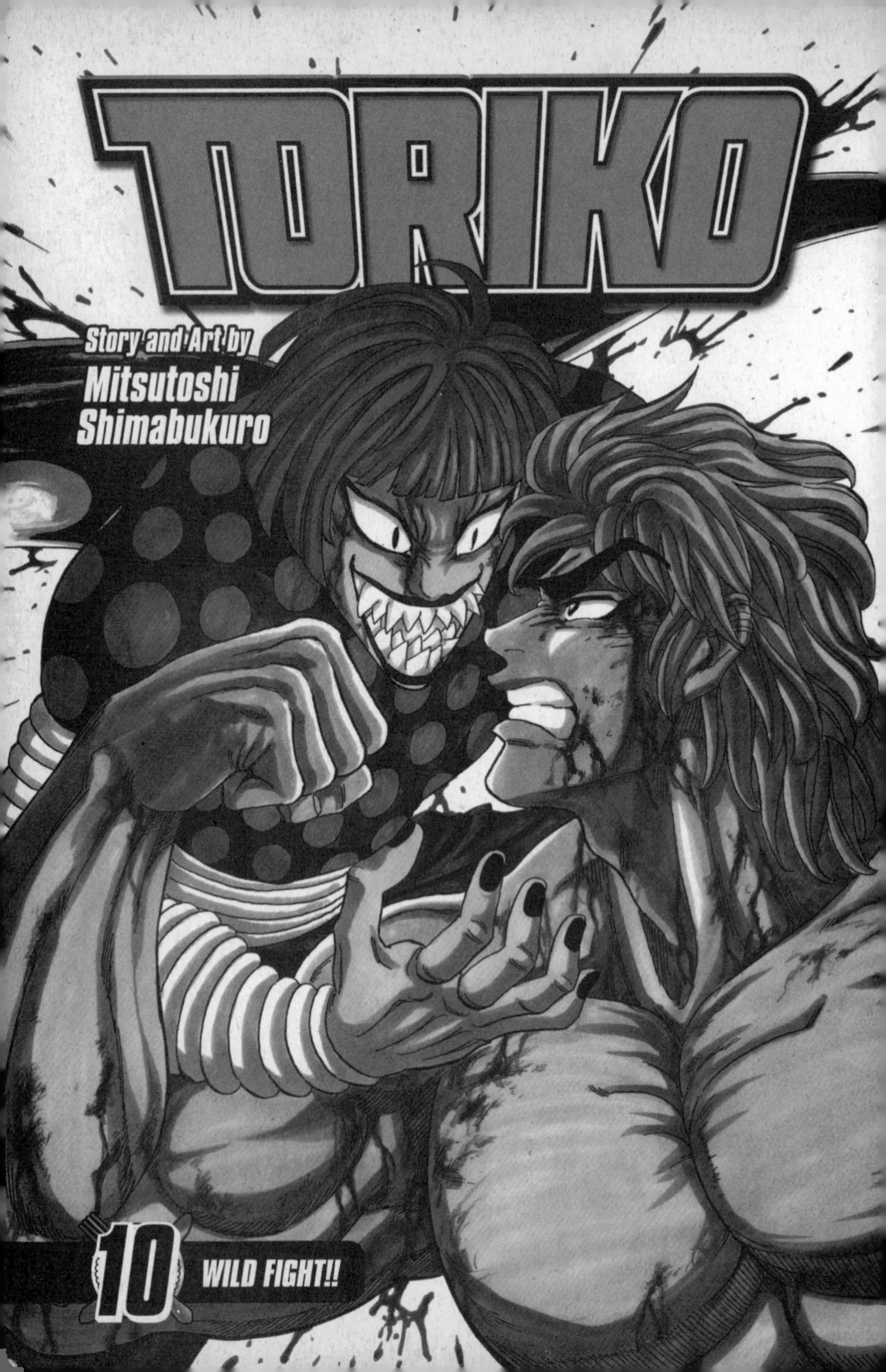
TORIKO
Story and Art by
Mitsutoshi Shimabukuro
10
WILD FIGHT!!

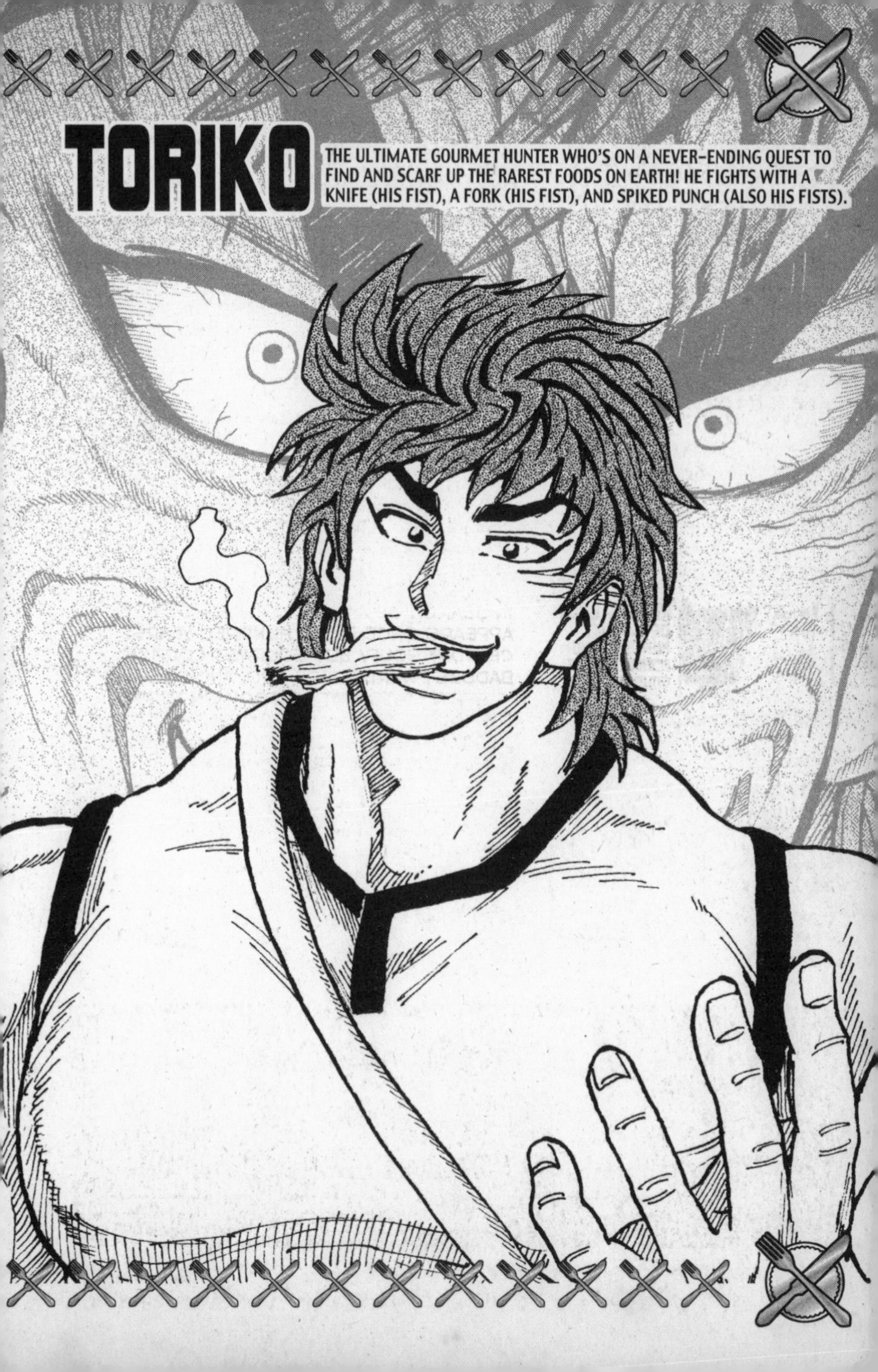
TORIKO
THE ULTIMATE GOURMET HUNTER WHO'S ON A NEVER-ENDING QUEST TO FIND AND SCARF UP THE RAREST FOODS ON EARTH! HE FIGHTS WITH A KNIFE (HIS FIST), A FORK (HIS FIST), AND SPIKED PUNCH (ALSO HIS FISTS).

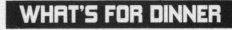

WHAT'S FOR DINNER

IT'S THE AGE OF GOURMET! KOMATSU, THE HEAD CHEF AT THE HOTEL OWNED BY THE IGO (INTERNATIONAL GOURMET ORGANIZATION), BECAME FAST FRIENDS WITH THE LEGENDARY GOURMET HUNTER TORIKO WHILE GATOR HUNTING. NOW KOMATSU ACCOMPANIES TORIKO ON HIS LIFELONG QUEST TO CREATE THE PERFECT FULL-COURSE MEAL.

AN EVIL ORGANIZATION KNOWN AS GOURMET CORP. IS OUT TO GET THE SAME FOODS AS THE IGO! IN THEIR FIRST BIG BATTLE, TORIKO DEFEATED THE GOURMET CORP.'S SUPER STRONG GT ROBOTS TO FILL HIS BELLY WITH JEWEL MEAT.

NEXT, TORIKO AND KOMATSU JOINED AN EXPEDITION WITH TAKIMARU, MATCH, AND A HORDE OF OTHER GOURMET HUNTERS ALL IN SEARCH OF A LEGENDARY SOUP THAT APPEARS ONCE EVERY HUNDRED YEARS: CENTURY SOUP! BUT GOURMET CORP.'S BADDEST WERE THERE TOO, AND BUG-PUPPETEER TOMMYROD TOOK ON TORIKO, THE HUMAN TANK BARRY GAMON WENT AFTER MATCH, AND THE BODYSNATCHING BOGIE WOODS FOUGHT TAKIMARU!

WHILE THEY FIGHT FOR THEIR LIVES, KOMATSU MAKES A BREAK FOR THE SOUP, ONLY TO ENCOUNTER A BIZARRE STRANGER. WHO COULD HE BE...?!

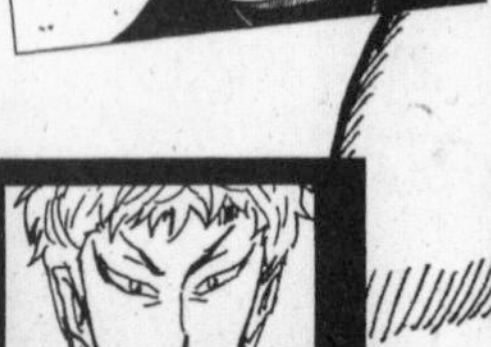
NOW WHAT IN THE WORLD IS THIS?!

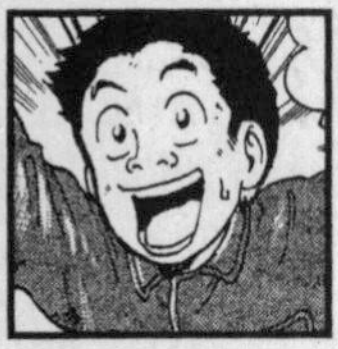

●KOMATSU
IGO HOTEL CHEF AND TORIKO'S #1 FAN.

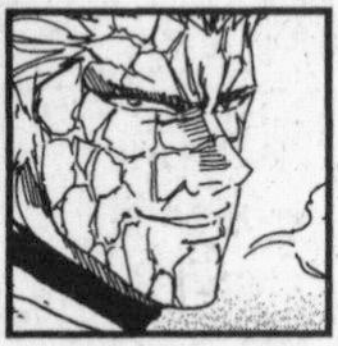

●MATCH
TRIPLE SLICIN' LIEUTENANT OF THE GOURMET MAFIA.

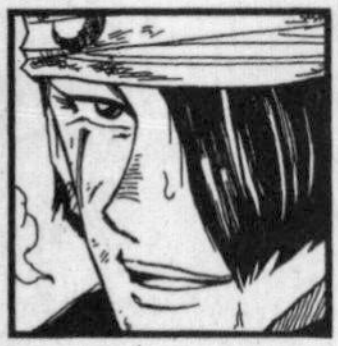

●TAKIMARU
A GOURMET KNIGHT, A GROUP OF GOURMET HUNTERS WHO ADHERE TO THE GOURMET FAITH.

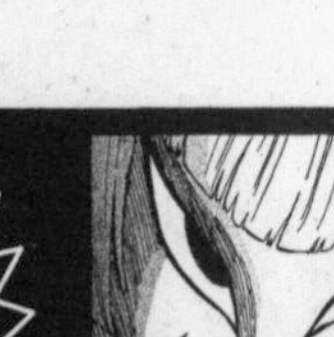

●COLONEL MOKKOI
PRESIDENT OF GOURMART, A COMPANY WITH AN ANNUAL TURNOVER OF TWENTY BILLION. SPONSOR OF THE QUEST FOR CENTURY SOUP.

GOURMET CORP.

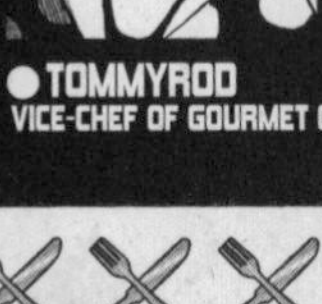

●TOMMYROD
VICE-CHEF OF GOURMET CORP.

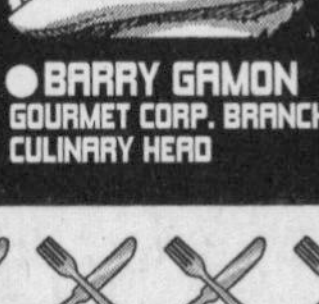

●BARRY GAMON
GOURMET CORP. BRANCH #4 CULINARY HEAD

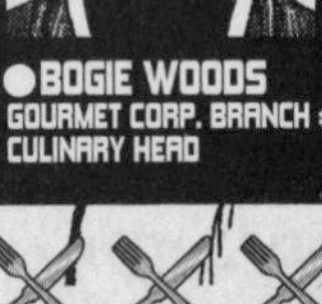

●BOGIE WOODS
GOURMET CORP. BRANCH #5 CULINARY HEAD

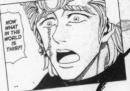

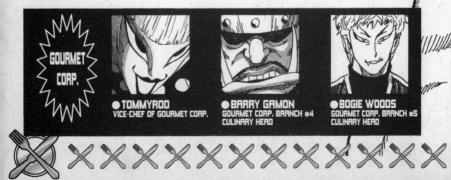

Contents

TORIKO

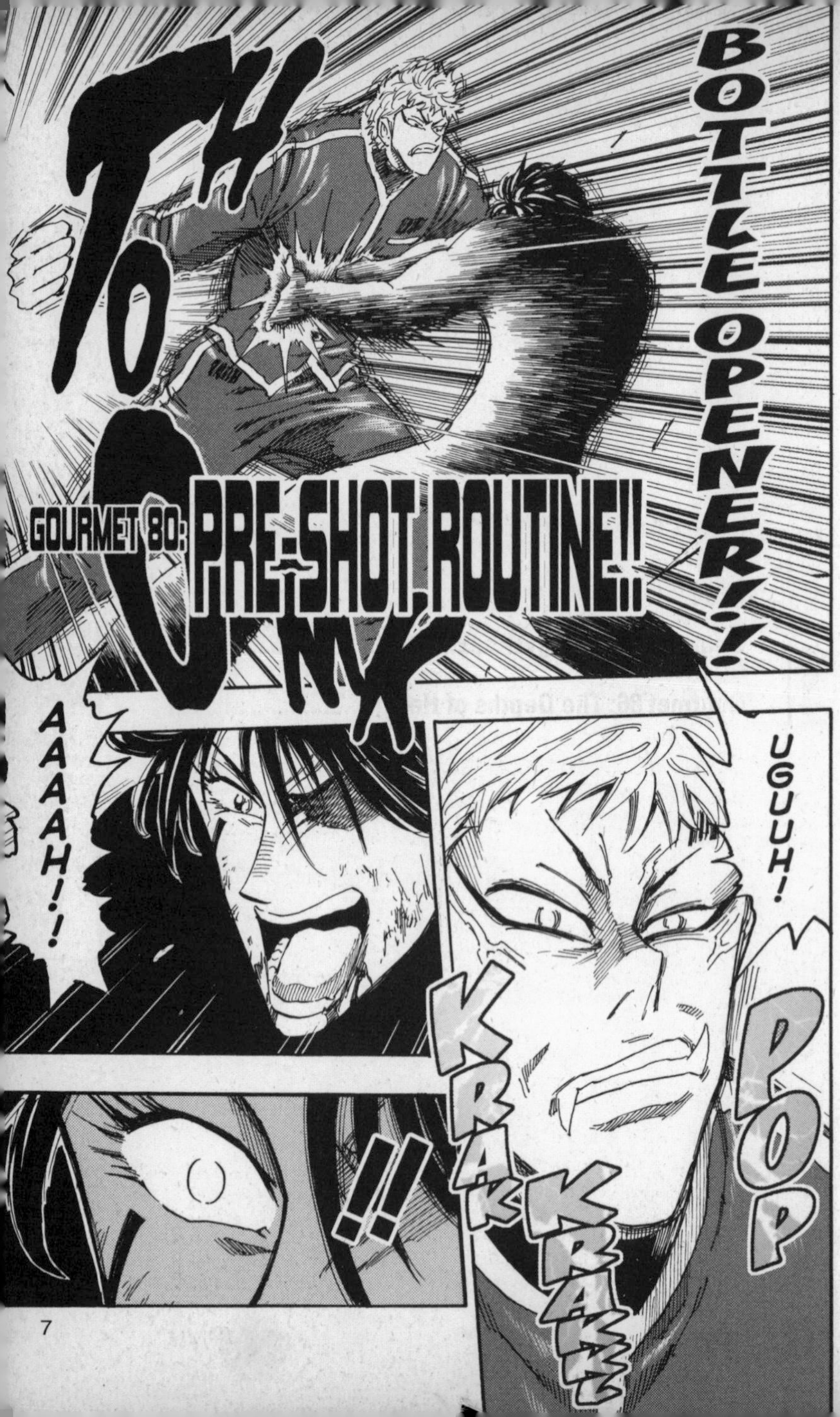
BOTTLE OPENER!!
GOURMET 80: PRE-SHOT ROUTINE!!
UGUUH!
AAAAH!!!
POP
KRAK
KRAKK
!!

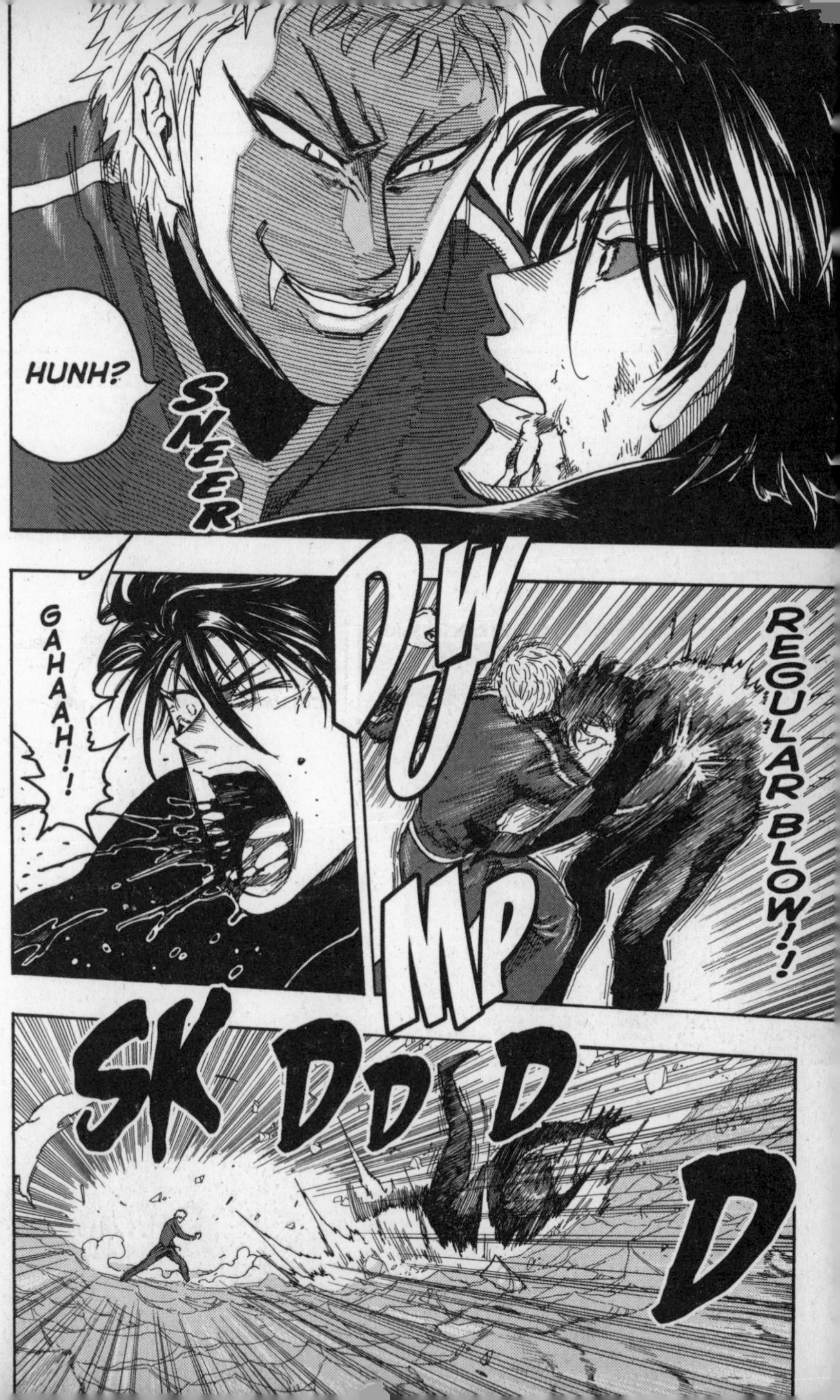
HUNH?
SNEER
REGULAR BLOW!!
DWUMP
GAHAAAH!!
SKDDDD

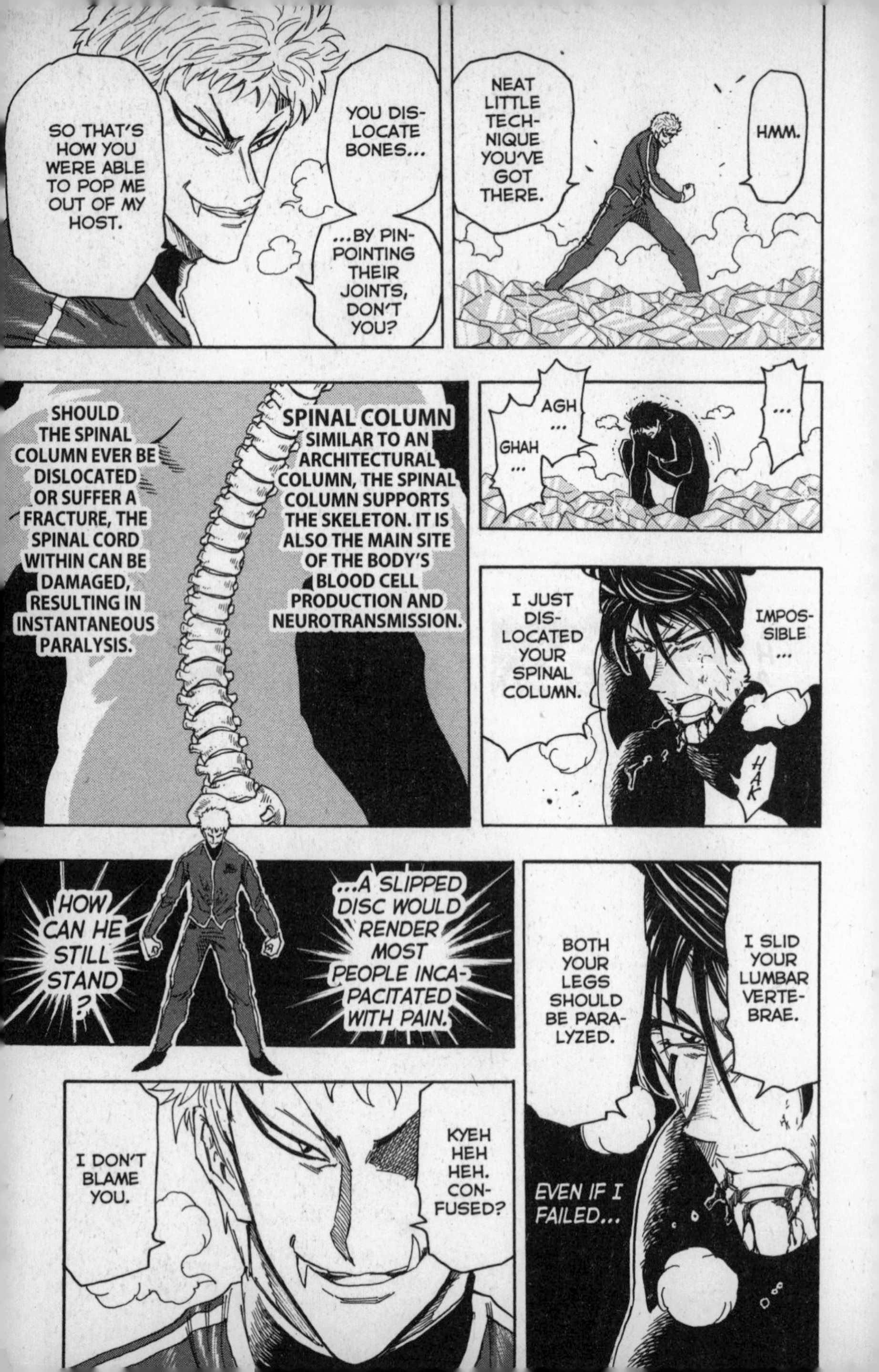
HMM.
NEAT LITTLE TECH-NIQUE YOU'VE GOT THERE.
YOU DIS-LOCATE BONES...
...BY PIN-POINTING THEIR JOINTS, DON'T YOU?
SO THAT'S HOW YOU WERE ABLE TO POP ME OUT OF MY HOST.
...
AGH...
GHAH...
IMPOS-SIBLE...
I JUST DIS-LOCATED YOUR SPINAL COLUMN.
HAK
SPINAL COLUMN
SIMILAR TO AN ARCHITECTURAL COLUMN, THE SPINAL COLUMN SUPPORTS THE SKELETON. IT IS ALSO THE MAIN SITE OF THE BODY'S BLOOD CELL PRODUCTION AND NEUROTRANSMISSION.
SHOULD THE SPINAL COLUMN EVER BE DISLOCATED OR SUFFER A FRACTURE, THE SPINAL CORD WITHIN CAN BE DAMAGED, RESULTING IN INSTANTANEOUS PARALYSIS.
I SLID YOUR LUMBAR VERTE-BRAE.
BOTH YOUR LEGS SHOULD BE PARA-LYZED.
EVEN IF I FAILED...
...A SLIPPED DISC WOULD RENDER MOST PEOPLE INCA-PACITATED WITH PAIN.
HOW CAN HE STILL STAND?
KYEH HEH HEH. CON-FUSED?
I DON'T BLAME YOU.

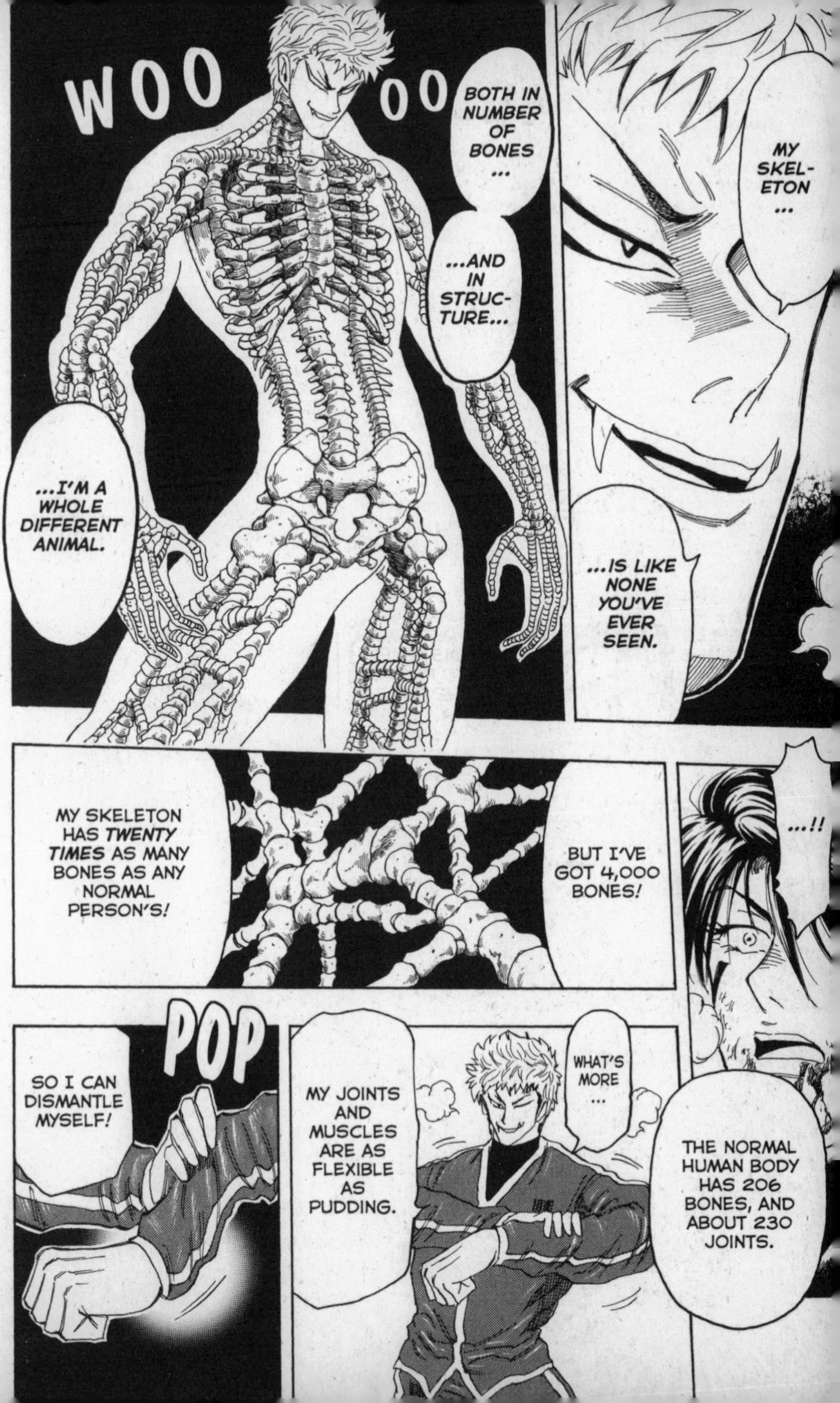
MY SKEL-ETON...
...IS LIKE NONE YOU'VE EVER SEEN.
WOO OO
BOTH IN NUMBER OF BONES...
...AND IN STRUCTURE...
...I'M A WHOLE DIFFERENT ANIMAL.
...!!
THE NORMAL HUMAN BODY HAS 206 BONES, AND ABOUT 230 JOINTS.
BUT I'VE GOT 4,000 BONES!
MY SKELETON HAS *TWENTY TIMES* AS MANY BONES AS ANY NORMAL PERSON'S!
WHAT'S MORE...
MY JOINTS AND MUSCLES ARE AS FLEXIBLE AS PUDDING.
POP
SO I CAN DISMANTLE MYSELF!

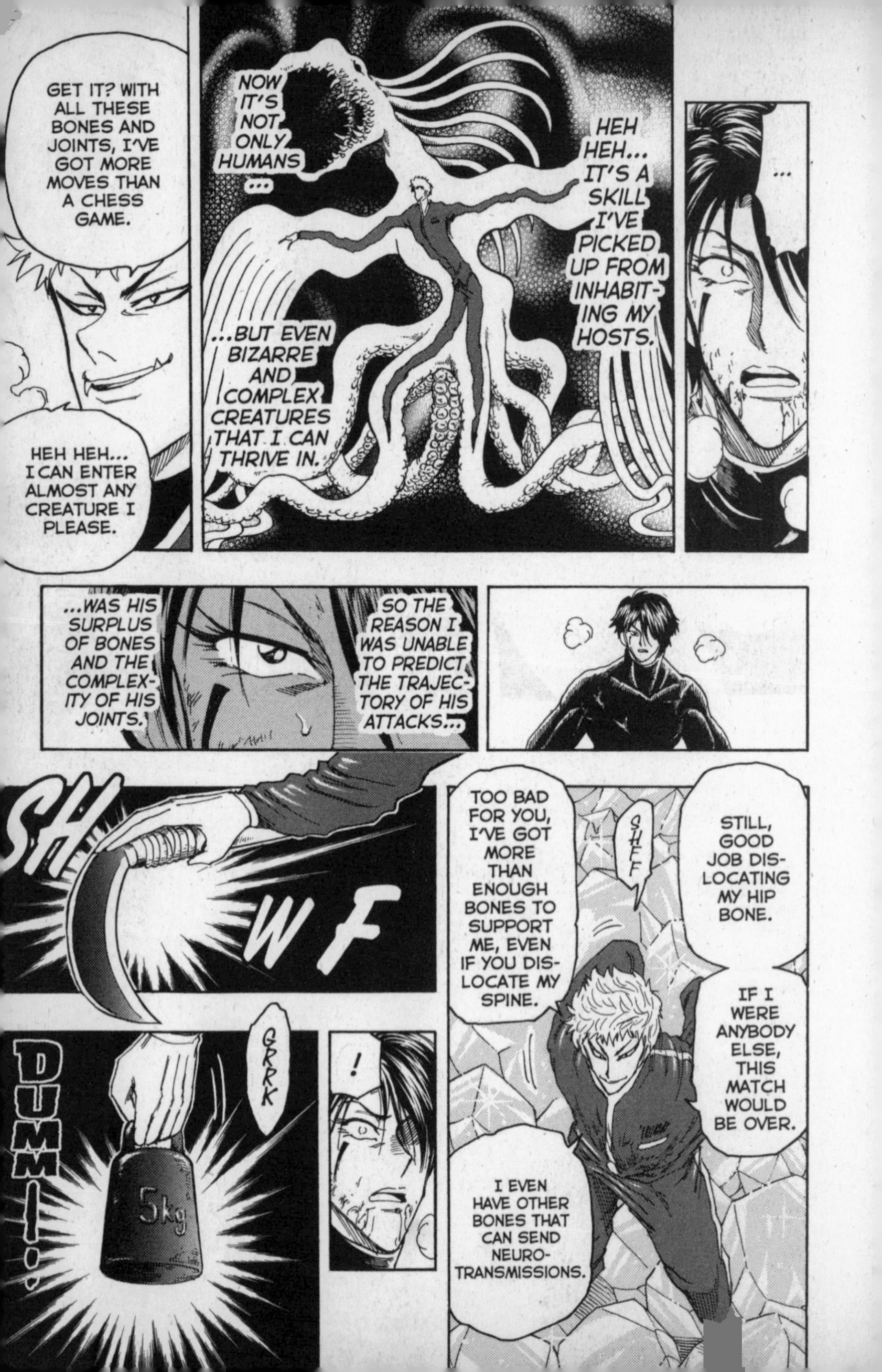
...
HEH HEH... IT'S A SKILL I'VE PICKED UP FROM INHABITING MY HOSTS.
NOW IT'S NOT ONLY HUMANS...
...BUT EVEN BIZARRE AND COMPLEX CREATURES THAT I CAN THRIVE IN.
GET IT? WITH ALL THESE BONES AND JOINTS, I'VE GOT MORE MOVES THAN A CHESS GAME.
HEH HEH... I CAN ENTER ALMOST ANY CREATURE I PLEASE.
SO THE REASON I WAS UNABLE TO PREDICT THE TRAJECTORY OF HIS ATTACKS...
...WAS HIS SURPLUS OF BONES AND THE COMPLEXITY OF HIS JOINTS.
STILL, GOOD JOB DISLOCATING MY HIP BONE.
IF I WERE ANYBODY ELSE, THIS MATCH WOULD BE OVER.
SHFF
TOO BAD FOR YOU, I'VE GOT MORE THAN ENOUGH BONES TO SUPPORT ME, EVEN IF YOU DISLOCATE MY SPINE.
I EVEN HAVE OTHER BONES THAT CAN SEND NEURO-TRANSMISSIONS.
SH
WF
!
GRRK
DUMM!!
5kg

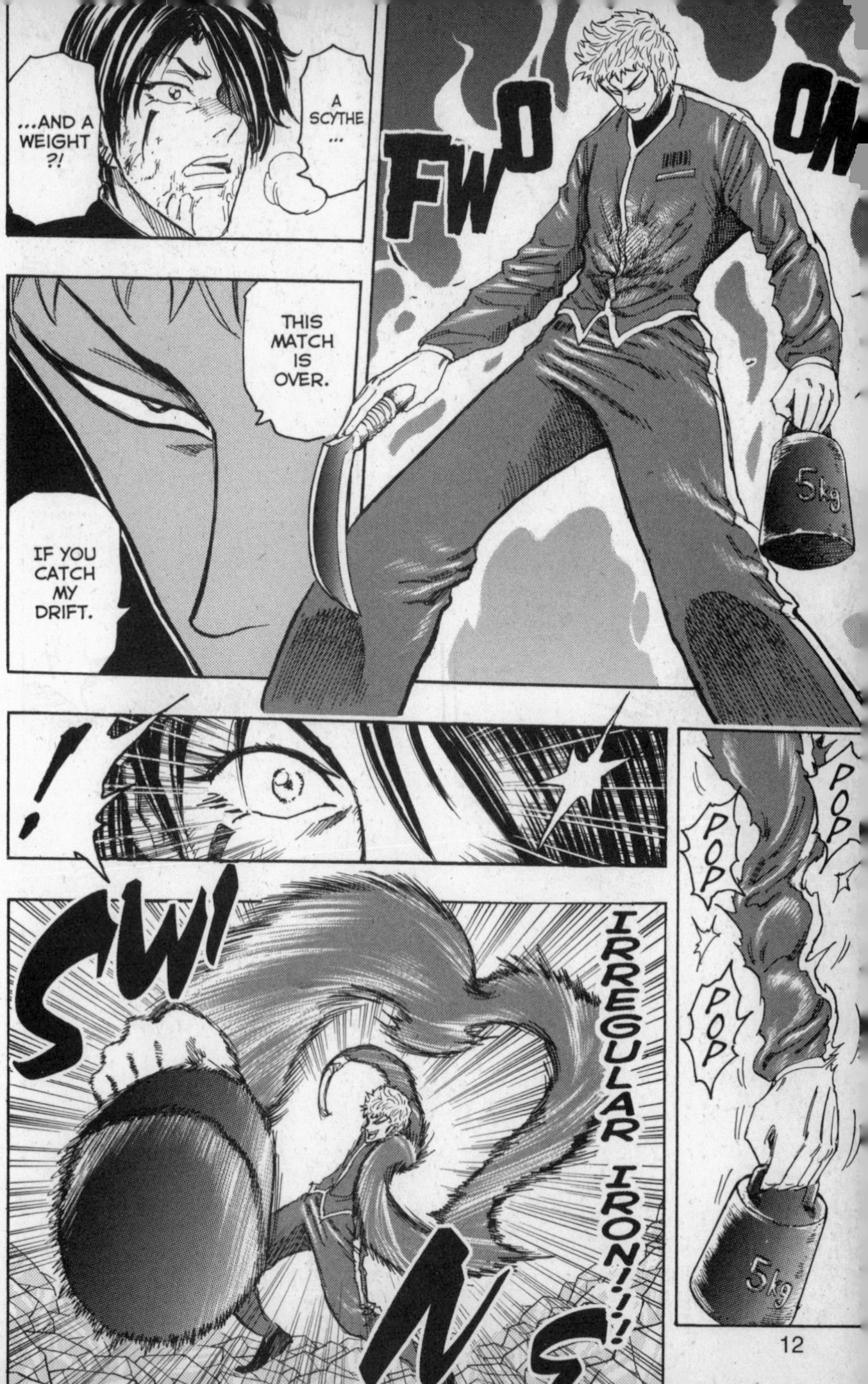
FWOOM
A SCYTHE ...
...AND A WEIGHT ?!
THIS MATCH IS OVER.
IF YOU CATCH MY DRIFT.
POP POP
POP POP
POP POP
!
SWING
IRREGULAR IRON!!!

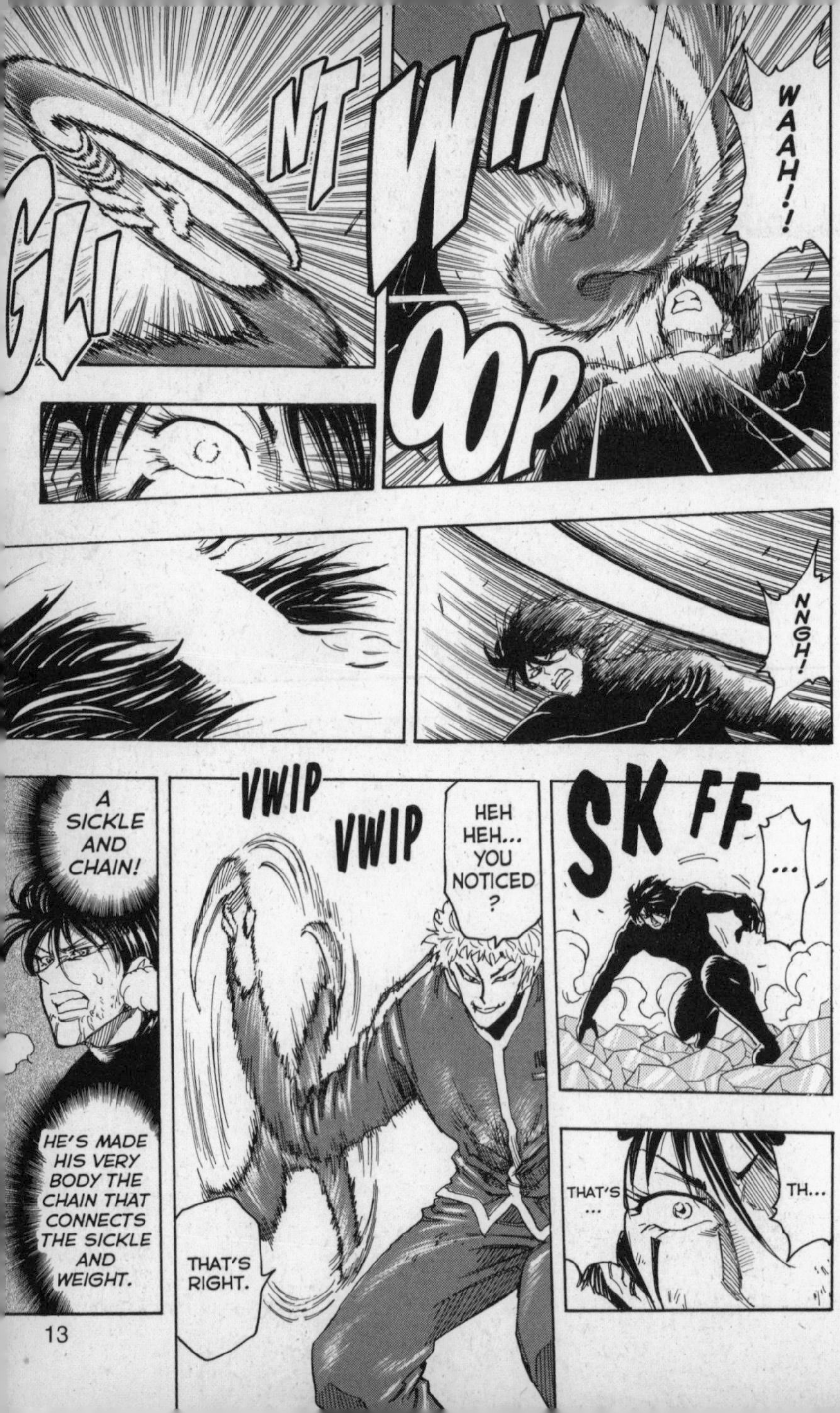
WAAAH!!
WHOOP
GLINT
NNGH!
SKFF
...
TH...
THAT'S ...
VWIP
VWIP
HEH HEH... YOU NOTICED?
THAT'S RIGHT.
A SICKLE AND CHAIN!
HE'S MADE HIS VERY BODY THE CHAIN THAT CONNECTS THE SICKLE AND WEIGHT.

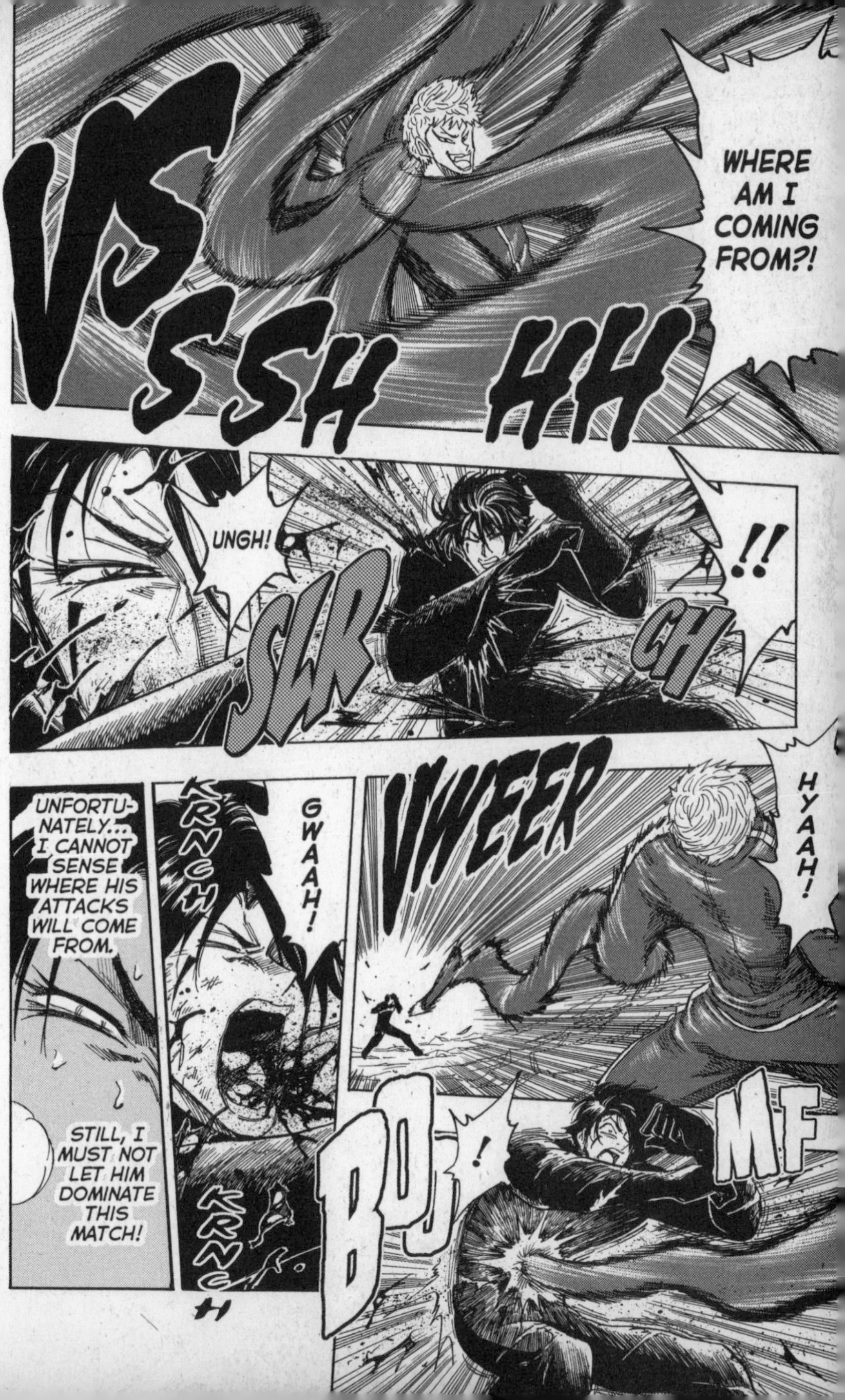
WHERE AM I COMING FROM?!
VSSSH HH
!!
UNGH!
SLURCH
HYAAH!
VWEER
GWAAH!
KRNCH
UNFORTU-NATELY... I CANNOT SENSE WHERE HIS ATTACKS WILL COME FROM.
BOMF
!
KRNCH
STILL, I MUST NOT LET HIM DOMINATE THIS MATCH!

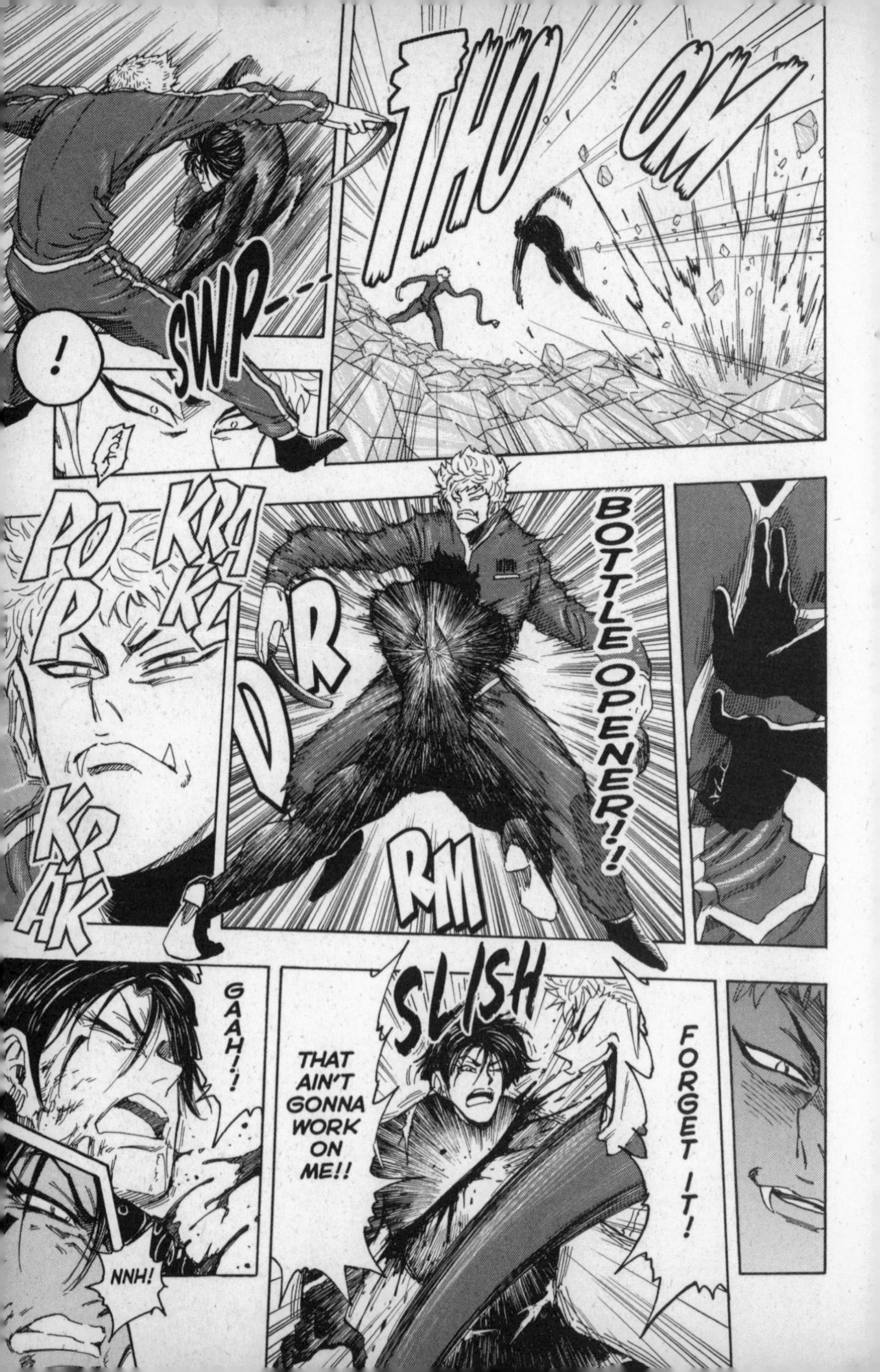
THO
OM
SWP---
!
ACK
BOTTLE OPENER!!
R
D
RM
KRA
KL
PO
P
KR
AK
FORGET IT!
SLISH
THAT AIN'T GONNA WORK ON ME!!
GAAH!!
NNH!

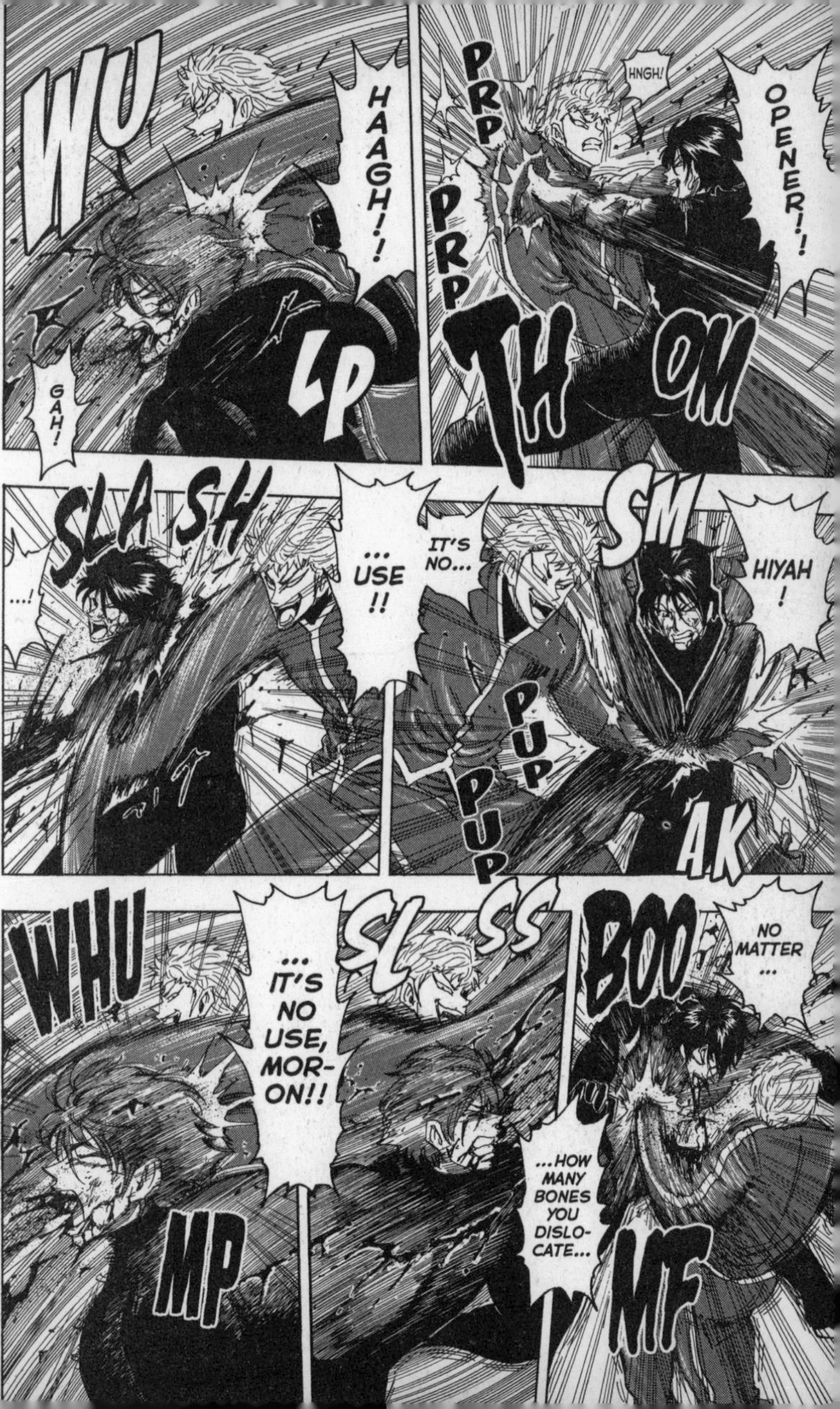
HNGH!
OPENER!!
PRP PRP PRP
TH OM
HAAGH!!
WU LP
GAH!
SM AK
HIYAH!
IT'S NO...
PUP PUP
PUP PUP
...USE!!
SLASH
...!
BOO MF
NO MATTER...
...HOW MANY BONES YOU DISLOCATE...
SL SS
...IT'S NO USE, MORON!!
WHU MP

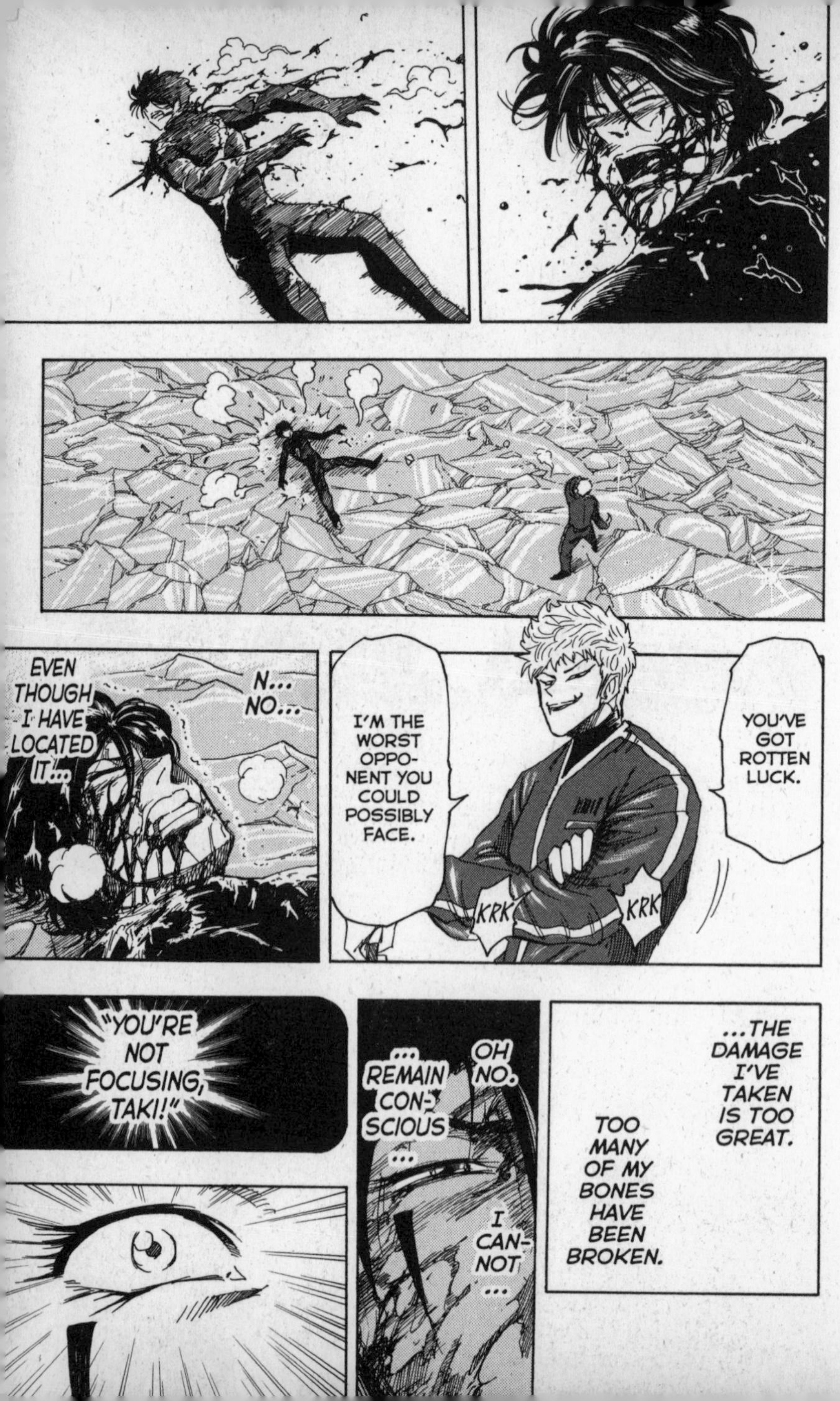
YOU'VE GOT ROTTEN LUCK.
I'M THE WORST OPPONENT YOU COULD POSSIBLY FACE.
KRK
KRK
N... NO...
EVEN THOUGH I HAVE LOCATED IT...
...THE DAMAGE I'VE TAKEN IS TOO GREAT.
TOO MANY OF MY BONES HAVE BEEN BROKEN.
OH NO.
...REMAIN CONSCIOUS...
I CANNOT...
"YOU'RE NOT FOCUSING, TAKI!"

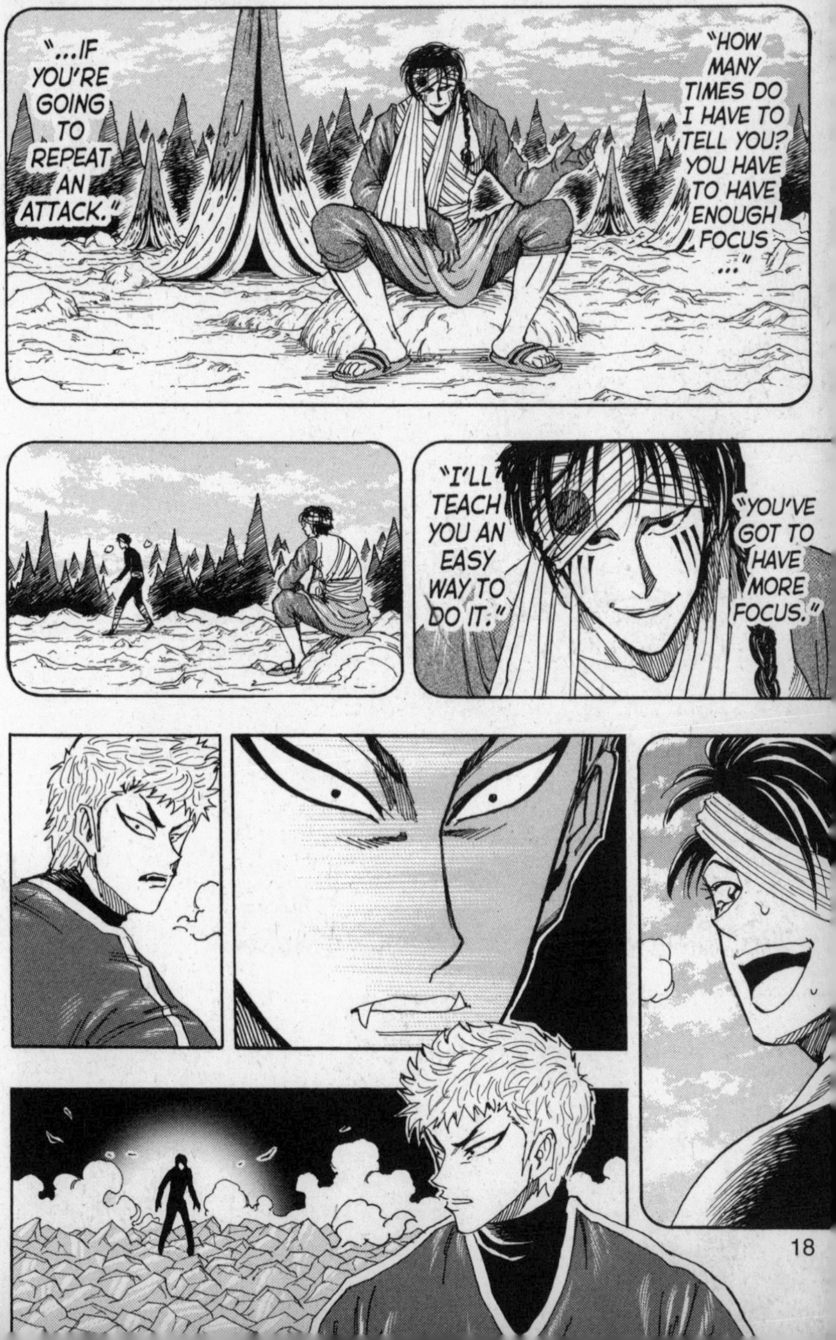
"HOW MANY TIMES DO I HAVE TO TELL YOU? YOU HAVE TO HAVE ENOUGH FOCUS ..."
"...IF YOU'RE GOING TO REPEAT AN ATTACK."
"YOU'VE GOT TO HAVE MORE FOCUS."
"I'LL TEACH YOU AN EASY WAY TO DO IT."

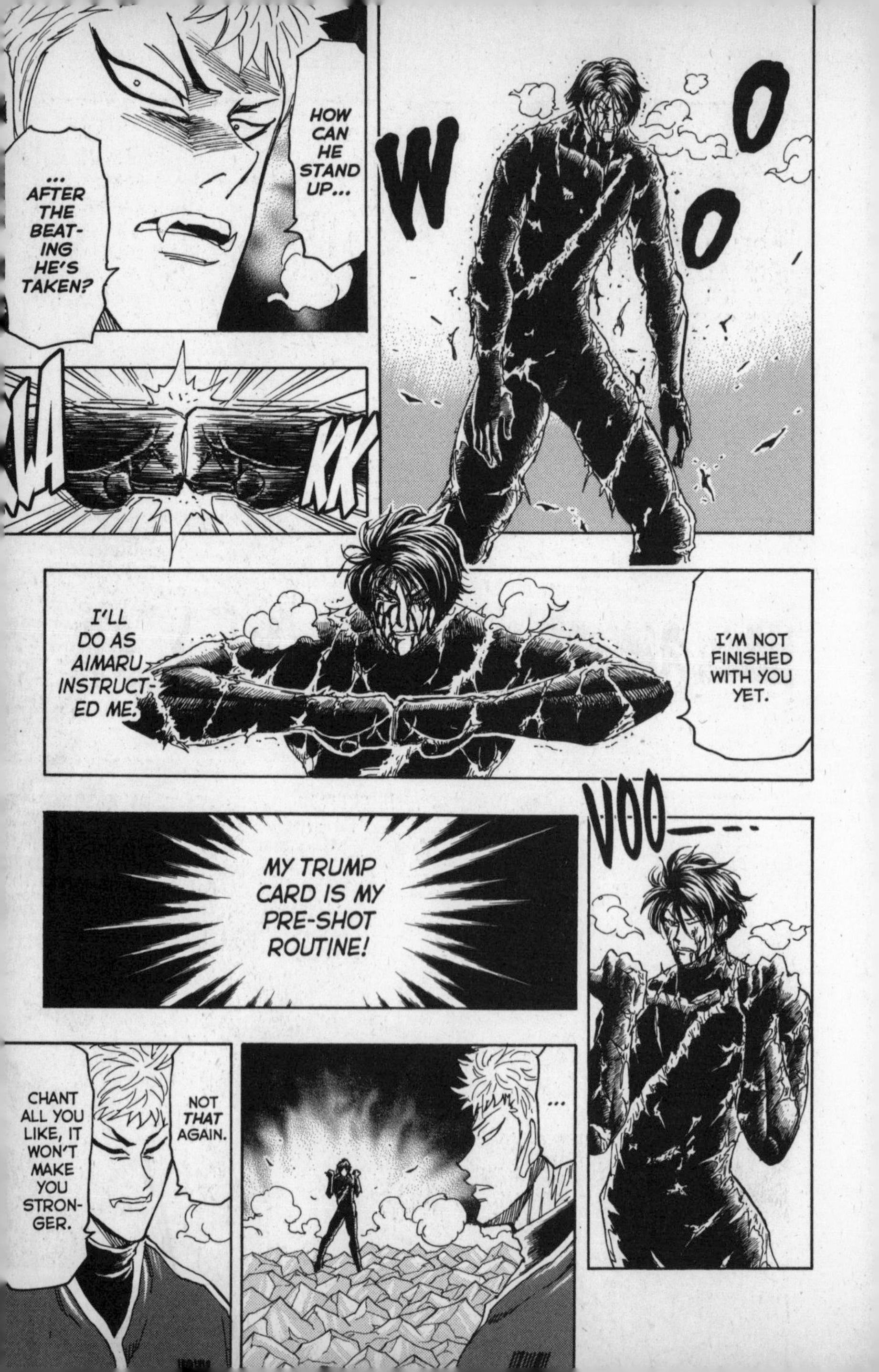
WOOO
HOW CAN HE STAND UP...
...AFTER THE BEATING HE'S TAKEN?
LAKK
I'M NOT FINISHED WITH YOU YET.
I'LL DO AS AIMARU INSTRUCTED ME.
VOO—
MY TRUMP CARD IS MY PRE-SHOT ROUTINE!
...
NOT *THAT* AGAIN.
CHANT ALL YOU LIKE, IT WON'T MAKE YOU STRONGER.

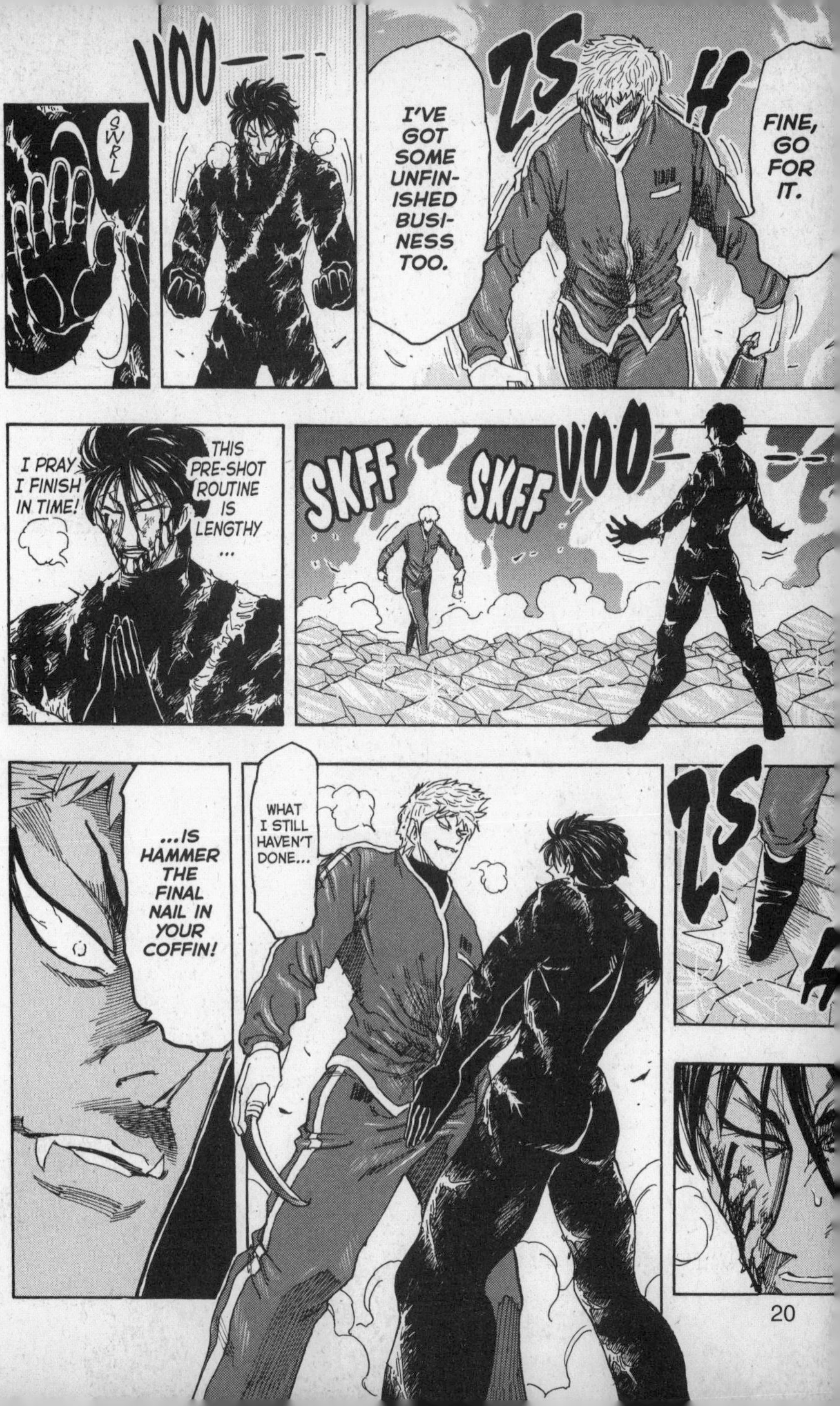
ZS
H
FINE, GO FOR IT.
I'VE GOT SOME UNFIN-ISHED BUSI-NESS TOO.
VOO—
SWRL
VOO—
SKFF
SKFF
THIS PRE-SHOT ROUTINE IS LENGTHY ...
I PRAY I FINISH IN TIME!
ZS
WHAT I STILL HAVEN'T DONE...
...IS HAMMER THE FINAL NAIL IN YOUR COFFIN!

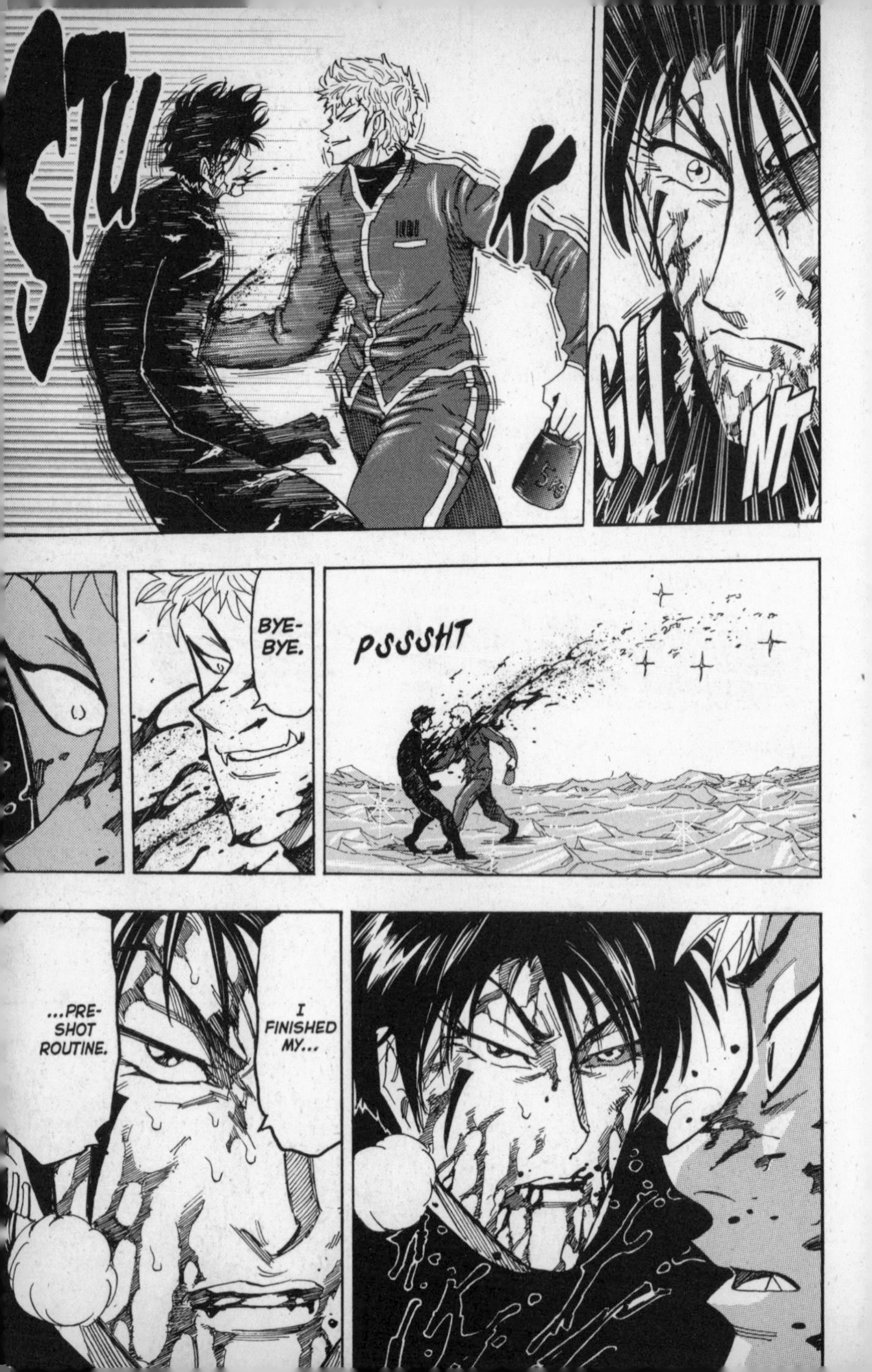
GLINT
STUK
PSSSHT
BYE-BYE.
I FINISHED MY...
...PRE-SHOT ROUTINE.

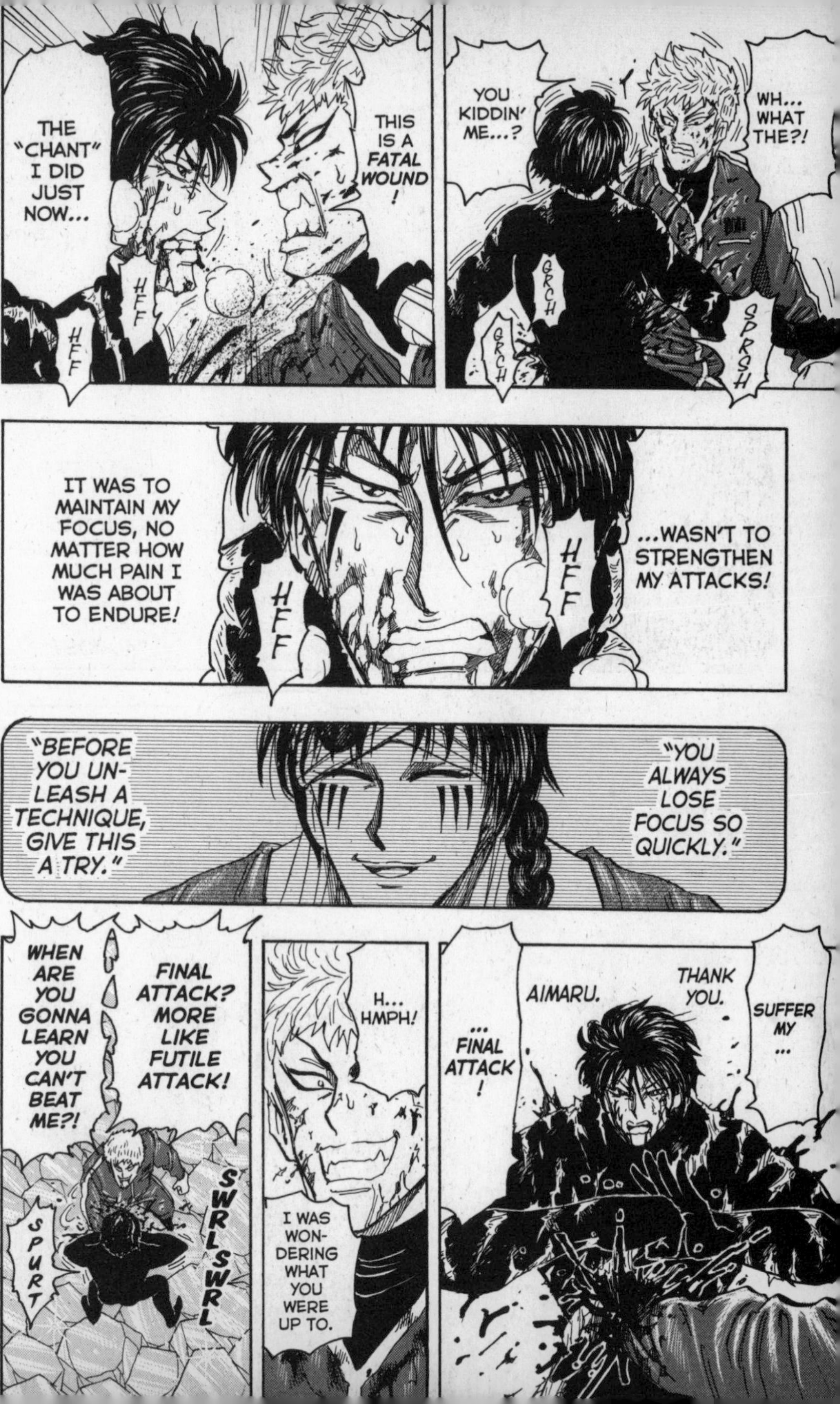
WH... WHAT THE?!
YOU KIDDIN' ME...?
GRCH
GRCH
SPRSH
THIS IS A FATAL WOUND!
THE "CHANT" I DID JUST NOW...
HFF
HFF
...WASN'T TO STRENGTHEN MY ATTACKS!
IT WAS TO MAINTAIN MY FOCUS, NO MATTER HOW MUCH PAIN I WAS ABOUT TO ENDURE!
HFF
HFF
"YOU ALWAYS LOSE FOCUS SO QUICKLY."
"BEFORE YOU UN-LEASH A TECHNIQUE, GIVE THIS A TRY."
SUFFER MY ...
THANK YOU.
AIMARU.
... FINAL ATTACK!
H... HMPH!
I WAS WON-DERING WHAT YOU WERE UP TO.
FINAL ATTACK? MORE LIKE FUTILE ATTACK!
WHEN ARE YOU GONNA LEARN YOU CAN'T BEAT ME?!
SWRL SWRL
SPURT

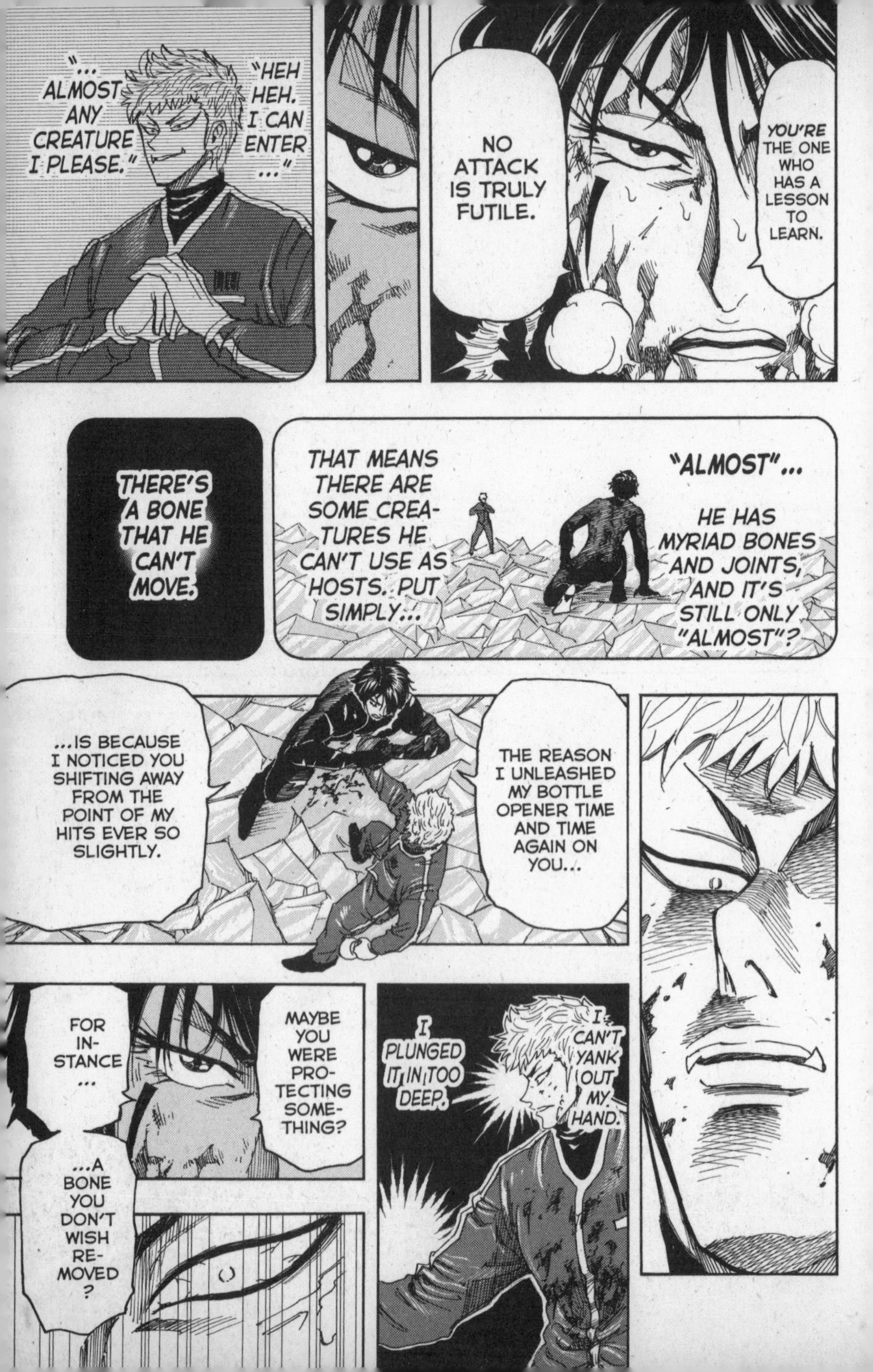
YOU'RE THE ONE WHO HAS A LESSON TO LEARN.
NO ATTACK IS TRULY FUTILE.
"HEH HEH. I CAN ENTER ..."
"... ALMOST ANY CREATURE I PLEASE."
"ALMOST"...
HE HAS MYRIAD BONES AND JOINTS, AND IT'S STILL ONLY "ALMOST"?
THAT MEANS THERE ARE SOME CREA- TURES HE CAN'T USE AS HOSTS. PUT SIMPLY...
THERE'S A BONE THAT HE CAN'T MOVE.
THE REASON I UNLEASHED MY BOTTLE OPENER TIME AND TIME AGAIN ON YOU...
...IS BECAUSE I NOTICED YOU SHIFTING AWAY FROM THE POINT OF MY HITS EVER SO SLIGHTLY.
I CAN'T YANK OUT MY HAND.
I PLUNGED IT IN TOO DEEP.
MAYBE YOU WERE PRO- TECTING SOME- THING?
FOR IN- STANCE ...
...A BONE YOU DON'T WISH RE- MOVED ?

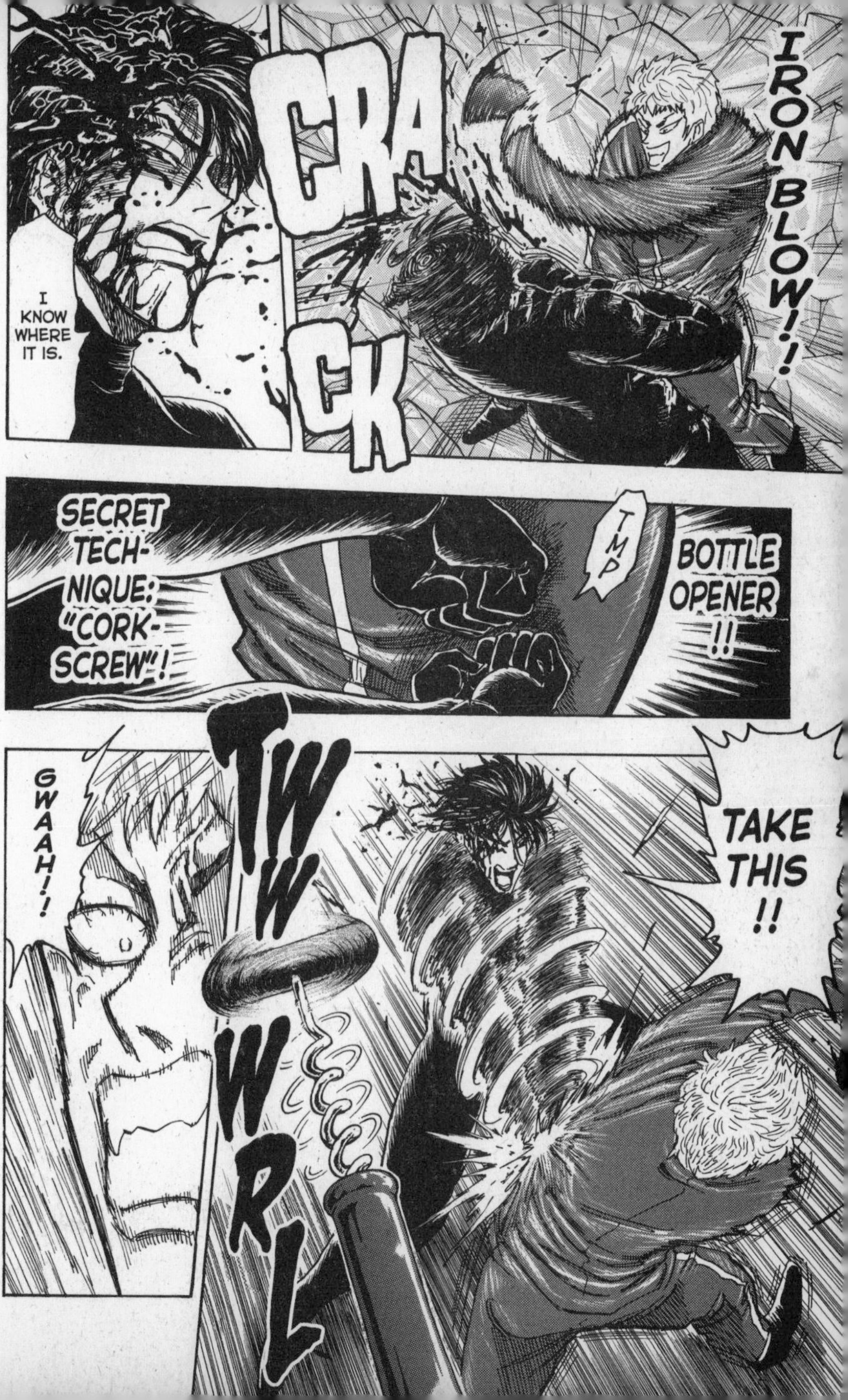
IRON BLOW!!
CRACK
I KNOW WHERE IT IS.
BOTTLE OPENER!!
TMP
SECRET TECHNIQUE: "CORKSCREW"!
TAKE THIS!!
TWWWRL
GWAAH!!

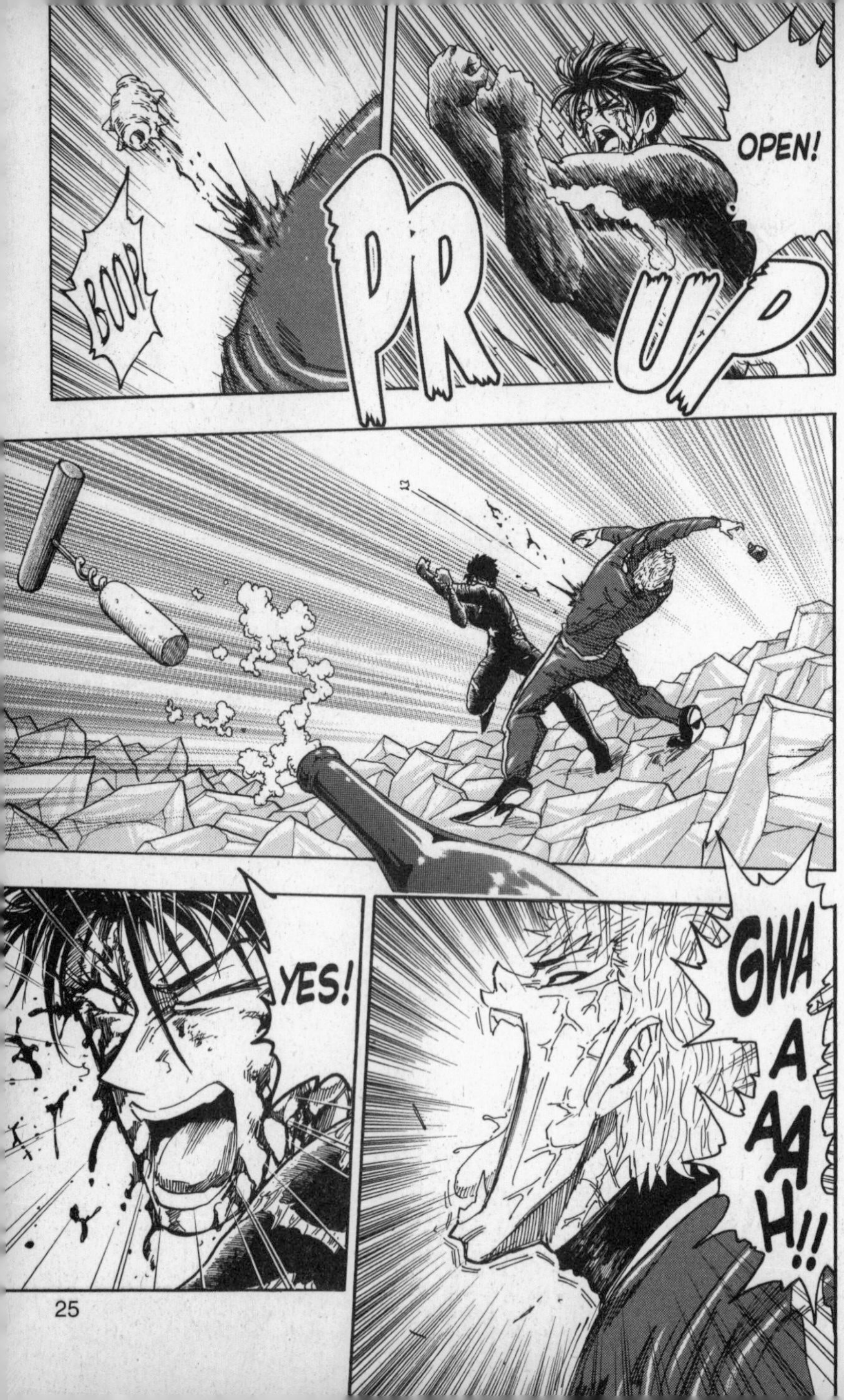
OPEN!
PR UP
BOOP
GWAAAH!!
YES!

TORIKO

GOURMET CHECKLIST

Vol. 078

JACK ELEPHANT
(INSECT-BEAST)

CAPTURE LEVEL: 85

HABITAT: UNKNOWN

LENGTH: 35 METERS

HEIGHT: ---

WEIGHT: 18 TONS

PRICE: NO VALUE AS A FOODSTUFF

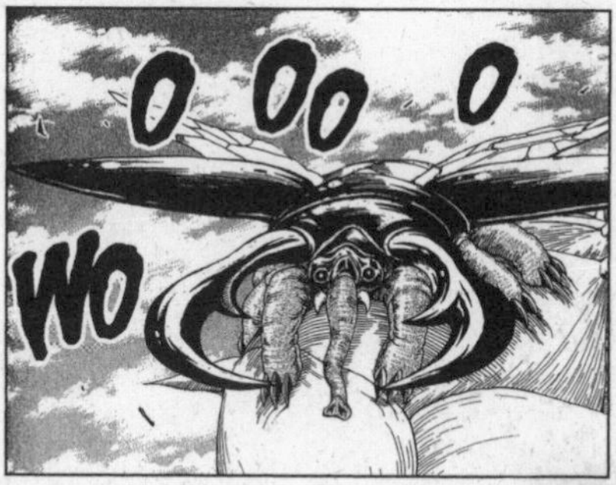
WO
O OO O

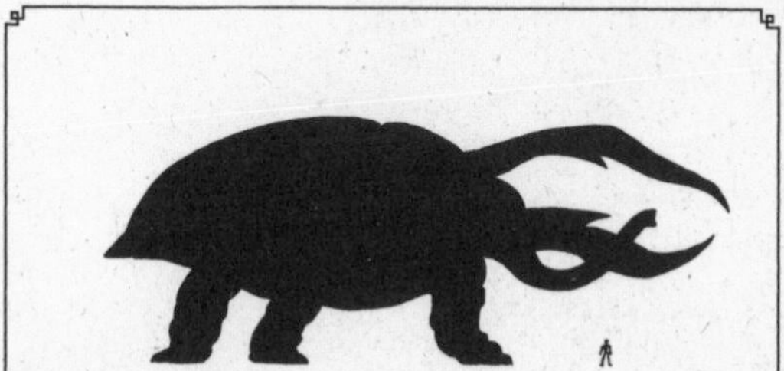

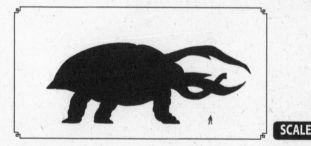

SCALE

VICE-CHEF OF GOURMET CORP., GRINPATCH, KEEPS THIS ELEPHANT-STAG BEETLE HYBRID AS A PET. ITS PINCERS CAN CLEAVE A SKYSCRAPER IN TWO; ITS SHELL IS TOUGH AS AN ELEPHANT'S HIDE AND A STAG BEETLE'S ARMOR-LIKE EXOSKELETON COMBINED. DESPITE ITS MASS, THE JACK ELEPHANT'S WINGS BEAT AT AN INCREDIBLE SPEED AND IT CAN TAKE TO THE AIR LIKE A JUMBO JET. WITH SERIOUS OFFENSIVE, DEFENSIVE, AND FLIGHT CAPABILITIES, THIS MOBILE FIGHTING MACHINE IS THE WHOLE PACKAGE!

GOURMET 81: BIG BLAST!!

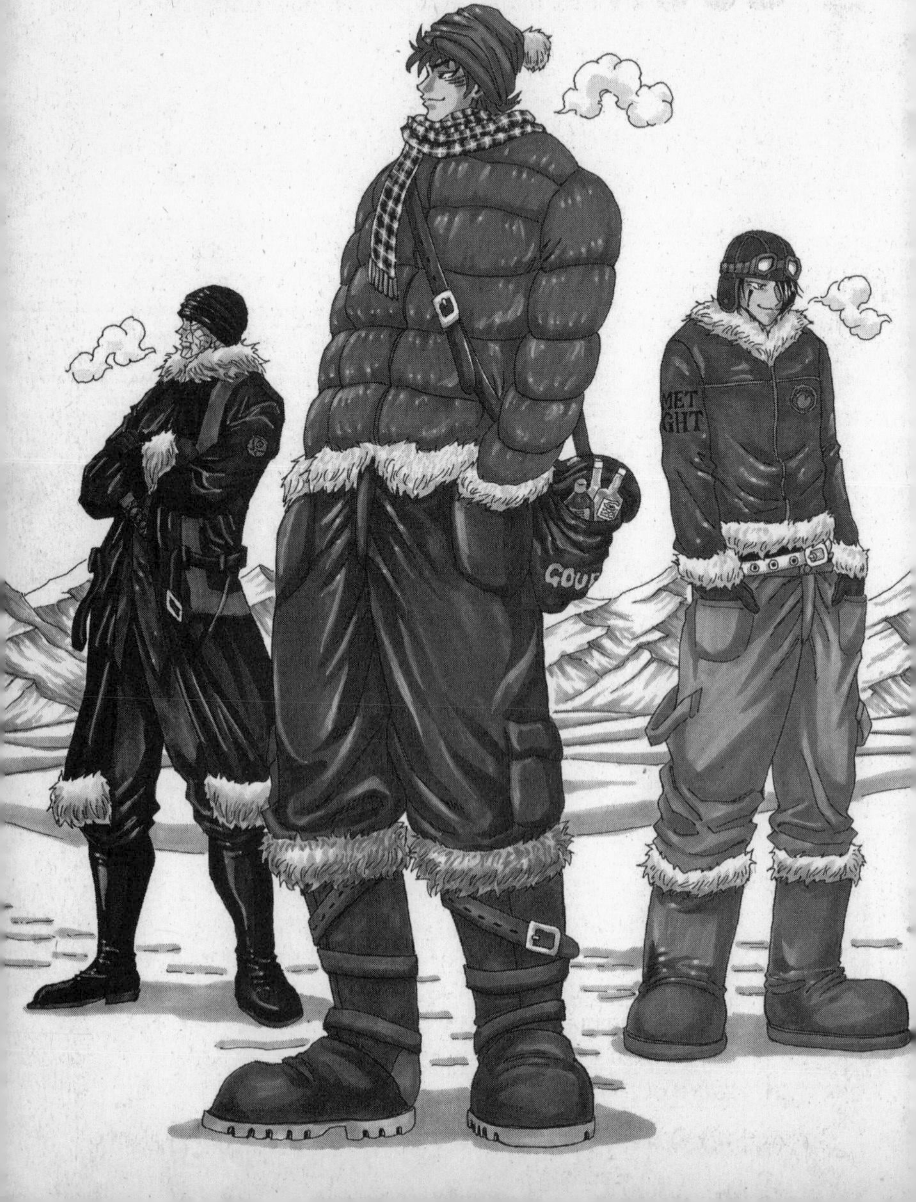

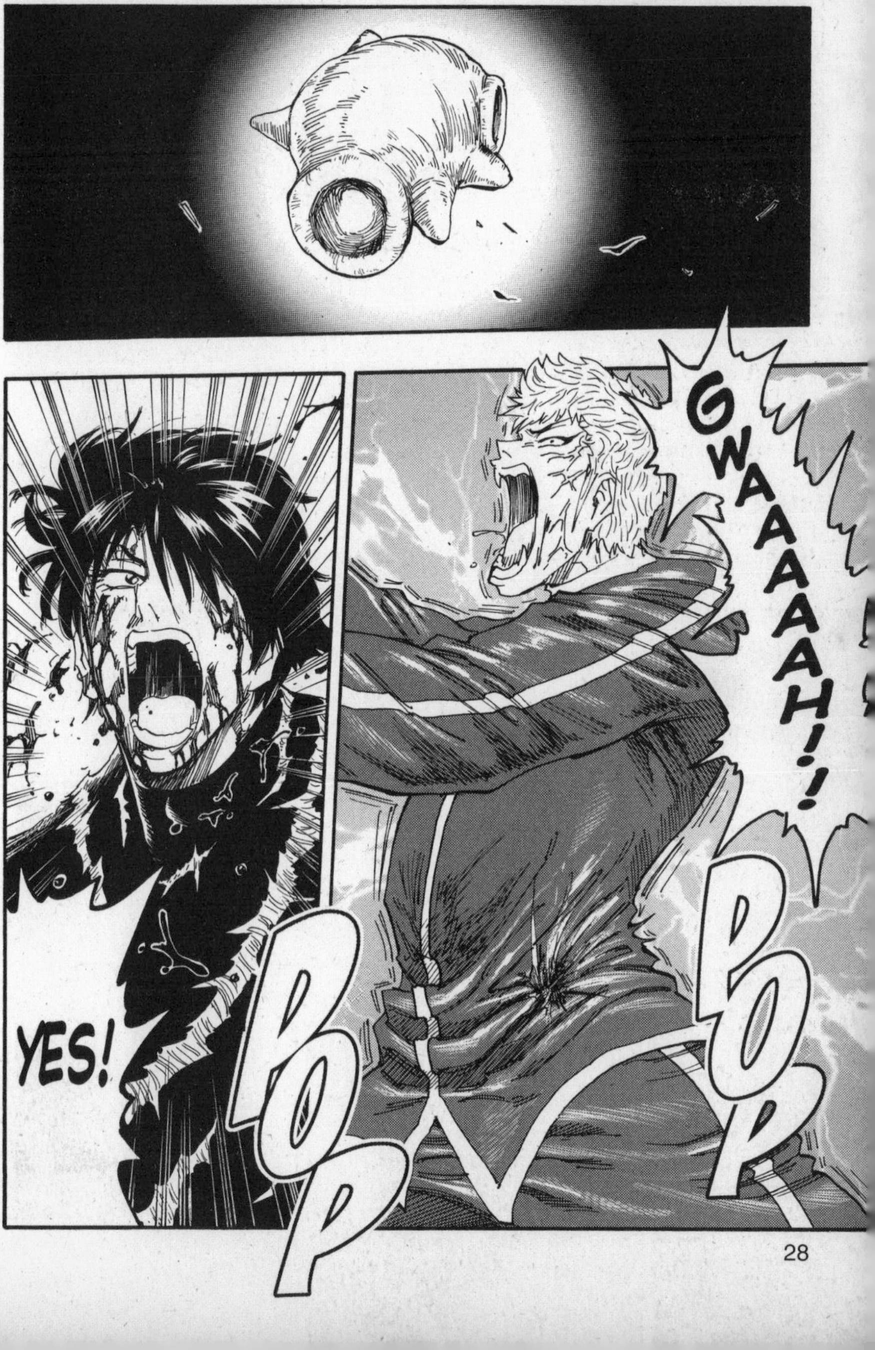
GWAAAAAH!!
POP
YES!
POP

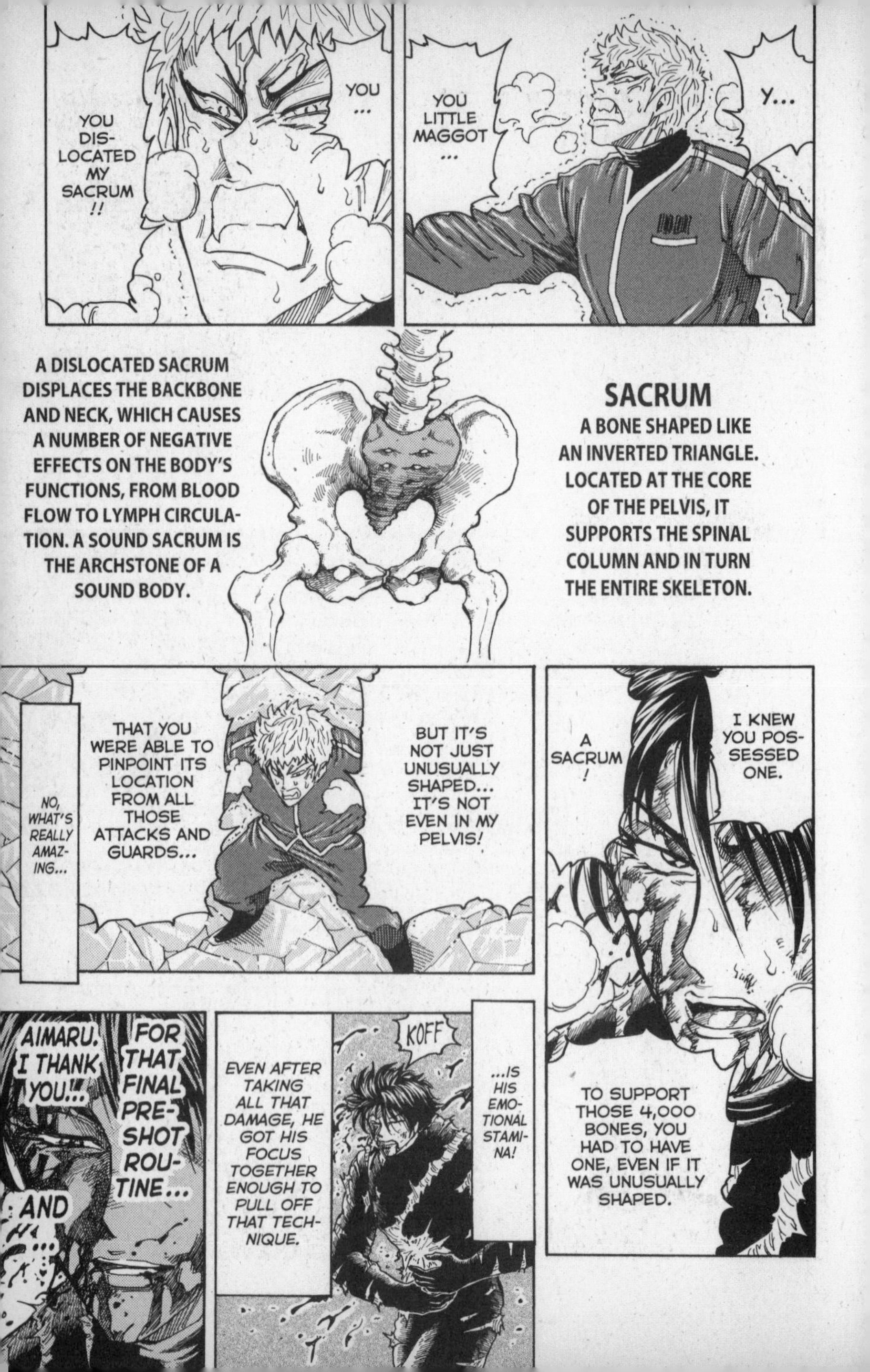
Y...
YOU LITTLE MAGGOT ...
YOU ...
YOU DIS-LOCATED MY SACRUM !!
SACRUM
A BONE SHAPED LIKE AN INVERTED TRIANGLE. LOCATED AT THE CORE OF THE PELVIS, IT SUPPORTS THE SPINAL COLUMN AND IN TURN THE ENTIRE SKELETON.
A DISLOCATED SACRUM DISPLACES THE BACKBONE AND NECK, WHICH CAUSES A NUMBER OF NEGATIVE EFFECTS ON THE BODY'S FUNCTIONS, FROM BLOOD FLOW TO LYMPH CIRCULA-TION. A SOUND SACRUM IS THE ARCHSTONE OF A SOUND BODY.
I KNEW YOU POS-SESSED ONE.
A SACRUM !
TO SUPPORT THOSE 4,000 BONES, YOU HAD TO HAVE ONE, EVEN IF IT WAS UNUSUALLY SHAPED.
BUT IT'S NOT JUST UNUSUALLY SHAPED... IT'S NOT EVEN IN MY PELVIS!
THAT YOU WERE ABLE TO PINPOINT ITS LOCATION FROM ALL THOSE ATTACKS AND GUARDS...
NO, WHAT'S REALLY AMAZ-ING...
...IS HIS EMO-TIONAL STAMI-NA!
KOFF
EVEN AFTER TAKING ALL THAT DAMAGE, HE GOT HIS FOCUS TOGETHER ENOUGH TO PULL OFF THAT TECH-NIQUE.
FOR THAT FINAL PRE-SHOT ROU-TINE...
AIMARU. I THANK YOU!!
AND

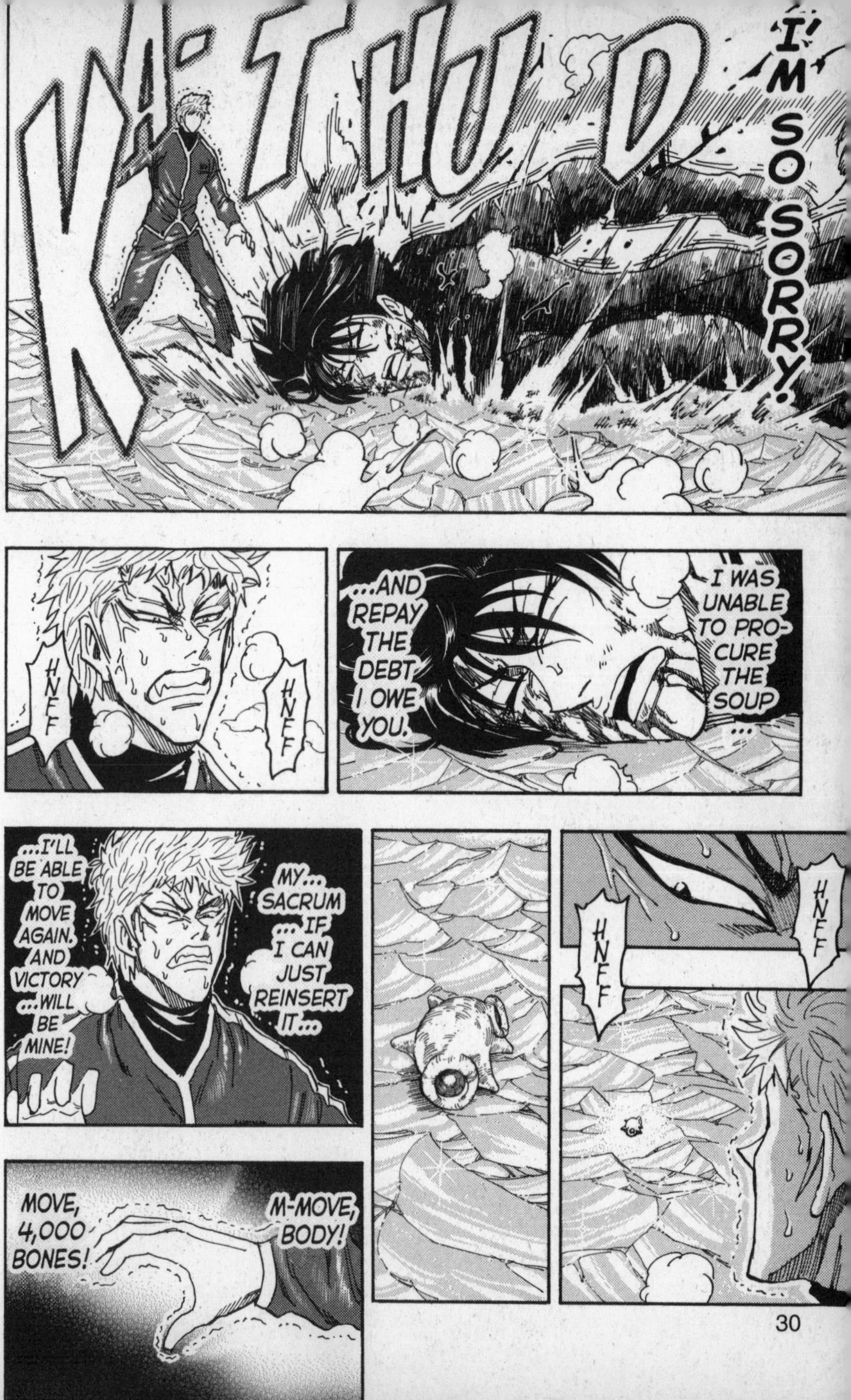
I'M SO SORRY!
KA-THUD
I WAS UNABLE TO PRO-CURE THE SOUP...
...AND REPAY THE DEBT I OWE YOU.
HNFF
HNFF
HNFF
HNFF
MY... SACRUM ...IF I CAN JUST REINSERT IT...
...I'LL BE ABLE TO MOVE AGAIN. AND VICTORY ...WILL BE MINE!
M-MOVE, BODY!
MOVE, 4,000 BONES!

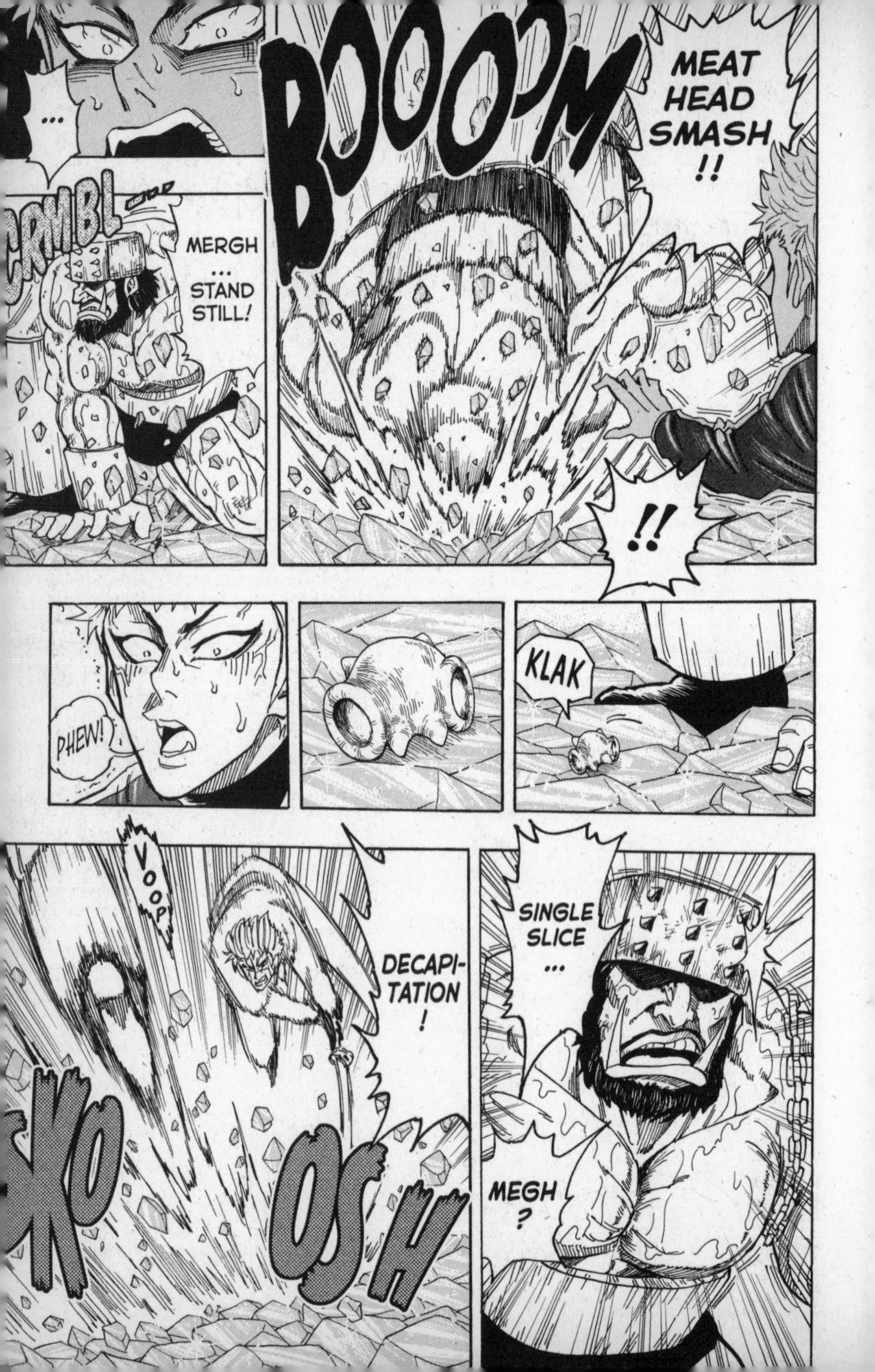
MEAT HEAD SMASH !!
BOOOM
!!
...
CRMBL
MERGH ... STAND STILL!
KLAK
PHEW!
SINGLE SLICE ...
MEGH ?
VOOOP
DECAPITATION !
KOOSH

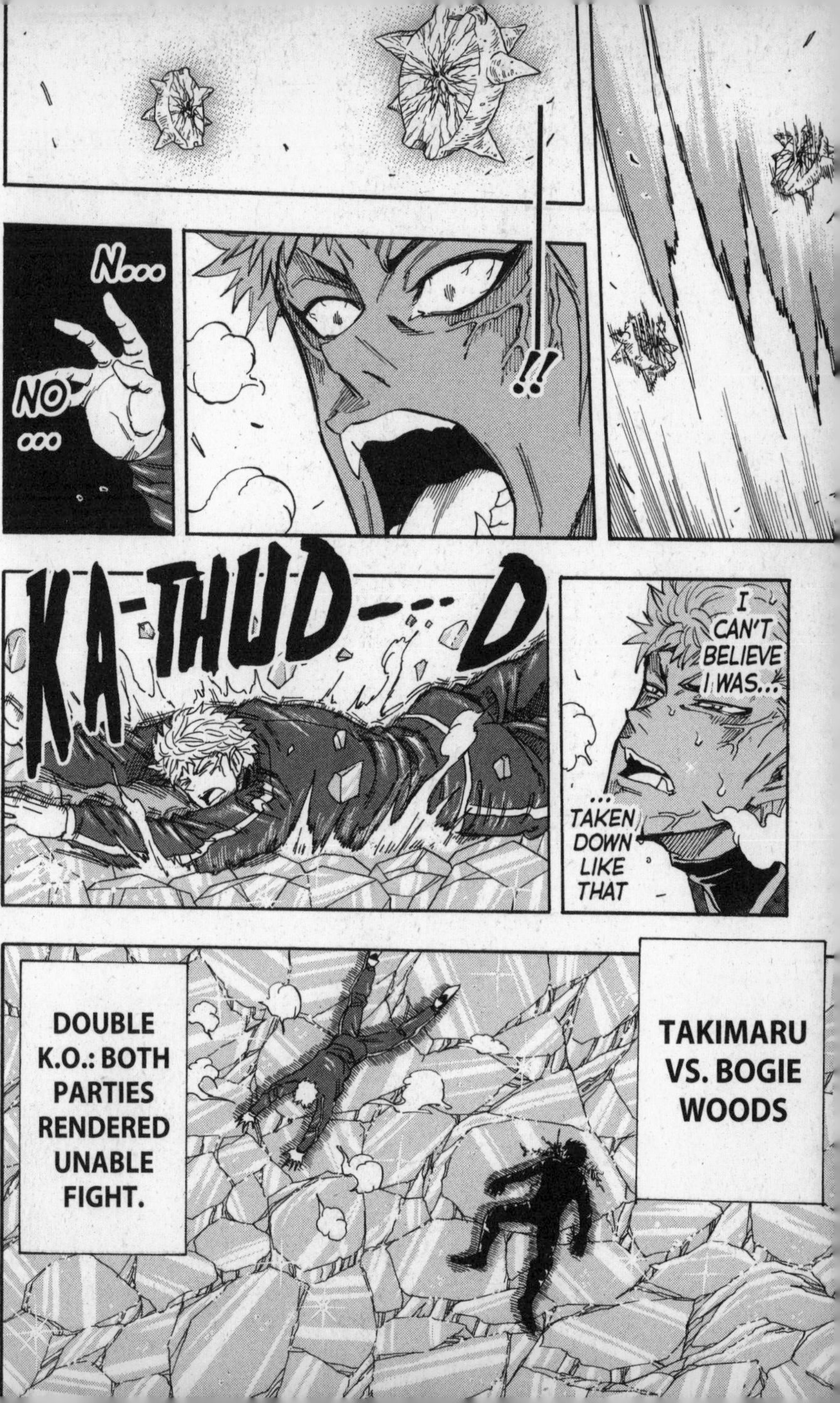
!!
N...
NO
...
I CAN'T BELIEVE I WAS...
...TAKEN DOWN LIKE THAT
KA-THUD---D
TAKIMARU VS. BOGIE WOODS
DOUBLE K.O.: BOTH PARTIES RENDERED UNABLE FIGHT.

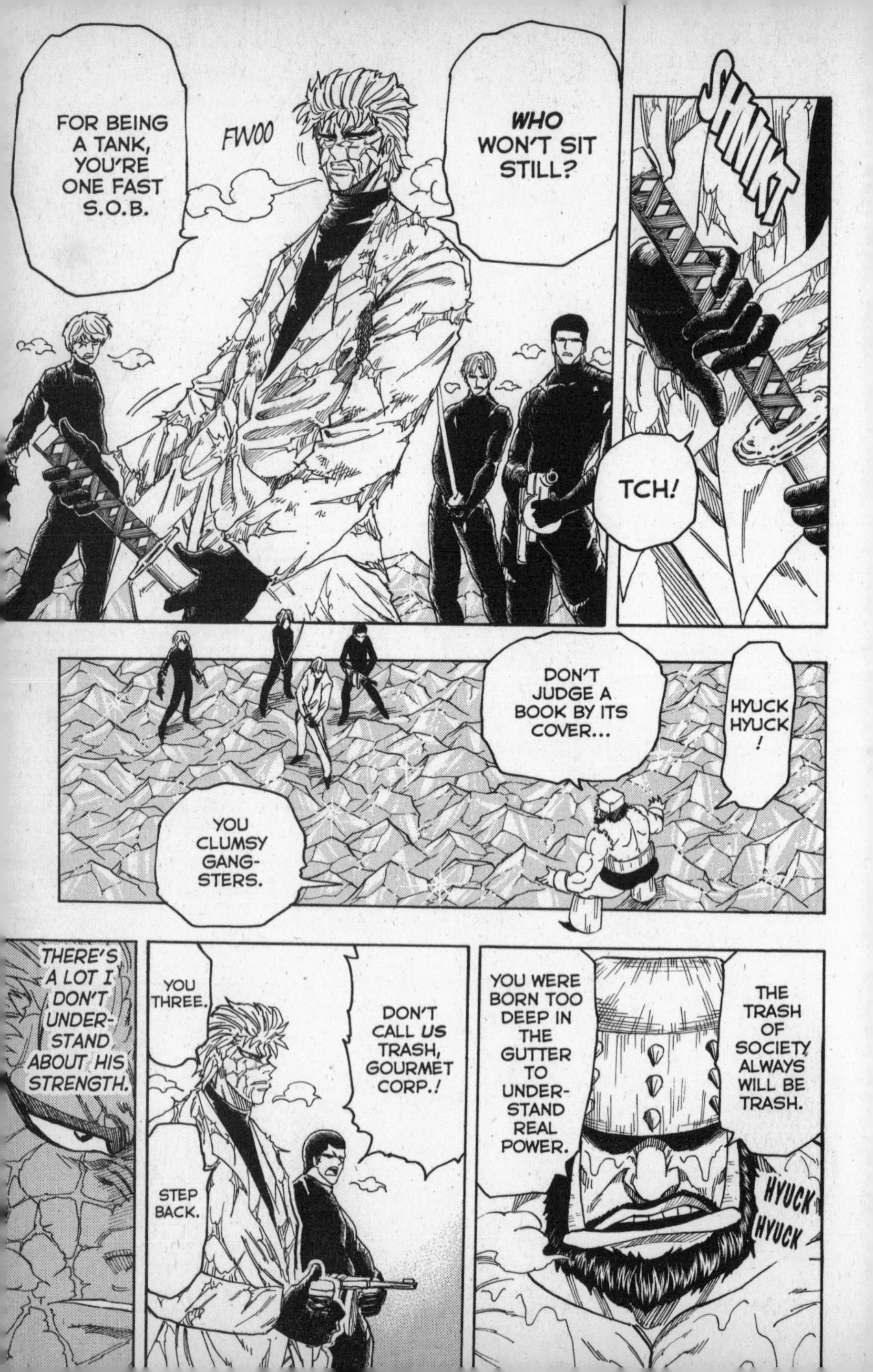
SHNKT
TCH!
WHO WON'T SIT STILL?
FWOO
FOR BEING A TANK, YOU'RE ONE FAST S.O.B.
HYUCK HYUCK!
DON'T JUDGE A BOOK BY ITS COVER...
YOU CLUMSY GANGSTERS.
THE TRASH OF SOCIETY ALWAYS WILL BE TRASH.
YOU WERE BORN TOO DEEP IN THE GUTTER TO UNDERSTAND REAL POWER.
HYUCK HYUCK
DON'T CALL US TRASH, GOURMET CORP.!
YOU THREE.
STEP BACK.
THERE'S A LOT I DON'T UNDERSTAND ABOUT HIS STRENGTH.

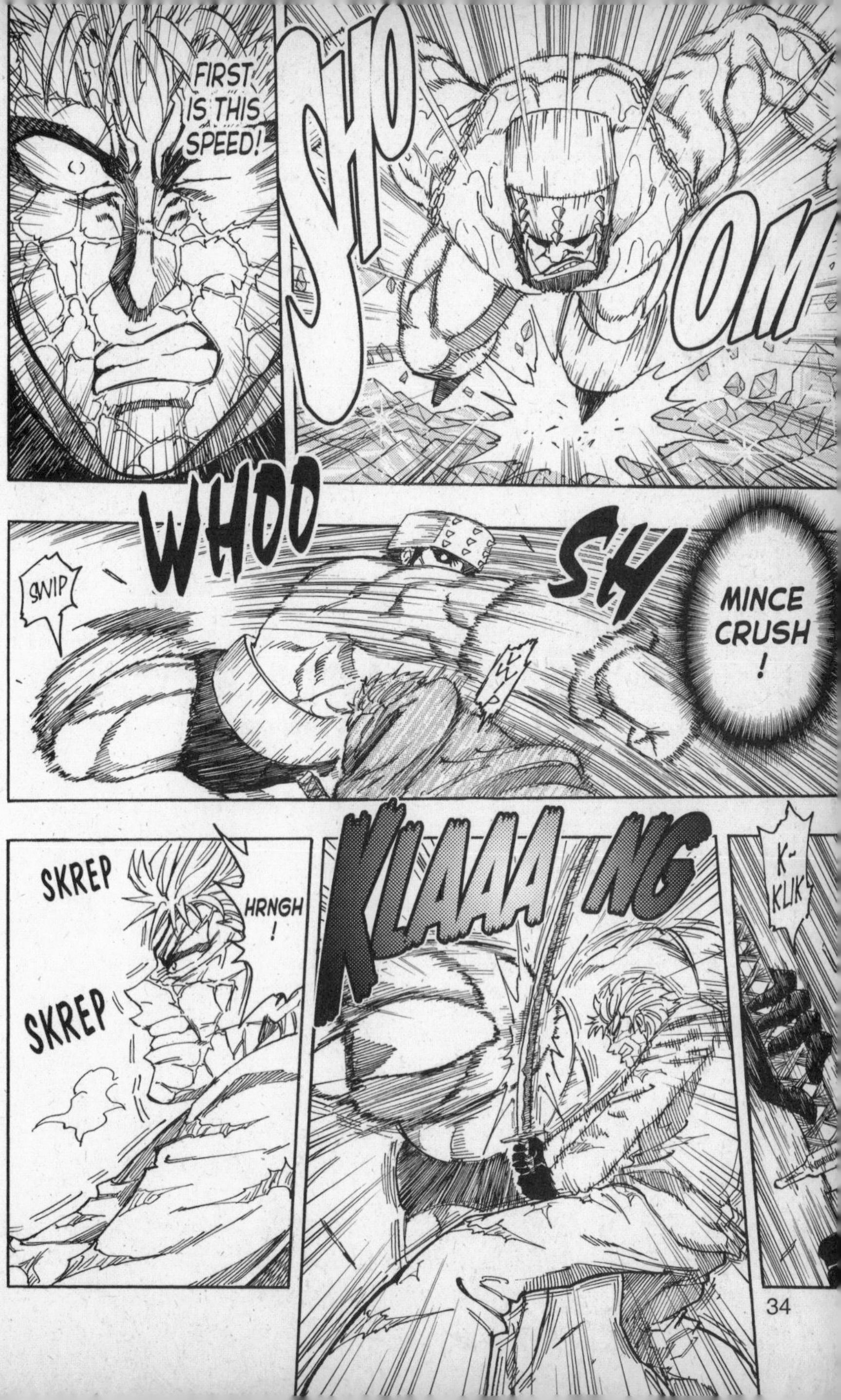
SHO OM
FIRST IS THIS SPEED!
WHOO SH
MINCE CRUSH!
SNIP
K-KLIK
KLAAA NG
SKREP
HRNGH!
SKREP

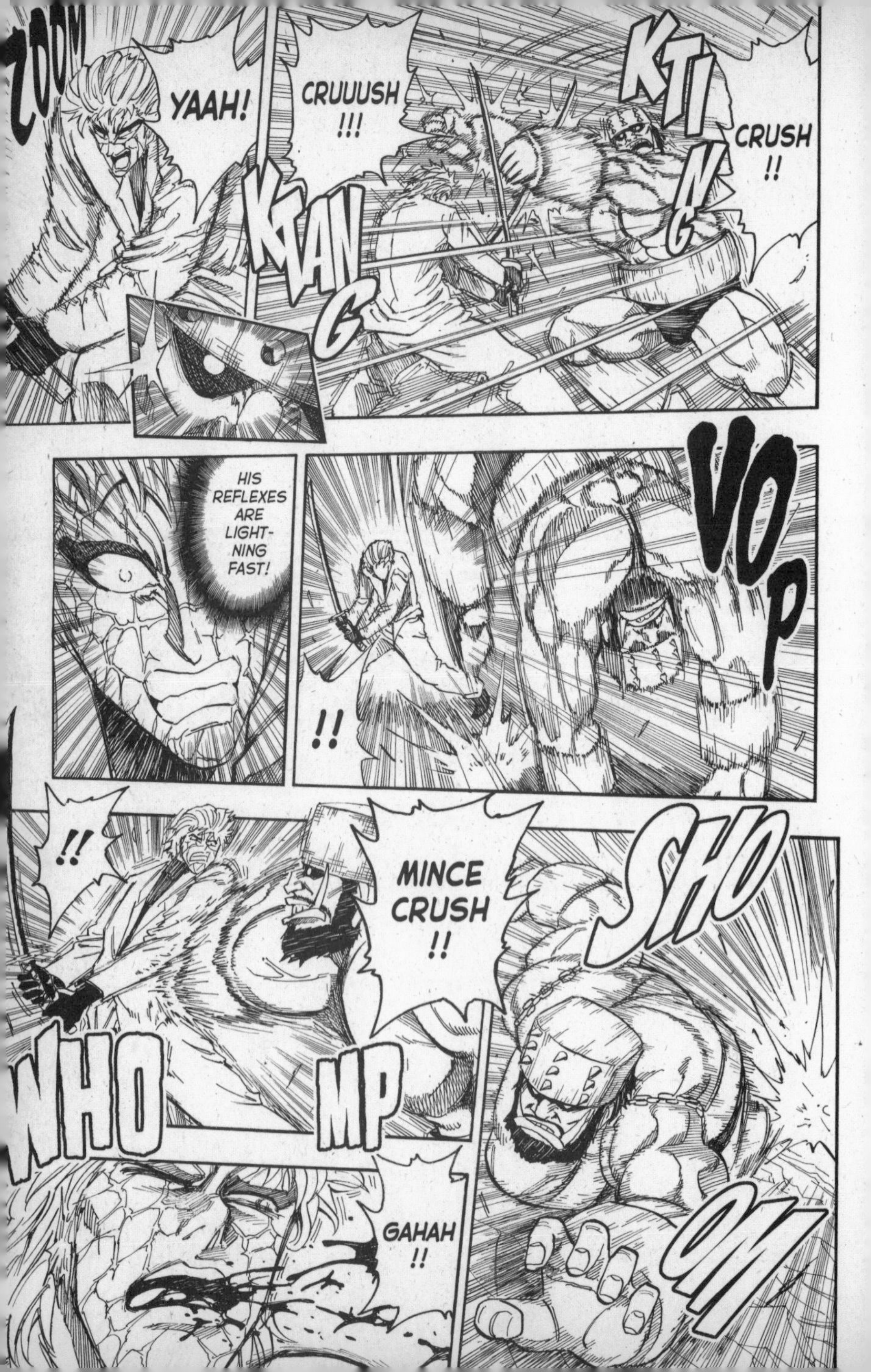
KTING
CRUSH !!
CRUUUSH !!!
KTANG
YAAH!
ZOOM
VOP
!!
HIS REFLEXES ARE LIGHTNING FAST!
SHOOM
MINCE CRUSH !!
!!
WHOMP
GAHAH !!

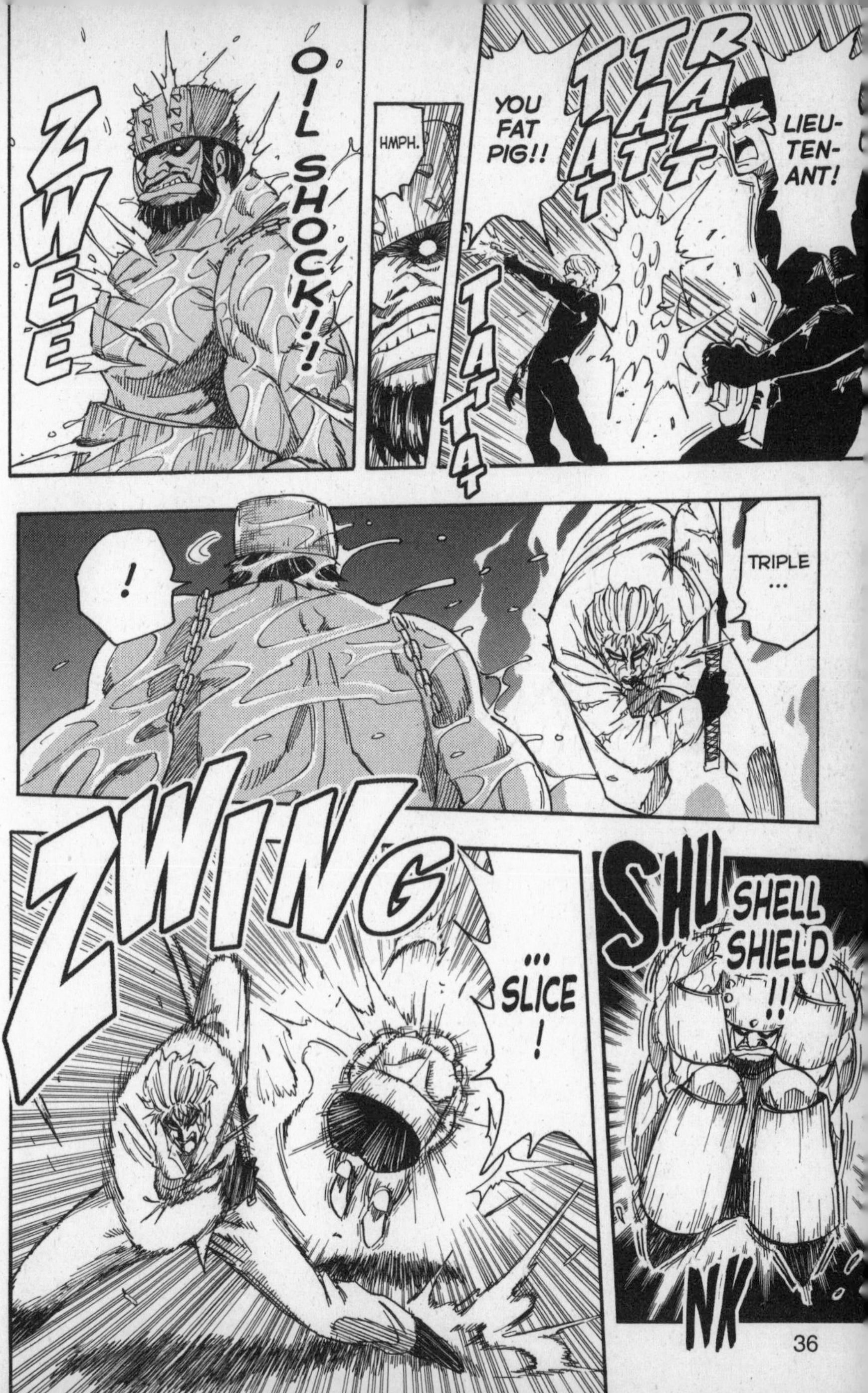
LIEU-TEN-ANT!
TTRATATATT
YOU FAT PIG!!
TATTATTAT
HMPH.
OIL SHOCK!!!
ZWEEE
TRIPLE...
!
SHUNK
SHELL SHIELD!!
ZWING
...SLICE!

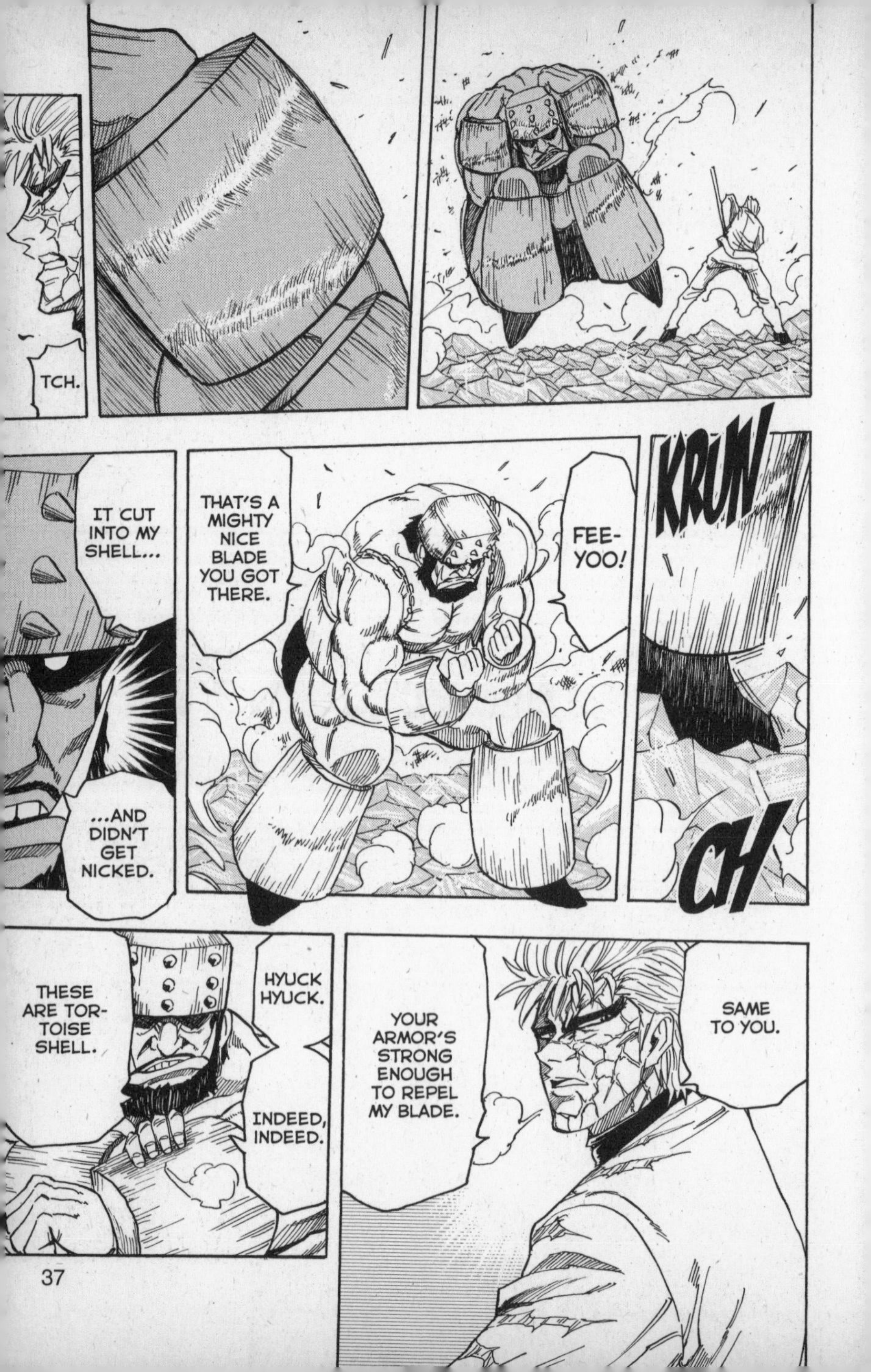
TCH.
KRUNCH
FEE-YOO!
THAT'S A MIGHTY NICE BLADE YOU GOT THERE.
IT CUT INTO MY SHELL...
...AND DIDN'T GET NICKED.
SAME TO YOU.
YOUR ARMOR'S STRONG ENOUGH TO REPEL MY BLADE.
HYUCK HYUCK.
THESE ARE TORTOISE SHELL.
INDEED, INDEED.

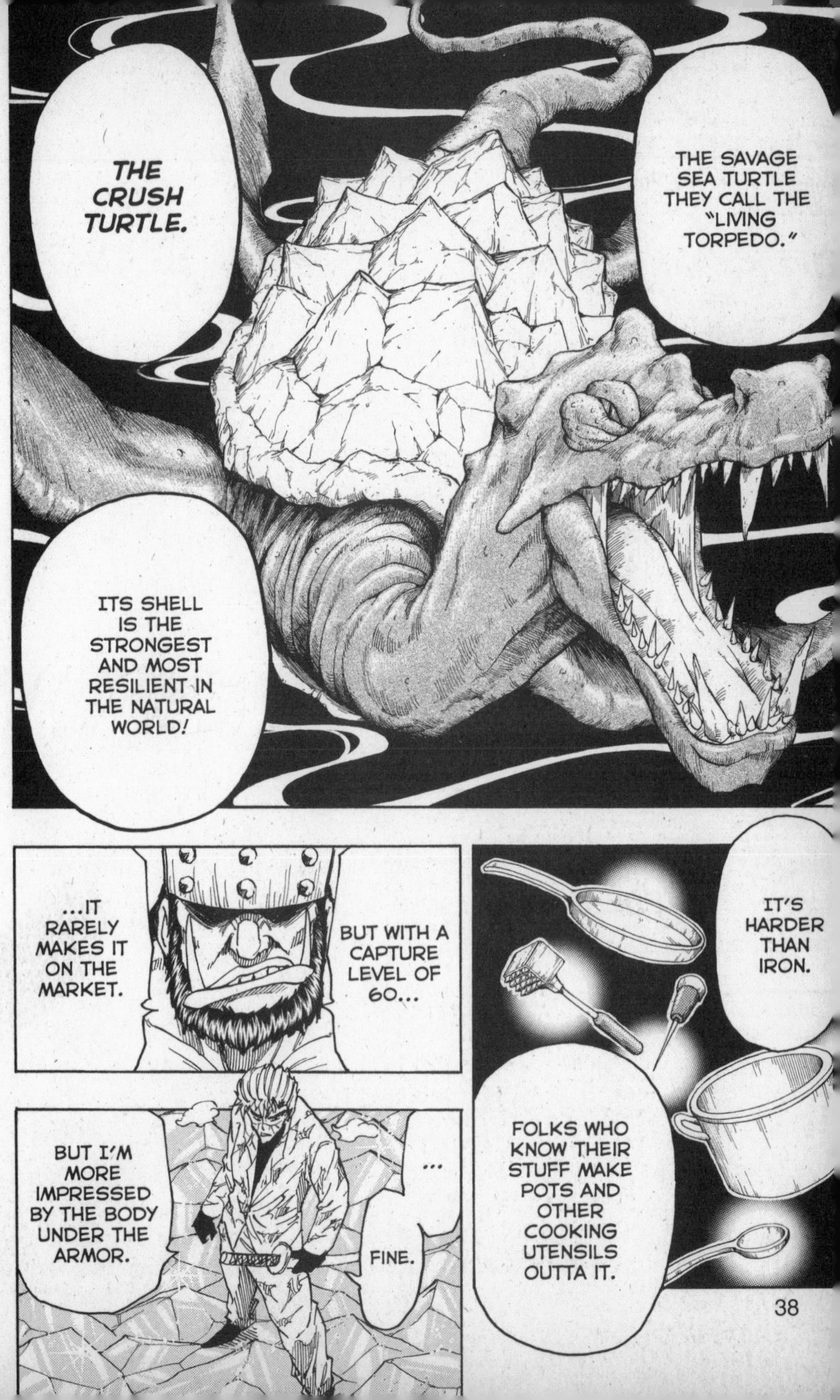
THE SAVAGE SEA TURTLE THEY CALL THE "LIVING TORPEDO."
THE CRUSH TURTLE.
ITS SHELL IS THE STRONGEST AND MOST RESILIENT IN THE NATURAL WORLD!
IT'S HARDER THAN IRON.
FOLKS WHO KNOW THEIR STUFF MAKE POTS AND OTHER COOKING UTENSILS OUTTA IT.
BUT WITH A CAPTURE LEVEL OF 60...
...IT RARELY MAKES IT ON THE MARKET.
...
FINE.
BUT I'M MORE IMPRESSED BY THE BODY UNDER THE ARMOR.

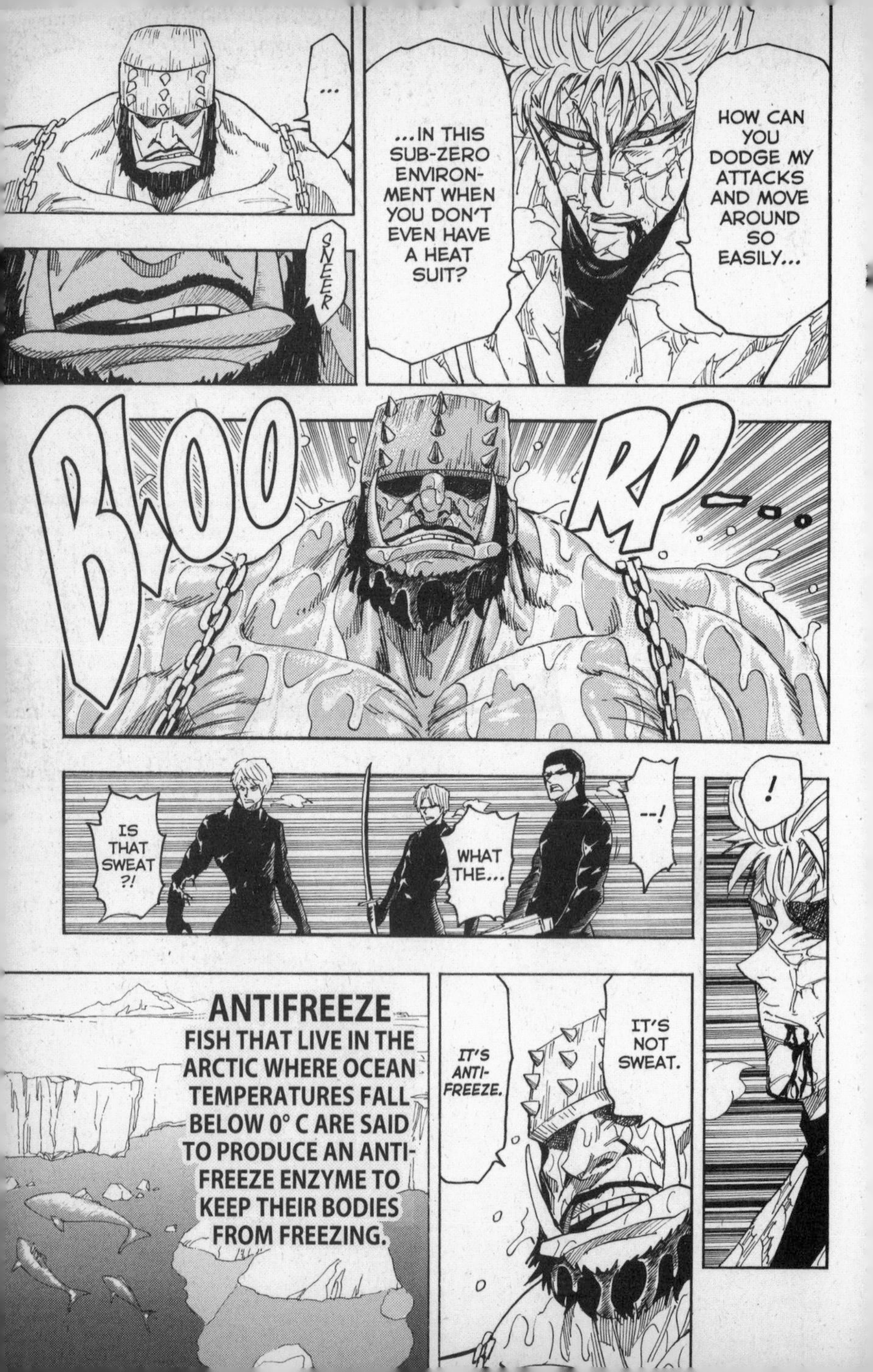
HOW CAN YOU DODGE MY ATTACKS AND MOVE AROUND SO EASILY...
...IN THIS SUB-ZERO ENVIRON-MENT WHEN YOU DON'T EVEN HAVE A HEAT SUIT?
...
SNEER
BLOORP--..
!
--!
WHAT THE...
IS THAT SWEAT?!
IT'S NOT SWEAT.
IT'S ANTI-FREEZE.
ANTIFREEZE
FISH THAT LIVE IN THE ARCTIC WHERE OCEAN TEMPERATURES FALL BELOW 0° C ARE SAID TO PRODUCE AN ANTI-FREEZE ENZYME TO KEEP THEIR BODIES FROM FREEZING.

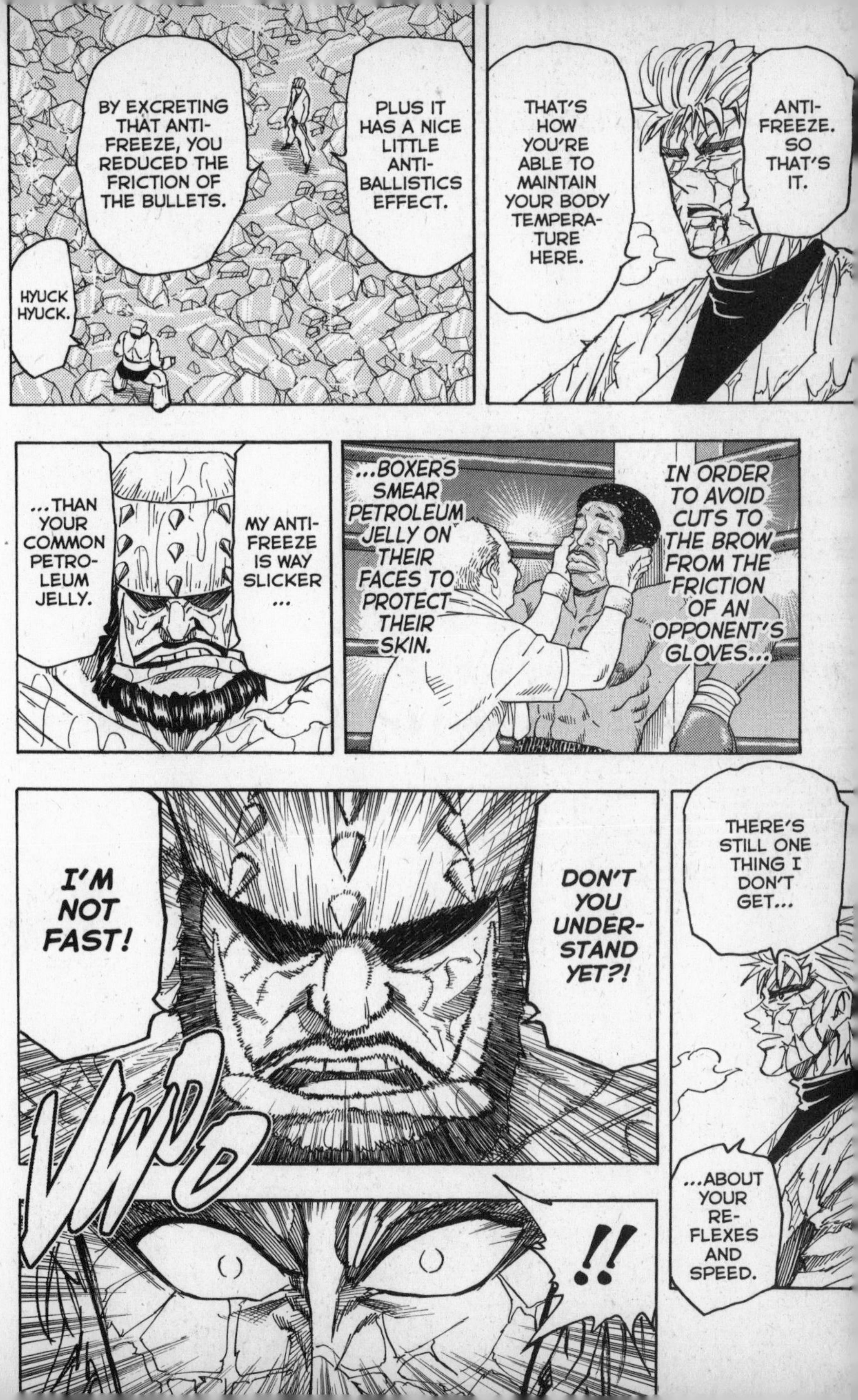
ANTI-FREEZE. SO THAT'S IT.
THAT'S HOW YOU'RE ABLE TO MAINTAIN YOUR BODY TEMPERATURE HERE.
PLUS IT HAS A NICE LITTLE ANTI-BALLISTICS EFFECT.
BY EXCRETING THAT ANTI-FREEZE, YOU REDUCED THE FRICTION OF THE BULLETS.
HYUCK HYUCK.
IN ORDER TO AVOID CUTS TO THE BROW FROM THE FRICTION OF AN OPPONENT'S GLOVES...
...BOXERS SMEAR PETROLEUM JELLY ON THEIR FACES TO PROTECT THEIR SKIN.
MY ANTI-FREEZE IS WAY SLICKER...
...THAN YOUR COMMON PETROLEUM JELLY.
THERE'S STILL ONE THING I DON'T GET...
...ABOUT YOUR REFLEXES AND SPEED.
DON'T YOU UNDERSTAND YET?!
I'M NOT FAST!
!!

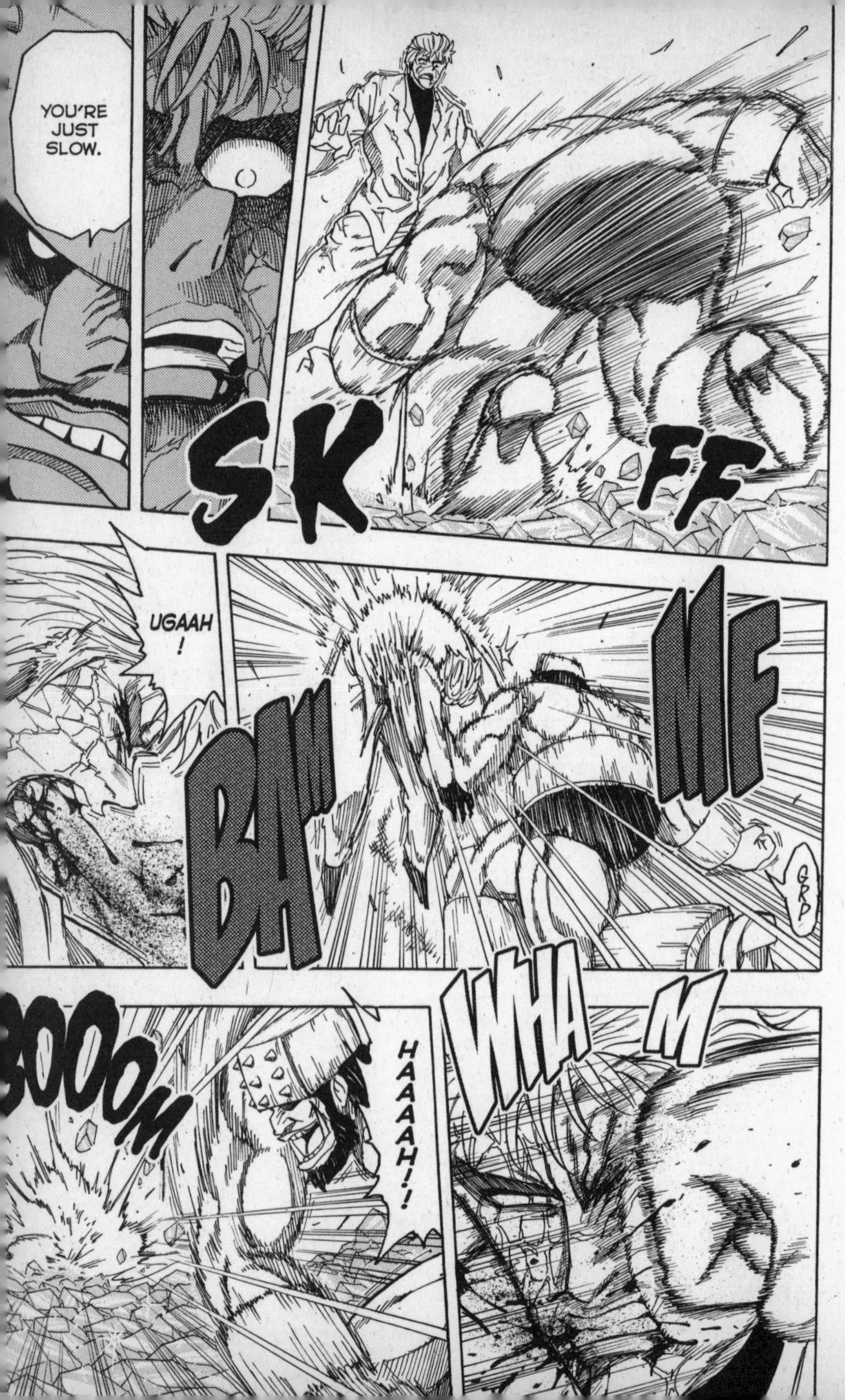
SK FF
YOU'RE JUST SLOW.
BAMMF
GRP
UGAAH!
WHA M
HAAAAAH!!
BOOOM

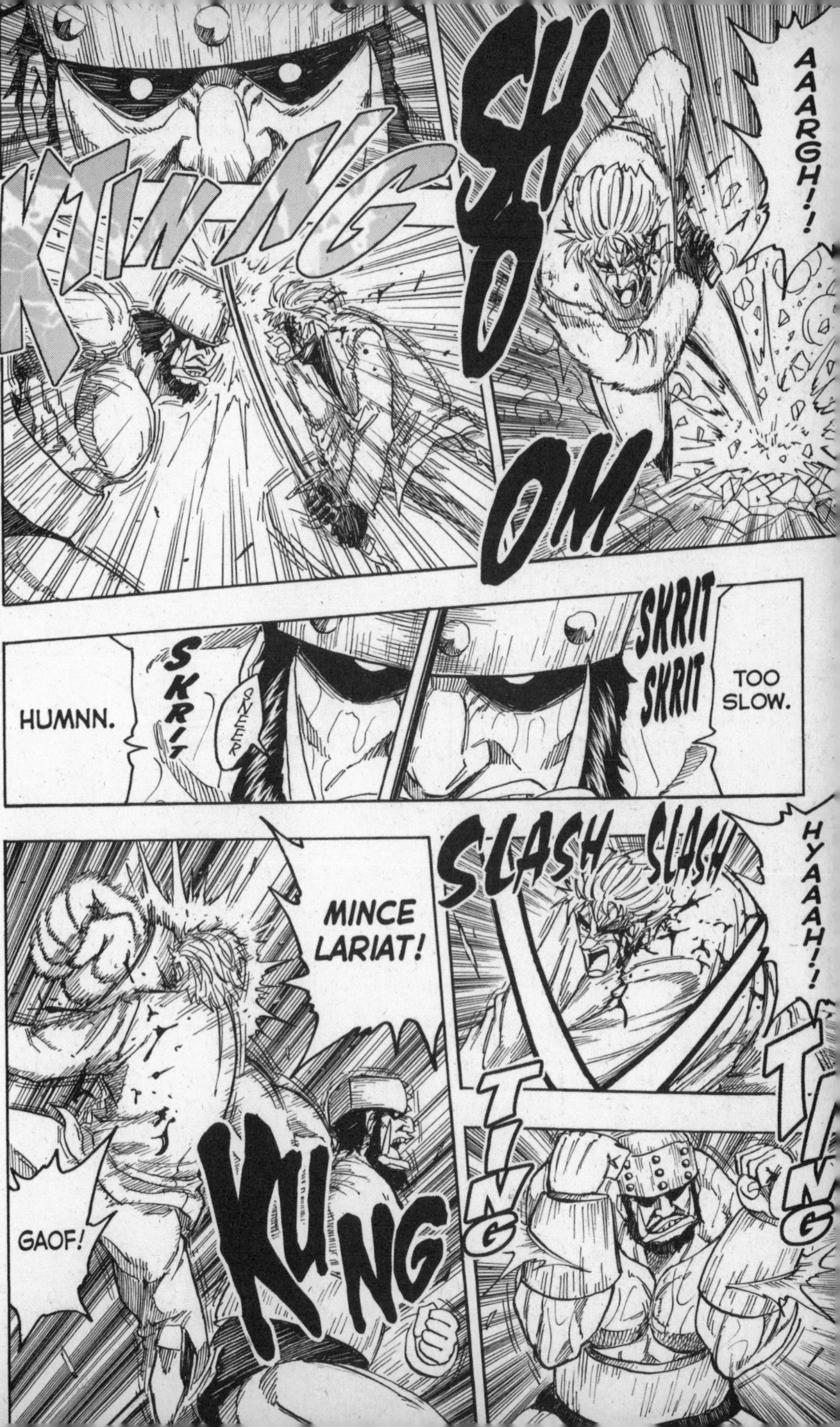
AAARGH!!
SHOOM
TOO SLOW.
SKRIT SKRIT
SNEER
SKRIT
HUMNN.
HYAAAAH!!
SLASH SLASH
TING
TING
MINCE LARIAT!
KUNG
GAOF!

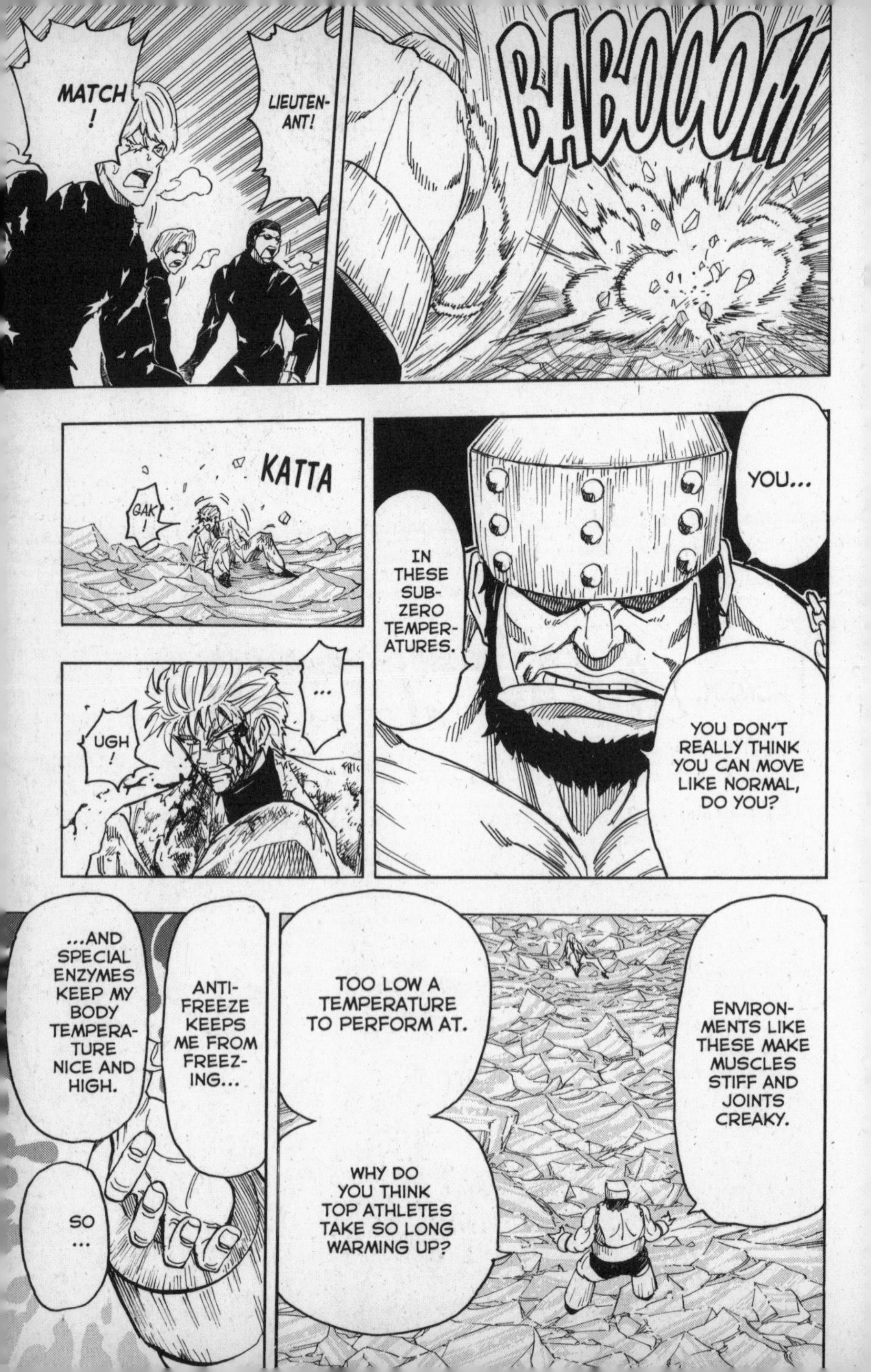
BABOOOM
LIEUTEN-ANT!
MATCH!
YOU...
IN THESE SUB-ZERO TEMPERATURES.
YOU DON'T REALLY THINK YOU CAN MOVE LIKE NORMAL, DO YOU?
KATTA
GAK!
...
UGH!
ENVIRONMENTS LIKE THESE MAKE MUSCLES STIFF AND JOINTS CREAKY.
TOO LOW A TEMPERATURE TO PERFORM AT.
WHY DO YOU THINK TOP ATHLETES TAKE SO LONG WARMING UP?
ANTI-FREEZE KEEPS ME FROM FREEZING...
...AND SPECIAL ENZYMES KEEP MY BODY TEMPERATURE NICE AND HIGH.
SO...

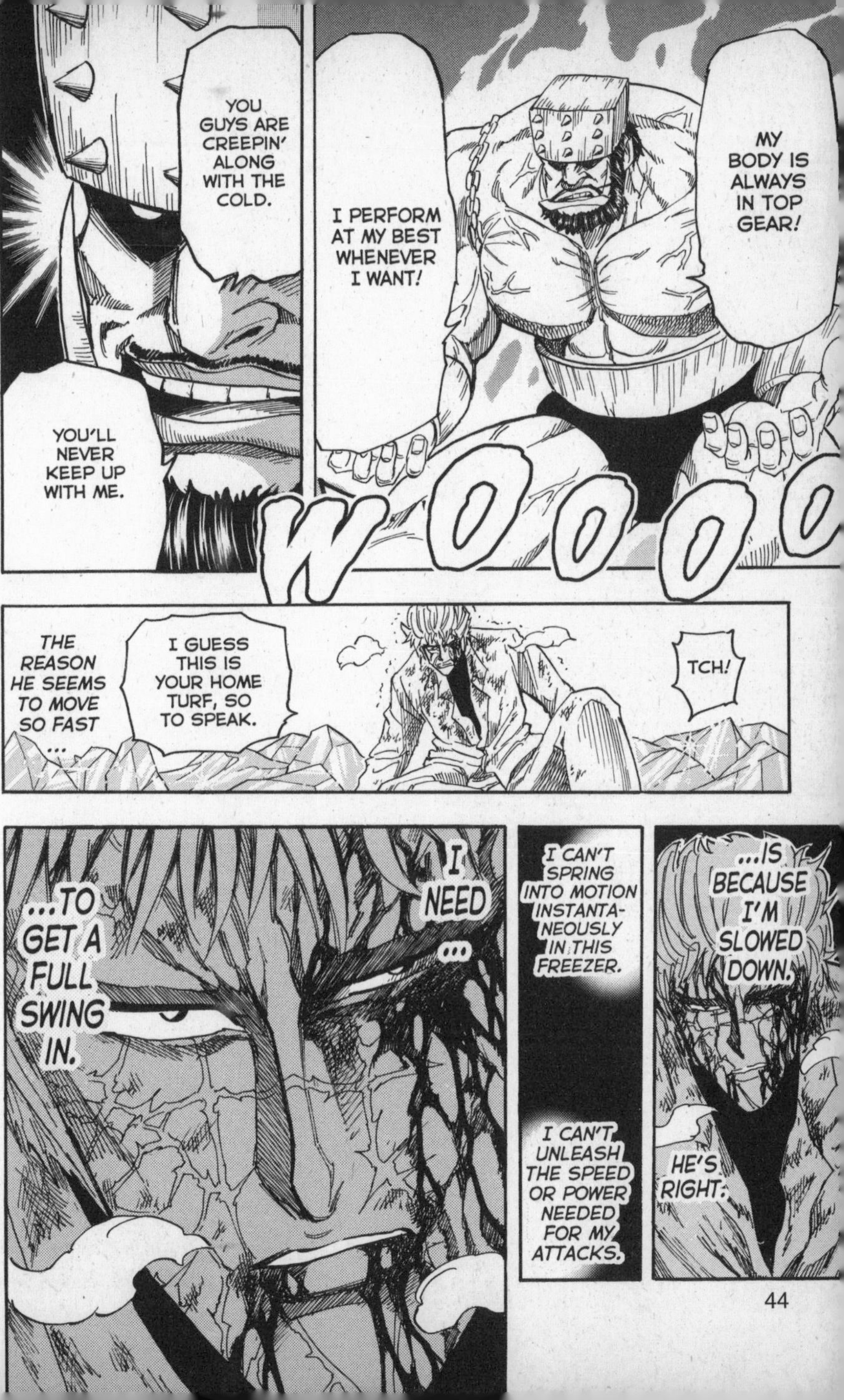
MY BODY IS ALWAYS IN TOP GEAR!
I PERFORM AT MY BEST WHENEVER I WANT!
WOOOOO
YOU GUYS ARE CREEPIN' ALONG WITH THE COLD.
YOU'LL NEVER KEEP UP WITH ME.
TCH!
I GUESS THIS IS YOUR HOME TURF, SO TO SPEAK.
THE REASON HE SEEMS TO MOVE SO FAST ...
...IS BECAUSE I'M SLOWED DOWN.
HE'S RIGHT.
I CAN'T SPRING INTO MOTION INSTANTA-NEOUSLY IN THIS FREEZER.
I CAN'T UNLEASH THE SPEED OR POWER NEEDED FOR MY ATTACKS.
I NEED ...
...TO GET A FULL SWING IN.

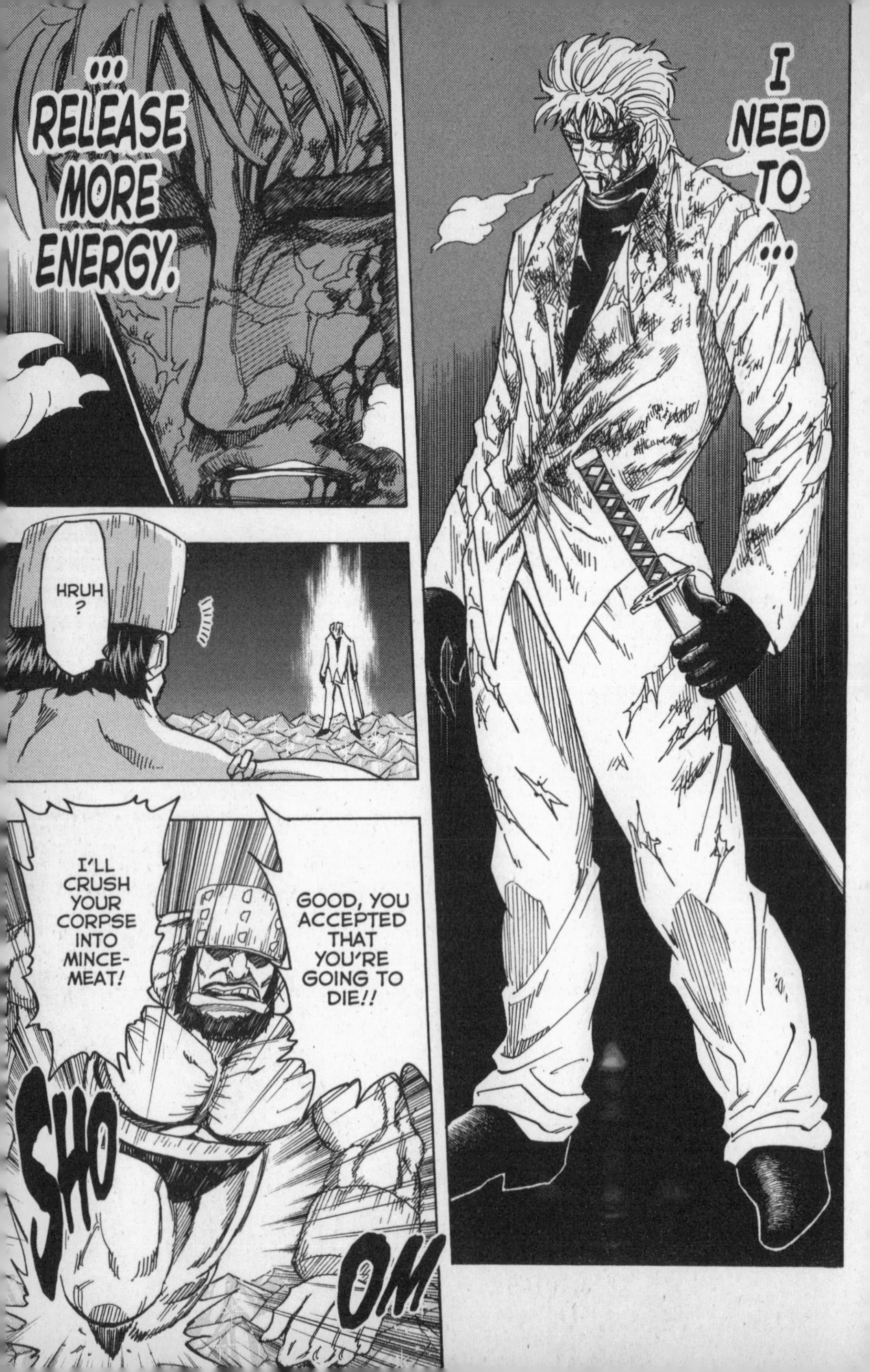
I NEED TO ...
... RELEASE MORE ENERGY.
HRUH ?
GOOD, YOU ACCEPTED THAT YOU'RE GOING TO DIE!!
I'LL CRUSH YOUR CORPSE INTO MINCE-MEAT!
SHOOM

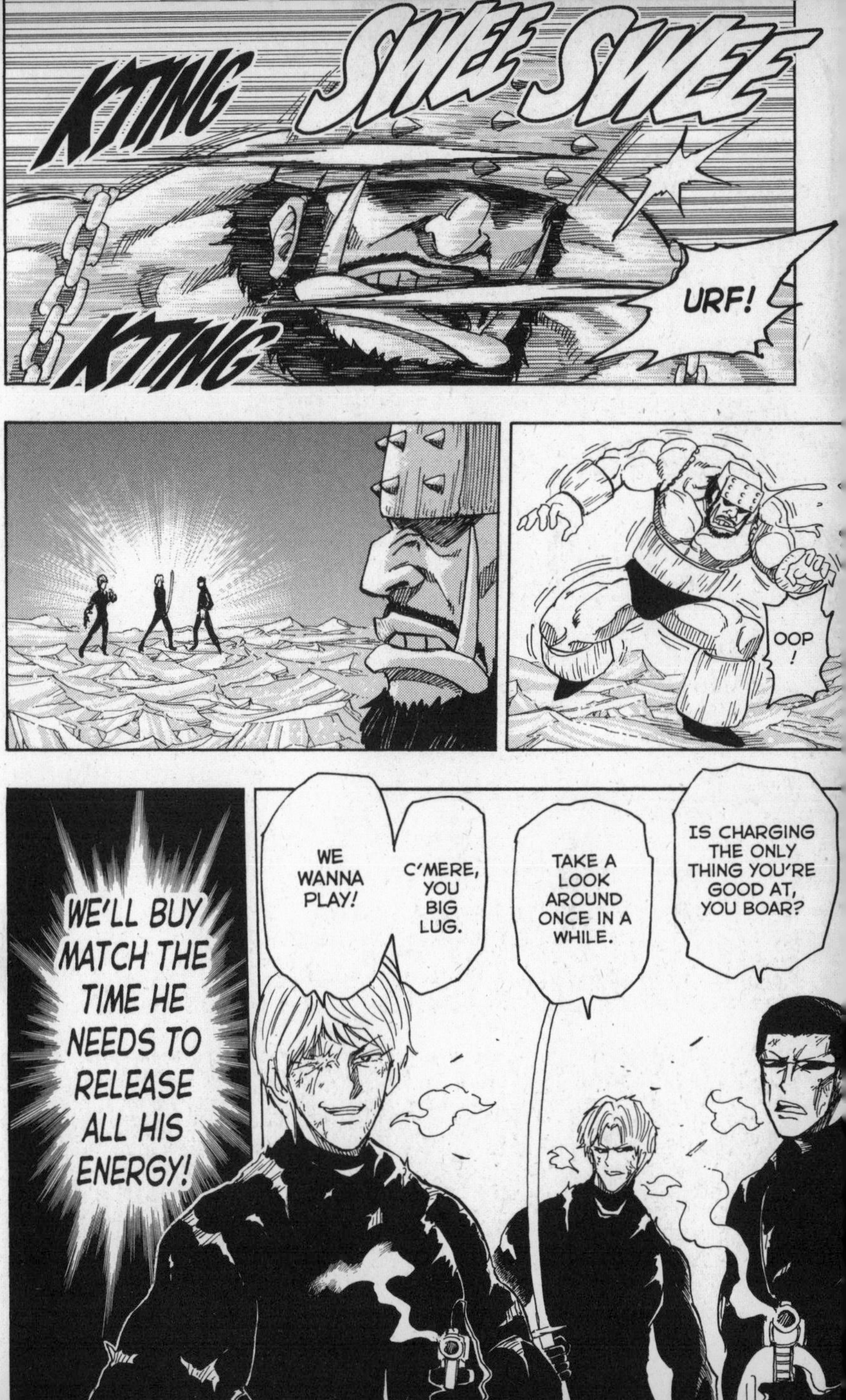
SWEE SWEE
K'TING
URF!
K'TING
OOP!
IS CHARGING THE ONLY THING YOU'RE GOOD AT, YOU BOAR?
TAKE A LOOK AROUND ONCE IN A WHILE.
C'MERE, YOU BIG LUG.
WE WANNA PLAY!
WE'LL BUY MATCH THE TIME HE NEEDS TO RELEASE ALL HIS ENERGY!

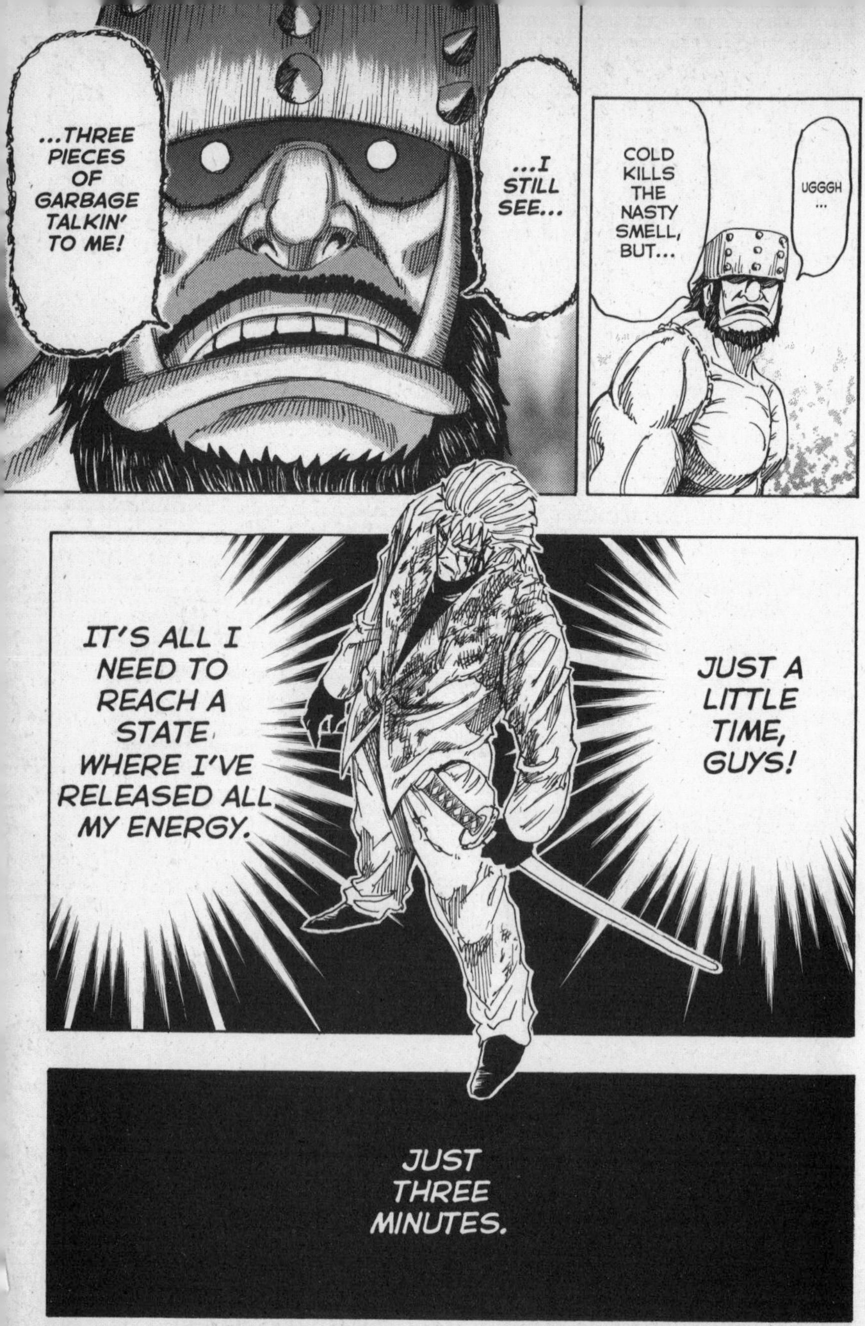
UGGGH ...
COLD KILLS THE NASTY SMELL, BUT...
...I STILL SEE...
...THREE PIECES OF GARBAGE TALKIN' TO ME!
JUST A LITTLE TIME, GUYS!
IT'S ALL I NEED TO REACH A STATE WHERE I'VE RELEASED ALL MY ENERGY.
JUST THREE MINUTES.

TORIKO

GOURMET CHECKLIST
Vol. 079

CRYSTAL COLA
(SOFT DRINK)

CAPTURE LEVEL: 19 (IN THE WILD)

HABITAT: GOURMET TOWN'S THREE-STAR

VENDING MACHINES

LENGTH: ---

HEIGHT: ---

WEIGHT: ---

PRICE: 100,000 YEN PER 350ML CAN

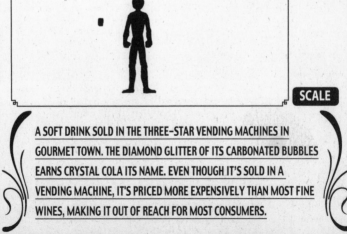

SCALE

A SOFT DRINK SOLD IN THE THREE-STAR VENDING MACHINES IN GOURMET TOWN. THE DIAMOND GLITTER OF ITS CARBONATED BUBBLES EARNS CRYSTAL COLA ITS NAME. EVEN THOUGH IT'S SOLD IN A VENDING MACHINE, IT'S PRICED MORE EXPENSIVELY THAN MOST FINE WINES, MAKING IT OUT OF REACH FOR MOST CONSUMERS.

GOURMET 82: TRASH!!

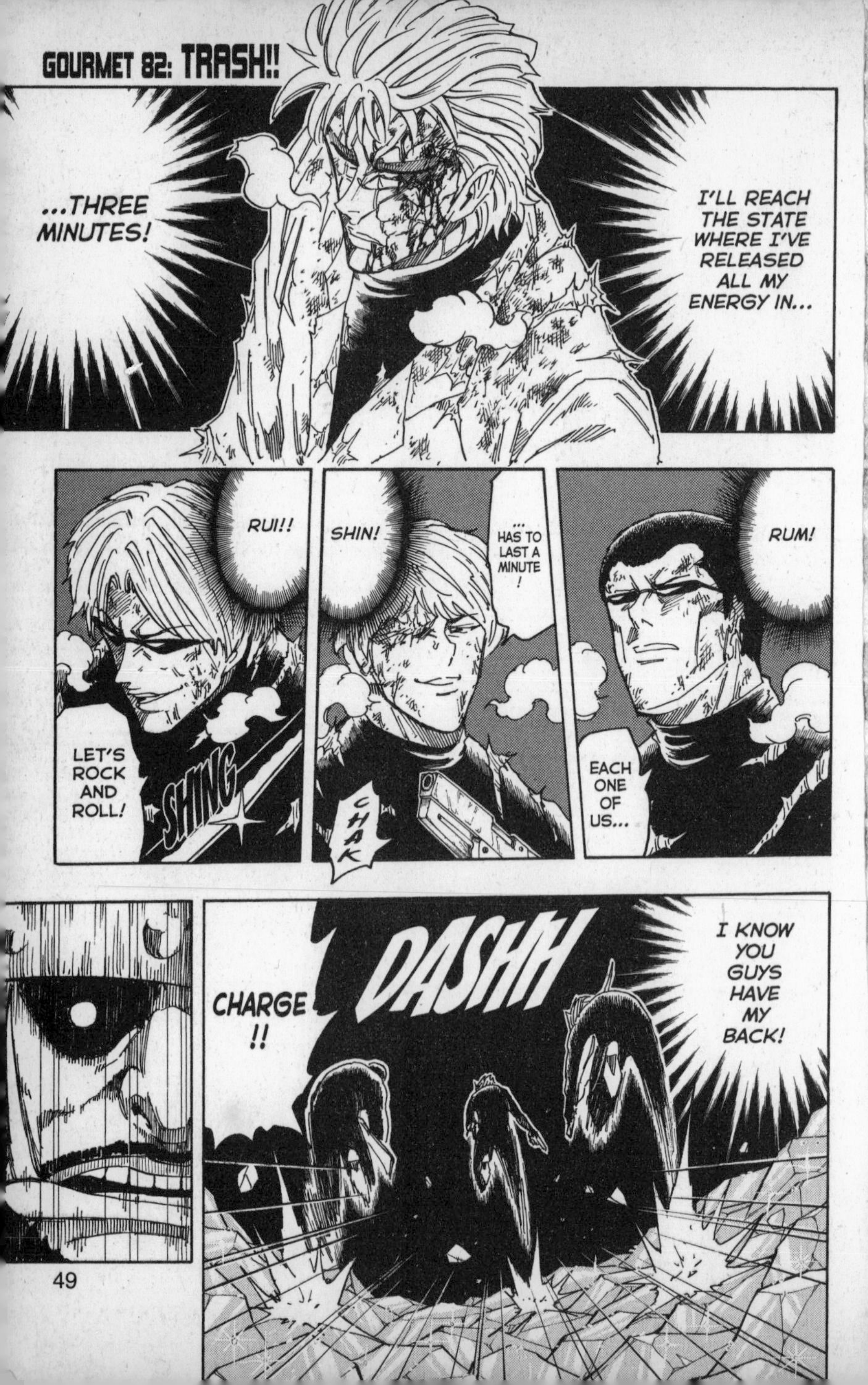

I'LL REACH THE STATE WHERE I'VE RELEASED ALL MY ENERGY IN...
...THREE MINUTES!
RUM!
EACH ONE OF US...
...HAS TO LAST A MINUTE!
SHIN!
CHAK
RUI!!
LET'S ROCK AND ROLL!
SHING
I KNOW YOU GUYS HAVE MY BACK!
DASHH
CHARGE!!

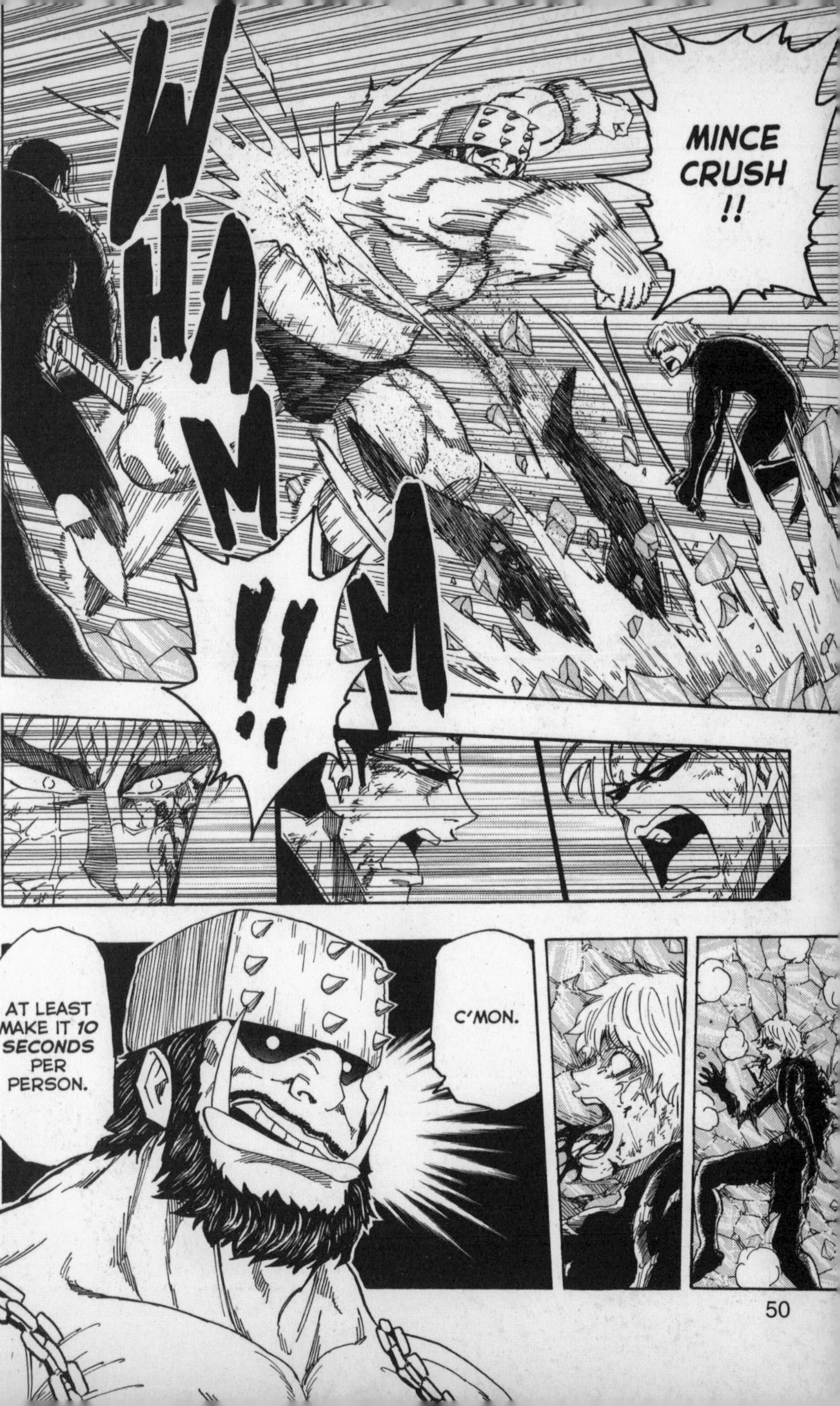
MINCE CRUSH !!
WHAMMM!!
C'MON.
AT LEAST MAKE IT *10 SECONDS* PER PERSON.

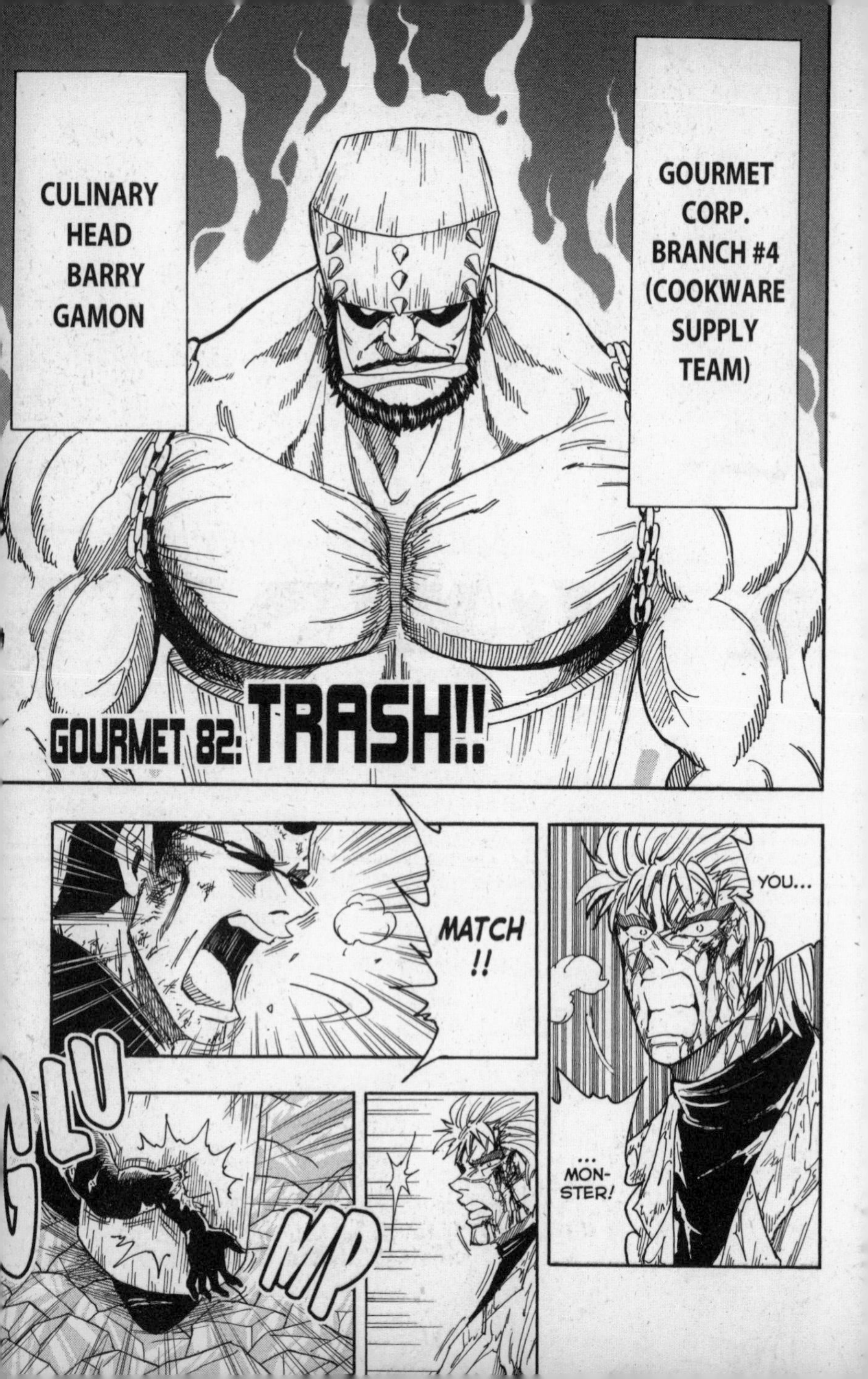
GOURMET CORP. BRANCH #4 (COOKWARE SUPPLY TEAM)
CULINARY HEAD BARRY GAMON
GOURMET 82: TRASH!!
YOU...
...MONSTER!
MATCH!!
GLUMP

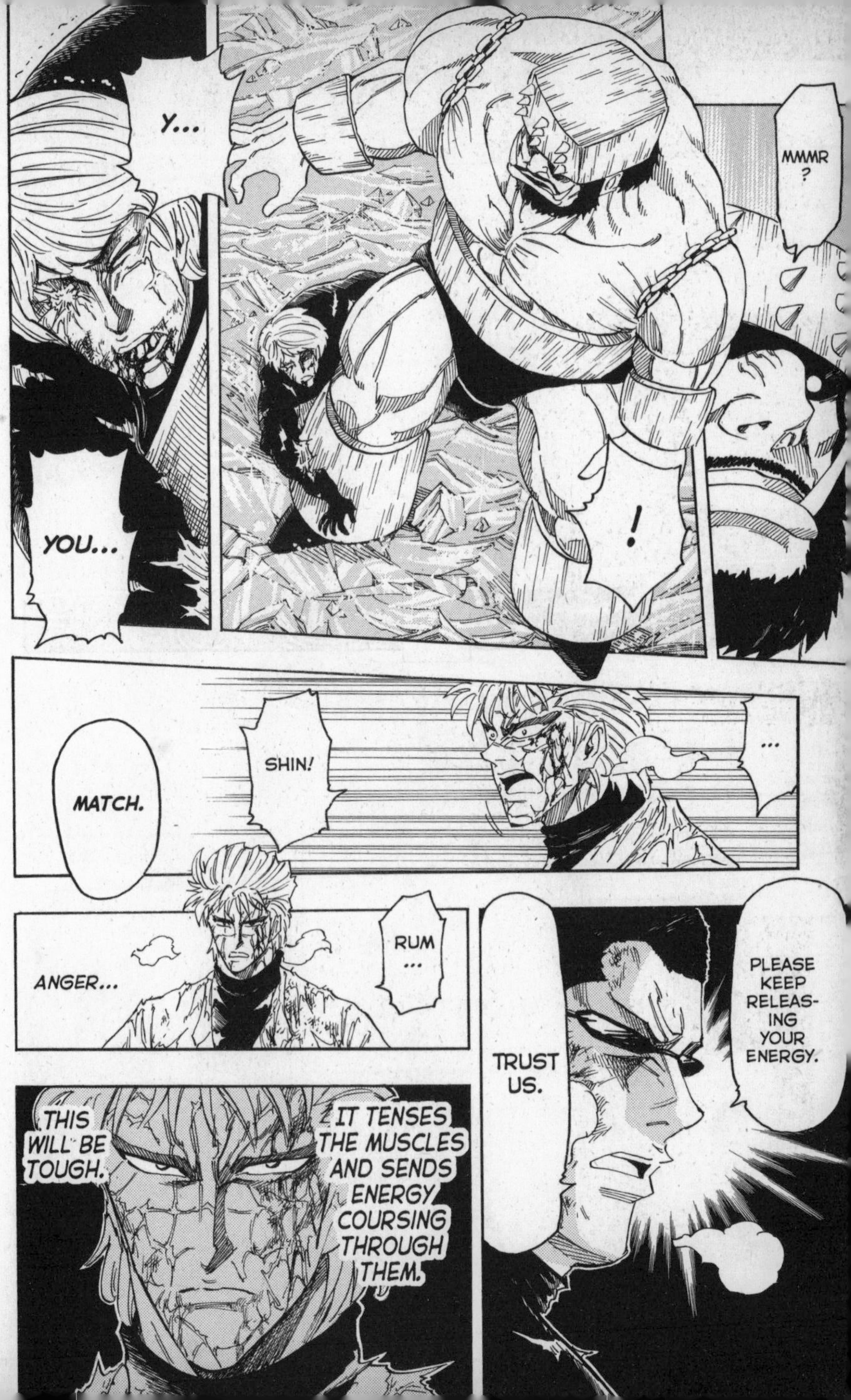
MMMR ?
!
Y...
YOU...
...
SHIN!
MATCH.
PLEASE KEEP RELEASING YOUR ENERGY.
TRUST US.
RUM ...
ANGER...
IT TENSES THE MUSCLES AND SENDS ENERGY COURSING THROUGH THEM.
THIS WILL BE TOUGH.

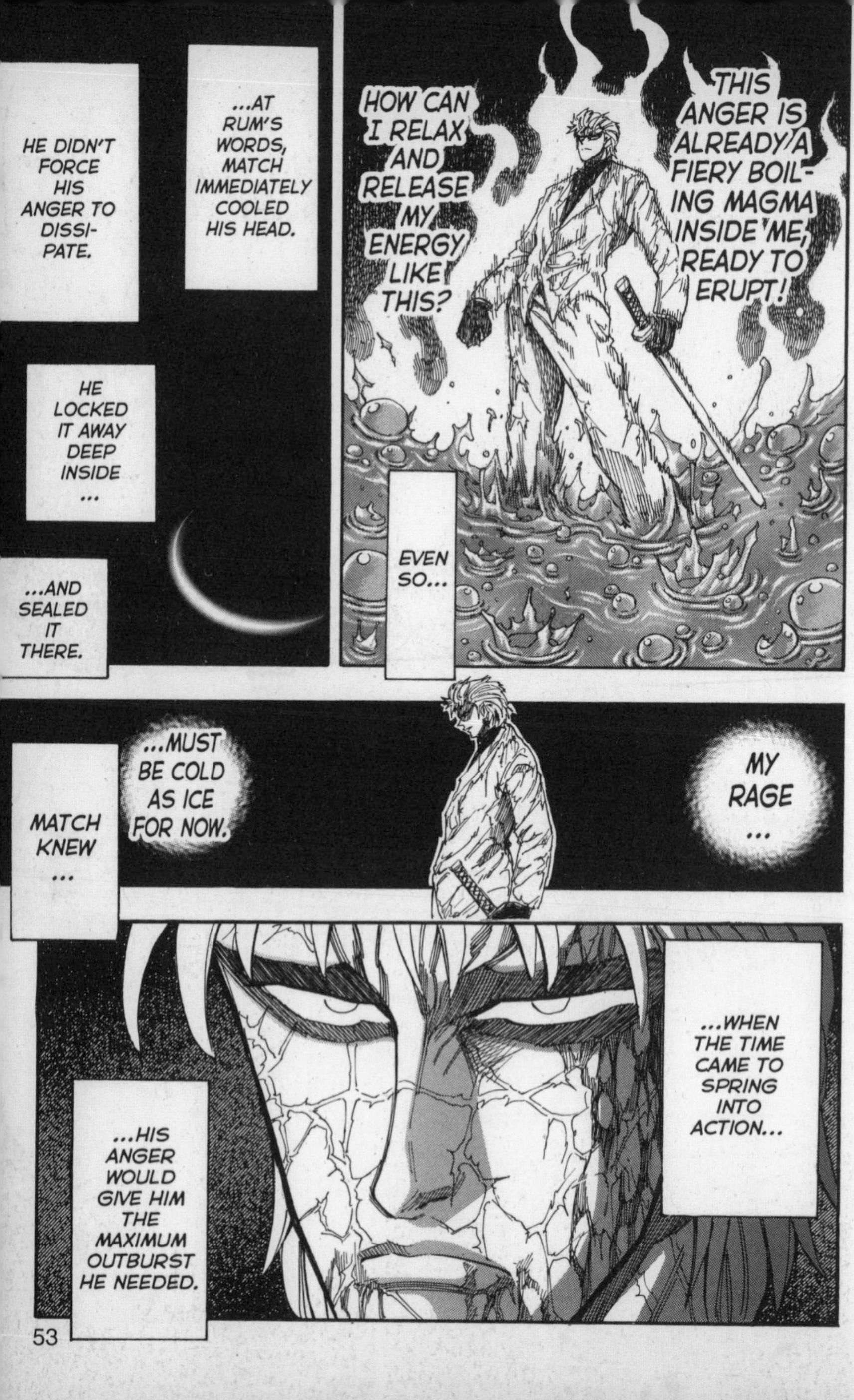
THIS ANGER IS ALREADY A FIERY BOIL-ING MAGMA INSIDE ME, READY TO ERUPT!
HOW CAN I RELAX AND RELEASE MY ENERGY LIKE THIS?
EVEN SO...
...AT RUM'S WORDS, MATCH IMMEDIATELY COOLED HIS HEAD.
HE DIDN'T FORCE HIS ANGER TO DISSI-PATE.
HE LOCKED IT AWAY DEEP INSIDE ...
...AND SEALED IT THERE.
MY RAGE ...
...MUST BE COLD AS ICE FOR NOW.
MATCH KNEW ...
...WHEN THE TIME CAME TO SPRING INTO ACTION...
...HIS ANGER WOULD GIVE HIM THE MAXIMUM OUTBURST HE NEEDED.

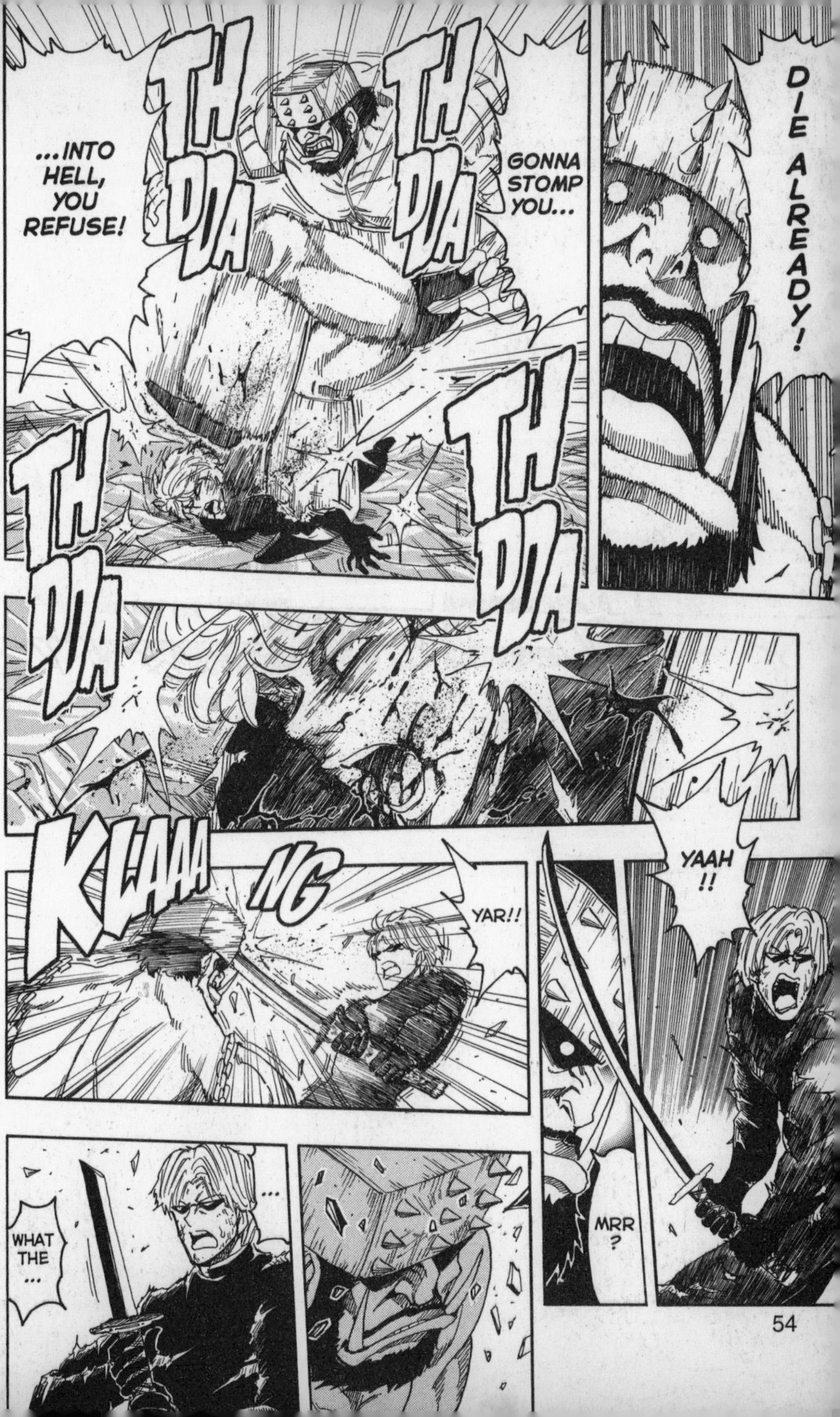

DIE ALREADY!
GONNA STOMP YOU...
...INTO HELL, YOU REFUSE!
THDDA
THDDA
THDDA
THDDA
YAAH!!
MRR?
KLAAANG
YAR!!
...
WHAT THE ...

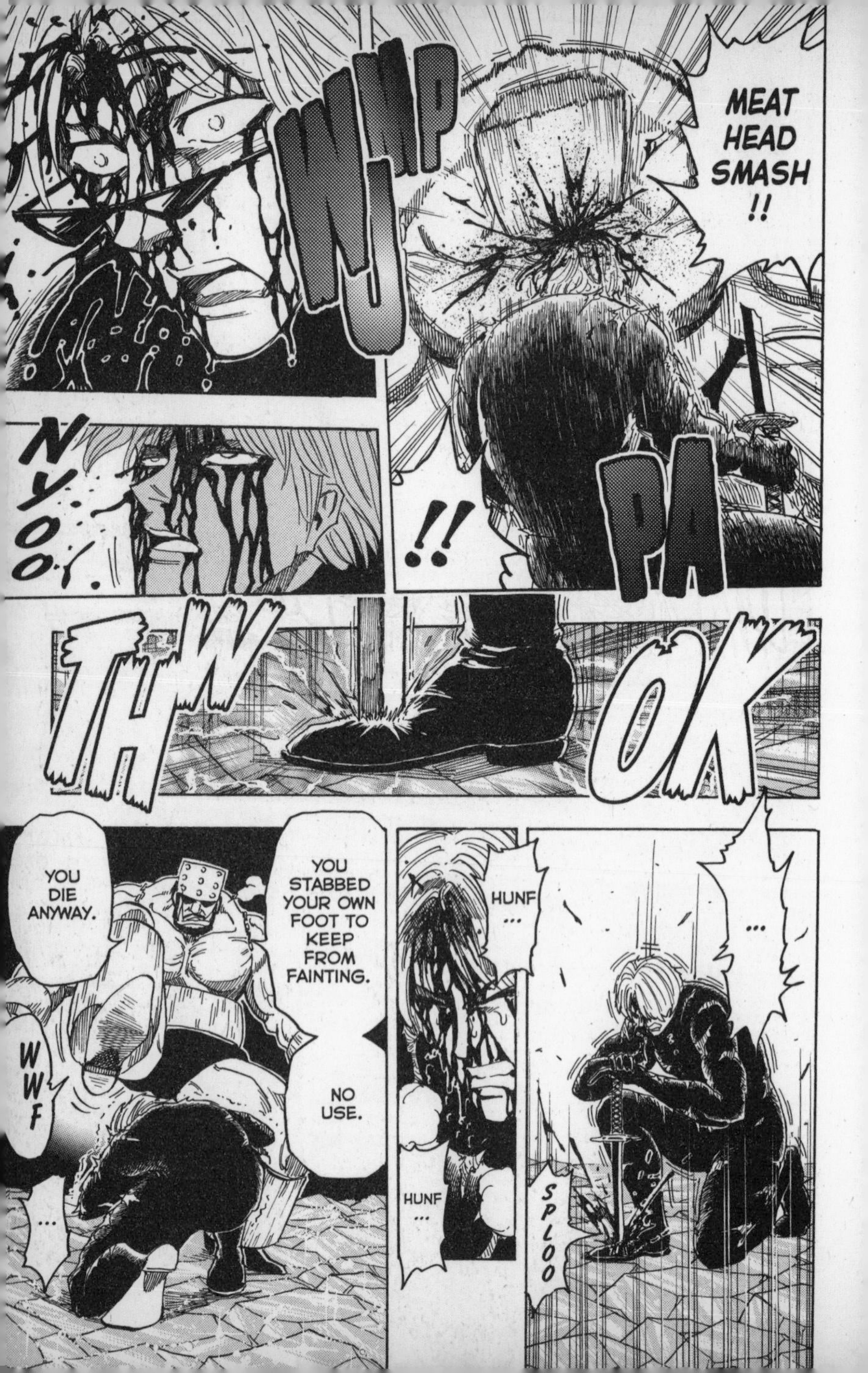
MEAT HEAD SMASH !!
!!
PA
WHUMP
NYOOO...
THWOK
...
SPLOO
HUNF ...
HUNF ...
YOU STABBED YOUR OWN FOOT TO KEEP FROM FAINTING.
NO USE.
YOU DIE ANYWAY.
WWF
...

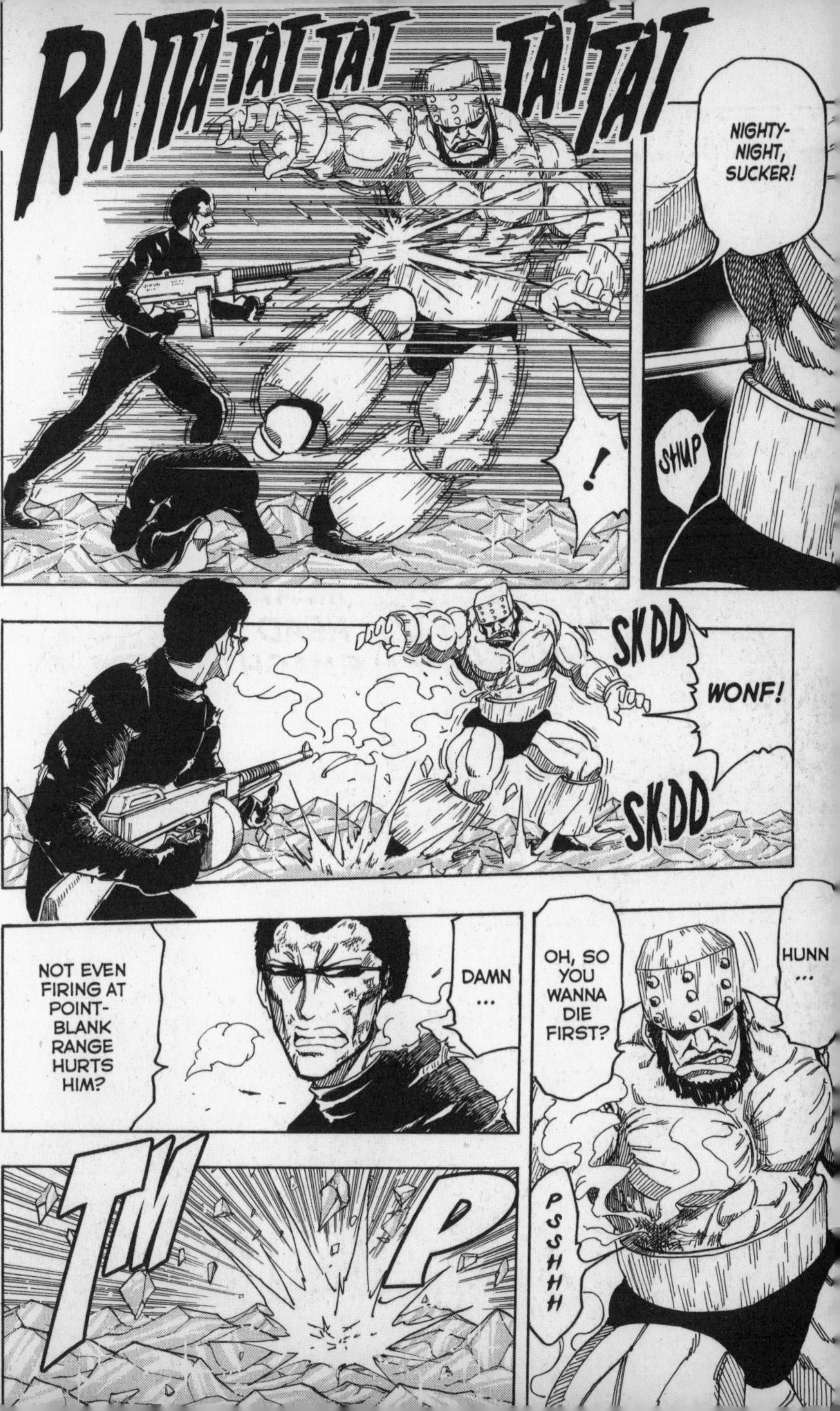
NIGHTY-NIGHT, SUCKER!
SHUP
RATTA TAT TAT
TAT TAT
!
SKDD
WONF!
SKDD
HUNN ...
OH, SO YOU WANNA DIE FIRST?
PSSHHH
DAMN ...
NOT EVEN FIRING AT POINT-BLANK RANGE HURTS HIM?
TMP

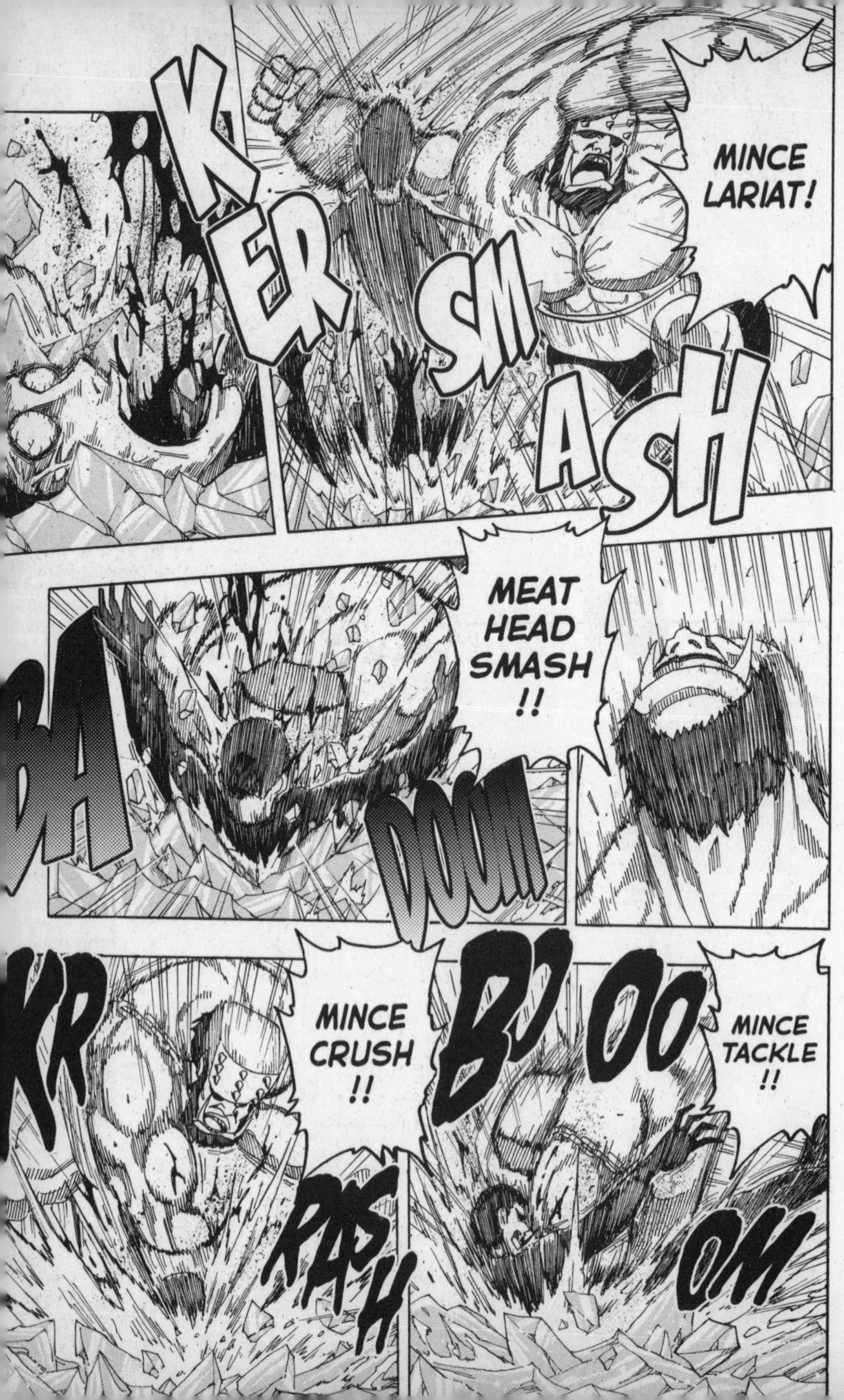
MINCE LARIAT!
KER SMASH
MEAT HEAD SMASH !!
BA DOOM
MINCE TACKLE !!
BOOO OOM
MINCE CRUSH !!
KR RASHH

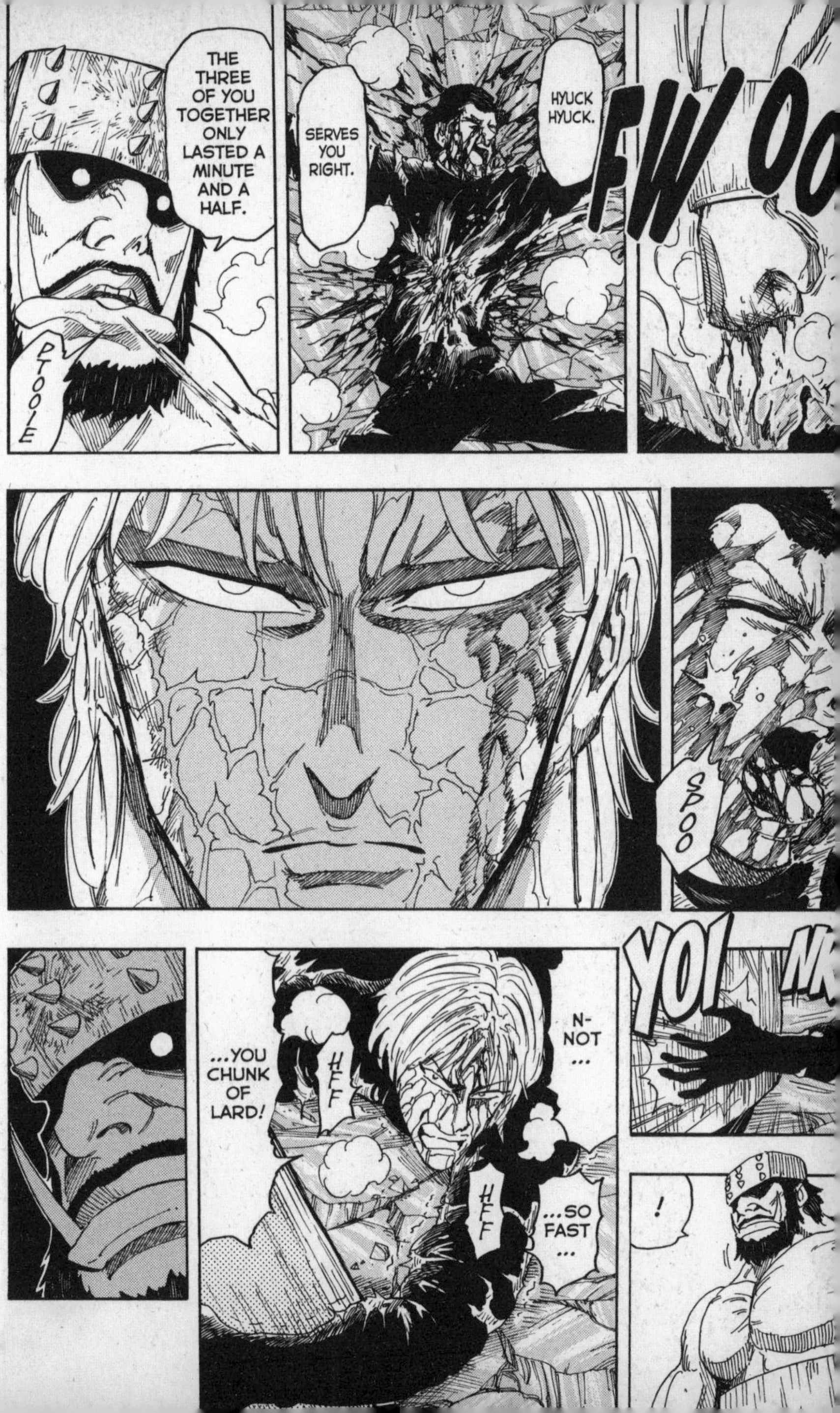

FWOO
HYUCK HYUCK.
SERVES YOU RIGHT.
THE THREE OF YOU TOGETHER ONLY LASTED A MINUTE AND A HALF.
PTOOIE
SPOO
YOI
NK
!
N-NOT ...
HFF
...SO FAST ...
HFF
...YOU CHUNK OF LARD!

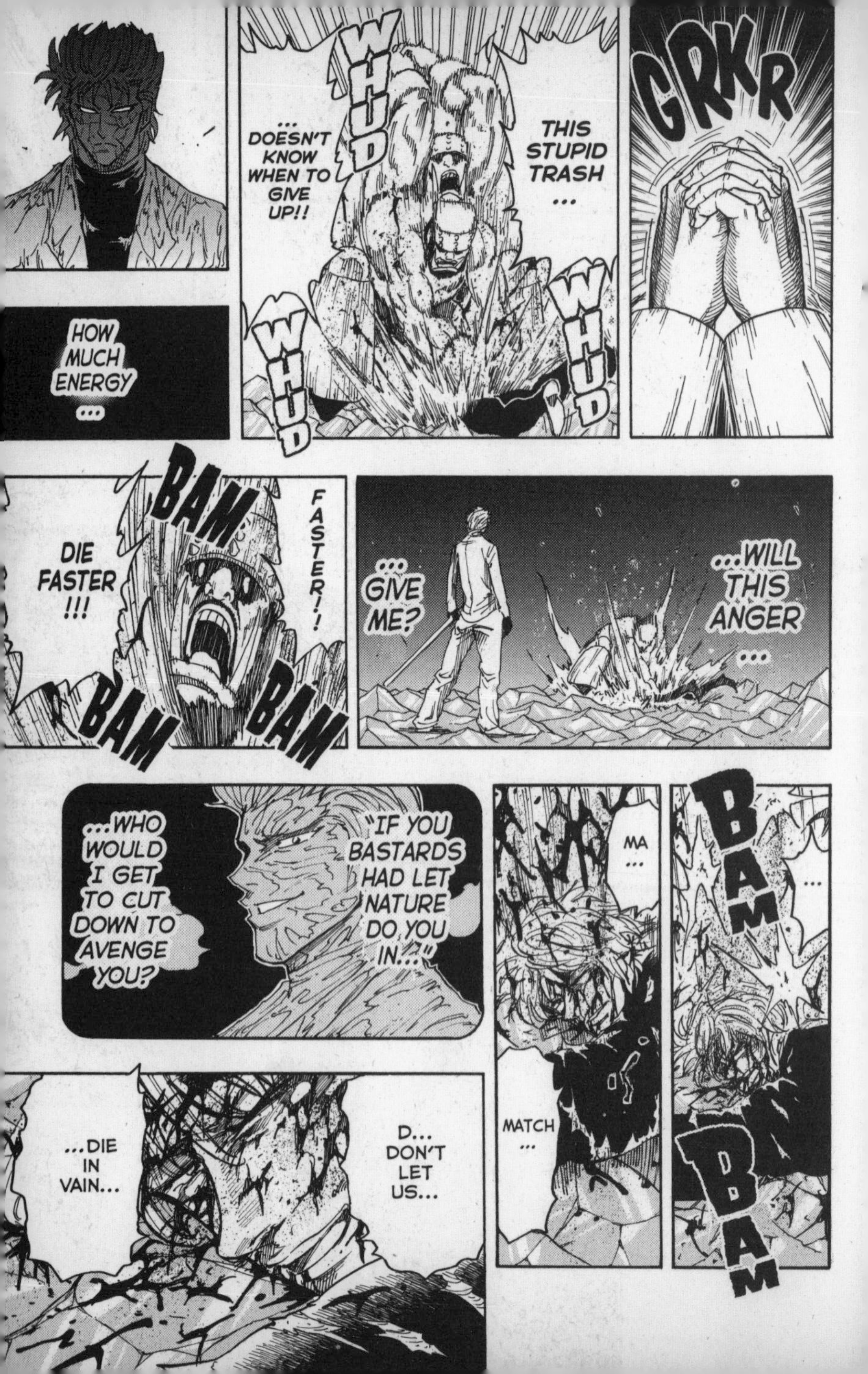
GRKR
THIS STUPID TRASH ...
... DOESN'T KNOW WHEN TO GIVE UP!!
WHUD
WHUD
WHUD
HOW MUCH ENERGY ...
...WILL THIS ANGER ...
... GIVE ME?
FASTER!!
BAM
DIE FASTER !!!
BAM
BAM
BAM
...
BAM
MA ...
MATCH ...
"IF YOU BASTARDS HAD LET NATURE DO YOU IN..."
...WHO WOULD I GET TO CUT DOWN TO AVENGE YOU?
D... DON'T LET US...
...DIE IN VAIN...

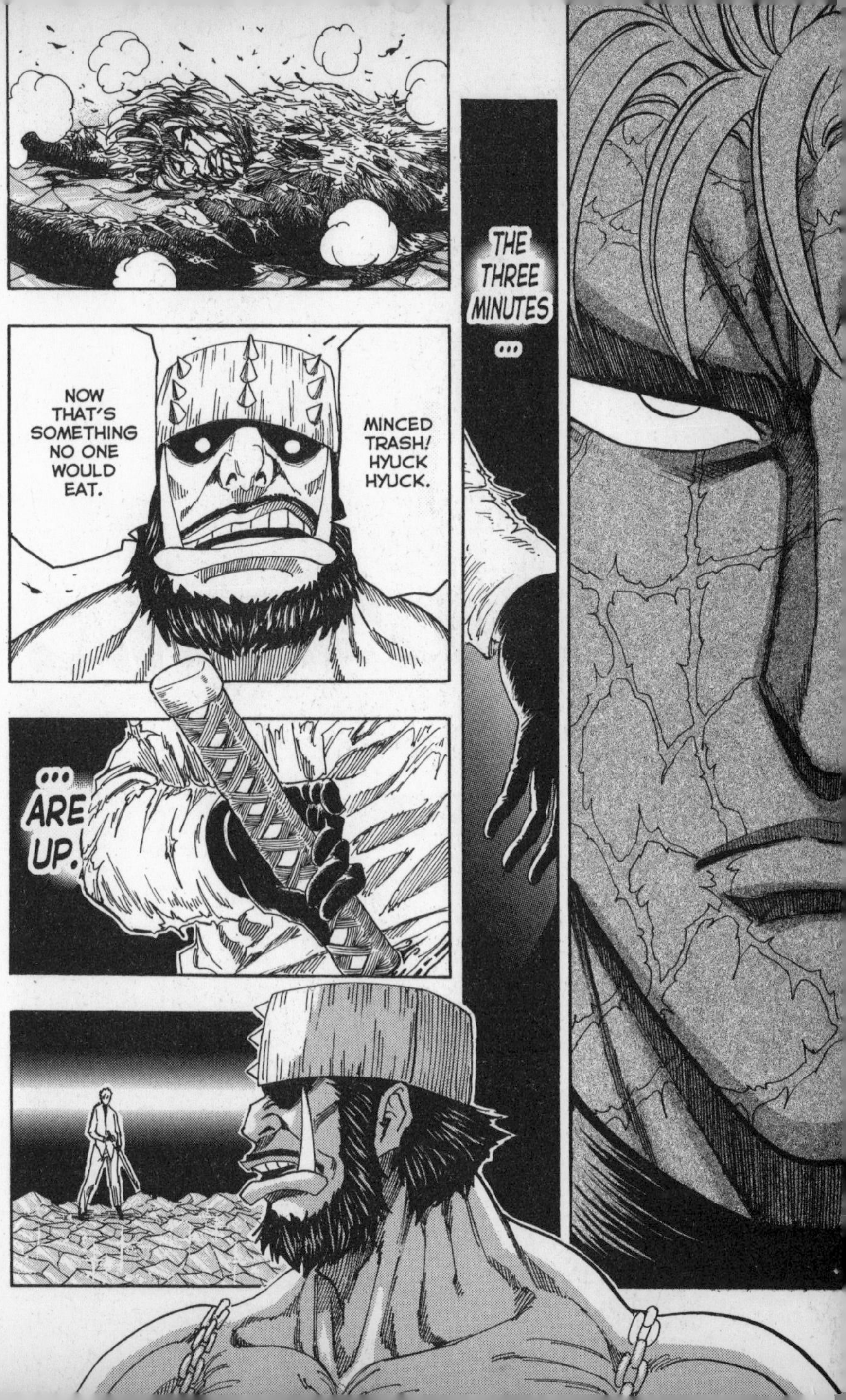
THE THREE MINUTES ...
MINCED TRASH! HYUCK HYUCK.
NOW THAT'S SOMETHING NO ONE WOULD EAT.
... ARE UP.

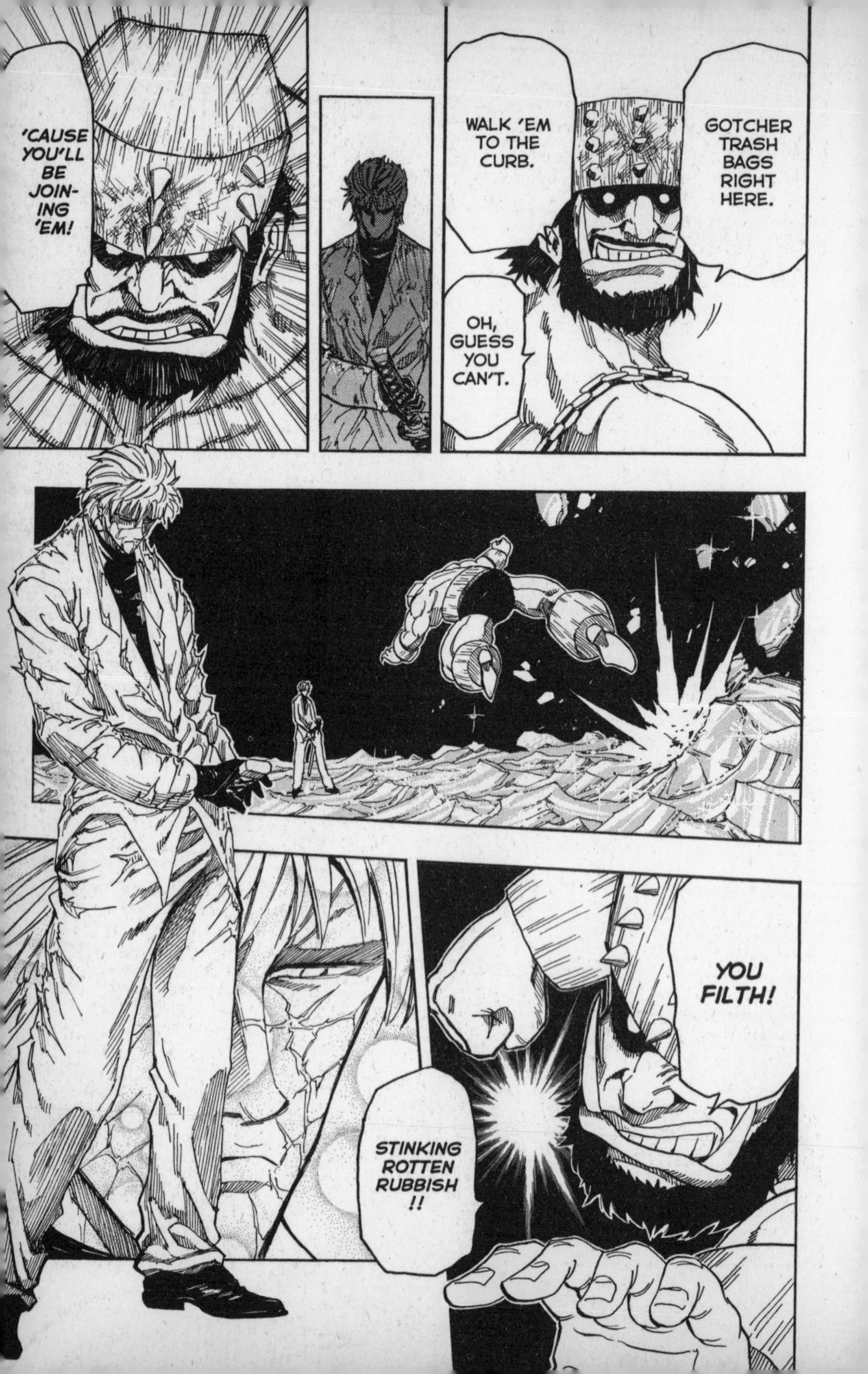
GOTCHER TRASH BAGS RIGHT HERE.
WALK 'EM TO THE CURB.
OH, GUESS YOU CAN'T.
'CAUSE YOU'LL BE JOIN-ING 'EM!
YOU FILTH!
STINKING ROTTEN RUBBISH !!

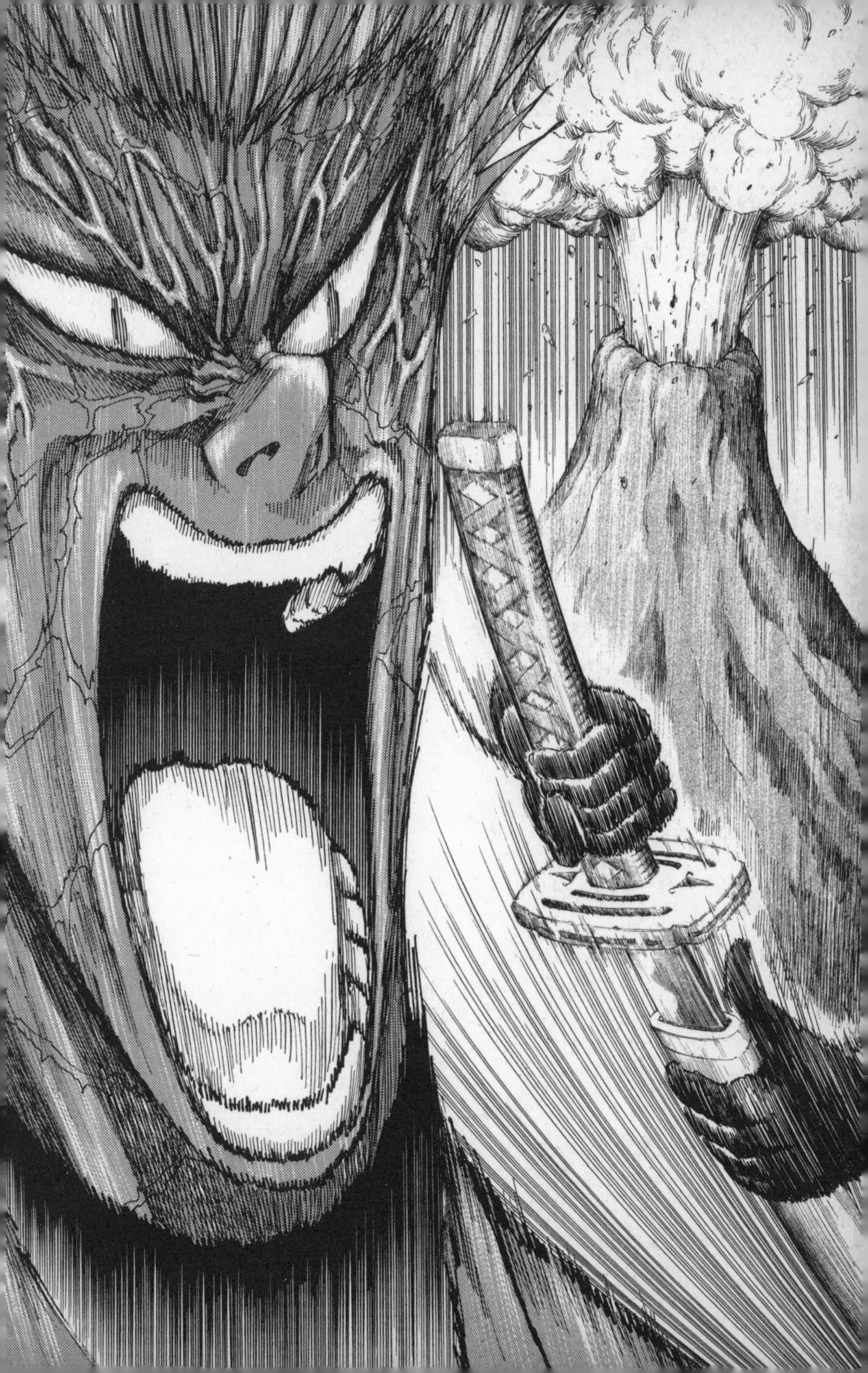

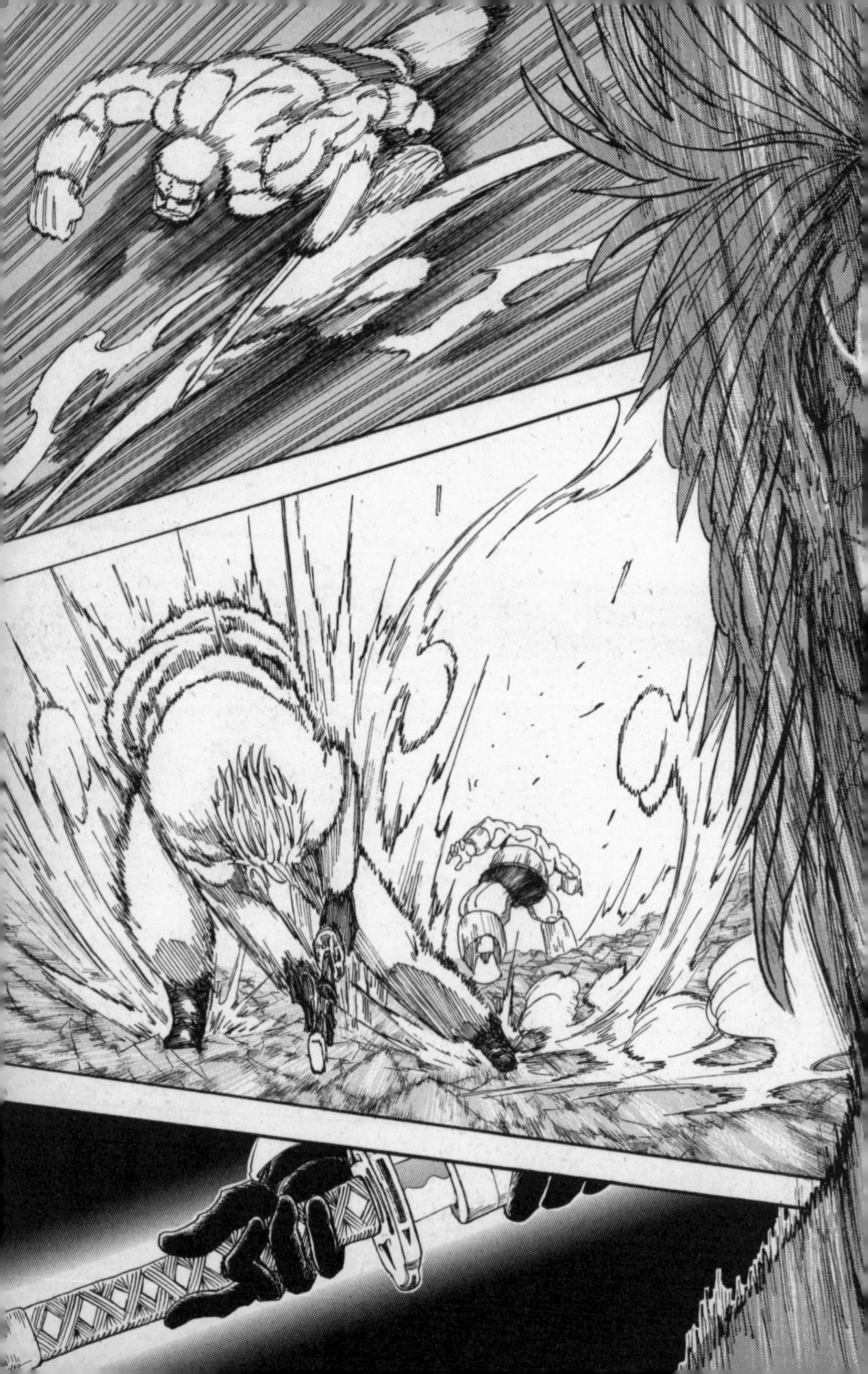

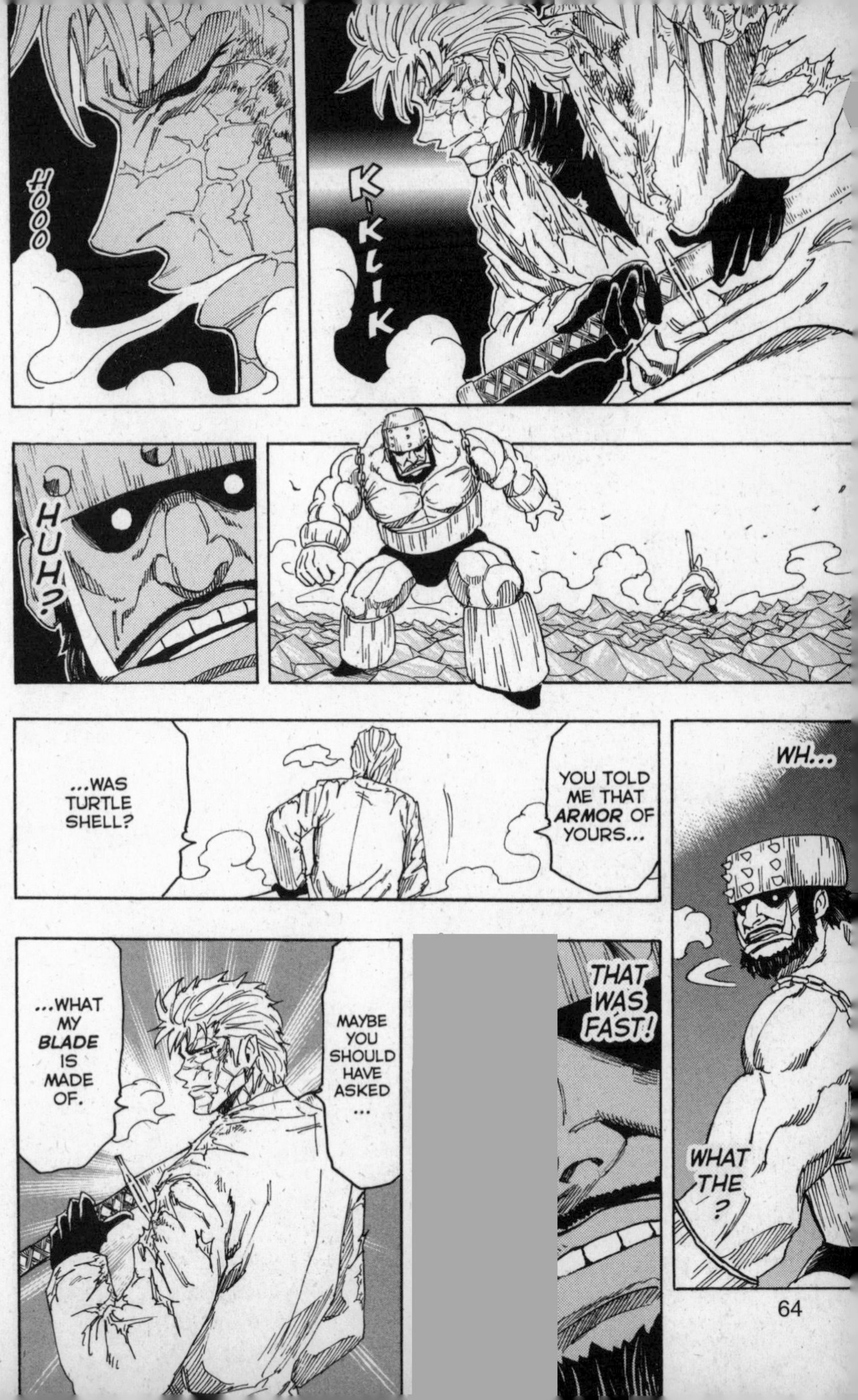
K-KLIK
HOOO
HUH?
WH...
WHAT THE?
YOU TOLD ME THAT ARMOR OF YOURS...
...WAS TURTLE SHELL?
THAT WAS FAST!
MAYBE YOU SHOULD HAVE ASKED...
...WHAT MY BLADE IS MADE OF.

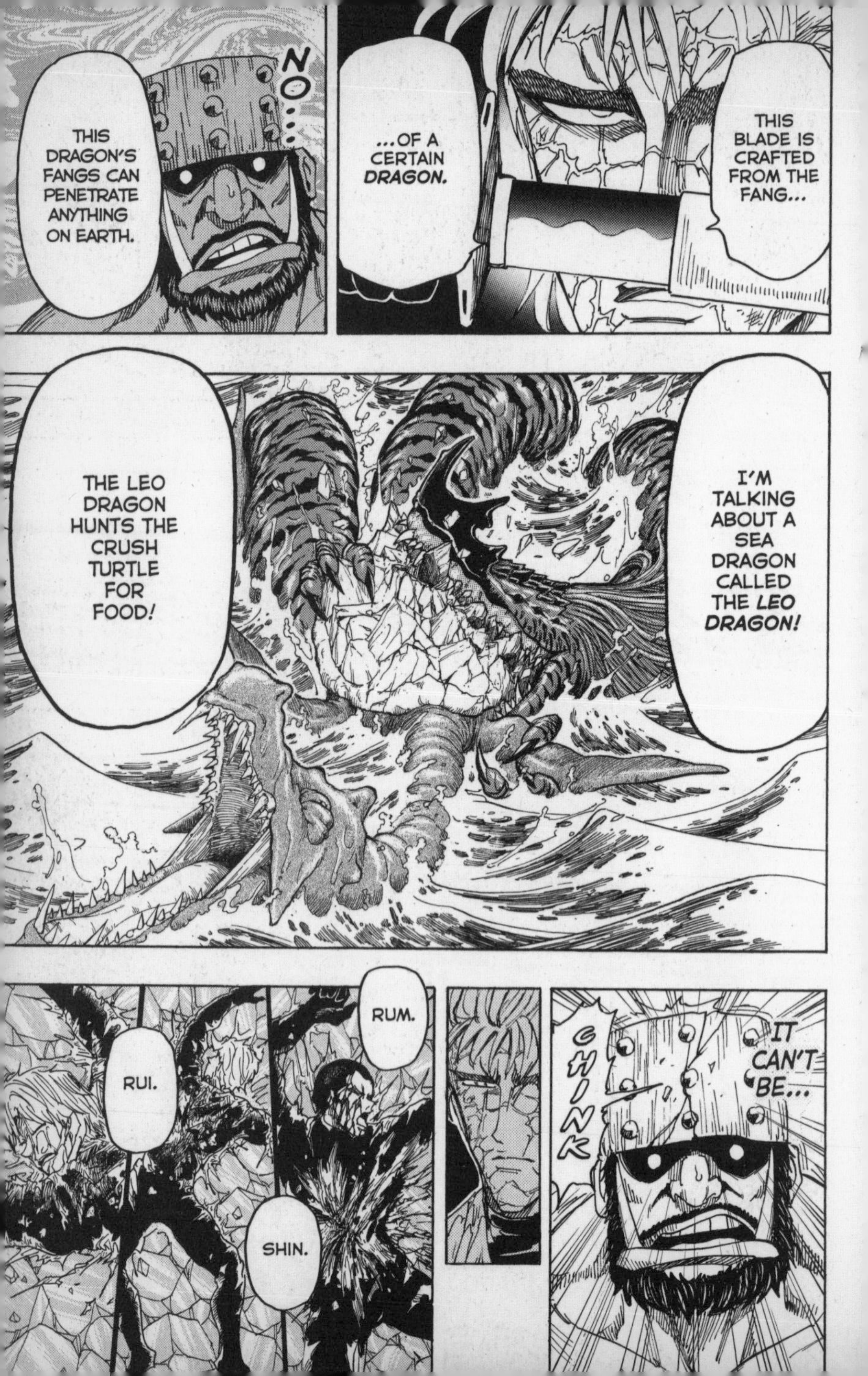
THIS BLADE IS CRAFTED FROM THE FANG...
...OF A CERTAIN *DRAGON.*
NO...
THIS DRAGON'S FANGS CAN PENETRATE ANYTHING ON EARTH.
I'M TALKING ABOUT A SEA DRAGON CALLED THE *LEO DRAGON!*
THE LEO DRAGON HUNTS THE CRUSH TURTLE FOR FOOD!
IT CAN'T BE...
CHINK
RUM.
RUI.
SHIN.

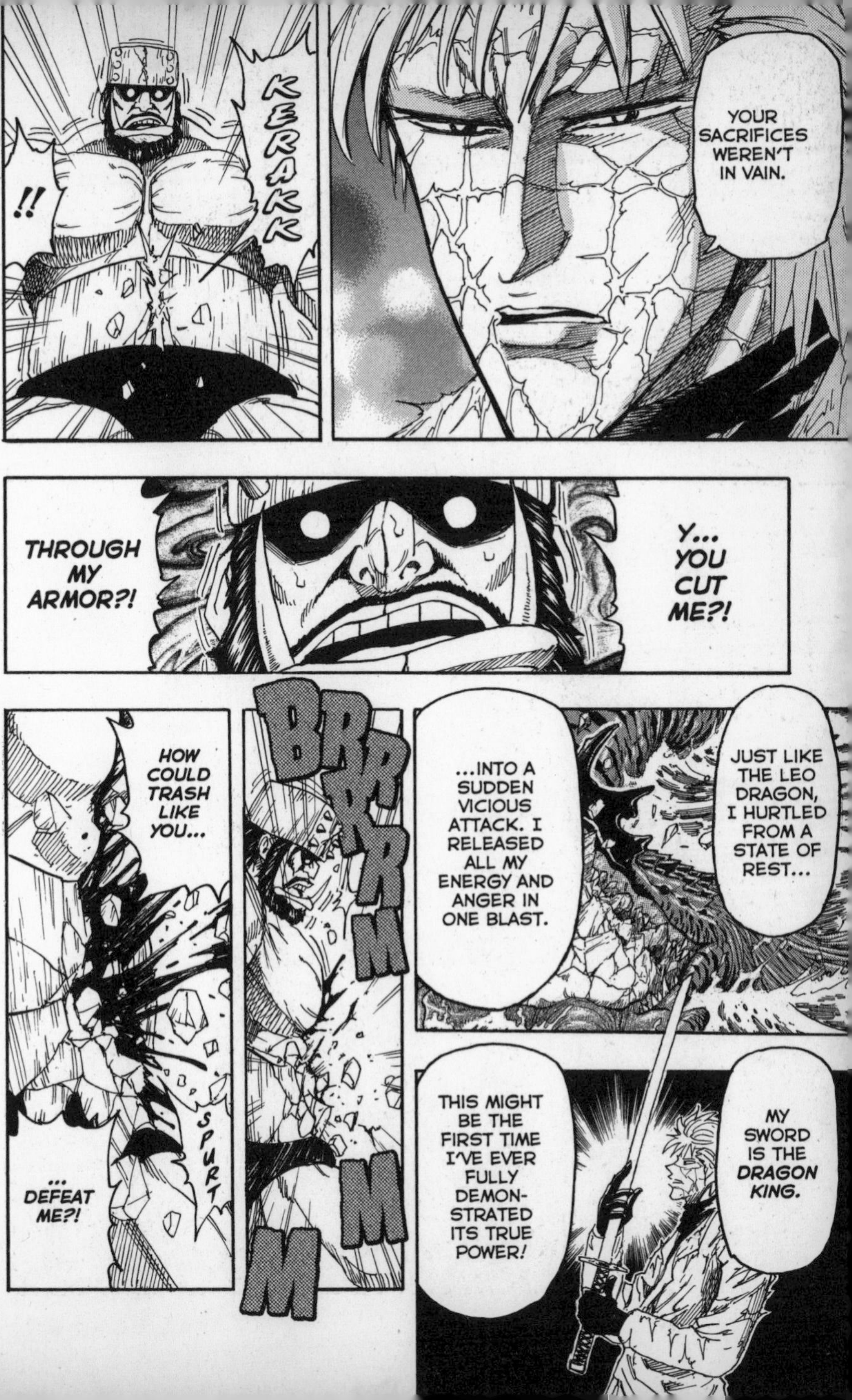
YOUR SACRIFICES WEREN'T IN VAIN.
KERAKK
!!
Y... YOU CUT ME?!
THROUGH MY ARMOR?!
JUST LIKE THE LEO DRAGON, I HURTLED FROM A STATE OF REST...
...INTO A SUDDEN VICIOUS ATTACK. I RELEASED ALL MY ENERGY AND ANGER IN ONE BLAST.
MY SWORD IS THE *DRAGON KING.*
THIS MIGHT BE THE FIRST TIME I'VE EVER FULLY DEMON-STRATED ITS TRUE POWER!
BRRRRMMM
HOW COULD TRASH LIKE YOU...
SPURT
...DEFEAT ME?!

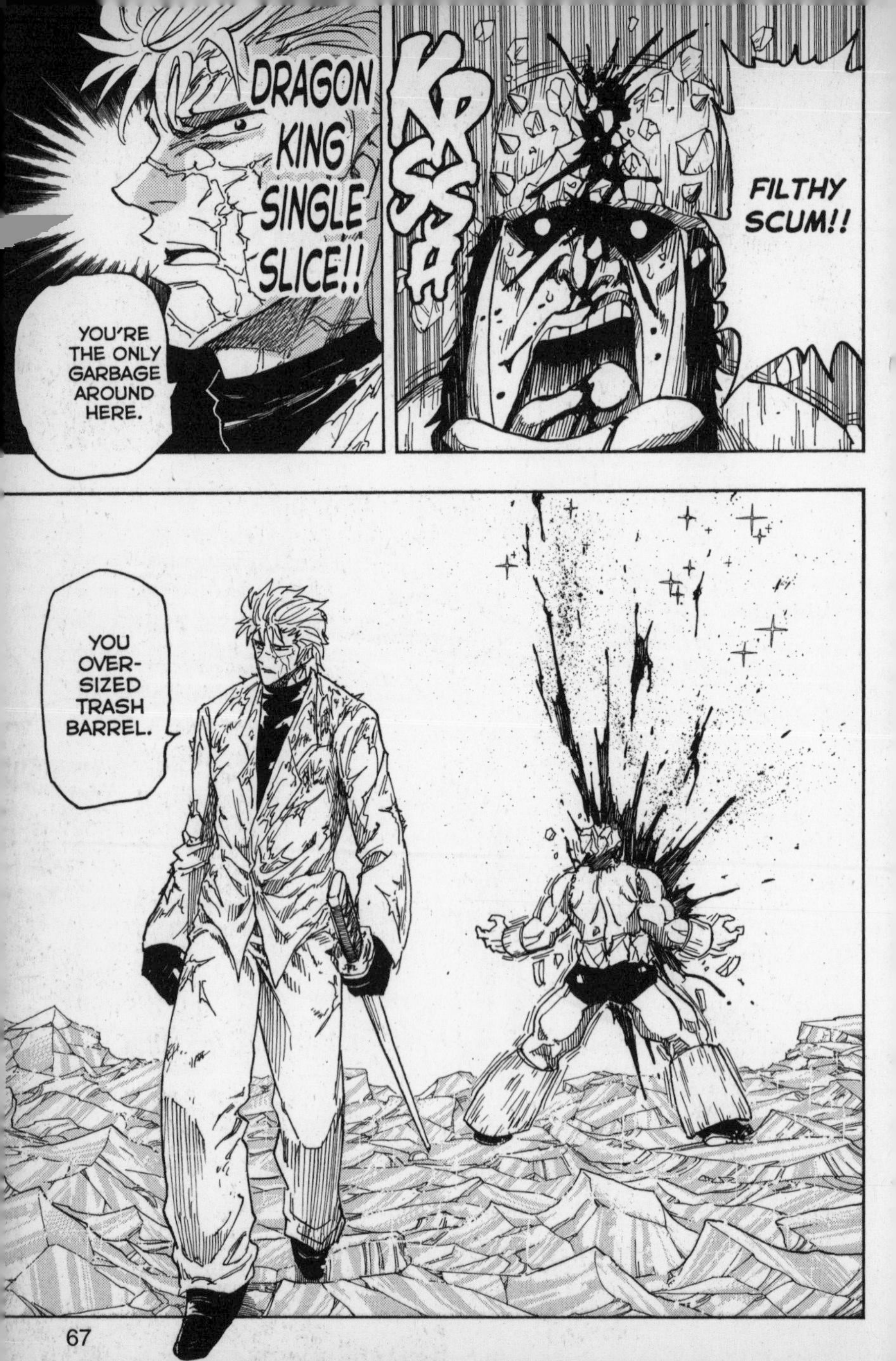
KDSA
FILTHY SCUM!!
DRAGON KING SINGLE SLICE!!
YOU'RE THE ONLY GARBAGE AROUND HERE.
YOU OVER-SIZED TRASH BARREL.

TORIKO

GOURMET CHECKLIST

Vol. 080

100% FRESH-SQUEEZED PEACH LEMON JUICE (SOFT DRINK)

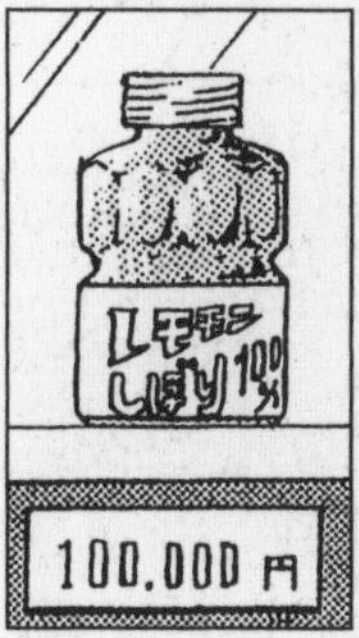
レモンしぼり 100%
100.000 円

CAPTURE LEVEL: 17 (IN THE WILD)

HABITAT: GOURMET TOWN'S THREE-STAR VENDING MACHINES

LENGTH: ---

HEIGHT: ---

WEIGHT: ---

PRICE: 100,000 YEN PER 350ML CAN

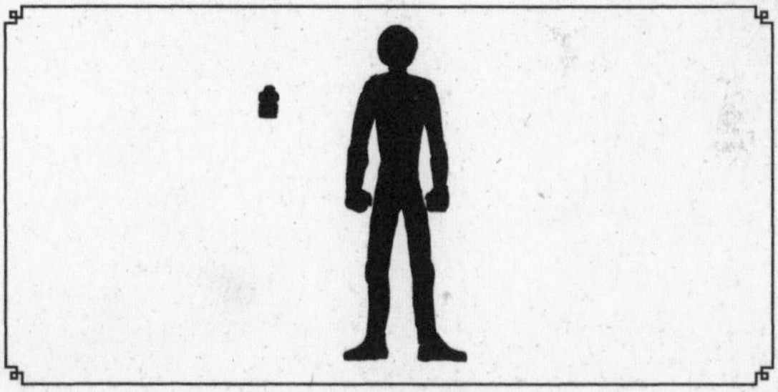

SCALE

A SOFT DRINK SOLD IN THE THREE-STAR VENDING MACHINES IN GOURMET TOWN. THE PEACH LEMON HAS A LEMON RIND BUT A PEACHY INTERIOR! ITS SWEETNESS HAS A HINT OF SOURNESS, WHICH GIVES IT A CURIOUS FLAVOR. IT'S ALSO VERY POPULAR AS AN INGREDIENT IN ALCOHOLIC LIQUEURS.

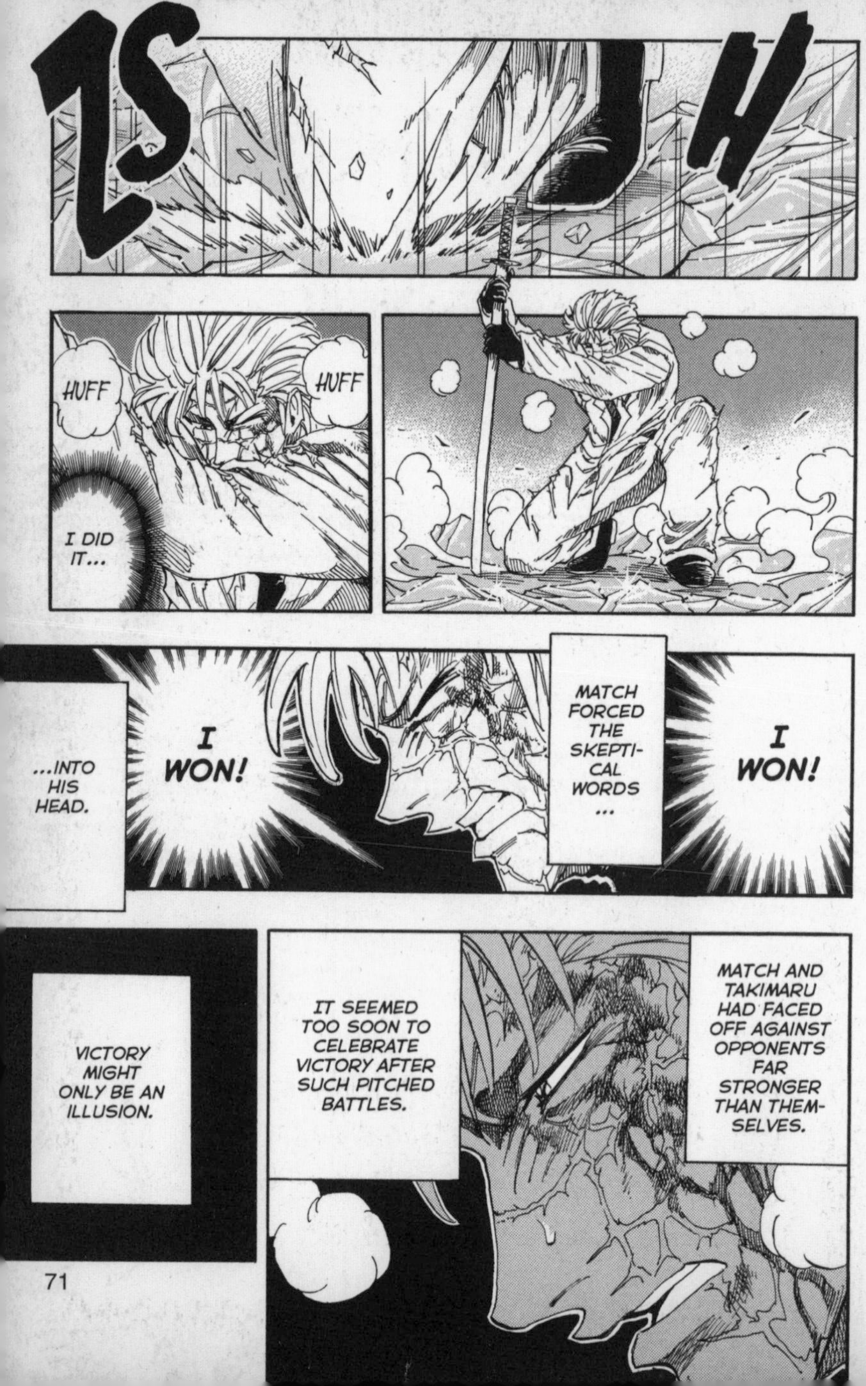
ZSH
HUFF
HUFF
I DID IT...
I WON!
MATCH FORCED THE SKEPTI-CAL WORDS ...
I WON!
...INTO HIS HEAD.
MATCH AND TAKIMARU HAD FACED OFF AGAINST OPPONENTS FAR STRONGER THAN THEM-SELVES.
IT SEEMED TOO SOON TO CELEBRATE VICTORY AFTER SUCH PITCHED BATTLES.
VICTORY MIGHT ONLY BE AN ILLUSION.

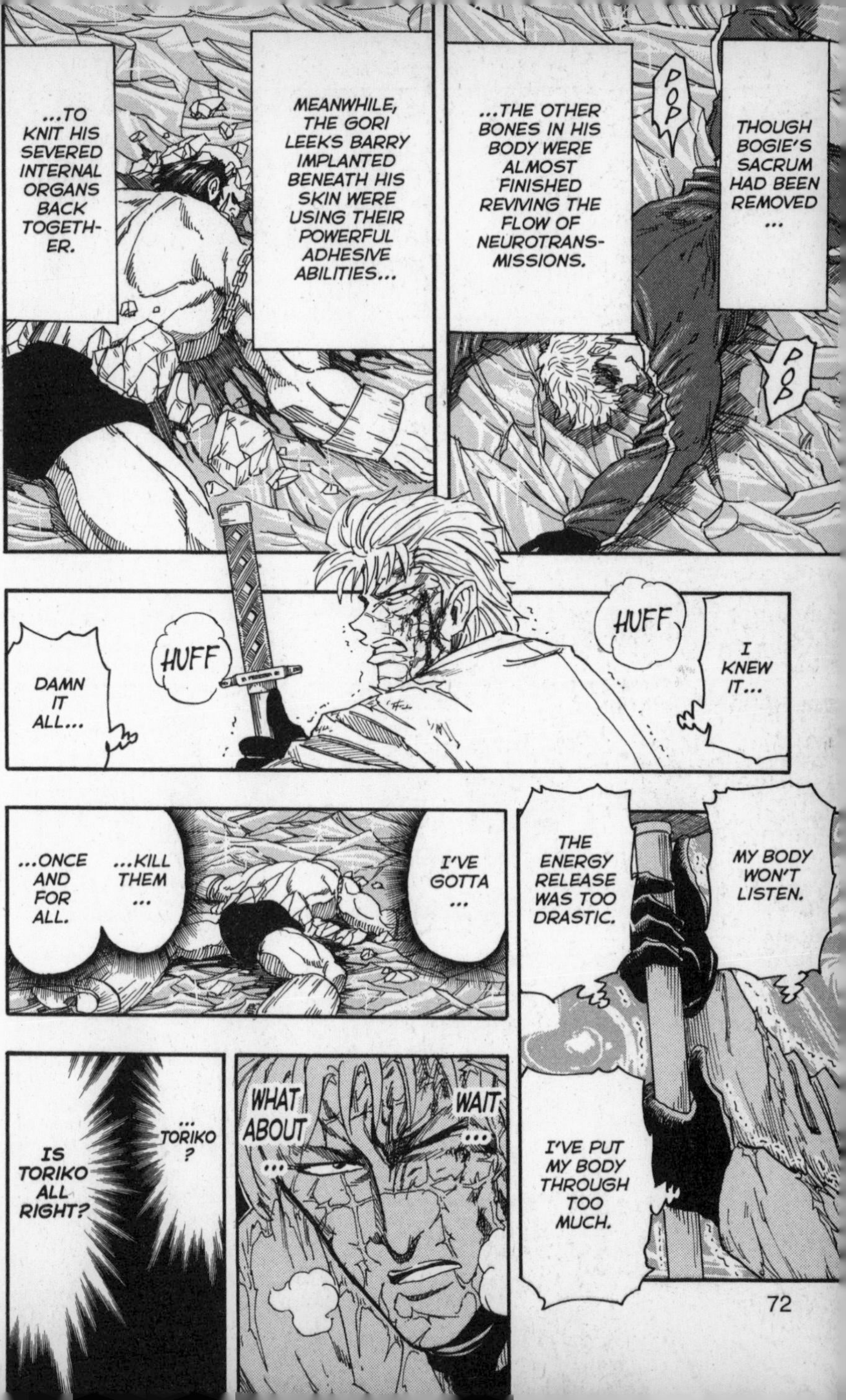
POP
THOUGH BOGIE'S SACRUM HAD BEEN REMOVED ...
POP
...THE OTHER BONES IN HIS BODY WERE ALMOST FINISHED REVIVING THE FLOW OF NEUROTRANSMISSIONS.
MEANWHILE, THE GORI LEEKS BARRY IMPLANTED BENEATH HIS SKIN WERE USING THEIR POWERFUL ADHESIVE ABILITIES...
...TO KNIT HIS SEVERED INTERNAL ORGANS BACK TOGETH-ER.
I KNEW IT...
HUFF
HUFF
DAMN IT ALL...
MY BODY WON'T LISTEN.
THE ENERGY RELEASE WAS TOO DRASTIC.
I'VE PUT MY BODY THROUGH TOO MUCH.
I'VE GOTTA ...
...KILL THEM ...
...ONCE AND FOR ALL.
WAIT ...
WHAT ABOUT ...
... TORIKO ?
IS TORIKO ALL RIGHT?

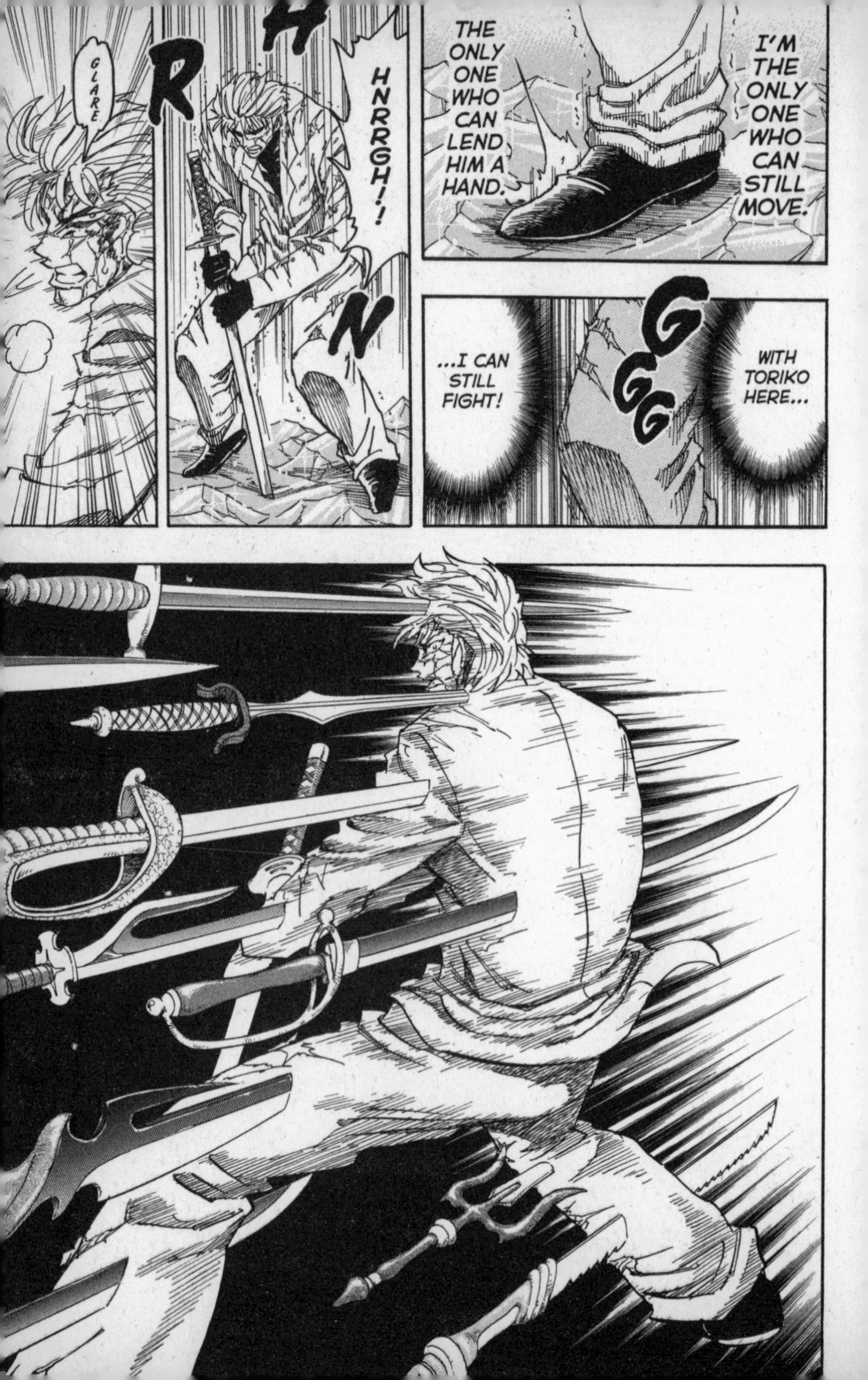
I'M THE ONLY ONE WHO CAN STILL MOVE.
THE ONLY ONE WHO CAN LEND HIM A HAND.
WITH TORIKO HERE...
GGG
...I CAN STILL FIGHT!
H
HNRRGH!!
R
N
GLARE

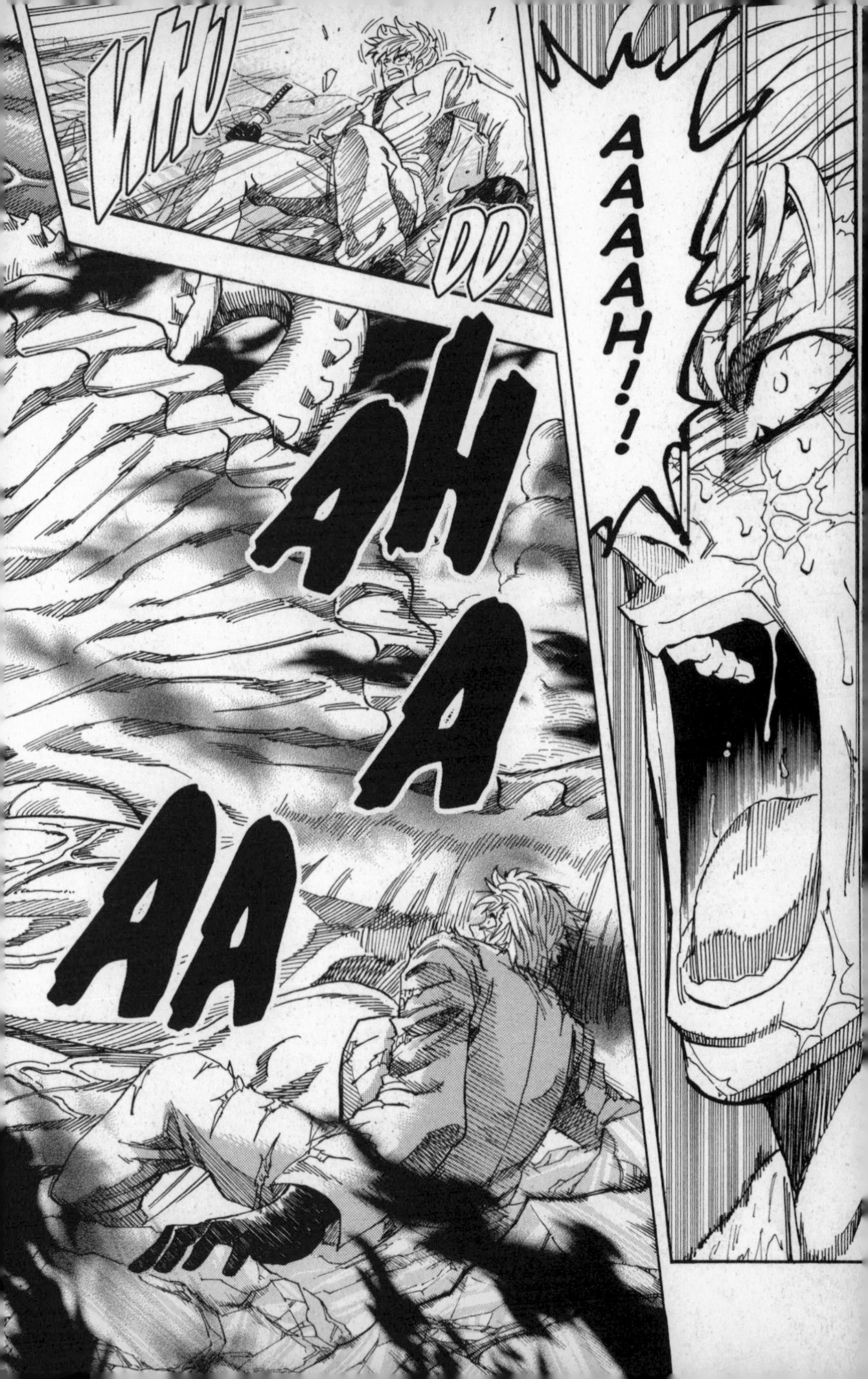
AAAAAH!!!
WHUDD
AAAAH

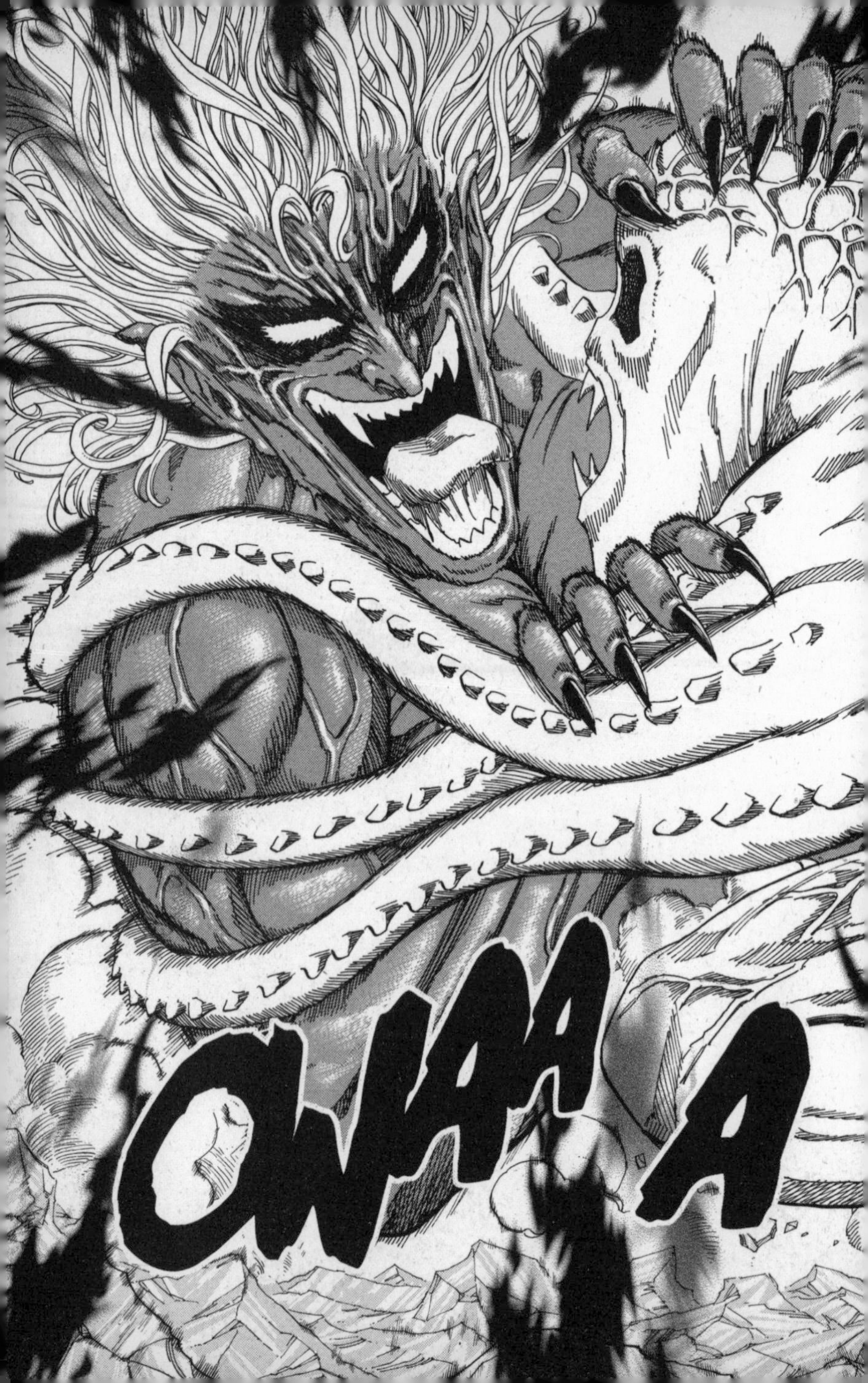
GWAA A

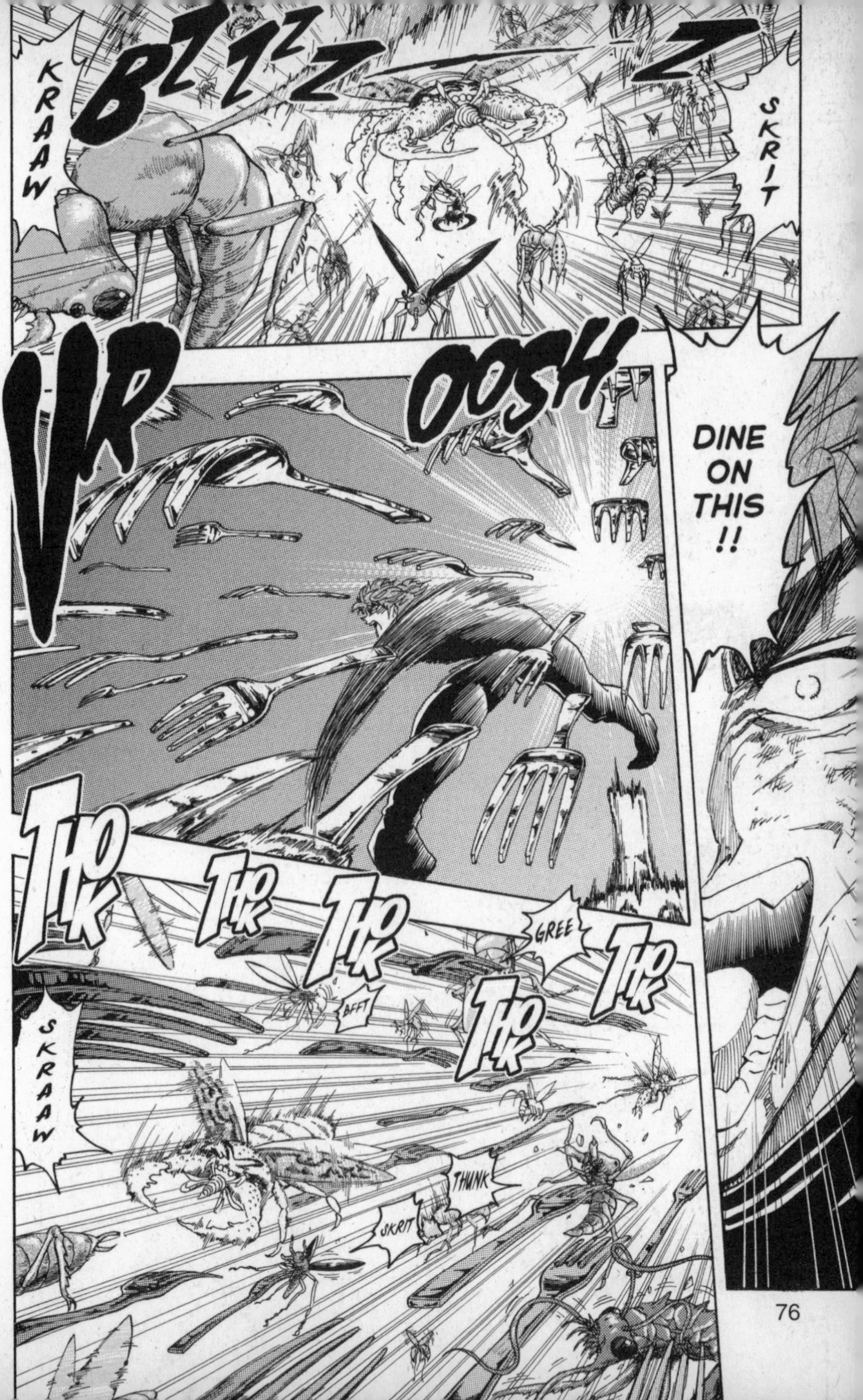
SKRIT
BZZZZZ
KRAAAW
DINE ON THIS!!
VROOSH
THOK
GREE
THOK
THOK
THOK
THOK
BFFT
SKRAAW
THUNK
SKRIT

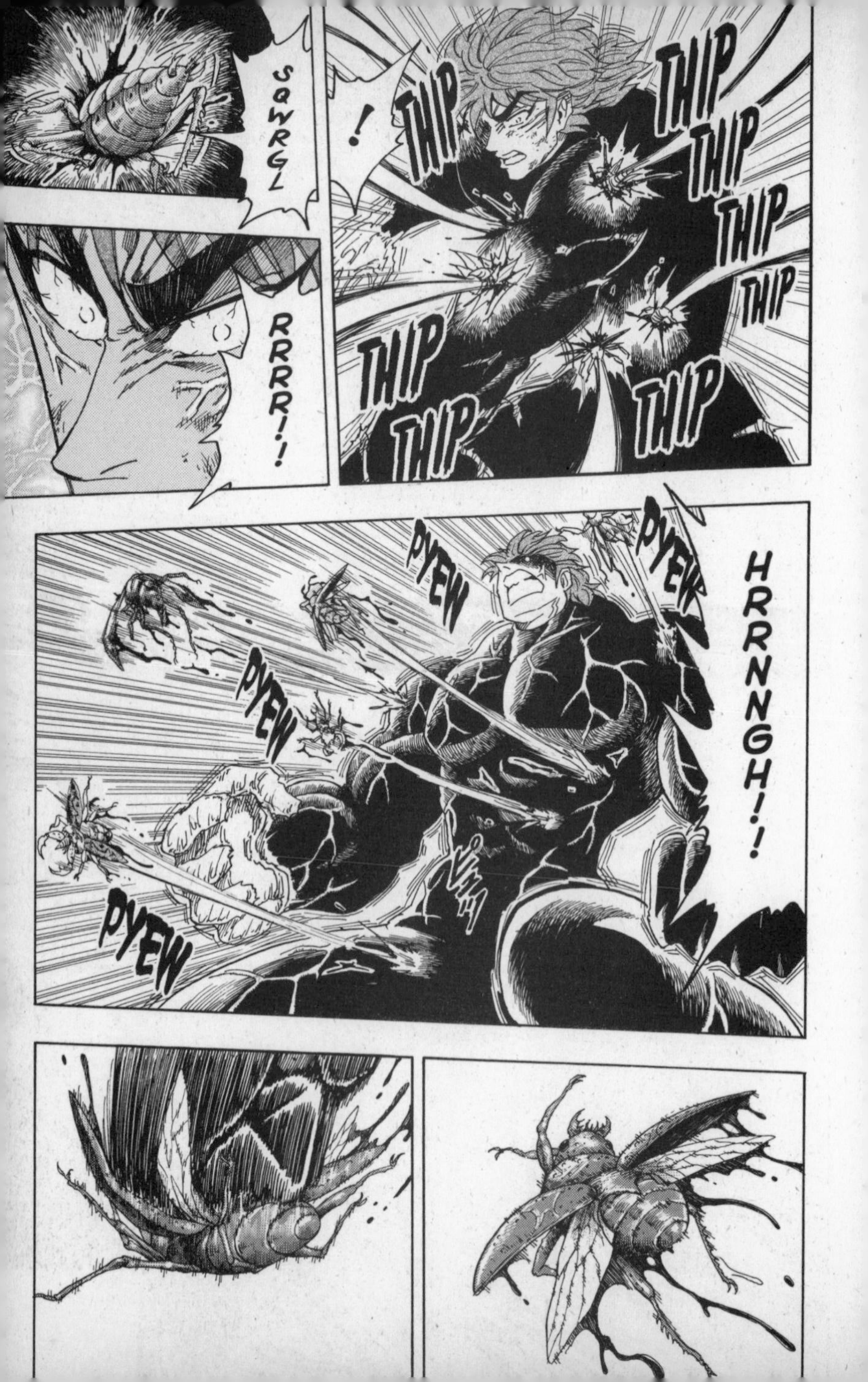
THIP
THIP
THIP
THIP
THIP
!
THIP
THIP
THIP
SQWRGL
RRRR!!
HRRNNNGH!!
PYEW
PYEW
PYEW
PYEW

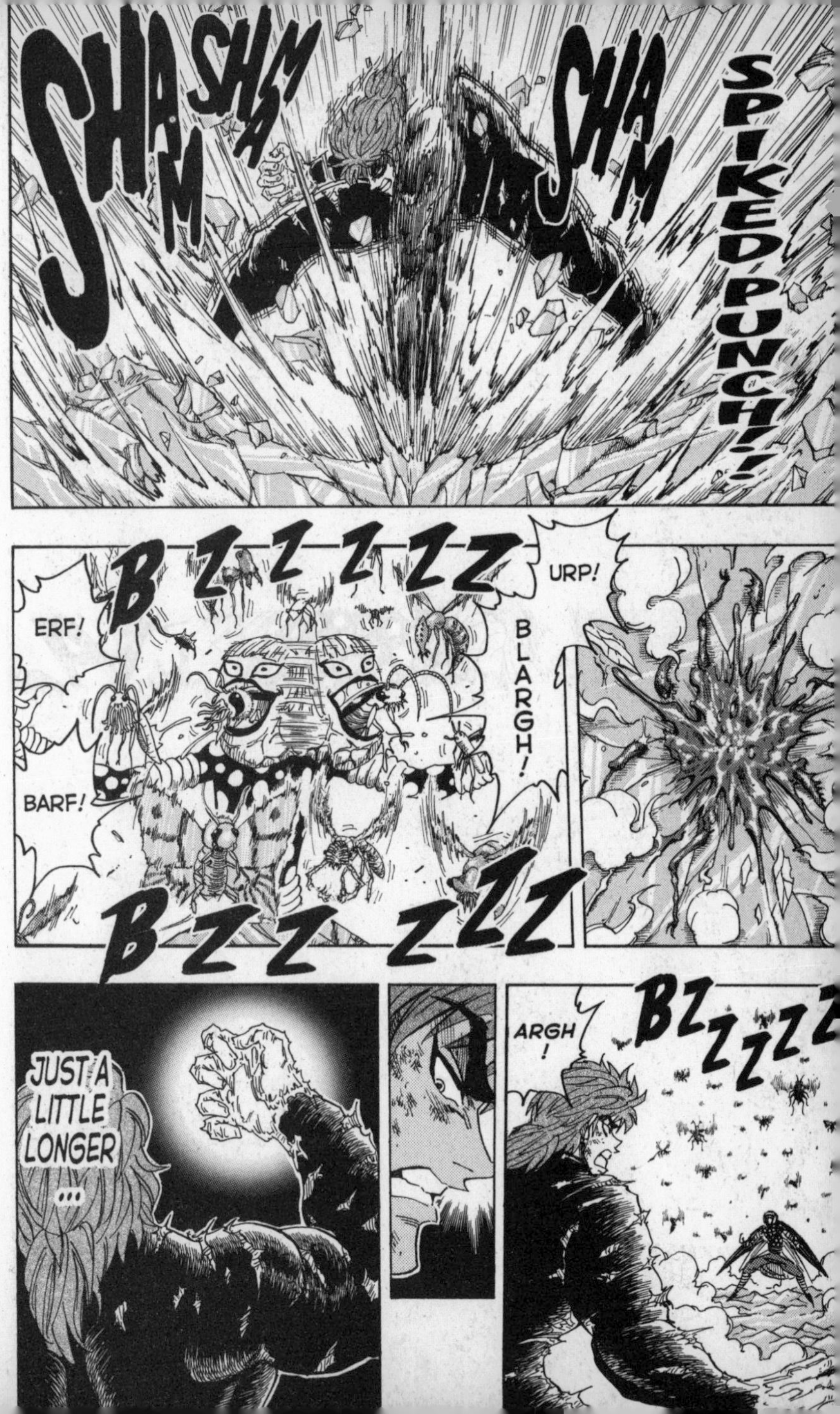
SPIKED PUNCH!!
SHASHAM
SHASHAM
URP!
BLARGH!
ERF!
BARF!
BZZZZZ
BZZZZZ
ARGH!
BZZZZZ
JUST A LITTLE LONGER...

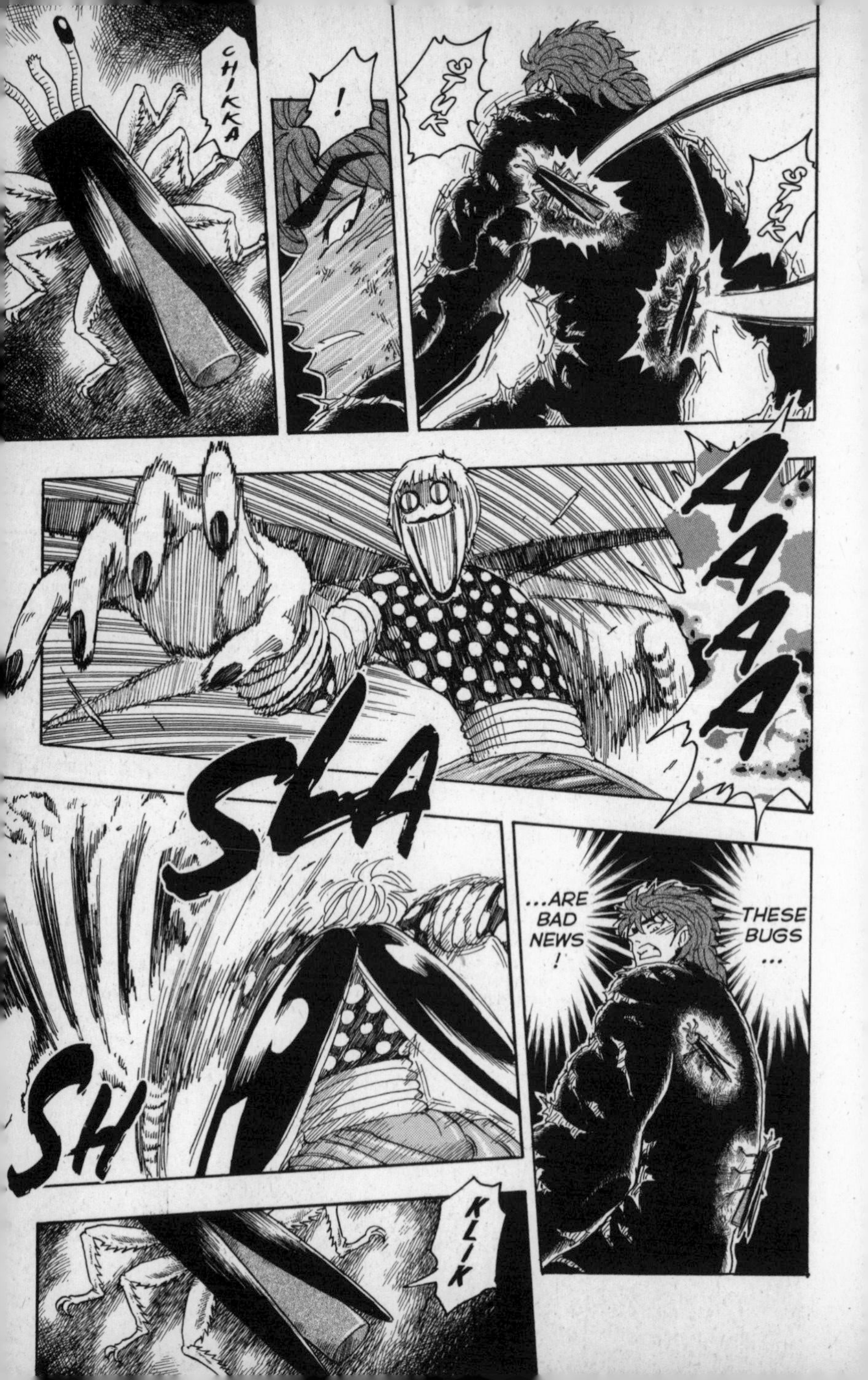
STUK
STUK
!
CHIKKA
AAAAA
THESE BUGS...
...ARE BAD NEWS!
SLASH
KLIK

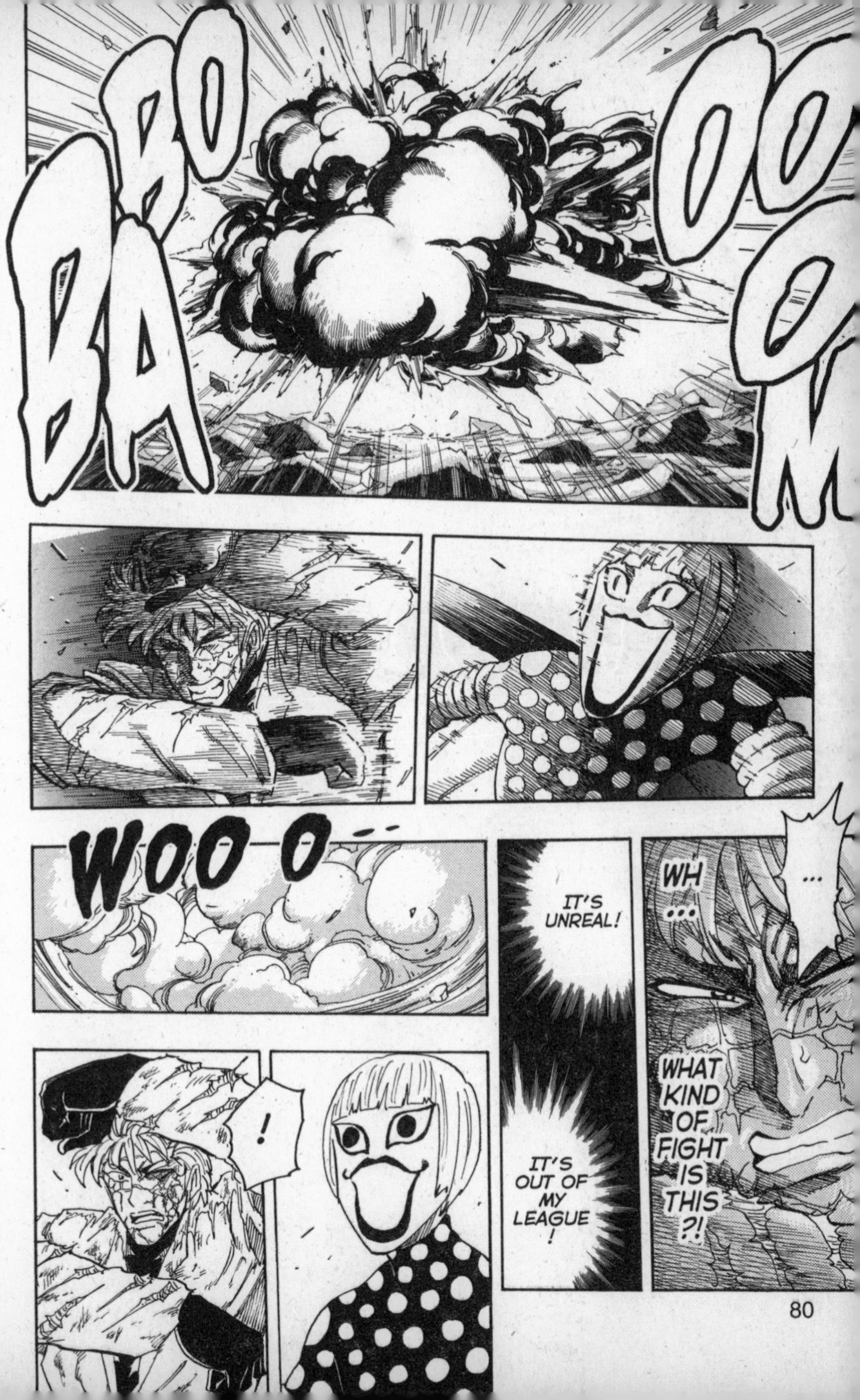
BA BOOOOM
WH ...
...
WHAT KIND OF FIGHT IS THIS?!
IT'S UNREAL!
IT'S OUT OF MY LEAGUE!
WOO O
!

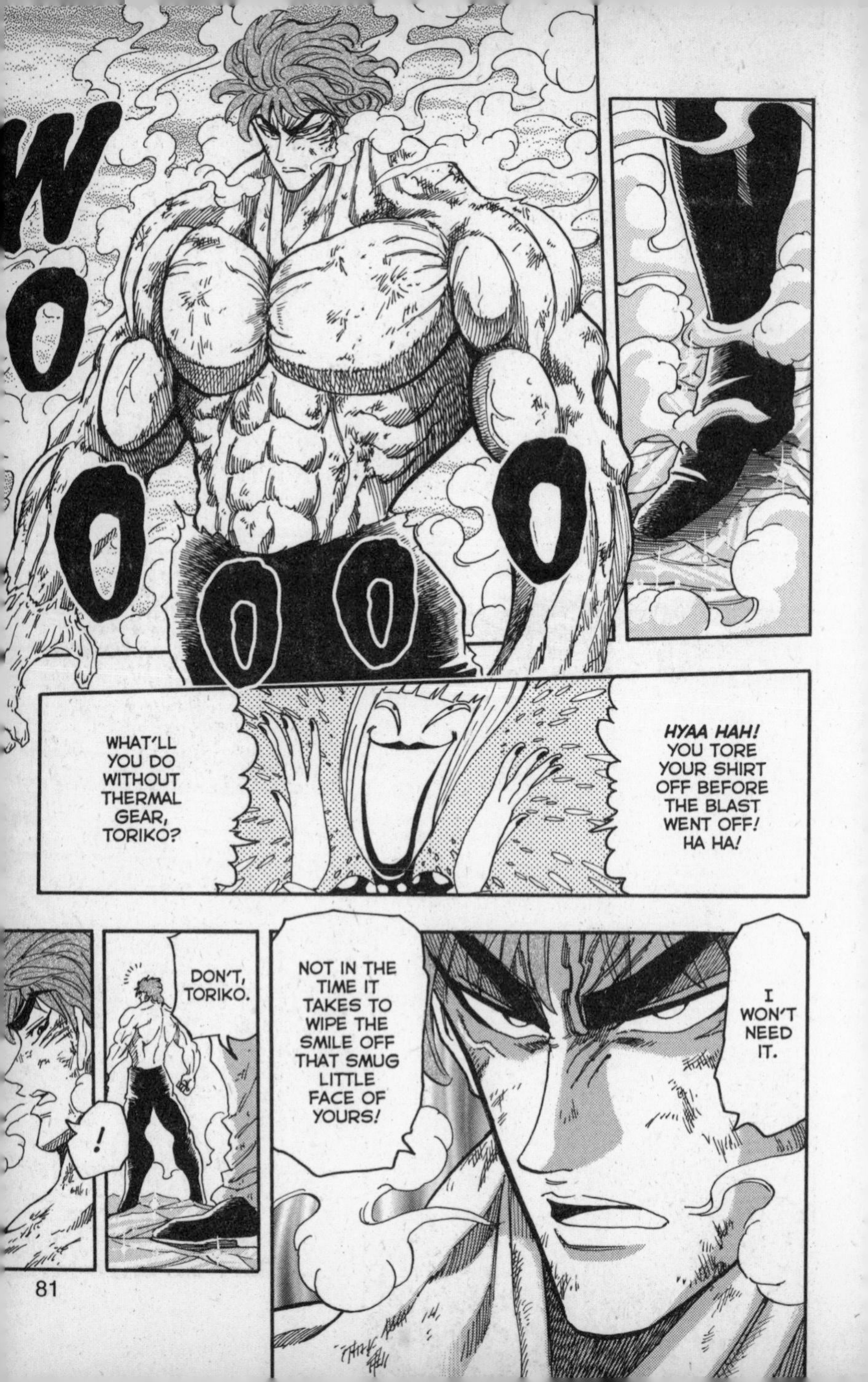
WOOOOOY
HYAA HAH! YOU TORE YOUR SHIRT OFF BEFORE THE BLAST WENT OFF! HA HA!
WHAT'LL YOU DO WITHOUT THERMAL GEAR, TORIKO?
I WON'T NEED IT.
NOT IN THE TIME IT TAKES TO WIPE THE SMILE OFF THAT SMUG LITTLE FACE OF YOURS!
DON'T, TORIKO.
!

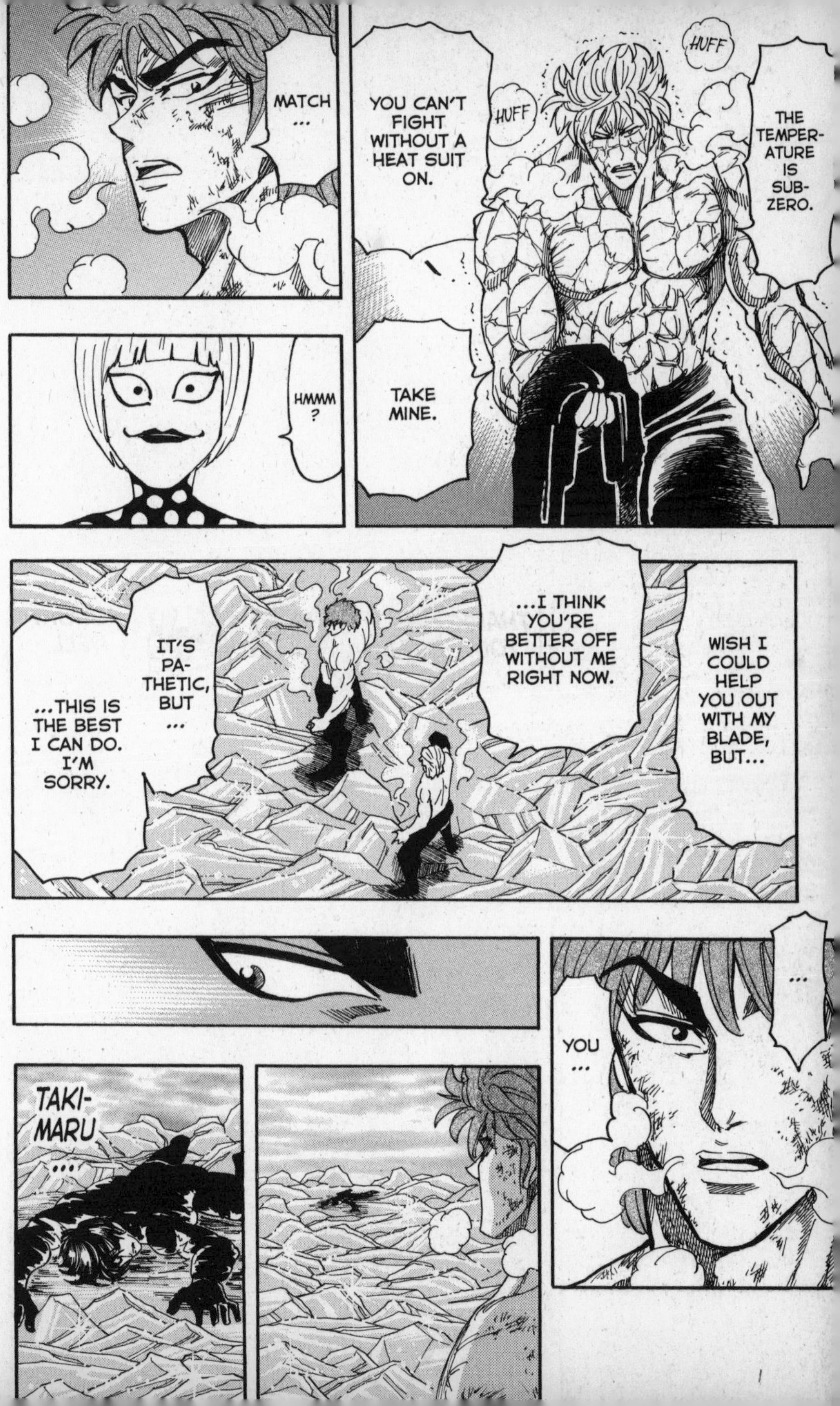
HUFF
HUFF
THE TEMPER-ATURE IS SUB-ZERO.
YOU CAN'T FIGHT WITHOUT A HEAT SUIT ON.
TAKE MINE.
MATCH ...
HMMM ?
WISH I COULD HELP YOU OUT WITH MY BLADE, BUT...
...I THINK YOU'RE BETTER OFF WITHOUT ME RIGHT NOW.
IT'S PA-THETIC, BUT ...
...THIS IS THE BEST I CAN DO. I'M SORRY.
...
YOU ...
TAKI-MARU
...

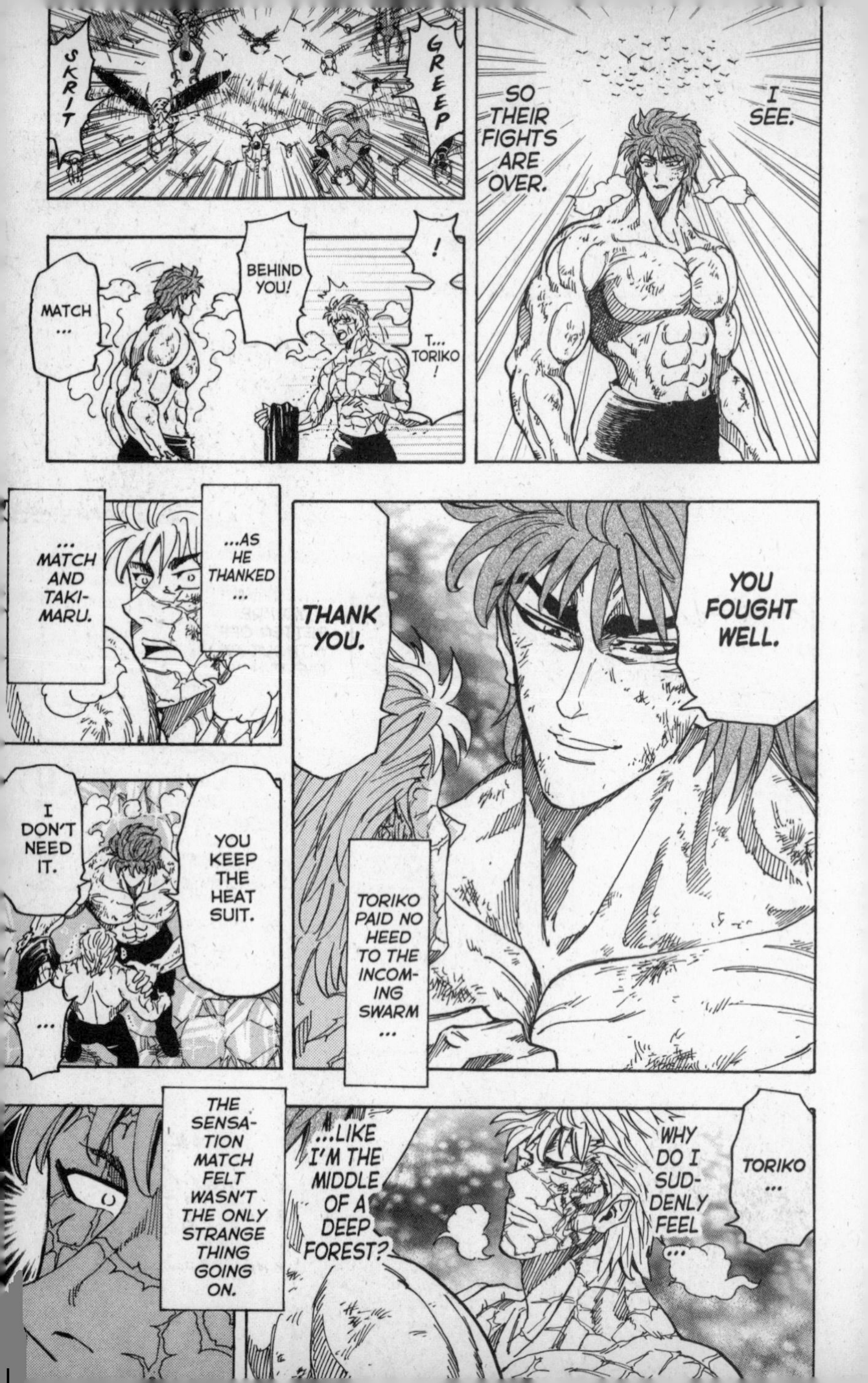
I SEE.
SO THEIR FIGHTS ARE OVER.
GREEP
SKRIT
!
T... TORIKO!
BEHIND YOU!
MATCH ...
YOU FOUGHT WELL.
THANK YOU.
TORIKO PAID NO HEED TO THE INCOMING SWARM ...
...AS HE THANKED ...
... MATCH AND TAKI-MARU.
YOU KEEP THE HEAT SUIT.
I DON'T NEED IT.
...
TORIKO ...
WHY DO I SUDDENLY FEEL ...
...LIKE I'M THE MIDDLE OF A DEEP FOREST?
THE SENSATION MATCH FELT WASN'T THE ONLY STRANGE THING GOING ON.

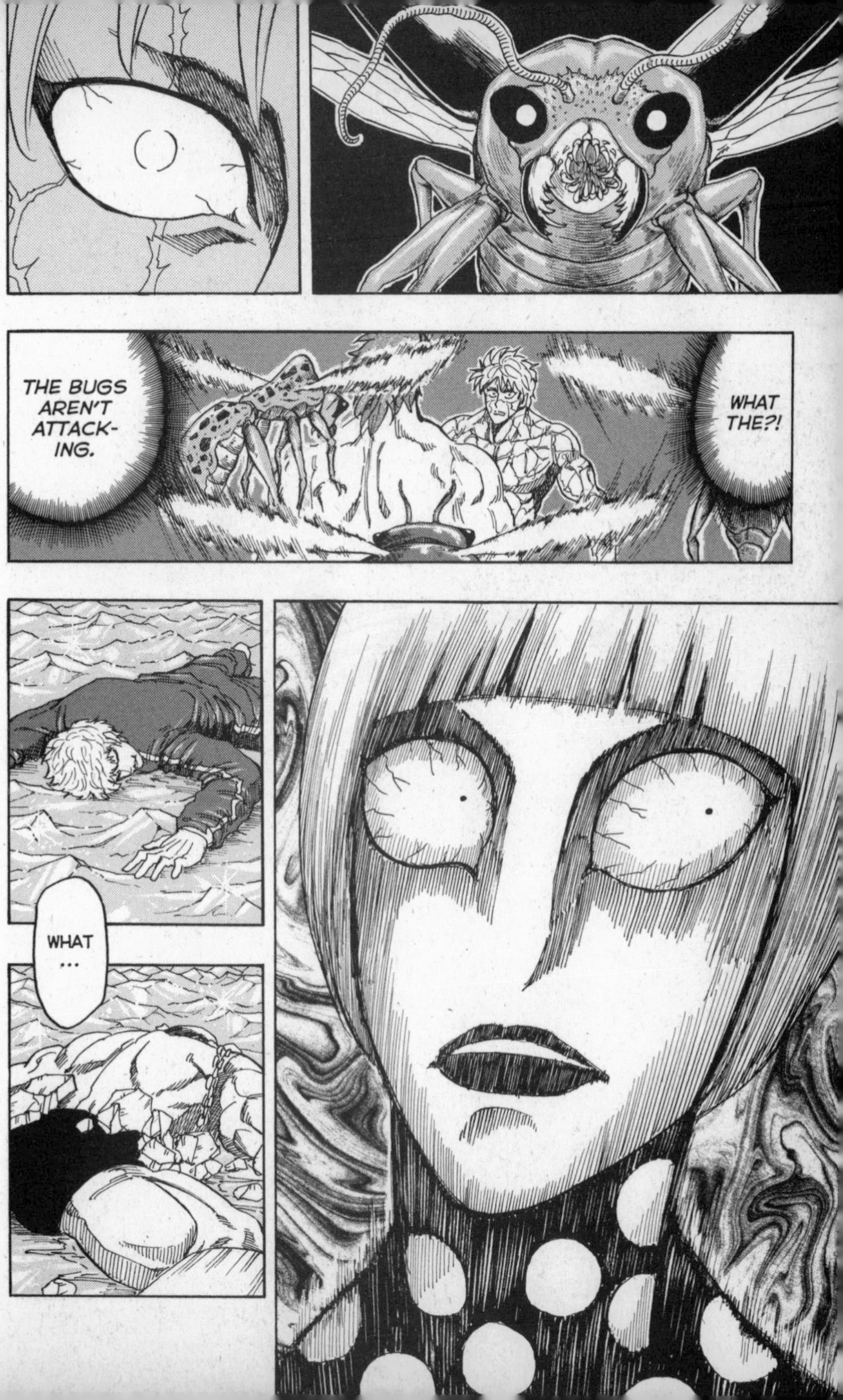
WHAT THE?!
THE BUGS AREN'T ATTACK-ING.
WHAT ...

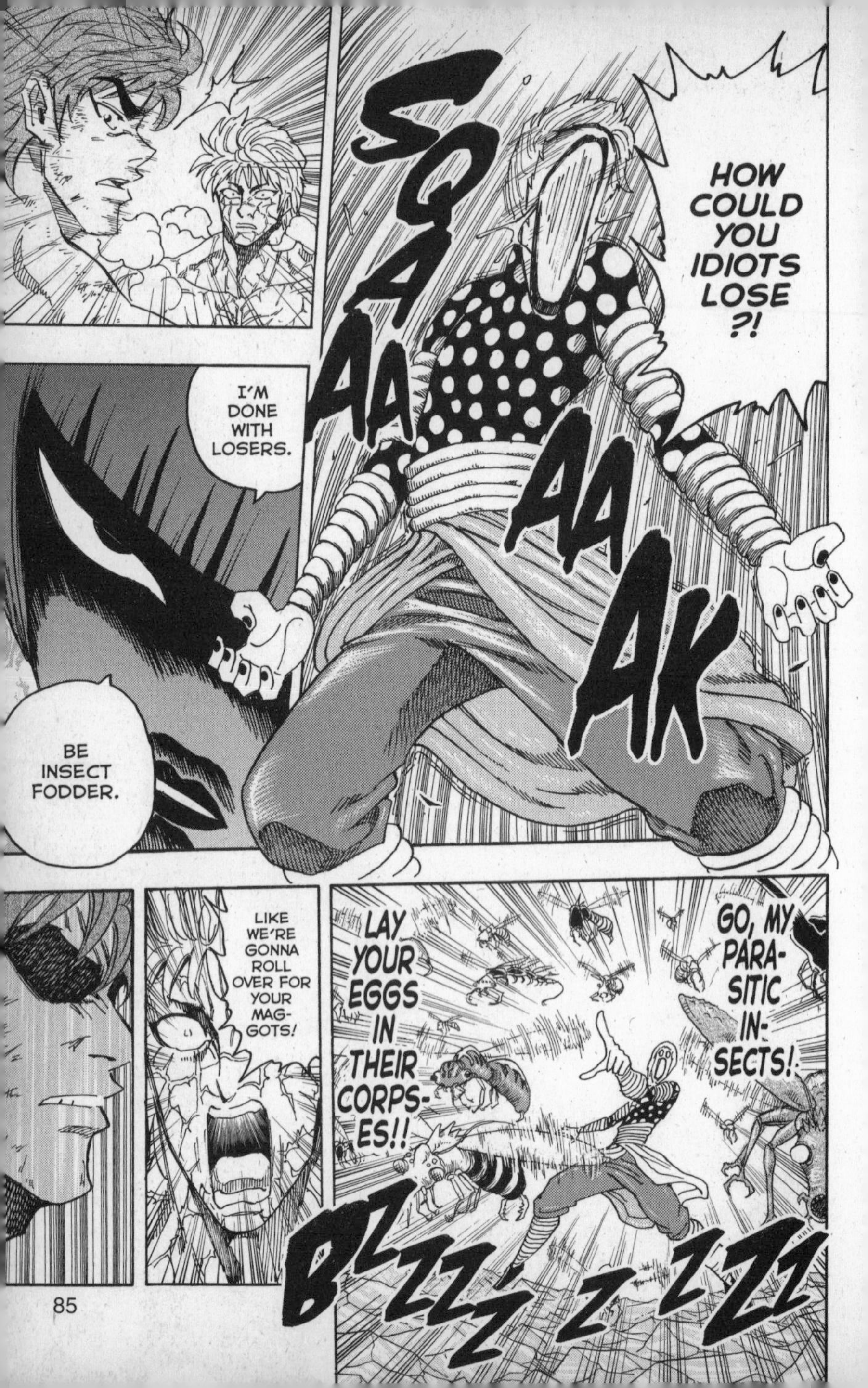
SQAAAAAAK
HOW COULD YOU IDIOTS LOSE?!
I'M DONE WITH LOSERS.
BE INSECT FODDER.
GO, MY PARASITIC INSECTS!
LAY YOUR EGGS IN THEIR CORPSES!!
BZZZZZZZ
LIKE WE'RE GONNA ROLL OVER FOR YOUR MAGGOTS!

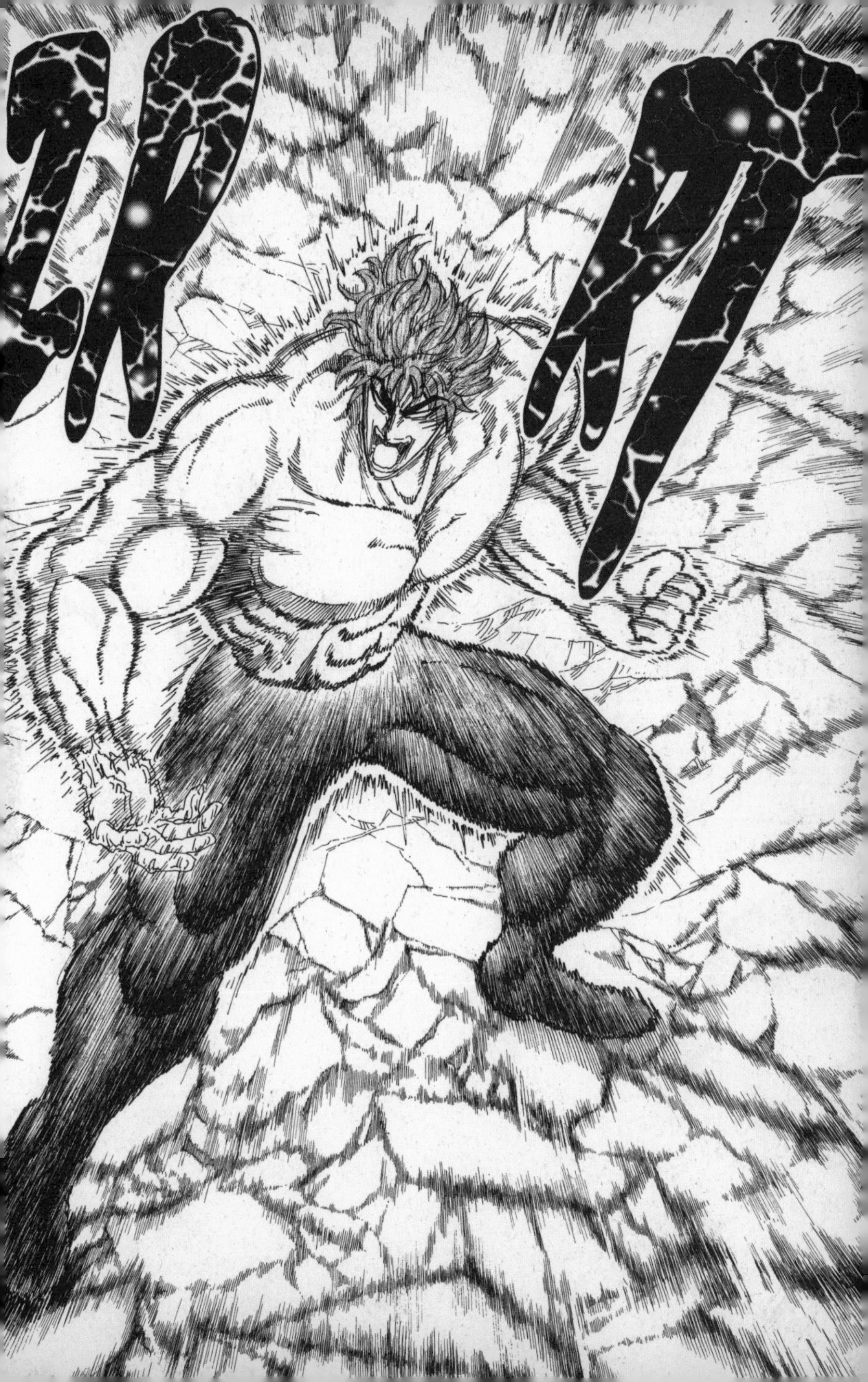

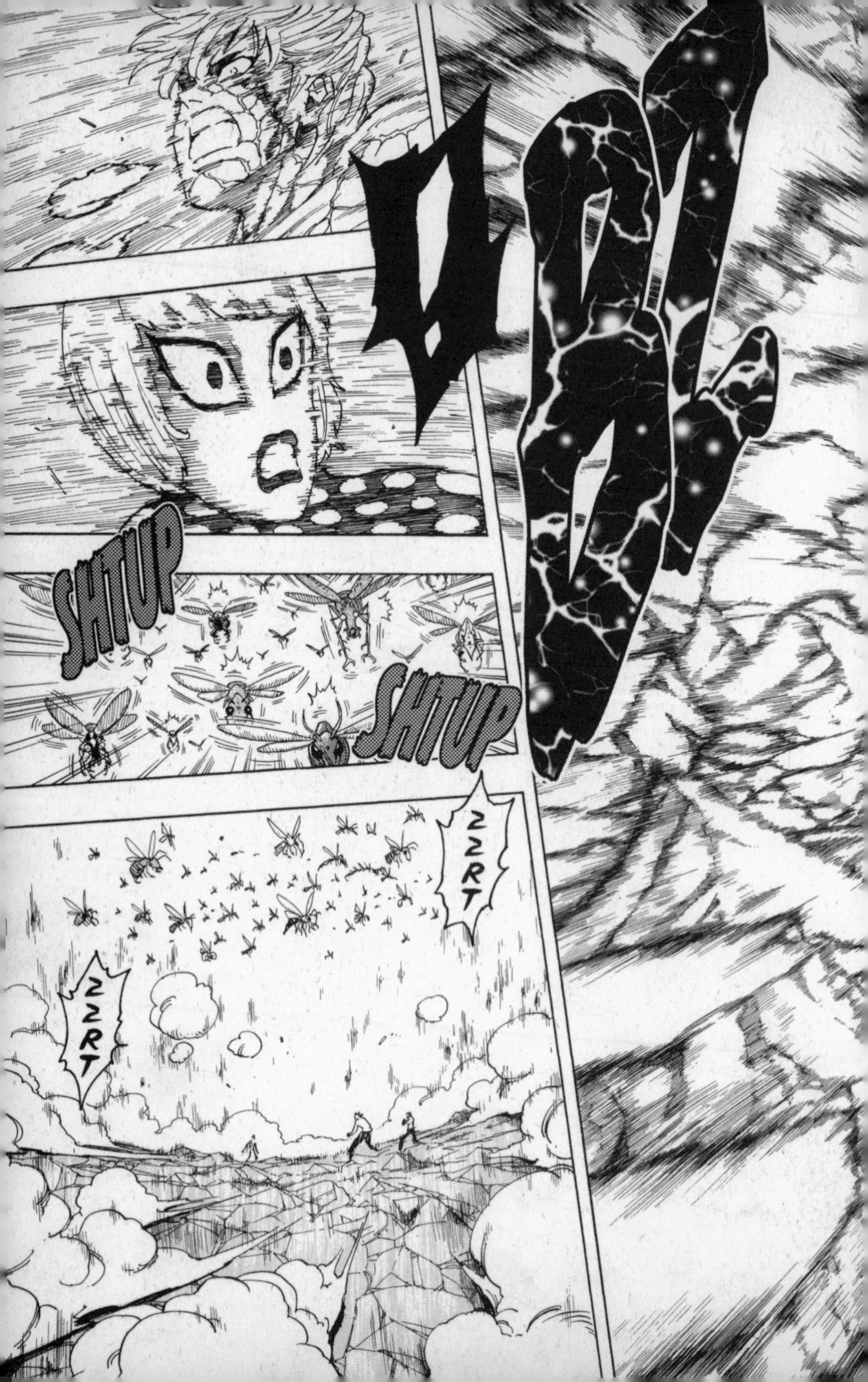
SHTUP
SHTUP
ZZRT
ZZRT

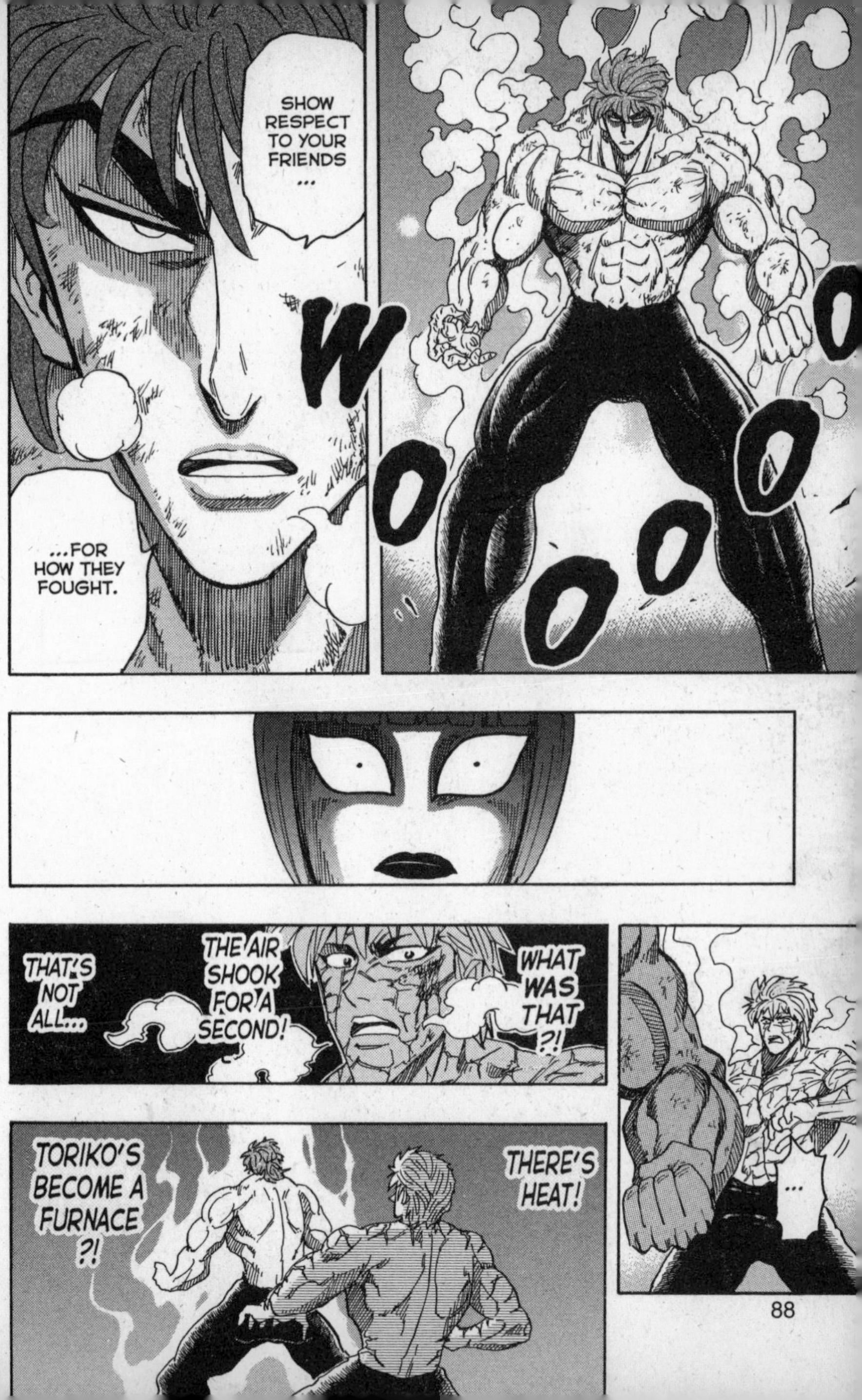
WOOOOO
SHOW RESPECT TO YOUR FRIENDS ...
...FOR HOW THEY FOUGHT.
...
WHAT WAS THAT?!
THE AIR SHOOK FOR A SECOND!
THAT'S NOT ALL...
THERE'S HEAT!
TORIKO'S BECOME A FURNACE?!

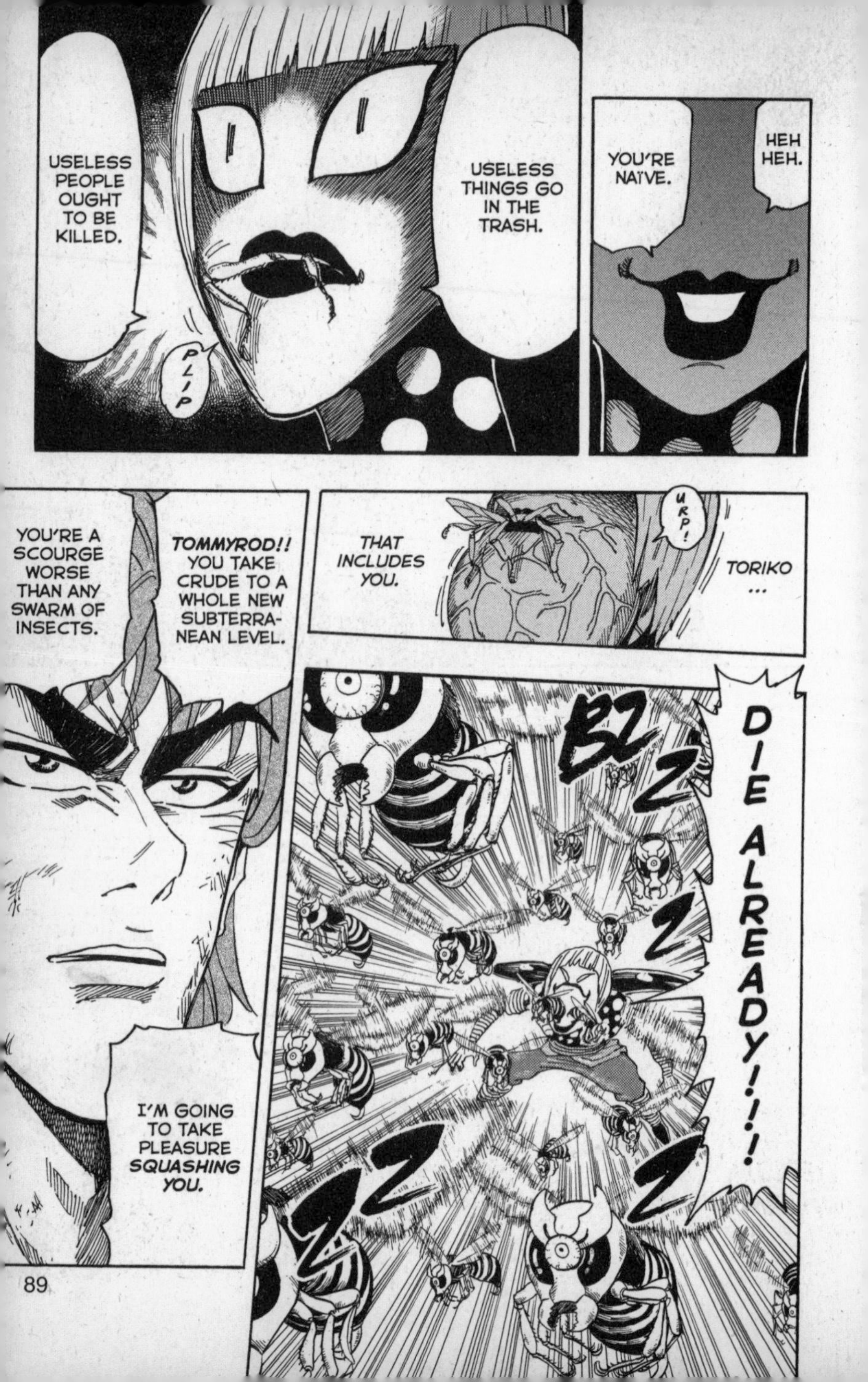
HEH HEH.
YOU'RE NAÏVE.
USELESS THINGS GO IN THE TRASH.
PLIP
USELESS PEOPLE OUGHT TO BE KILLED.
TORIKO ...
URP!
THAT INCLUDES YOU.
DIE ALREADY!!!!
BZZZZZ
TOMMYROD!! YOU TAKE CRUDE TO A WHOLE NEW SUBTERRA-NEAN LEVEL.
YOU'RE A SCOURGE WORSE THAN ANY SWARM OF INSECTS.
I'M GOING TO TAKE PLEASURE SQUASHING YOU.

TORIKO

GOURMET CHECKLIST

Vol. 082

GARI BOX

(PLANT / PALATE-CLEANSING GINGER)

CAPTURE LEVEL: LESS THAN 1

HABITAT: FIELDS (CAN ALSO BE ARTIFICIALLY CULTIVATED)

LENGTH: ---

HEIGHT: 60~70 CM

WEIGHT: ---

PRICE: 500 YEN PER SLICE (AS A SEASONING). OFFERED FREE IN GOURMET TOWN AS A PALATE-CLEANSER.

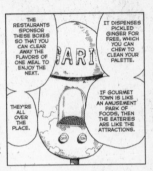

IT DISPENSES PICKLED GINGER FOR FREE, WHICH YOU CAN CHEW TO CLEAN YOUR PALETTE.
THE RESTAURANTS SPONSOR THESE BOXES SO THAT YOU CAN CLEAR AWAY THE FLAVORS OF ONE MEAL TO ENJOY THE NEXT.
GARI
IF GOURMET TOWN IS LIKE AN AMUSEMENT PARK OF FOODS, THEN THE EATERIES ARE LIKE THE ATTRACTIONS.
THEY'RE ALL OVER THE PLACE.
OFF
ON

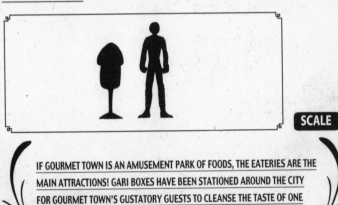

SCALE

IF GOURMET TOWN IS AN AMUSEMENT PARK OF FOODS, THE EATERIES ARE THE MAIN ATTRACTIONS! GARI BOXES HAVE BEEN STATIONED AROUND THE CITY FOR GOURMET TOWN'S GUSTATORY GUESTS TO CLEANSE THE TASTE OF ONE MEAL FROM THEIR MOUTHS AS THEY HEAD TO THE NEXT. IN THIS FASHION, THESE GINGER SNACKS HELP KEEP COMPETITION FAIR AND HEALTHY.

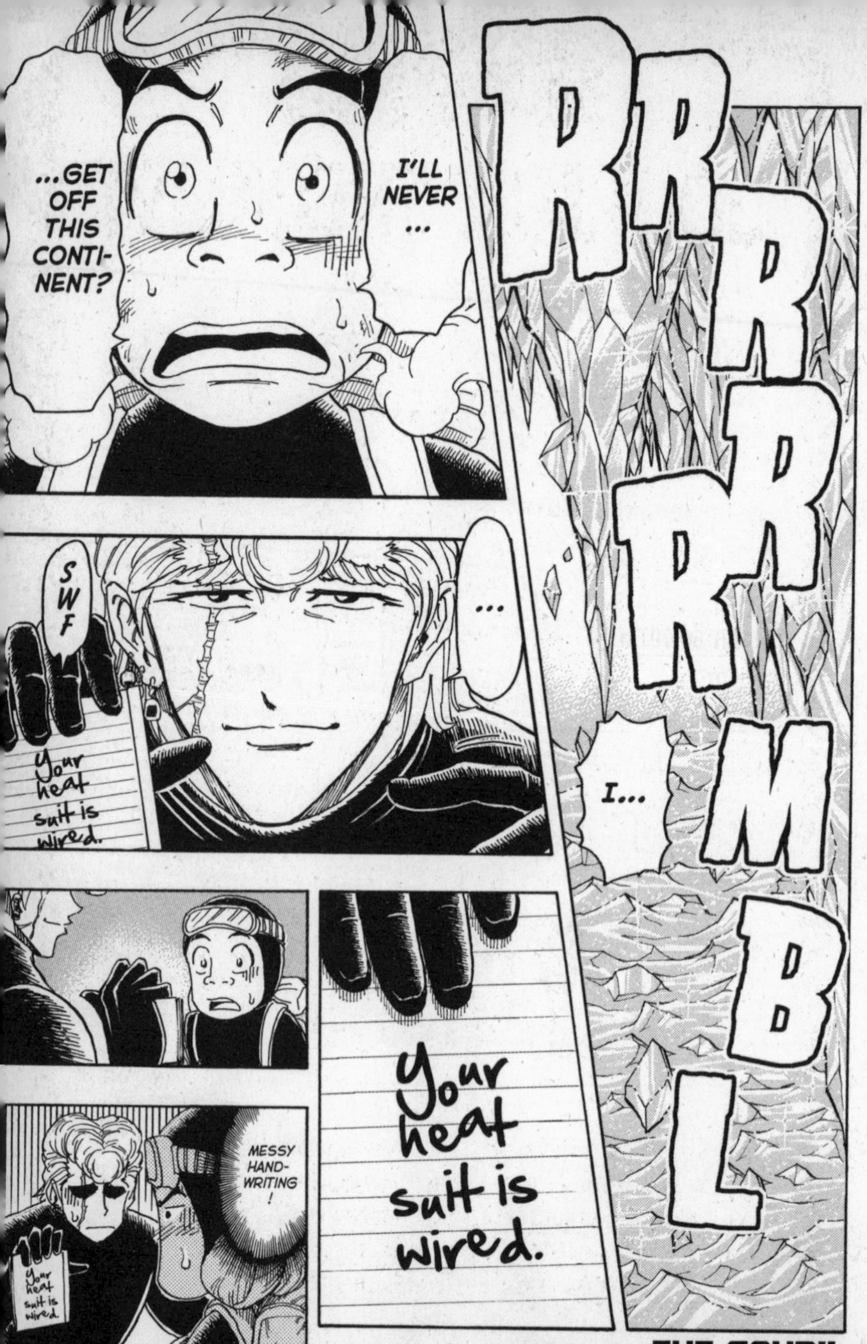
RRRRRMBL
I...
I'LL NEVER ...
...GET OFF THIS CONTI-NENT?
...
SWF
Your heat suit is wired.
Your heat suit is wired.
MESSY HAND-WRITING!
Your heat suit is wired.

GOURMET 84: THE SOUP!!

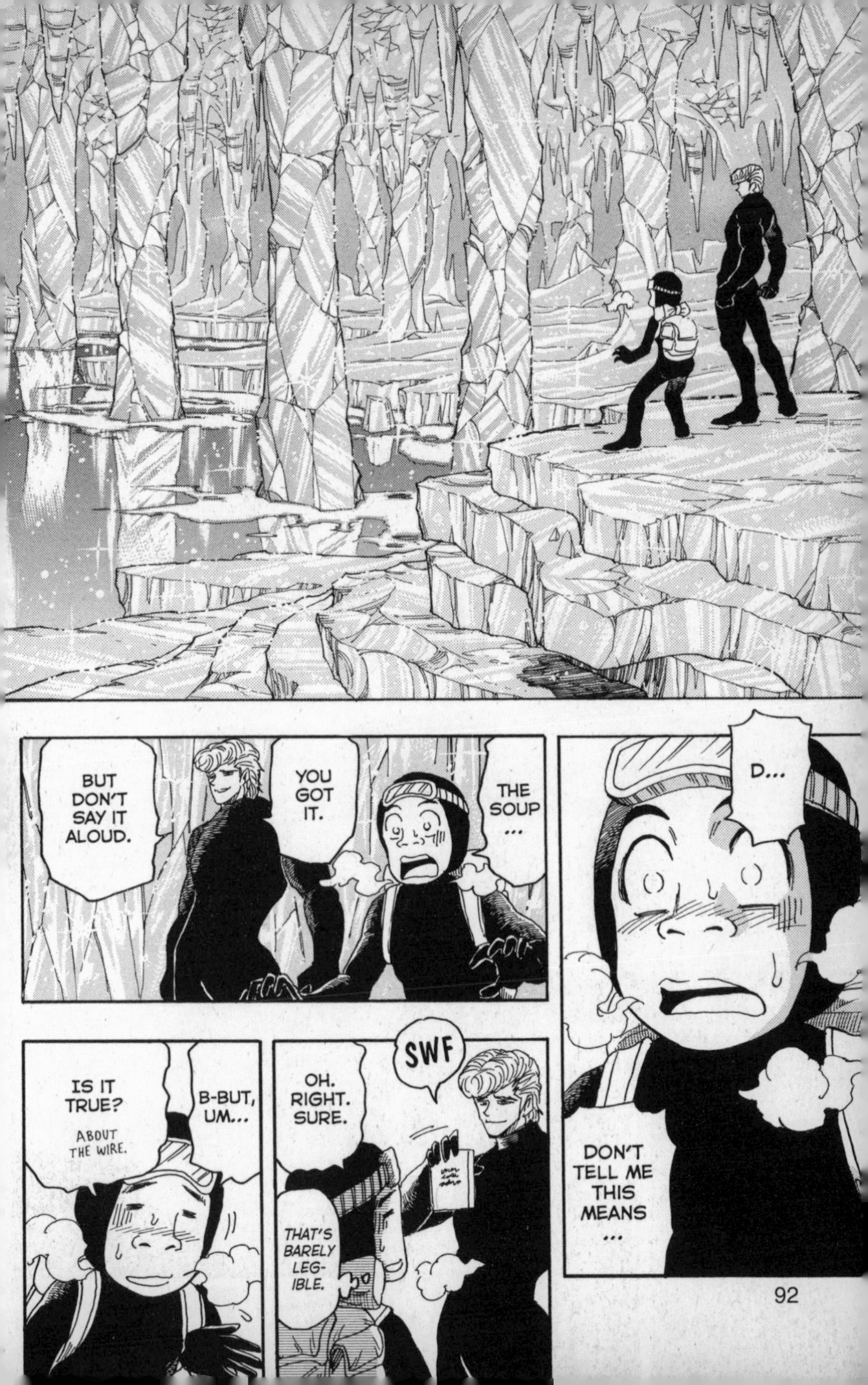
D...
DON'T TELL ME THIS MEANS ...
THE SOUP ...
YOU GOT IT.
BUT DON'T SAY IT ALOUD.
SWF
OH. RIGHT. SURE.
THAT'S BARELY LEGIBLE.
B-BUT, UM...
IS IT TRUE?
ABOUT THE WIRE.

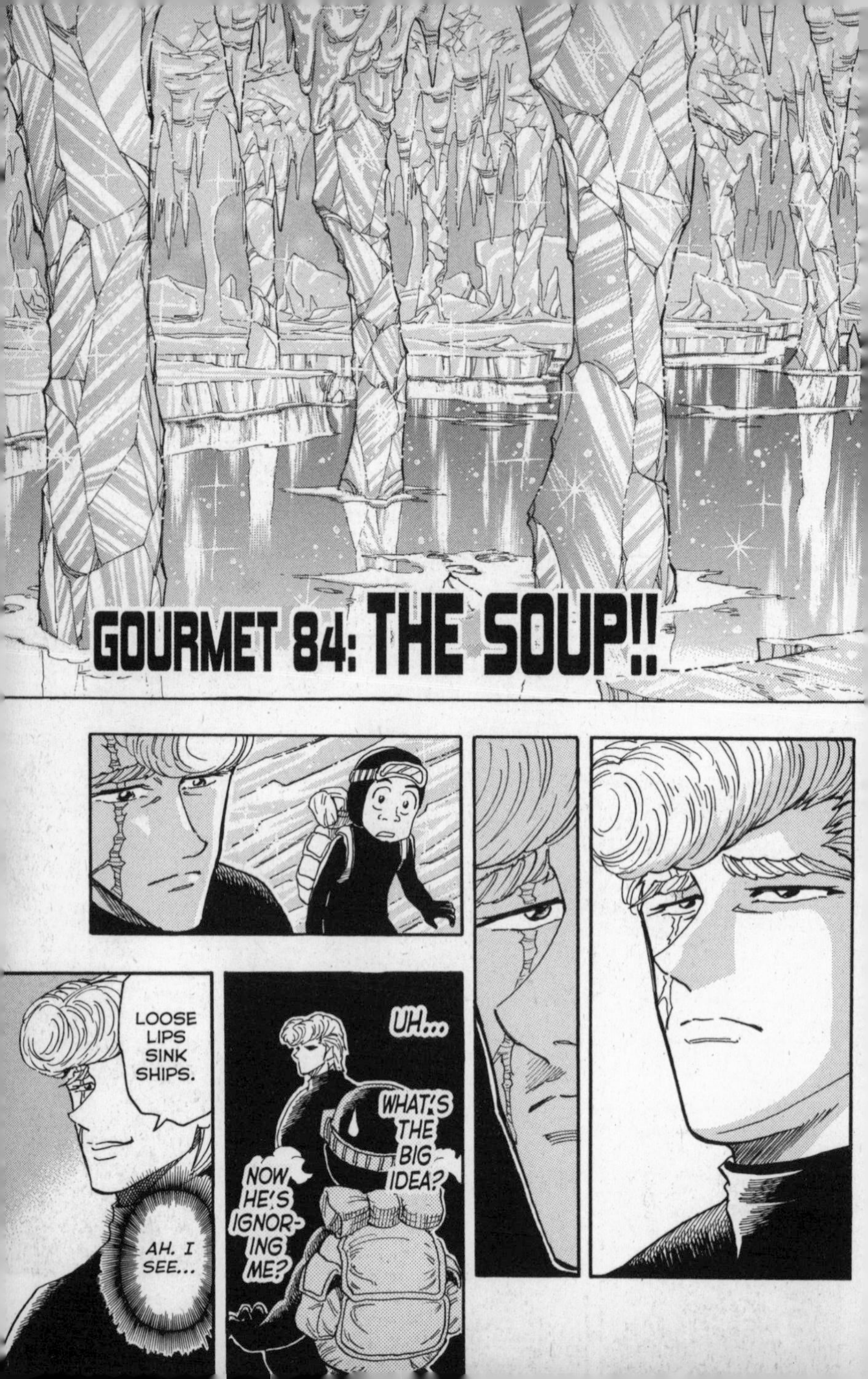
GOURMET 84: THE SOUP!!
UH...
WHAT'S THE BIG IDEA?
NOW HE'S IGNORING ME?
LOOSE LIPS SINK SHIPS.
AH. I SEE...

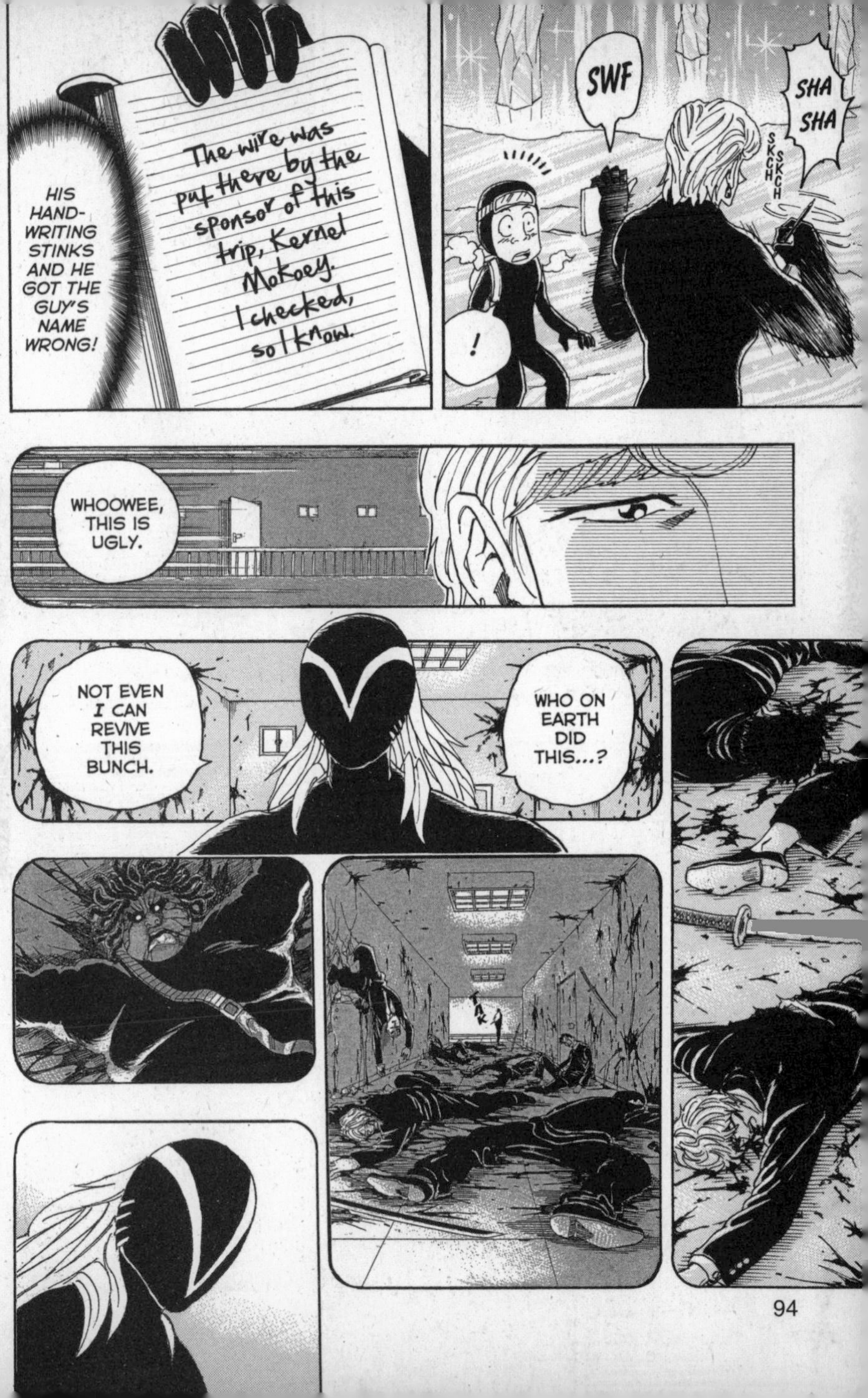
SWF
SHA SHA
SKCH SKCH
!
The wire was put there by the sponsor of this trip, Kernel Mokoey. I checked, so I know.
HIS HANDWRITING STINKS AND HE GOT THE GUY'S NAME WRONG!
WHOOWEE, THIS IS UGLY.
WHO ON EARTH DID THIS...?
NOT EVEN I CAN REVIVE THIS BUNCH.
TAK

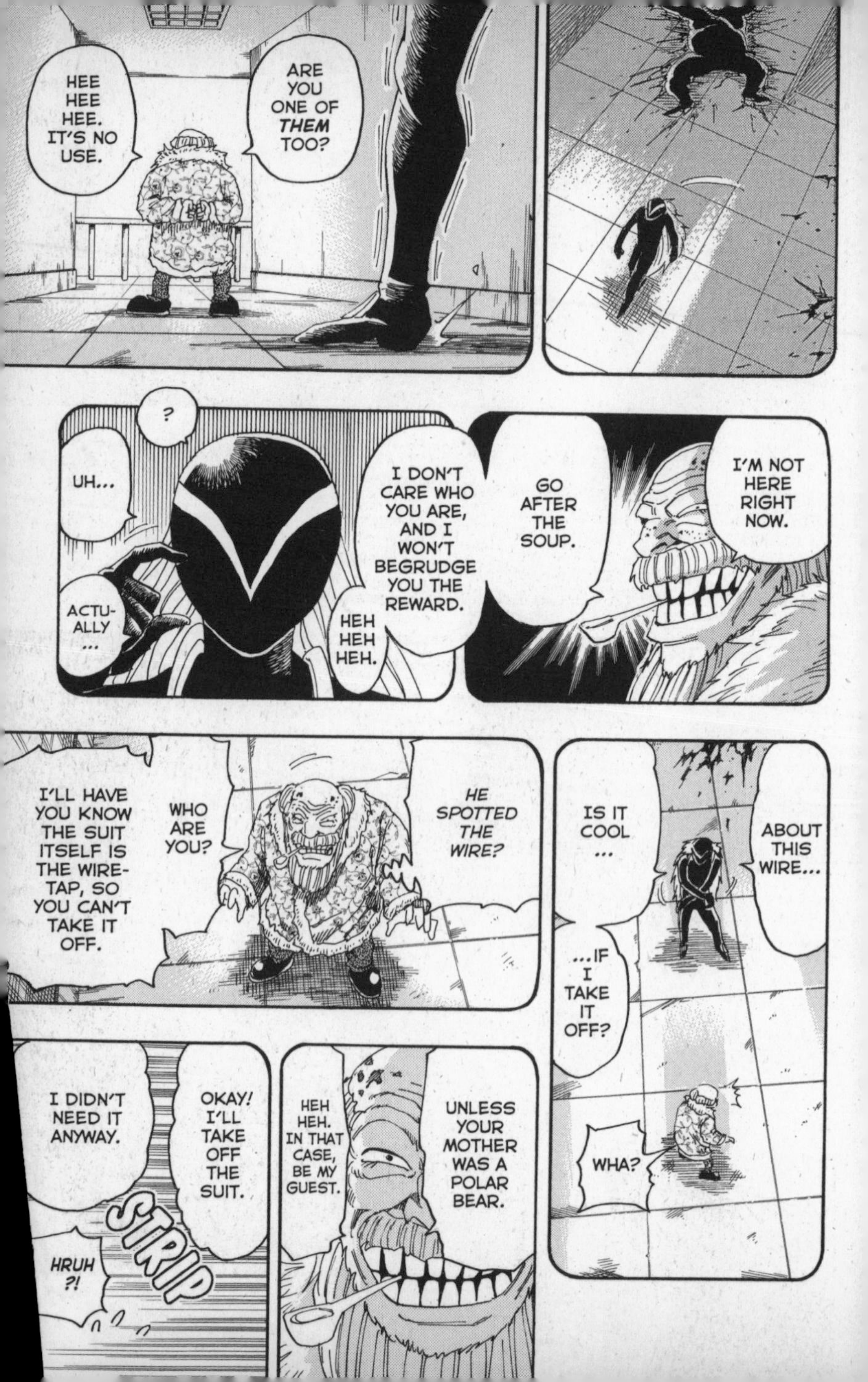

ARE YOU ONE OF *THEM* TOO?
HEE HEE HEE. IT'S NO USE.
I'M NOT HERE RIGHT NOW.
GO AFTER THE SOUP.
I DON'T CARE WHO YOU ARE, AND I WON'T BEGRUDGE YOU THE REWARD.
HEH HEH HEH.
?
UH...
ACTU-ALLY...
ABOUT THIS WIRE...
IS IT COOL...
...IF I TAKE IT OFF?
WHA?
HE SPOTTED THE WIRE?
WHO ARE YOU?
I'LL HAVE YOU KNOW THE SUIT ITSELF IS THE WIRE-TAP, SO YOU CAN'T TAKE IT OFF.
UNLESS YOUR MOTHER WAS A POLAR BEAR.
HEH HEH. IN THAT CASE, BE MY GUEST.
OKAY! I'LL TAKE OFF THE SUIT.
I DIDN'T NEED IT ANYWAY.
STRIP
HRUH ?!

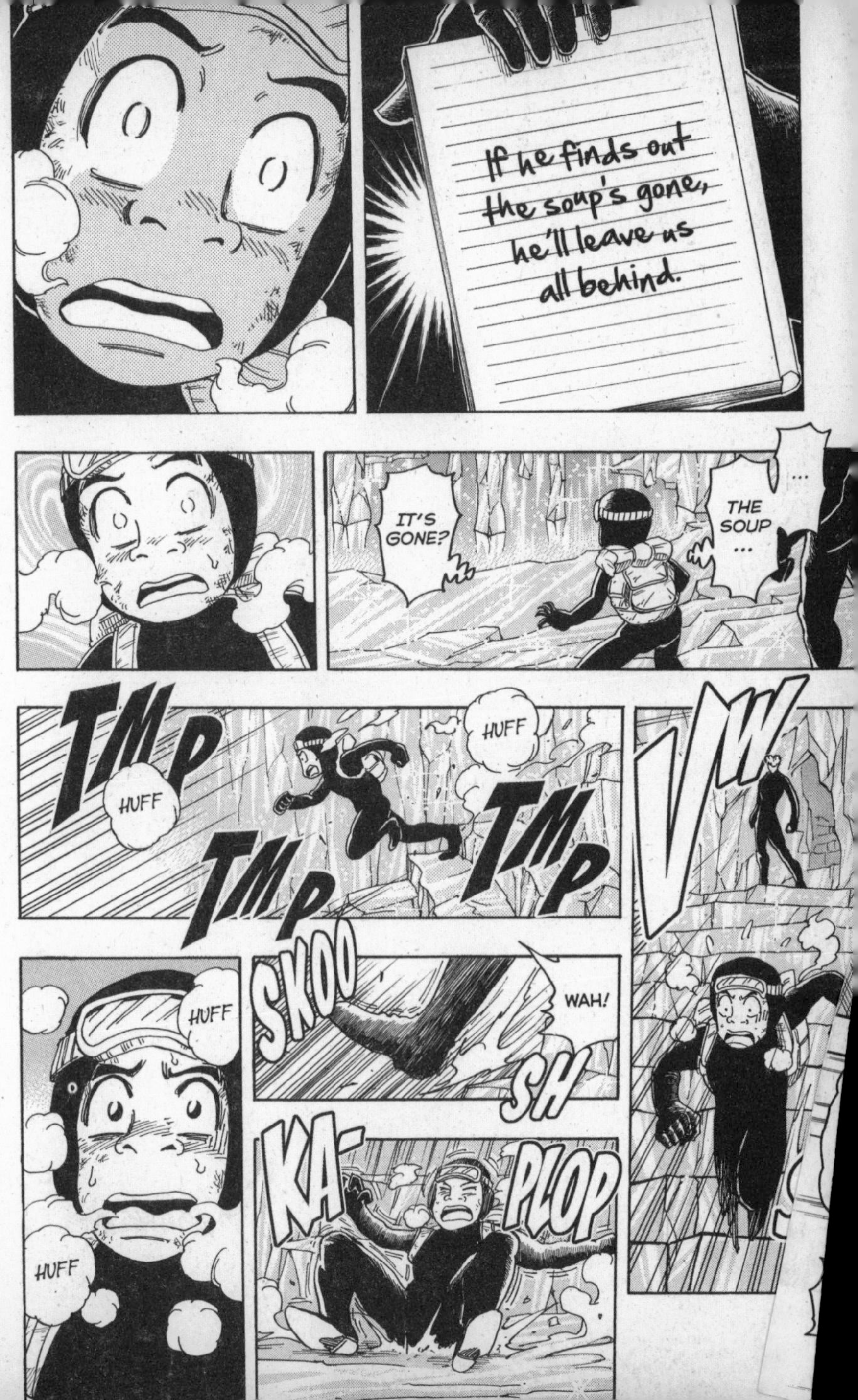
If he finds out the soup's gone, he'll leave us all behind.
...
THE SOUP ...
IT'S GONE?
VW
HUFF
TMP
TMP
HUFF
TMP
WAH!
SKOO
SH
KA-PLOP
HUFF
HUFF

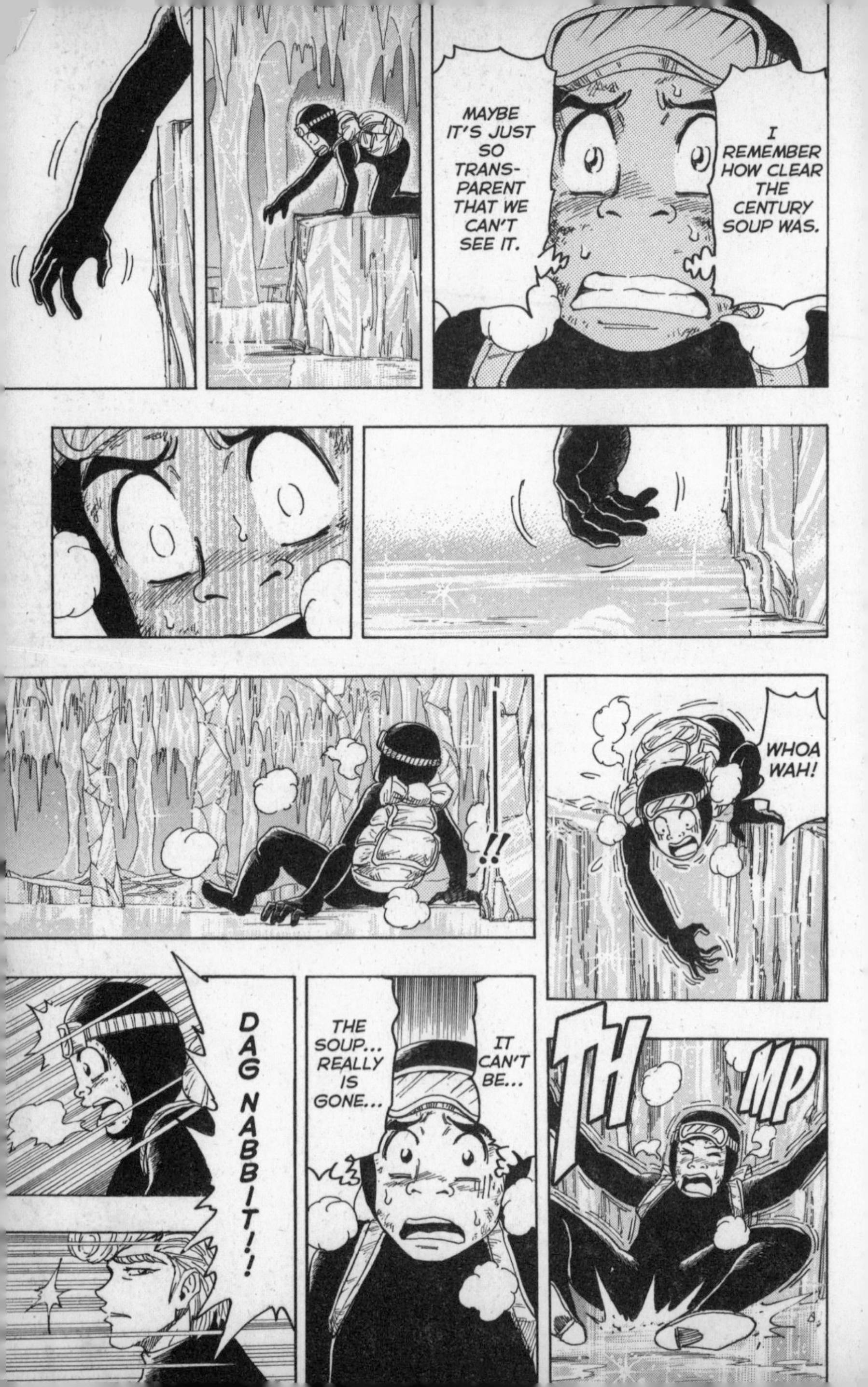
I REMEMBER HOW CLEAR THE CENTURY SOUP WAS.
MAYBE IT'S JUST SO TRANS-PARENT THAT WE CAN'T SEE IT.
!!
WHOA WAH!
THUMP
IT CAN'T BE...
THE SOUP... REALLY IS GONE...
DAG NABBIT!!!

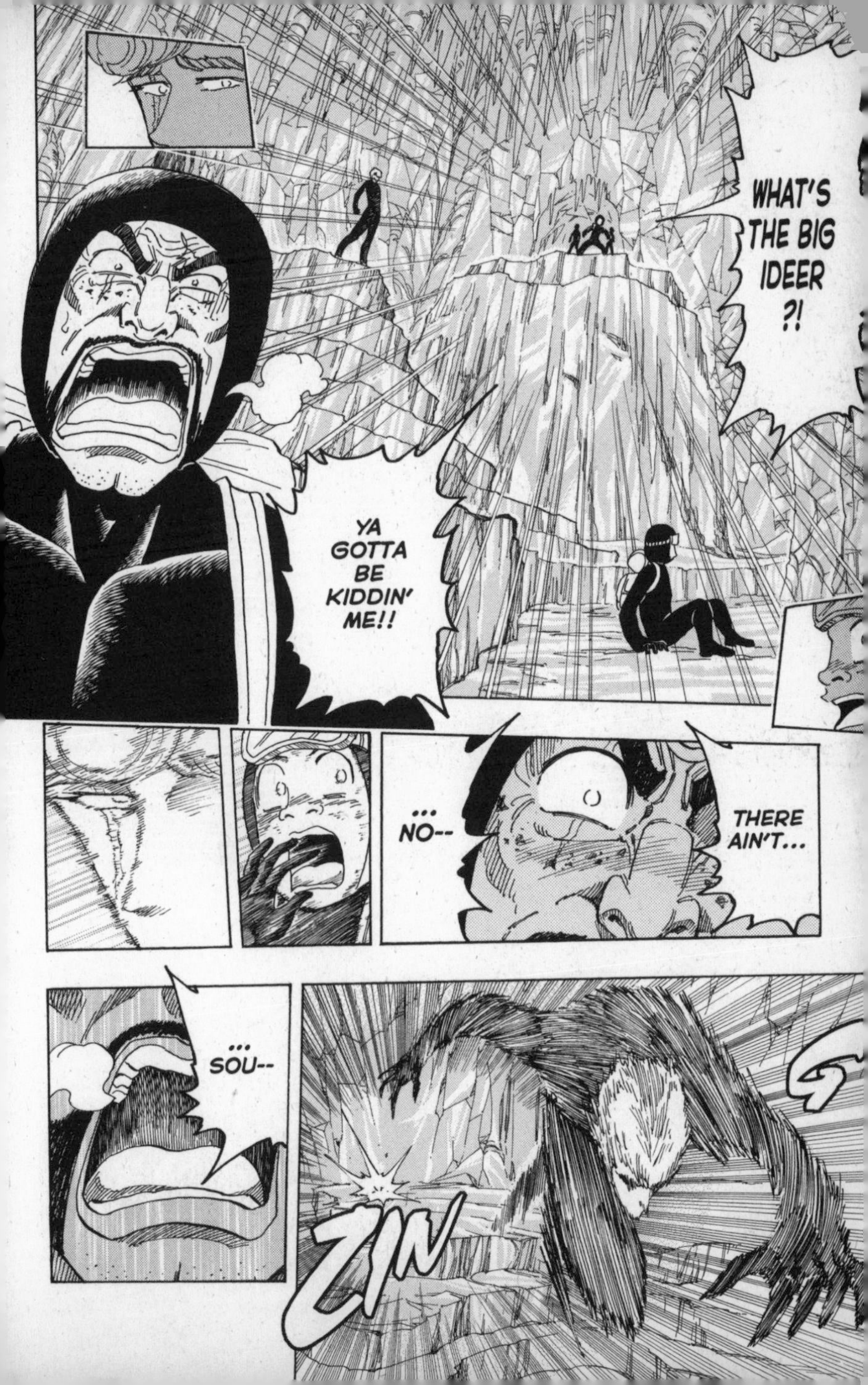
WHAT'S THE BIG IDEER ?!
YA GOTTA BE KIDDIN' ME!!
THERE AIN'T...
... NO--
... SOU--
G
ZIN

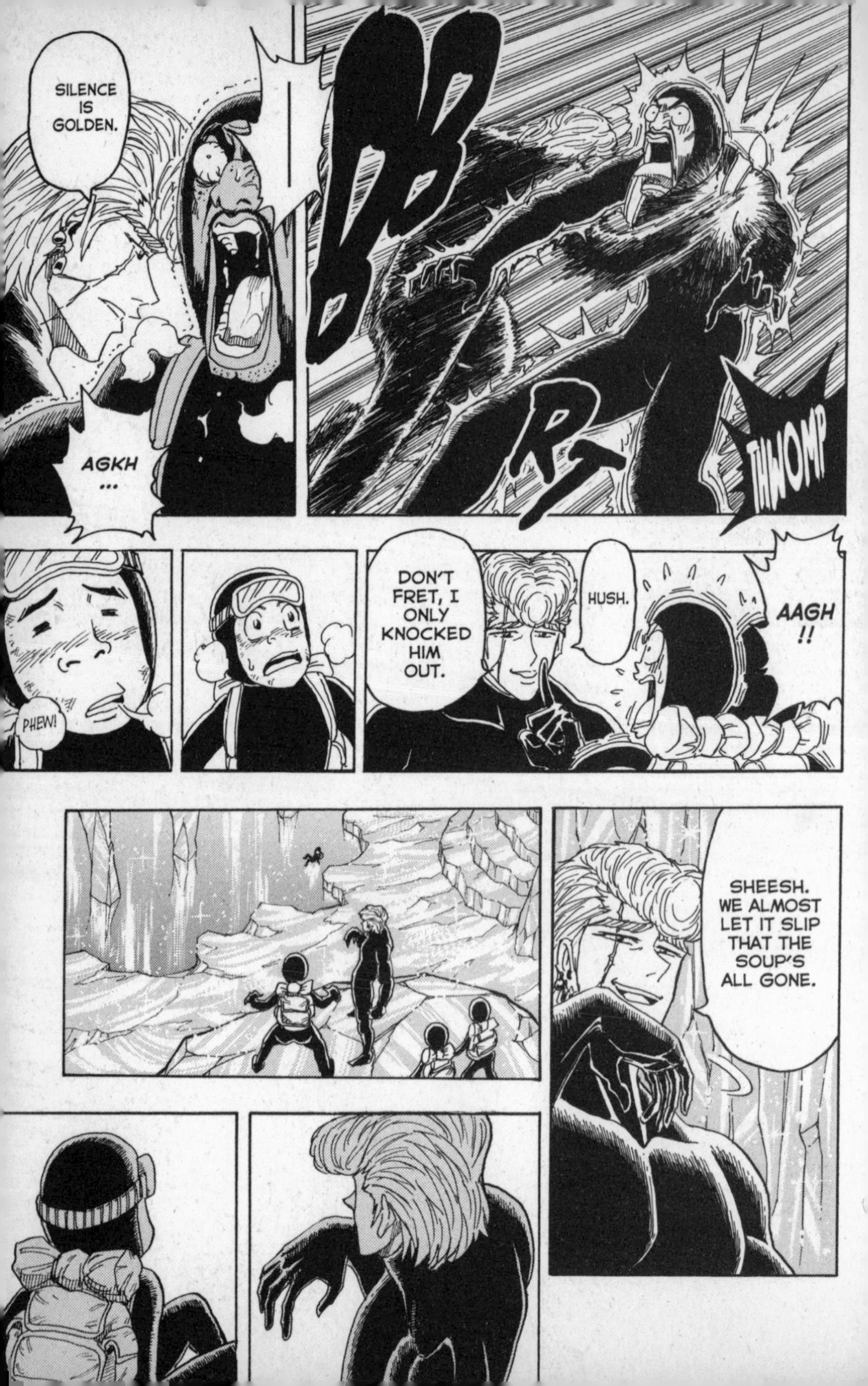
THWOMP
DB
R
SILENCE IS GOLDEN.
AGKH ...
AAGH !!
HUSH.
DON'T FRET, I ONLY KNOCKED HIM OUT.
PHEW!
SHEESH. WE ALMOST LET IT SLIP THAT THE SOUP'S ALL GONE.

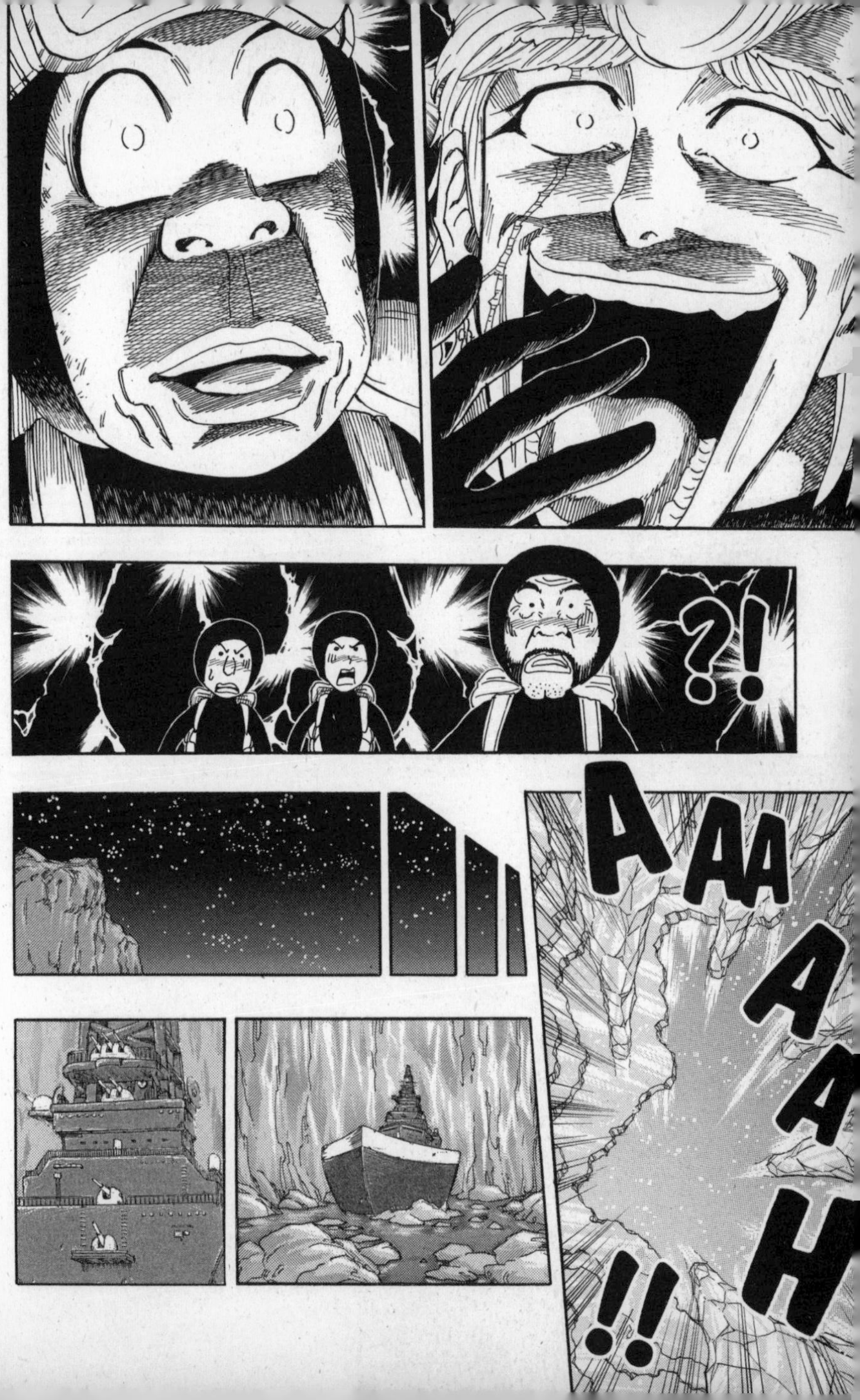

?!
AAAAAH!!

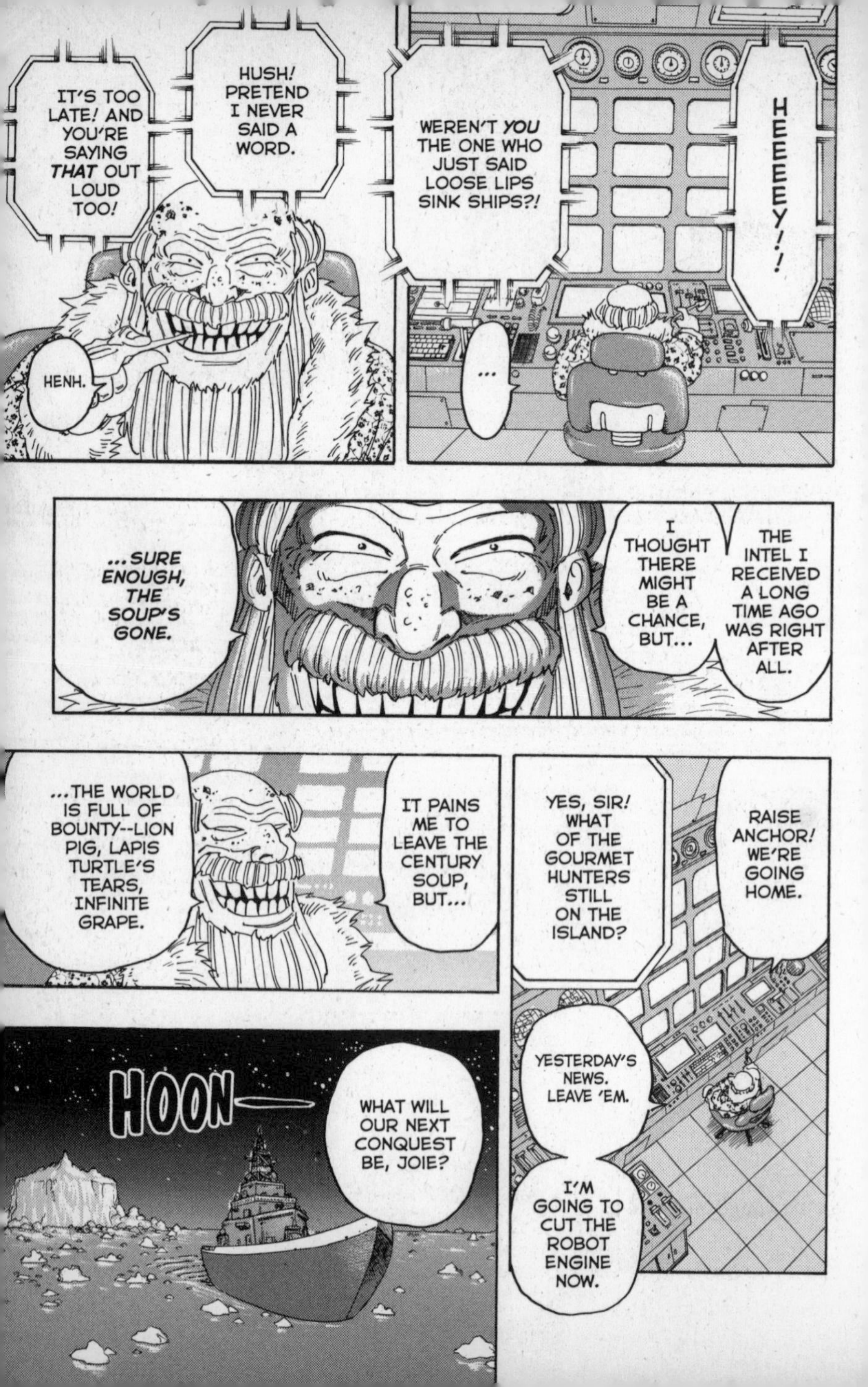
HEEEEY!!
WEREN'T *YOU* THE ONE WHO JUST SAID LOOSE LIPS SINK SHIPS?!
...
HUSH! PRETEND I NEVER SAID A WORD.
IT'S TOO LATE! AND YOU'RE SAYING *THAT* OUT LOUD TOO!
HENH.
THE INTEL I RECEIVED A LONG TIME AGO WAS RIGHT AFTER ALL.
I THOUGHT THERE MIGHT BE A CHANCE, BUT...
...SURE ENOUGH, THE SOUP'S GONE.
RAISE ANCHOR! WE'RE GOING HOME.
YES, SIR! WHAT OF THE GOURMET HUNTERS STILL ON THE ISLAND?
YESTERDAY'S NEWS. LEAVE 'EM.
I'M GOING TO CUT THE ROBOT ENGINE NOW.
IT PAINS ME TO LEAVE THE CENTURY SOUP, BUT...
...THE WORLD IS FULL OF BOUNTY--LION PIG, LAPIS TURTLE'S TEARS, INFINITE GRAPE.
HOON
WHAT WILL OUR NEXT CONQUEST BE, JOIE?

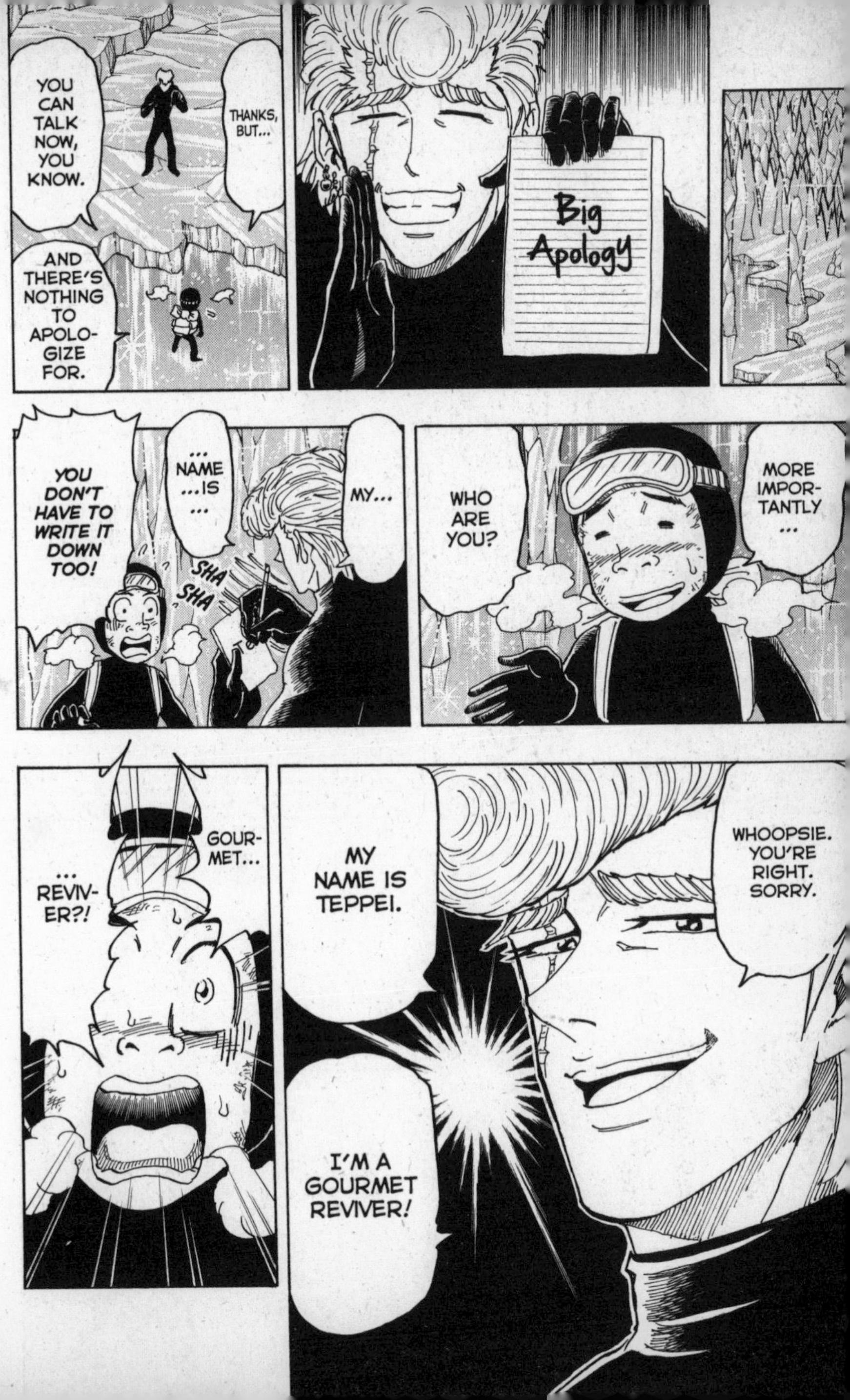
Big Apology
THANKS, BUT...
YOU CAN TALK NOW, YOU KNOW.
AND THERE'S NOTHING TO APOLOGIZE FOR.
MORE IMPORTANTLY...
WHO ARE YOU?
MY...
...NAME ...IS ...
SHA SHA
YOU DON'T HAVE TO WRITE IT DOWN TOO!
WHOOPSIE. YOU'RE RIGHT. SORRY.
MY NAME IS TEPPEI.
I'M A GOURMET REVIVER!
GOURMET...
...REVIVER?!

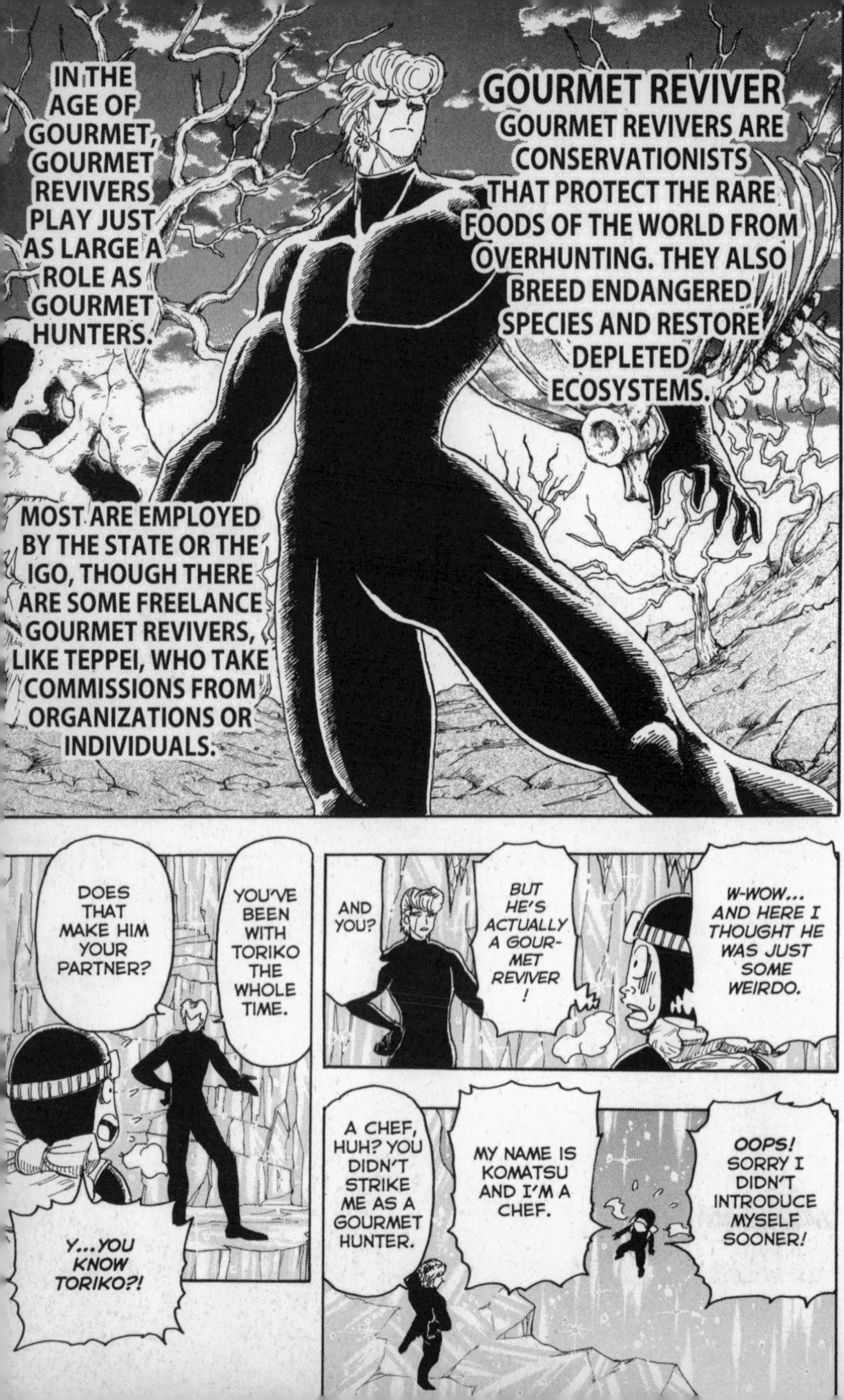
GOURMET REVIVER
GOURMET REVIVERS ARE CONSERVATIONISTS THAT PROTECT THE RARE FOODS OF THE WORLD FROM OVERHUNTING. THEY ALSO BREED ENDANGERED SPECIES AND RESTORE DEPLETED ECOSYSTEMS.
IN THE AGE OF GOURMET, GOURMET REVIVERS PLAY JUST AS LARGE A ROLE AS GOURMET HUNTERS.
MOST ARE EMPLOYED BY THE STATE OR THE IGO, THOUGH THERE ARE SOME FREELANCE GOURMET REVIVERS, LIKE TEPPEI, WHO TAKE COMMISSIONS FROM ORGANIZATIONS OR INDIVIDUALS.
W-WOW... AND HERE I THOUGHT HE WAS JUST SOME WEIRDO.
BUT HE'S ACTUALLY A GOURMET REVIVER!
AND YOU?
OOPS! SORRY I DIDN'T INTRODUCE MYSELF SOONER!
MY NAME IS KOMATSU AND I'M A CHEF.
A CHEF, HUH? YOU DIDN'T STRIKE ME AS A GOURMET HUNTER.
YOU'VE BEEN WITH TORIKO THE WHOLE TIME.
DOES THAT MAKE HIM YOUR PARTNER?
Y...YOU KNOW TORIKO?!

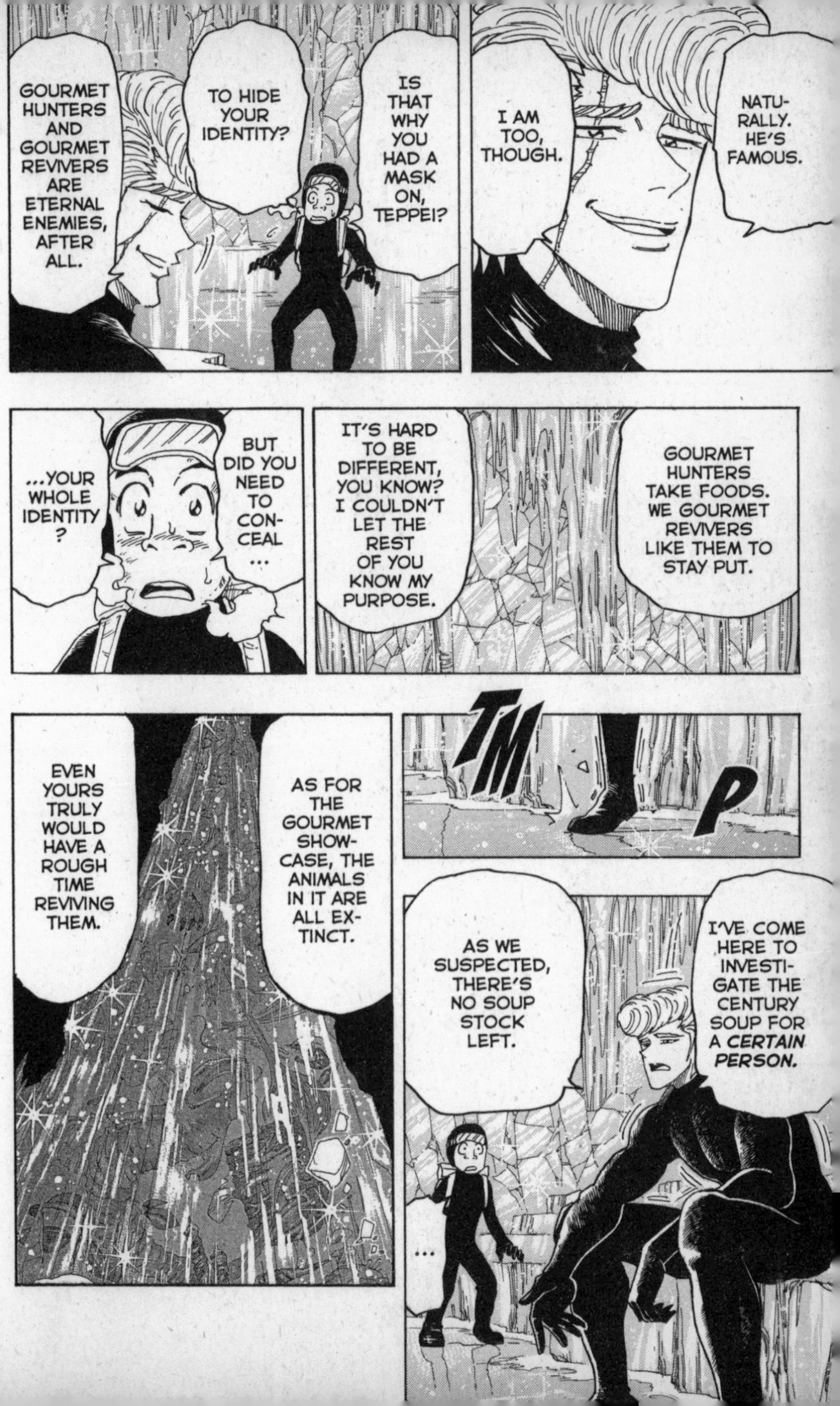
NATU-RALLY. HE'S FAMOUS.
I AM TOO, THOUGH.
IS THAT WHY YOU HAD A MASK ON, TEPPEI?
TO HIDE YOUR IDENTITY?
GOURMET HUNTERS AND GOURMET REVIVERS ARE ETERNAL ENEMIES, AFTER ALL.
GOURMET HUNTERS TAKE FOODS. WE GOURMET REVIVERS LIKE THEM TO STAY PUT.
IT'S HARD TO BE DIFFERENT, YOU KNOW? I COULDN'T LET THE REST OF YOU KNOW MY PURPOSE.
BUT DID YOU NEED TO CON-CEAL...
...YOUR WHOLE IDENTITY?
TMP
I'VE COME HERE TO INVESTI-GATE THE CENTURY SOUP FOR A *CERTAIN PERSON.*
AS WE SUSPECTED, THERE'S NO SOUP STOCK LEFT.
...
AS FOR THE GOURMET SHOW-CASE, THE ANIMALS IN IT ARE ALL EX-TINCT.
EVEN YOURS TRULY WOULD HAVE A ROUGH TIME REVIVING THEM.

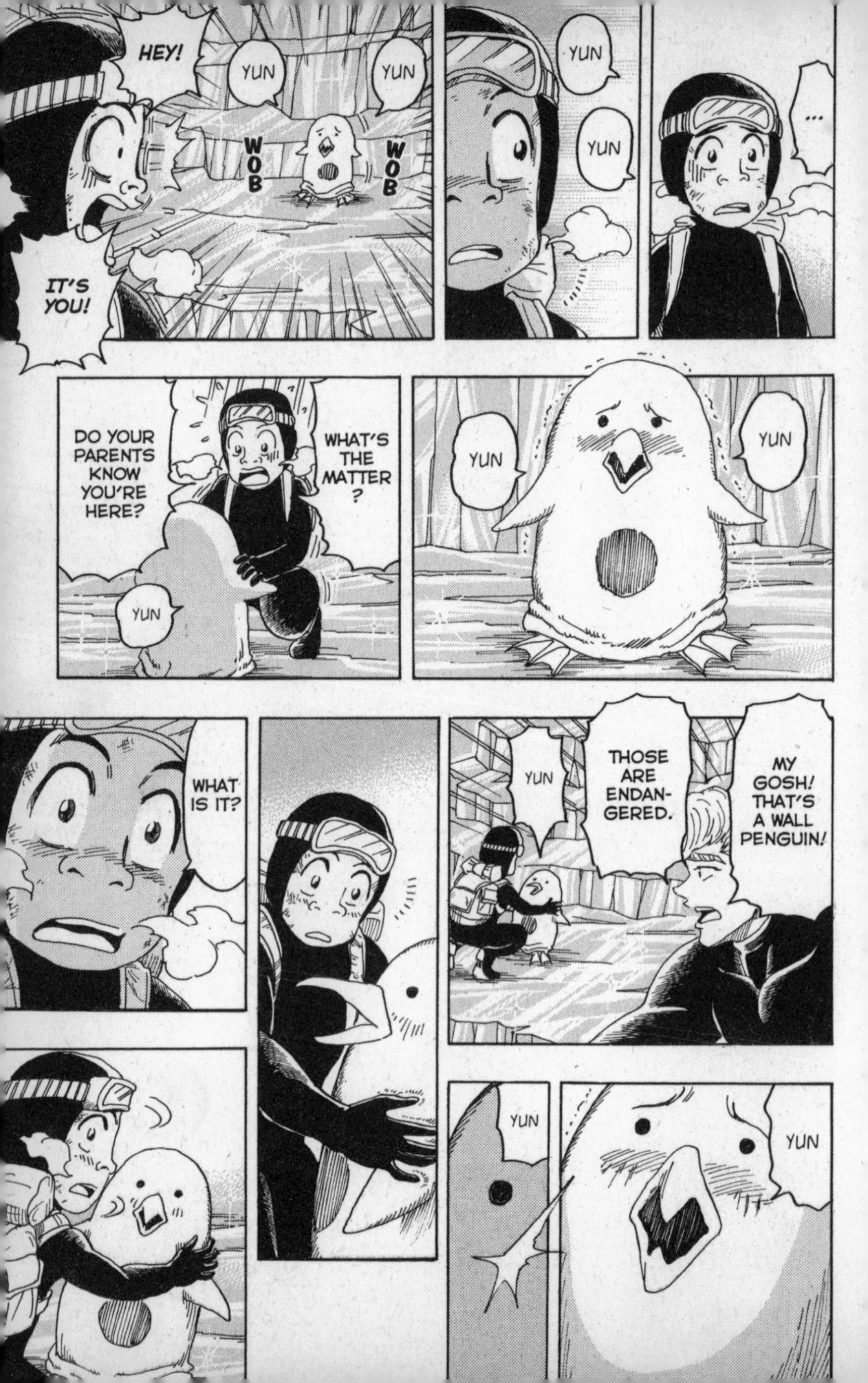
...
YUN
YUN
YUN
YUN
HEY!
WOB
WOB
IT'S YOU!
YUN
YUN
WHAT'S THE MATTER?
DO YOUR PARENTS KNOW YOU'RE HERE?
YUN
MY GOSH! THAT'S A WALL PENGUIN!
THOSE ARE ENDANGERED.
YUN
WHAT IS IT?
YUN
YUN

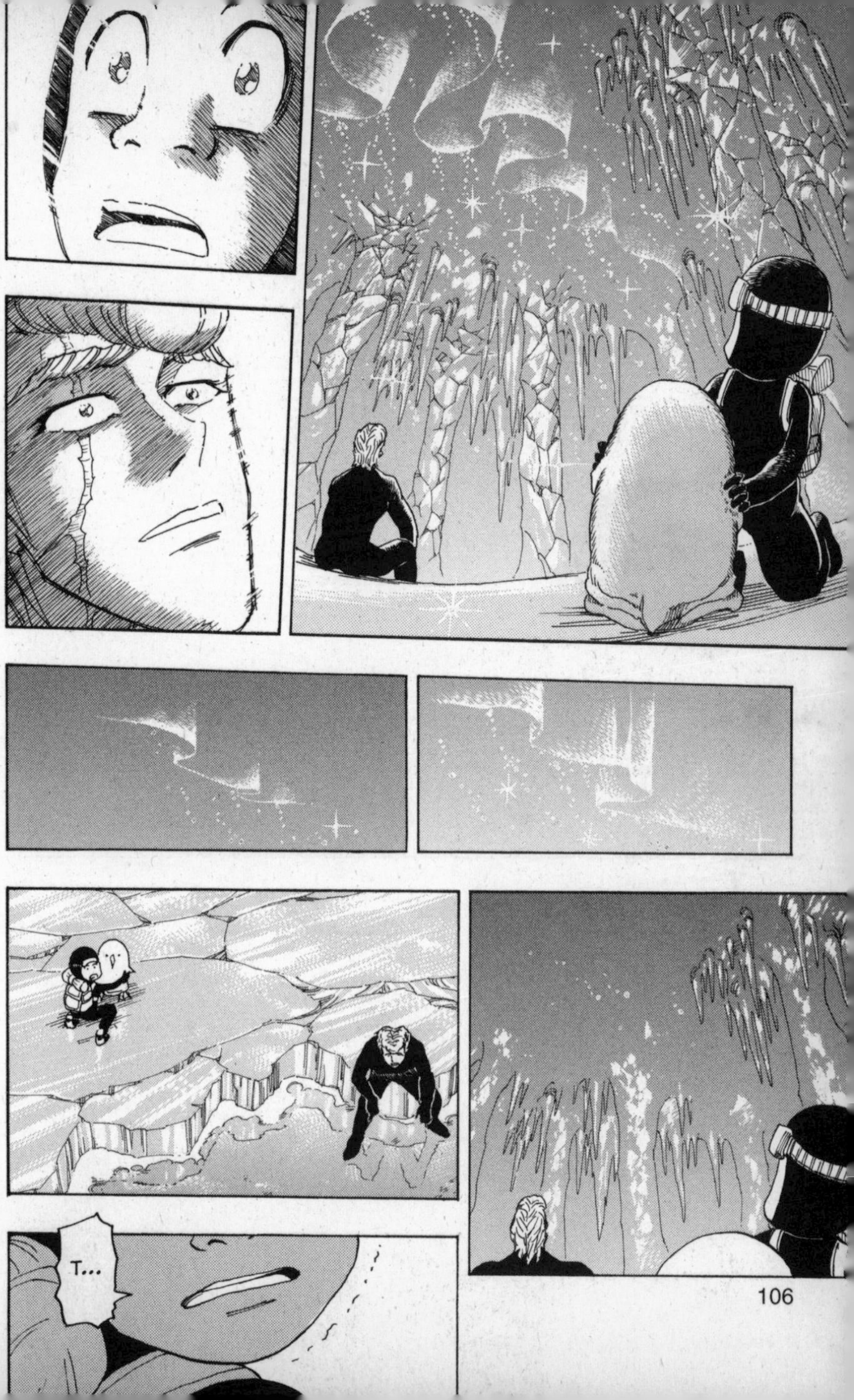
T...

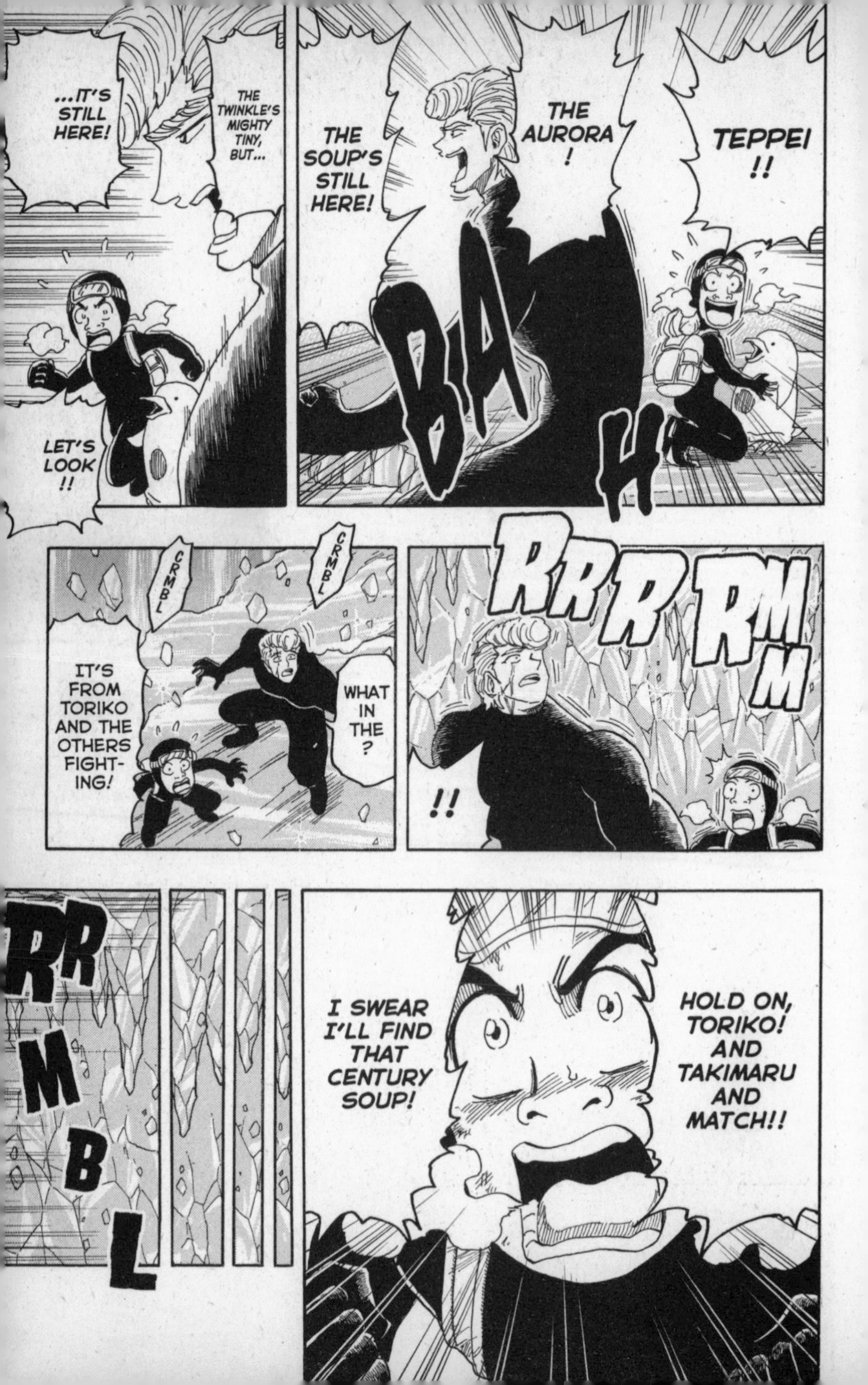
TEPPEI!!
THE AURORA!
THE SOUP'S STILL HERE!
BAAH
THE TWINKLE'S MIGHTY TINY, BUT...
...IT'S STILL HERE!
LET'S LOOK!!
RRRRMM
!!
CRMBL
CRMBL
WHAT IN THE?
IT'S FROM TORIKO AND THE OTHERS FIGHTING!
HOLD ON, TORIKO! AND TAKIMARU AND MATCH!!
I SWEAR I'LL FIND THAT CENTURY SOUP!
RRMBL

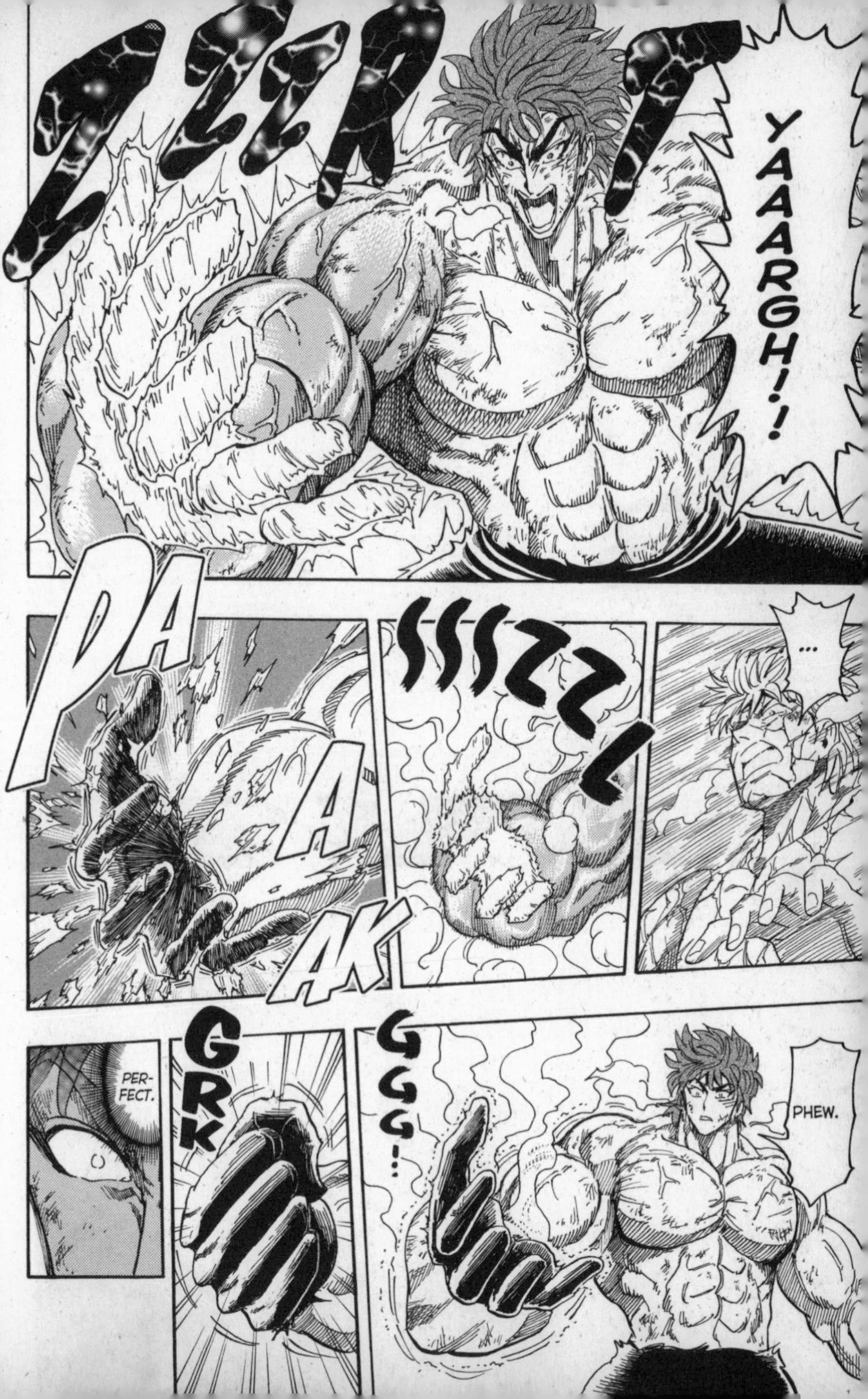

ZZZRT
YAAARGH!!
...
SSSZZL
DAAAK
PHEW.
GGG...
GRK
PER-FECT.

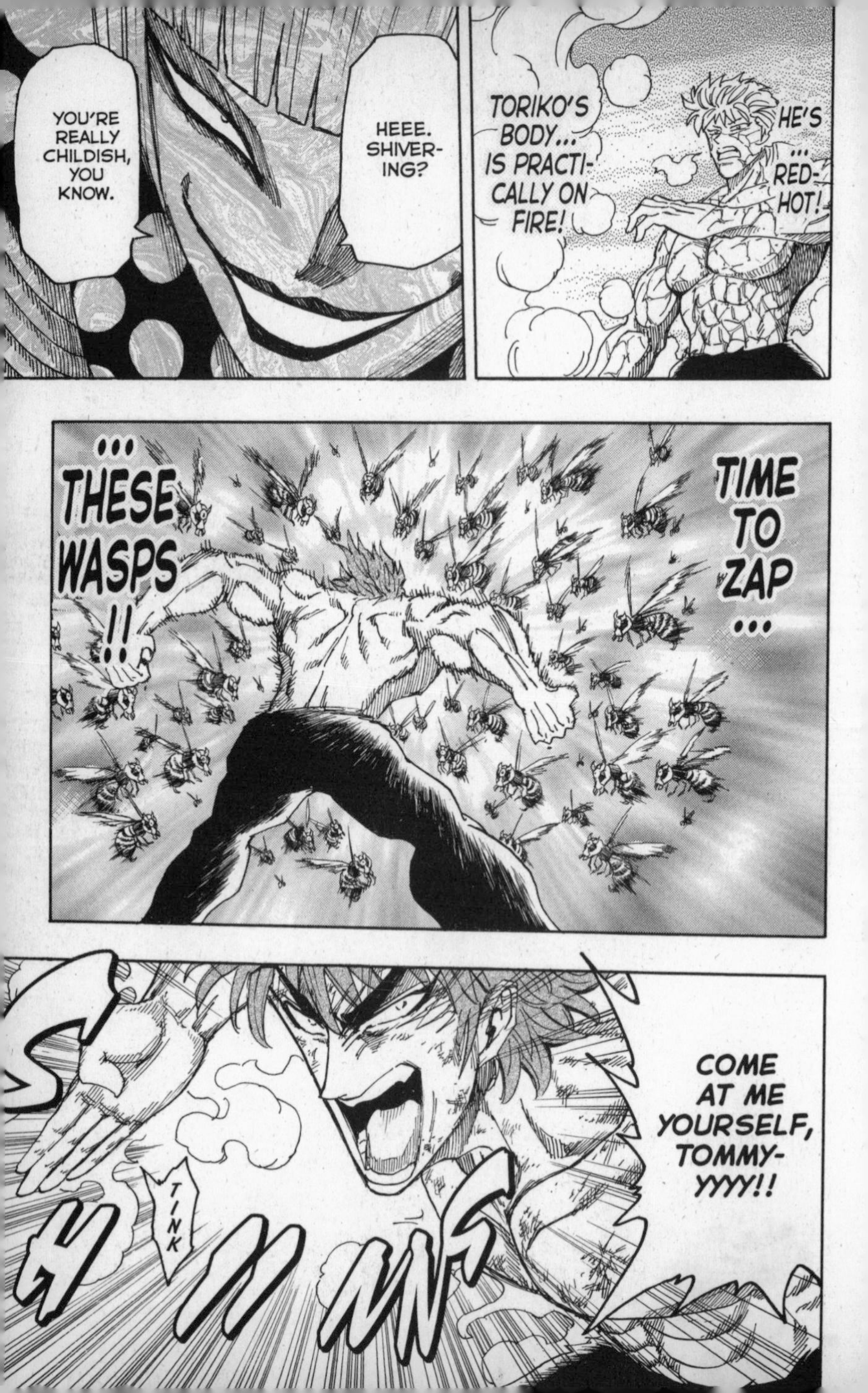
HE'S ... RED-HOT!
TORIKO'S BODY... IS PRACTICALLY ON FIRE!
HEEE. SHIVERING?
YOU'RE REALLY CHILDISH, YOU KNOW.
TIME TO ZAP ...
... THESE WASPS !!
COME AT ME YOURSELF, TOMMY-YYYY!!
TINK

TORIKO

GOURMET CHECKLIST

Vol. 083

AIR AQUA
(WATER)

CAPTURE LEVEL: 68

HABITAT: AQUA MOUNTAIN

LENGTH: ---

HEIGHT: ---

WEIGHT: ---

PRICE: 120,000 YEN PER 2 LITER BOTTLE

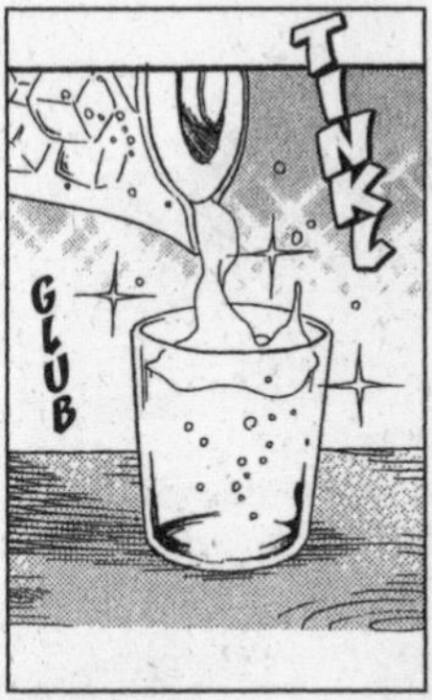
TINKL
GLUB

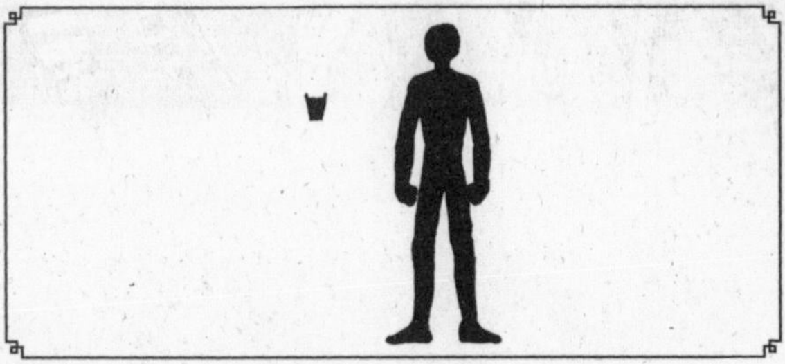

SCALE

THE SPRING WATER FROM AQUA MOUNTAIN, A TOWERING PEAK OF 10,000 METERS, RANKS AMONG THE TOP FIVE THIRST QUENCHING DRINKS IN THE WORLD. AFTER ALL, IT GOES DOWN AS LIGHT AS AIR! TOP CHEFS EVERYWHERE LOVE HAVING THIS CRYSTAL CLEAR FLUID IN THEIR KITCHENS, NO MATTER WHAT SORT OF CUISINE THEY'RE PREPARING!

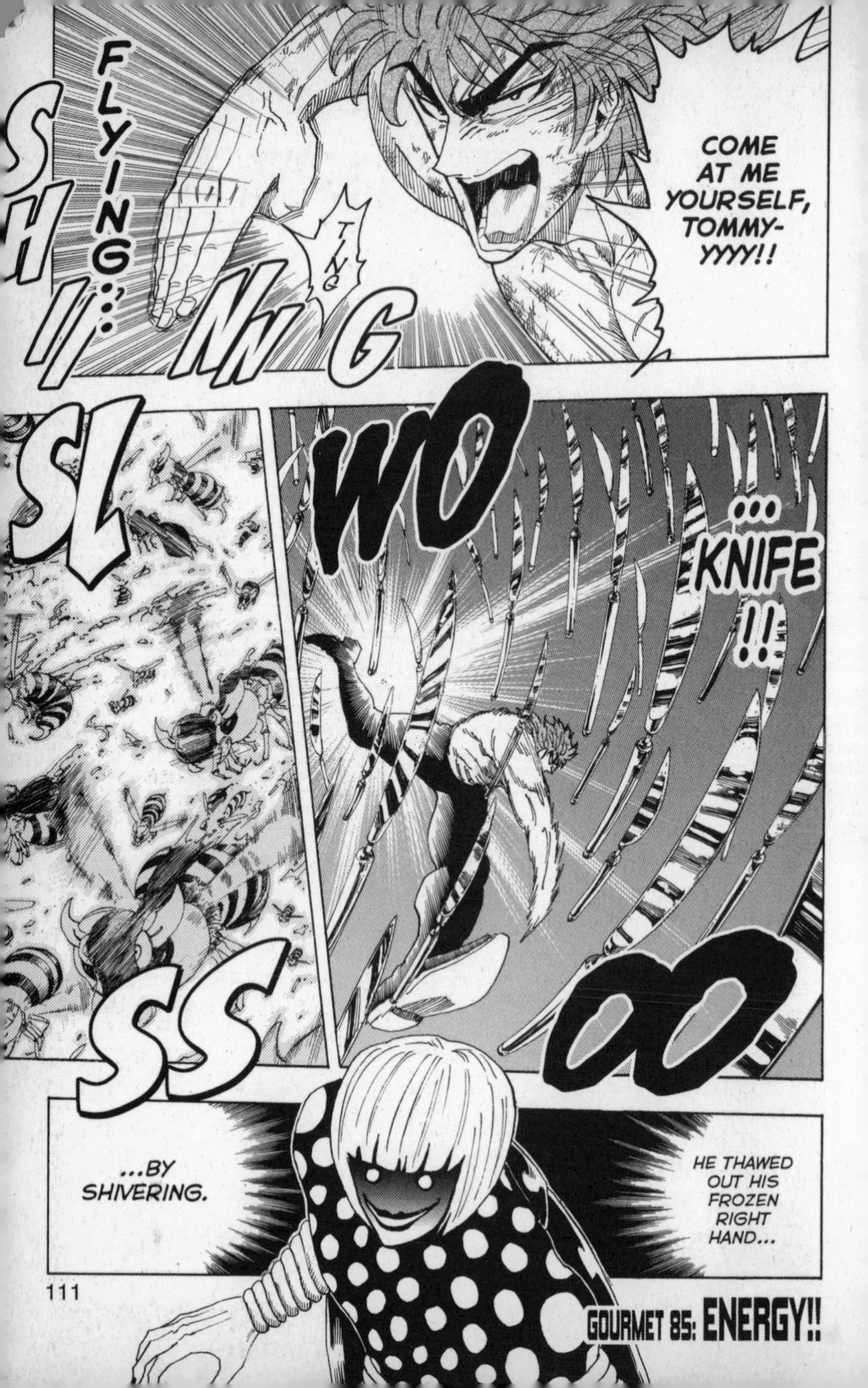
COME AT ME YOURSELF, TOMMY-YYYY!!
TING
FLYING...
SHINNG
WO
...KNIFE!!
OO
SL
SS
HE THAWED OUT HIS FROZEN RIGHT HAND...
...BY SHIVERING.
GOURMET 85: ENERGY!!

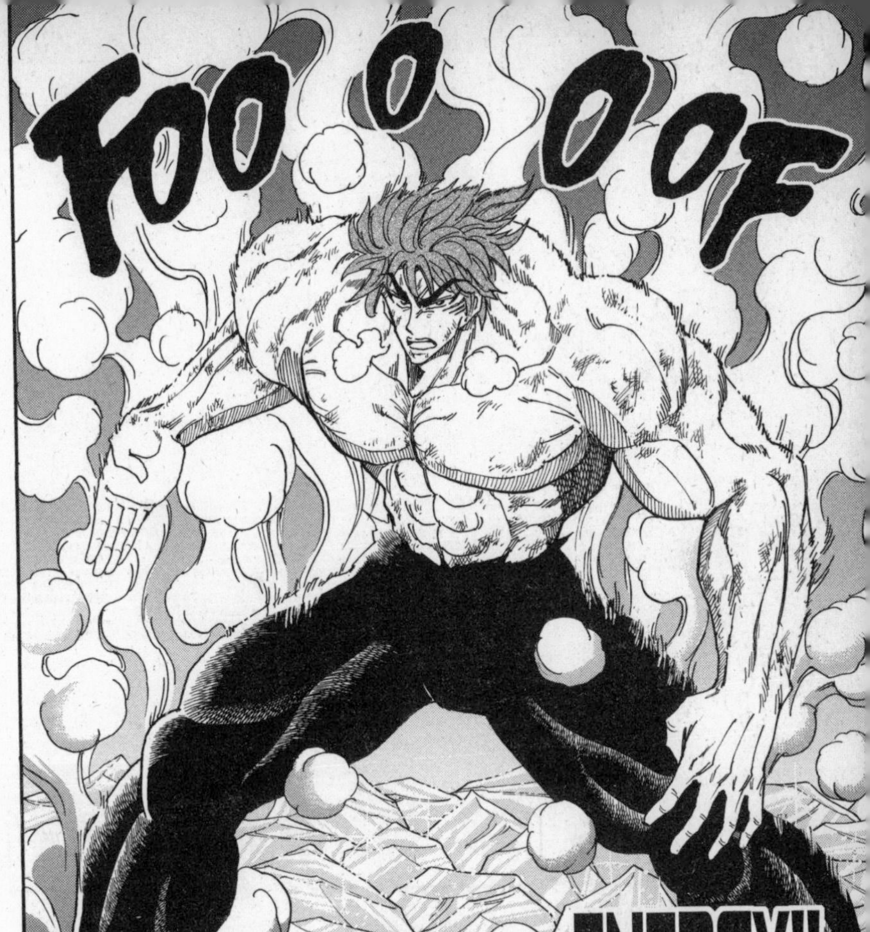
FOOOOOOF
GOURMET 85: ENERGY!!
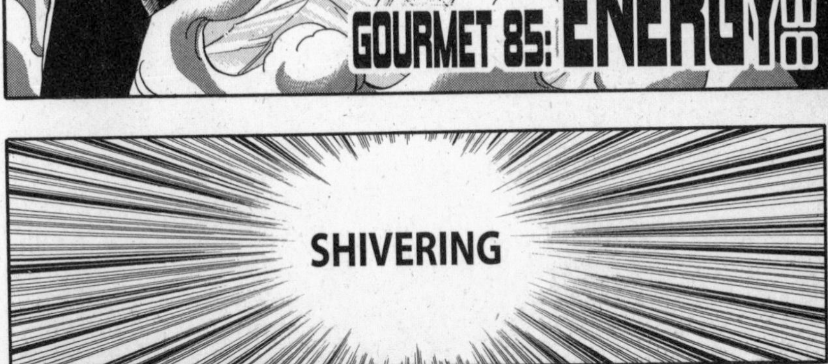
SHIVERING

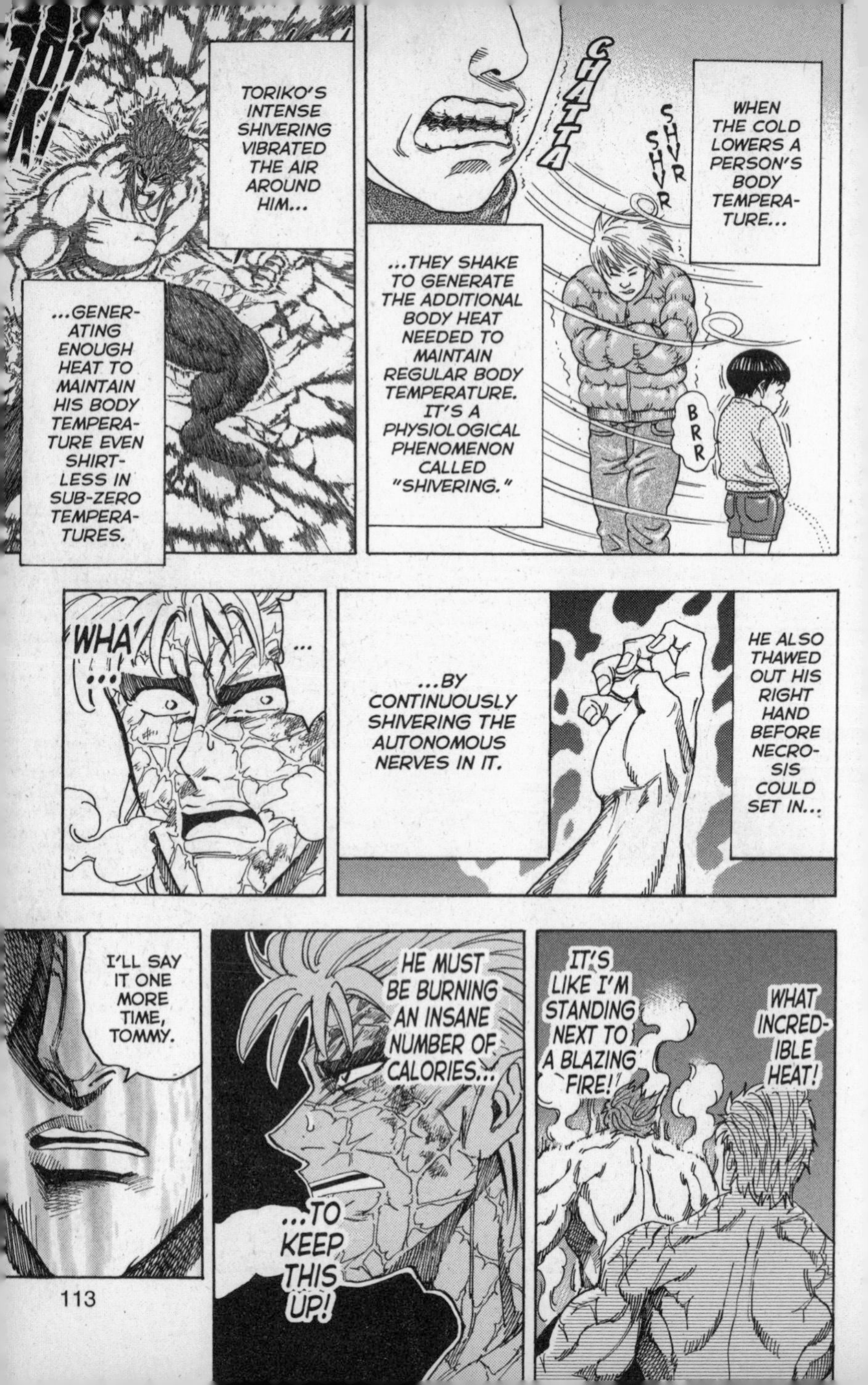
WHEN THE COLD LOWERS A PERSON'S BODY TEMPERATURE...
CHATTA
SHVR SHVR
...THEY SHAKE TO GENERATE THE ADDITIONAL BODY HEAT NEEDED TO MAINTAIN REGULAR BODY TEMPERATURE. IT'S A PHYSIOLOGICAL PHENOMENON CALLED "SHIVERING."
BRR
TORIKO'S INTENSE SHIVERING VIBRATED THE AIR AROUND HIM...
...GENERATING ENOUGH HEAT TO MAINTAIN HIS BODY TEMPERATURE EVEN SHIRTLESS IN SUB-ZERO TEMPERATURES.
HE ALSO THAWED OUT HIS RIGHT HAND BEFORE NECROSIS COULD SET IN...
...BY CONTINUOUSLY SHIVERING THE AUTONOMOUS NERVES IN IT.
WHA...
...
WHAT INCREDIBLE HEAT!
IT'S LIKE I'M STANDING NEXT TO A BLAZING FIRE!
HE MUST BE BURNING AN INSANE NUMBER OF CALORIES...
...TO KEEP THIS UP!
I'LL SAY IT ONE MORE TIME, TOMMY.

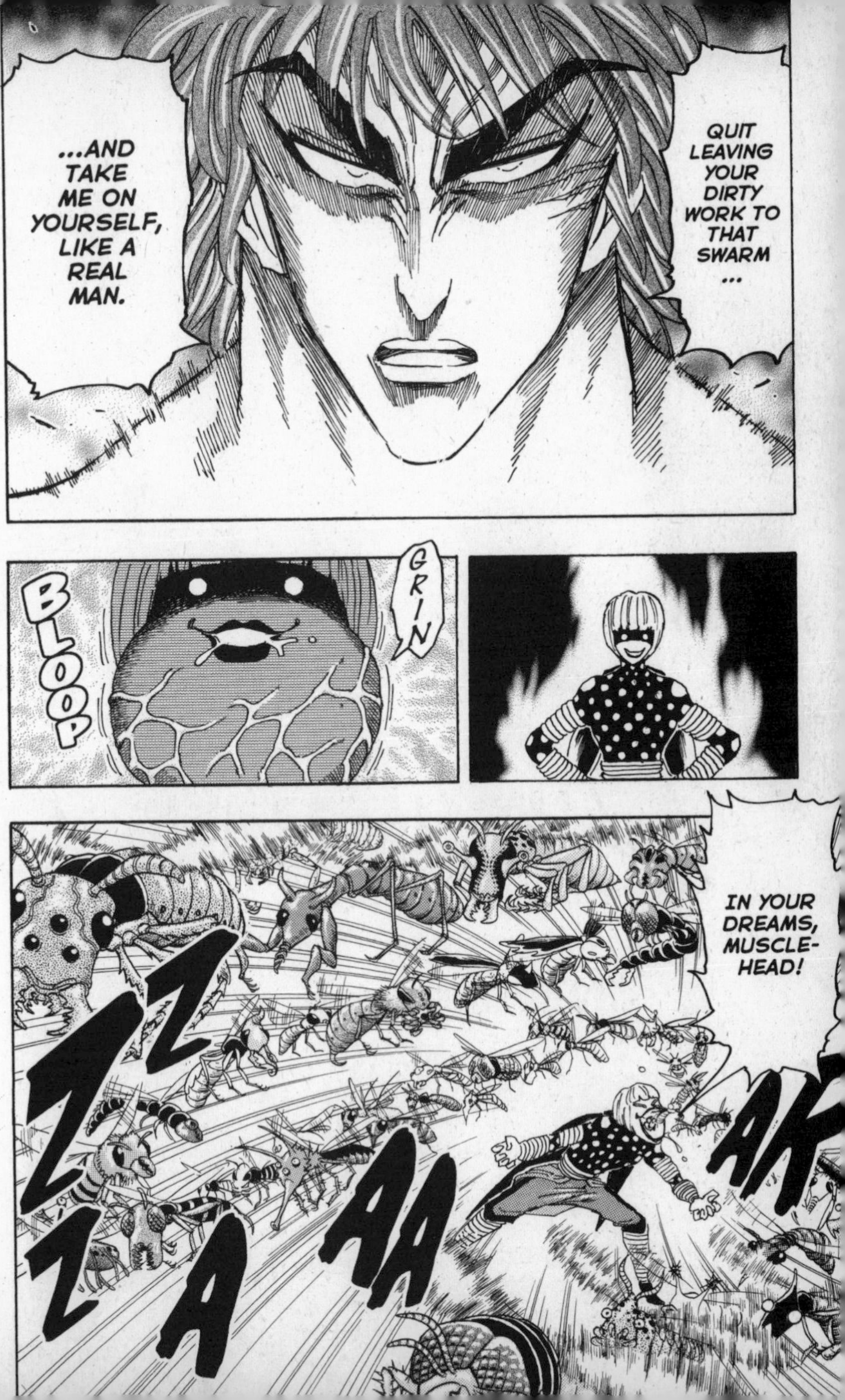
QUIT LEAVING YOUR DIRTY WORK TO THAT SWARM...
...AND TAKE ME ON YOURSELF, LIKE A REAL MAN.
GRIN
BLOOP
IN YOUR DREAMS, MUSCLE-HEAD!
AK
AAAA
ZZZZ

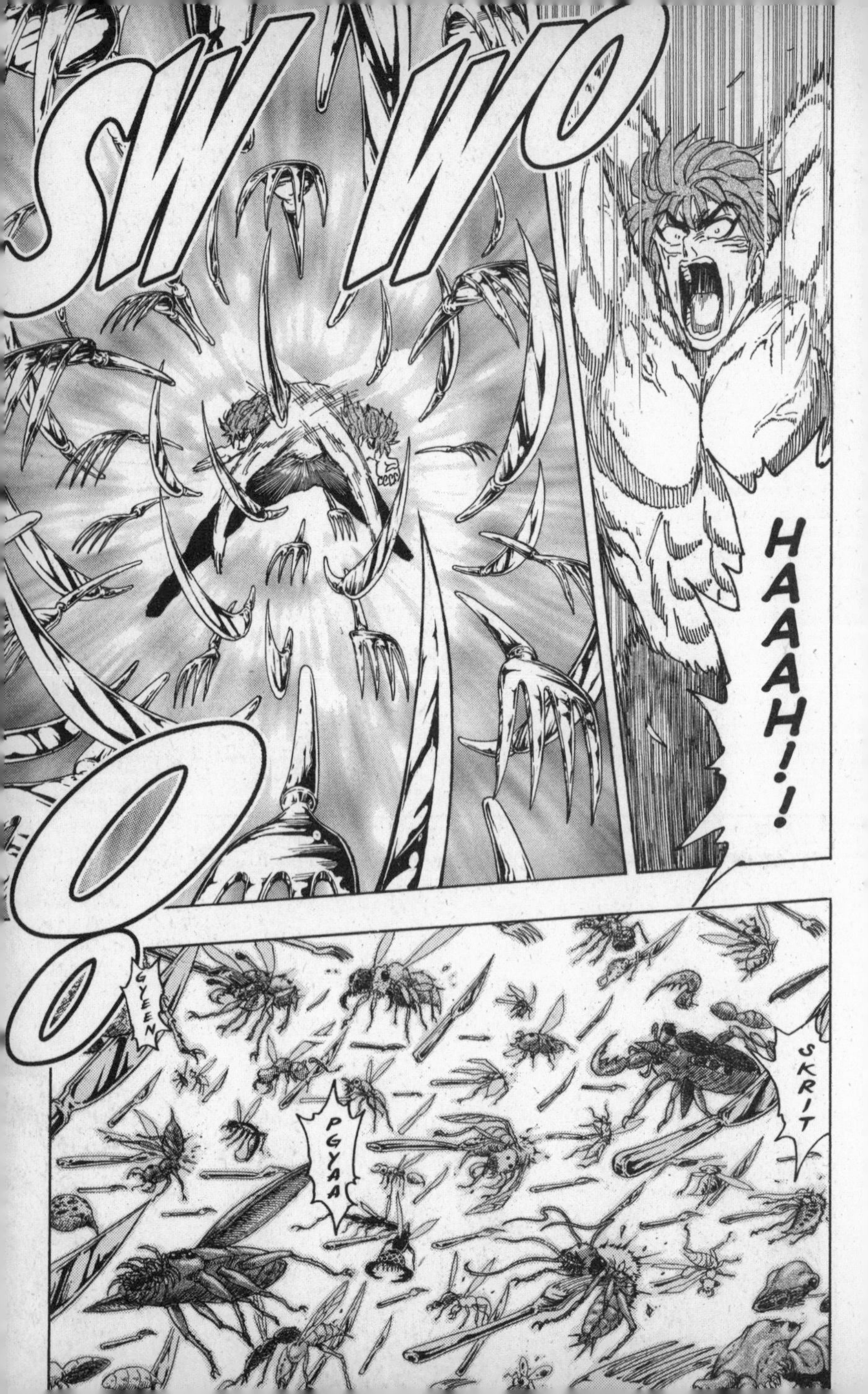
SHWOOO
HAAAAH!!
SKRIT
GYEEN
PGYAA

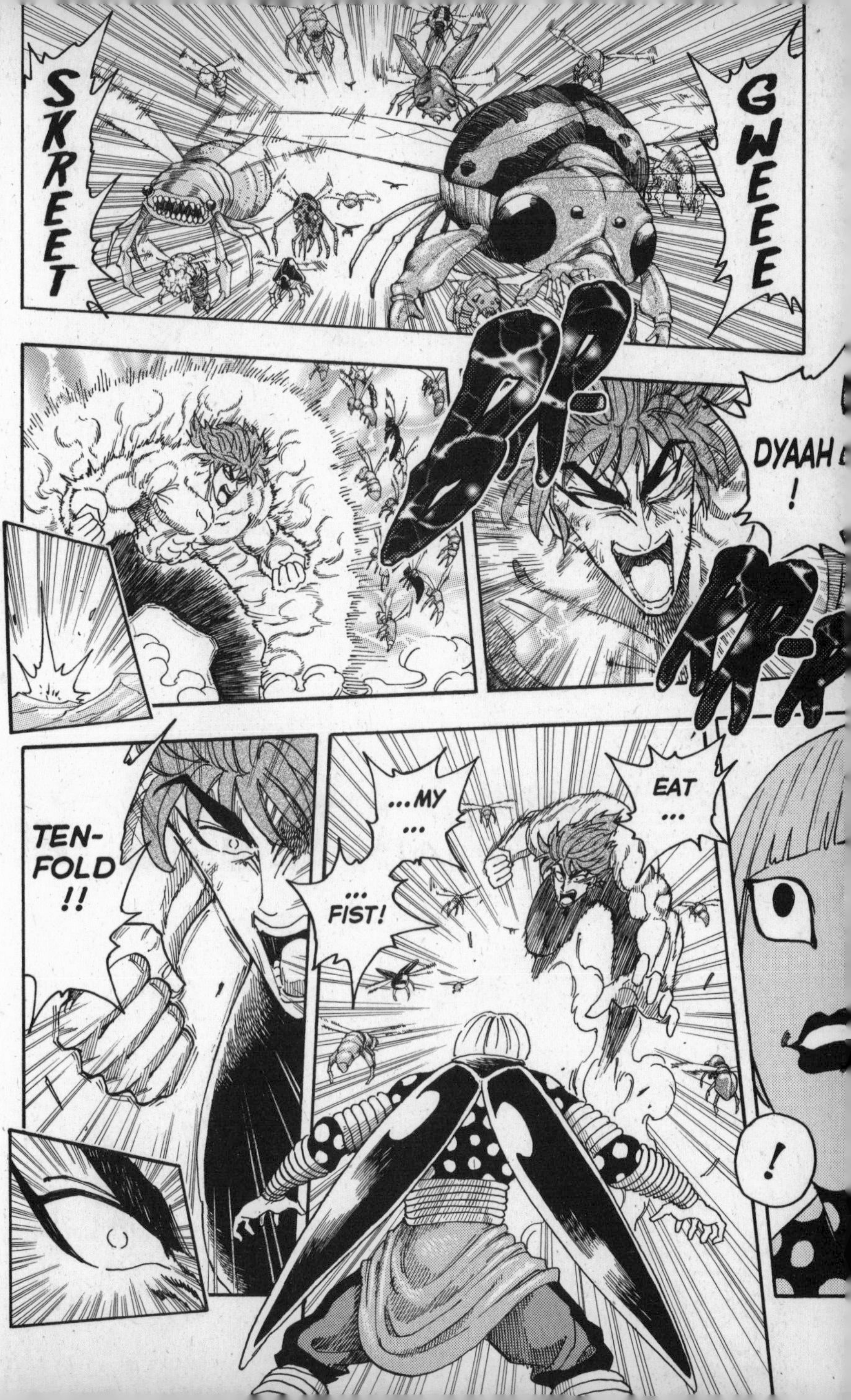
GWEEE
SKREET
DYAAH!
!
EAT ...
...MY ...
... FIST!
TEN-FOLD!!

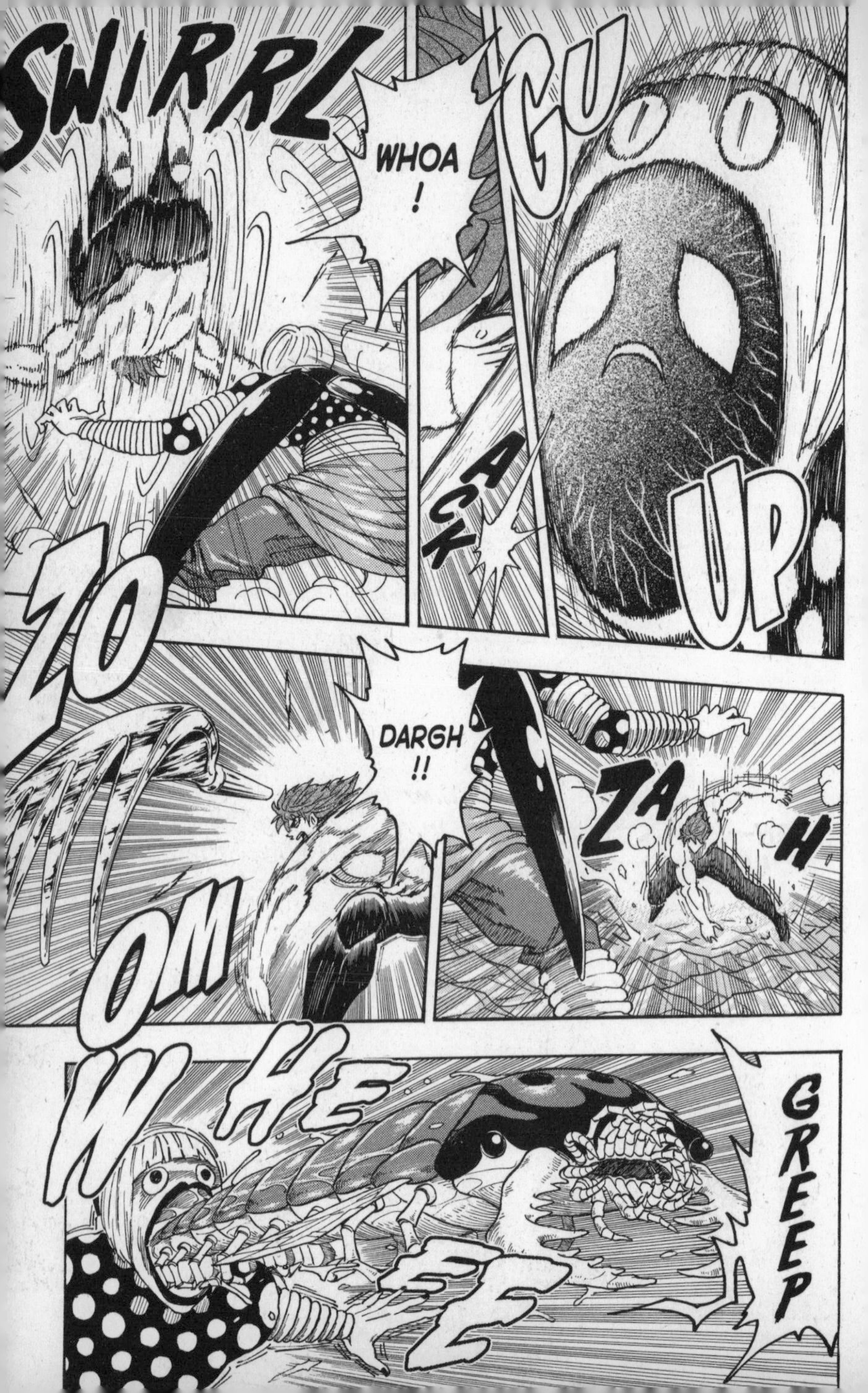
GU
UP
ACK
WHOA!
SWIRRL
ZAH
DARGH!!
ZOOM
GREEP
WHEE

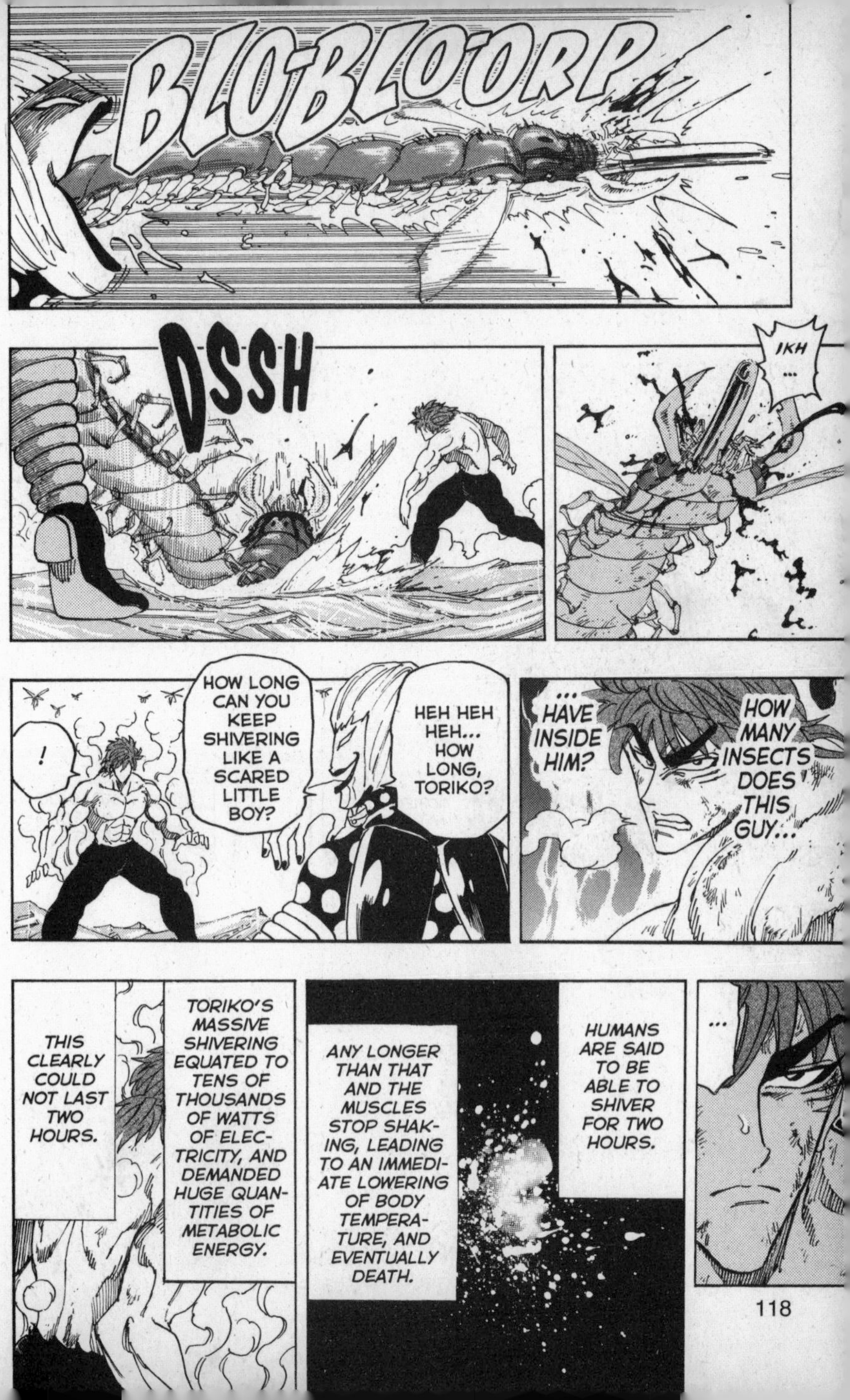
BLO-BLO-ORP
IKH...
DSSH
HOW MANY INSECTS DOES THIS GUY...
...HAVE INSIDE HIM?
HEH HEH HEH... HOW LONG, TORIKO?
HOW LONG CAN YOU KEEP SHIVERING LIKE A SCARED LITTLE BOY?
!
...
HUMANS ARE SAID TO BE ABLE TO SHIVER FOR TWO HOURS.
ANY LONGER THAN THAT AND THE MUSCLES STOP SHAKING, LEADING TO AN IMMEDIATE LOWERING OF BODY TEMPERATURE, AND EVENTUALLY DEATH.
TORIKO'S MASSIVE SHIVERING EQUATED TO TENS OF THOUSANDS OF WATTS OF ELECTRICITY, AND DEMANDED HUGE QUANTITIES OF METABOLIC ENERGY.
THIS CLEARLY COULD NOT LAST TWO HOURS.

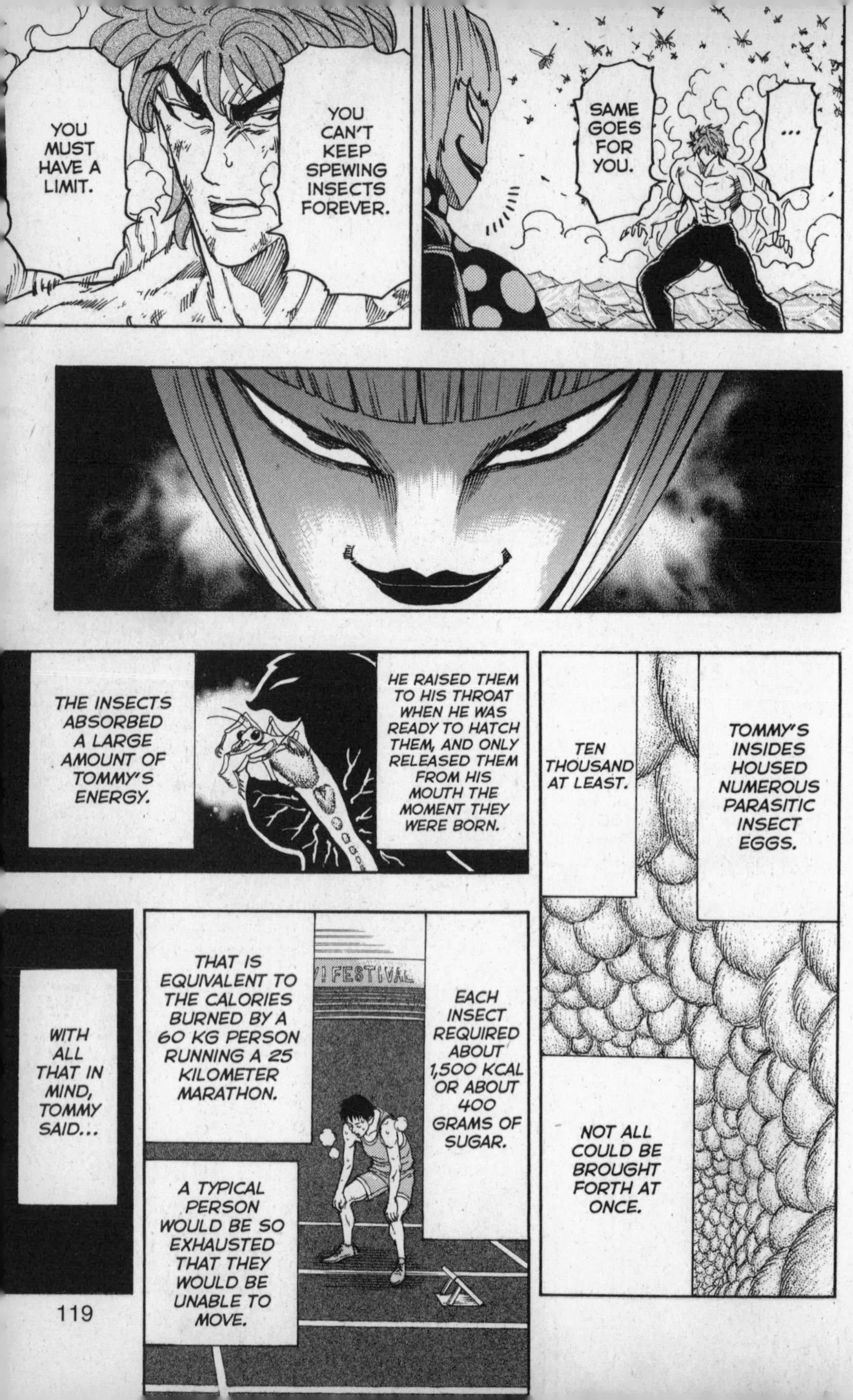
...
SAME GOES FOR YOU.
YOU CAN'T KEEP SPEWING INSECTS FOREVER.
YOU MUST HAVE A LIMIT.
TOMMY'S INSIDES HOUSED NUMEROUS PARASITIC INSECT EGGS.
TEN THOUSAND AT LEAST.
NOT ALL COULD BE BROUGHT FORTH AT ONCE.
HE RAISED THEM TO HIS THROAT WHEN HE WAS READY TO HATCH THEM, AND ONLY RELEASED THEM FROM HIS MOUTH THE MOMENT THEY WERE BORN.
THE INSECTS ABSORBED A LARGE AMOUNT OF TOMMY'S ENERGY.
EACH INSECT REQUIRED ABOUT 1,500 KCAL OR ABOUT 400 GRAMS OF SUGAR.
THAT IS EQUIVALENT TO THE CALORIES BURNED BY A 60 KG PERSON RUNNING A 25 KILOMETER MARATHON.
A TYPICAL PERSON WOULD BE SO EXHAUSTED THAT THEY WOULD BE UNABLE TO MOVE.
WITH ALL THAT IN MIND, TOMMY SAID...

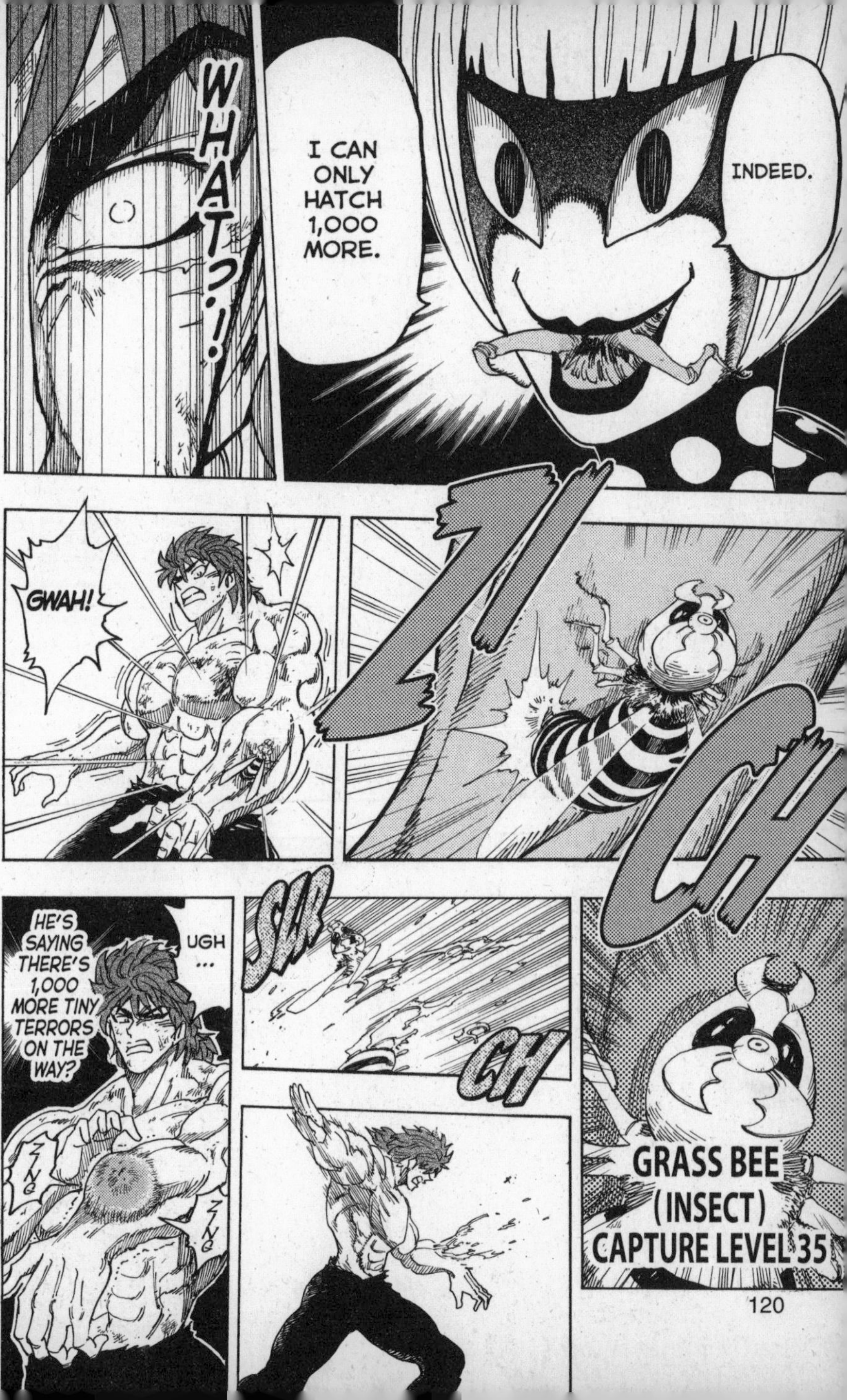
INDEED.
I CAN ONLY HATCH 1,000 MORE.
WHAT?!
GWAH!
GRASS BEE (INSECT) CAPTURE LEVEL 35
SHR
CH
UGH ...
HE'S SAYING THERE'S 1,000 MORE TINY TERRORS ON THE WAY?
ZING
ZING

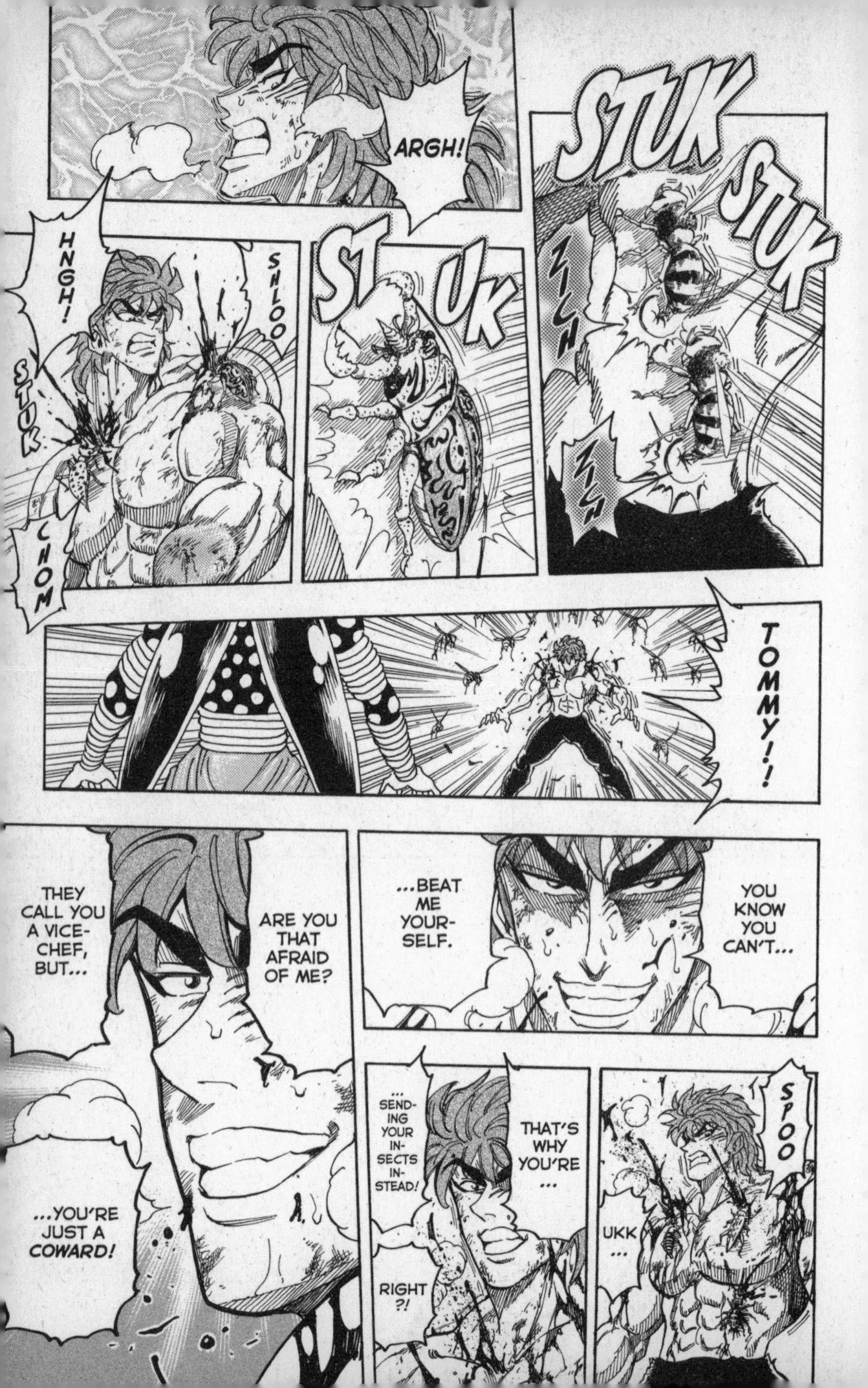
STUK
STUK
ZIZH
ZIZH
ARGH!
ST UK
SHLOO
HNGH!
STUK
CHOM
TOMMY!!
YOU KNOW YOU CAN'T...
...BEAT ME YOURSELF.
SPOO
UKK...
THAT'S WHY YOU'RE...
...SENDING YOUR INSECTS INSTEAD!
RIGHT?!
ARE YOU THAT AFRAID OF ME?
THEY CALL YOU A VICE-CHEF, BUT...
...YOU'RE JUST A COWARD!

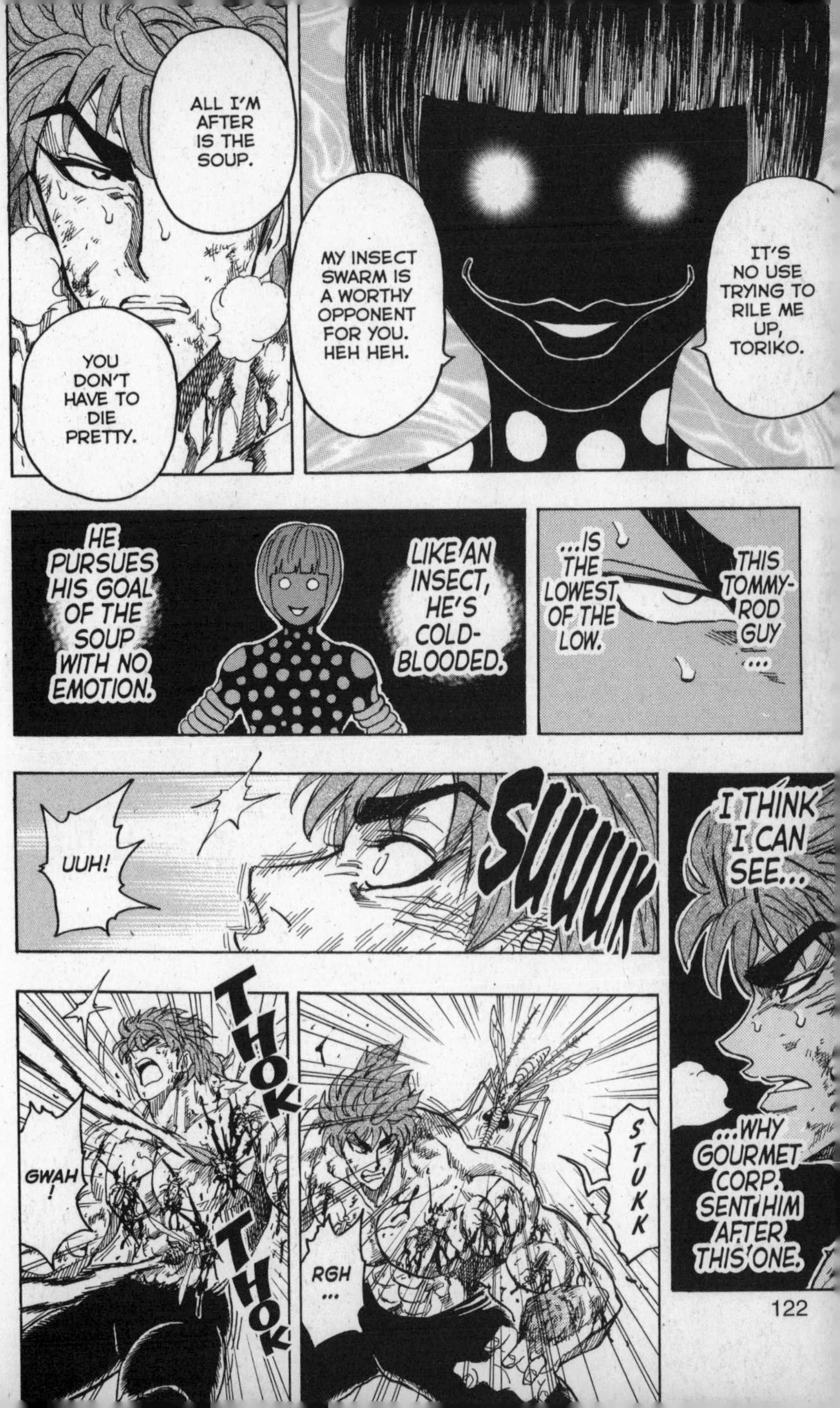

IT'S NO USE TRYING TO RILE ME UP, TORIKO.
MY INSECT SWARM IS A WORTHY OPPONENT FOR YOU. HEH HEH.
ALL I'M AFTER IS THE SOUP.
YOU DON'T HAVE TO DIE PRETTY.
THIS TOMMY-ROD GUY...
...IS THE LOWEST OF THE LOW.
LIKE AN INSECT, HE'S COLD-BLOODED.
HE PURSUES HIS GOAL OF THE SOUP WITH NO EMOTION.
I THINK I CAN SEE...
...WHY GOURMET CORP. SENT HIM AFTER THIS ONE.
SUUUK
UUH!
STUKK
RGH...
THOK
THOK
GWAH!

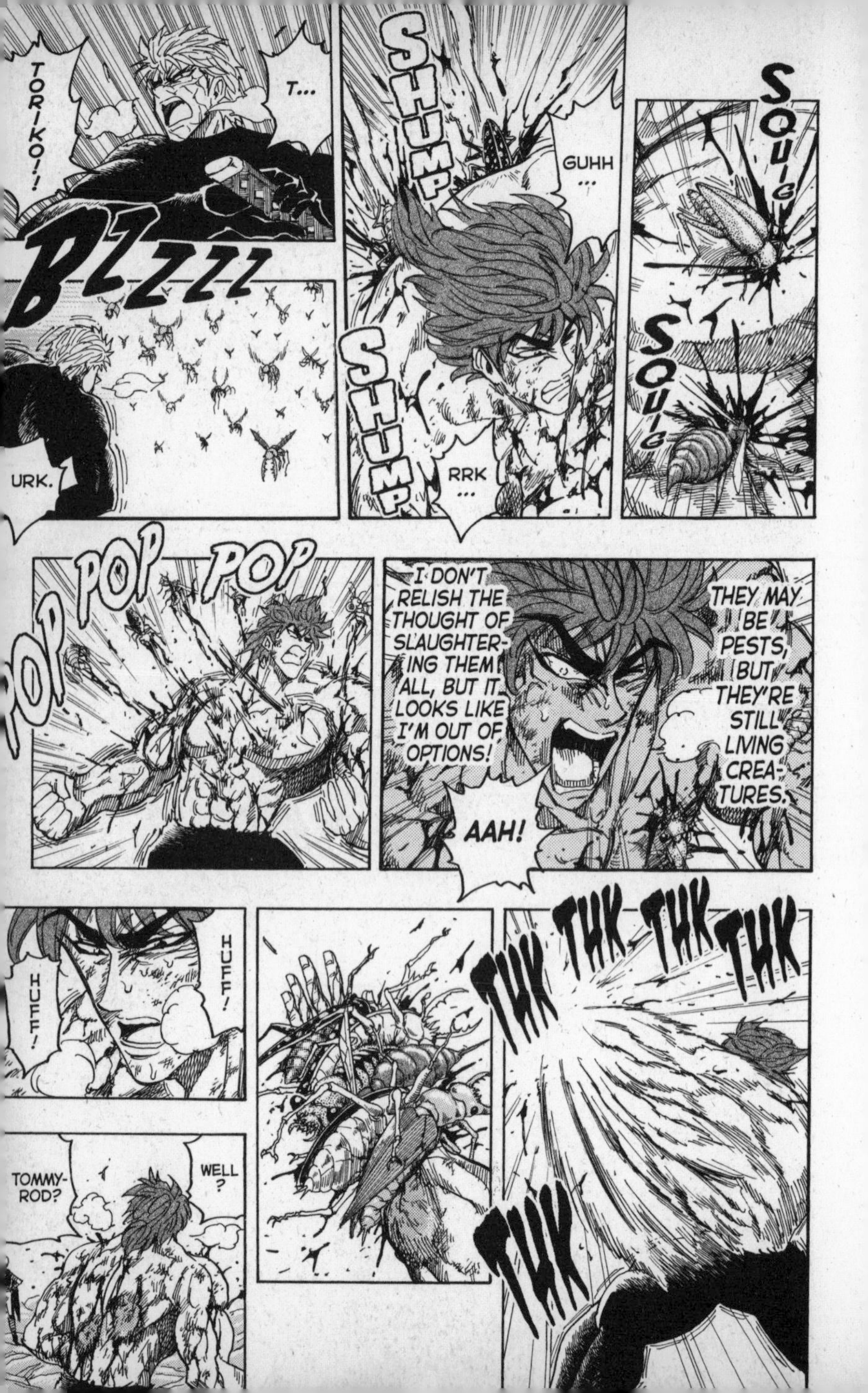
SQUIG
SQUIG
SHUMP
GUHH...
SHUMP
RRK...
T...
TORIKO!!
BZZZZ
URK.
THEY MAY BE PESTS, BUT THEY'RE STILL LIVING CREATURES.
I DON'T RELISH THE THOUGHT OF SLAUGHTERING THEM ALL, BUT IT LOOKS LIKE I'M OUT OF OPTIONS!
AAH!
POP POP POP
THK THK THK THK
THK
HUFF!
HUFF!
WELL?
TOMMY-ROD?

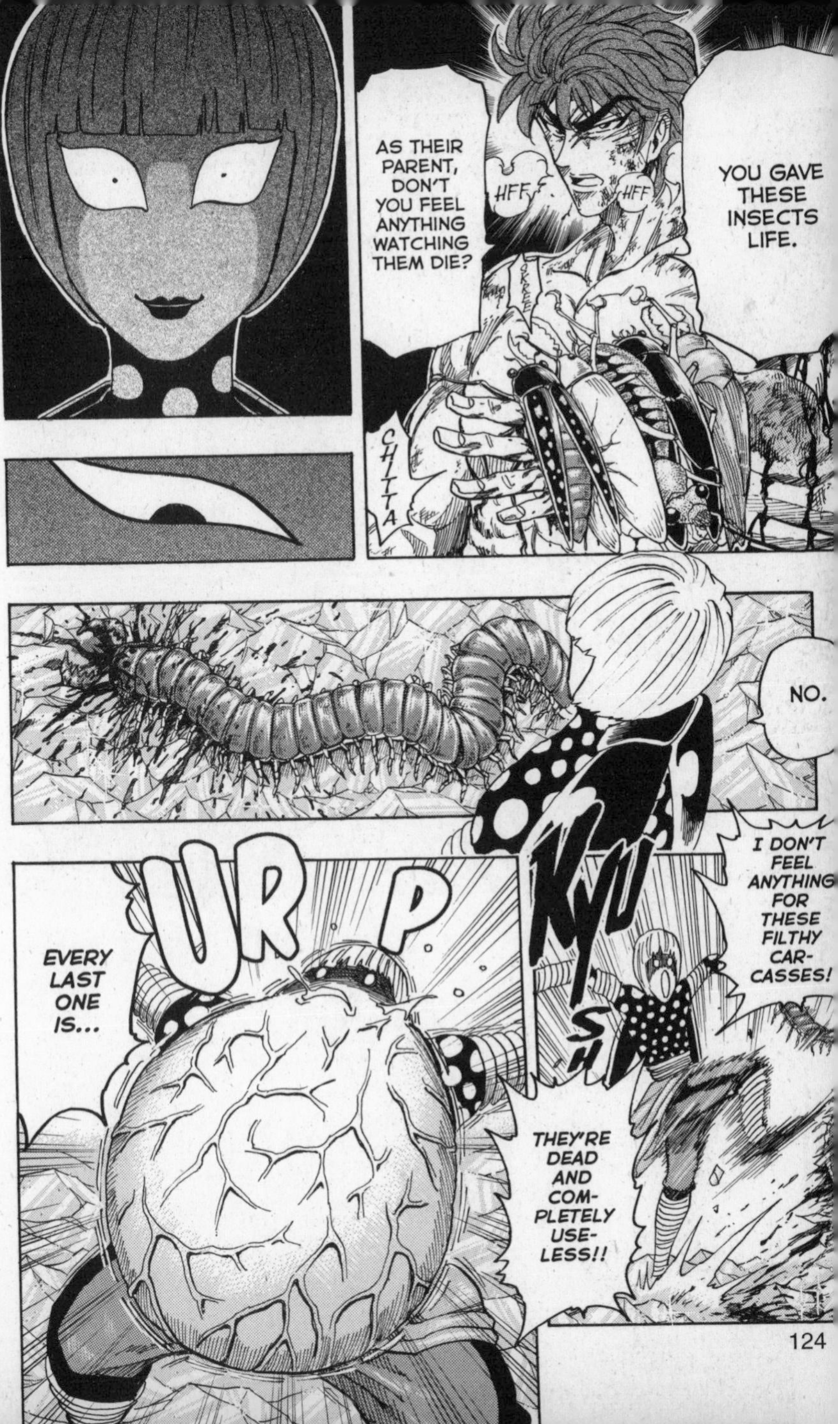
YOU GAVE THESE INSECTS LIFE.
HFF
HFF
AS THEIR PARENT, DON'T YOU FEEL ANYTHING WATCHING THEM DIE?
CHITTA
NO.
I DON'T FEEL ANYTHING FOR THESE FILTHY CAR-CASSES!
KYU
SH
EVERY LAST ONE IS...
URP
THEY'RE DEAD AND COM-PLETELY USE-LESS!!

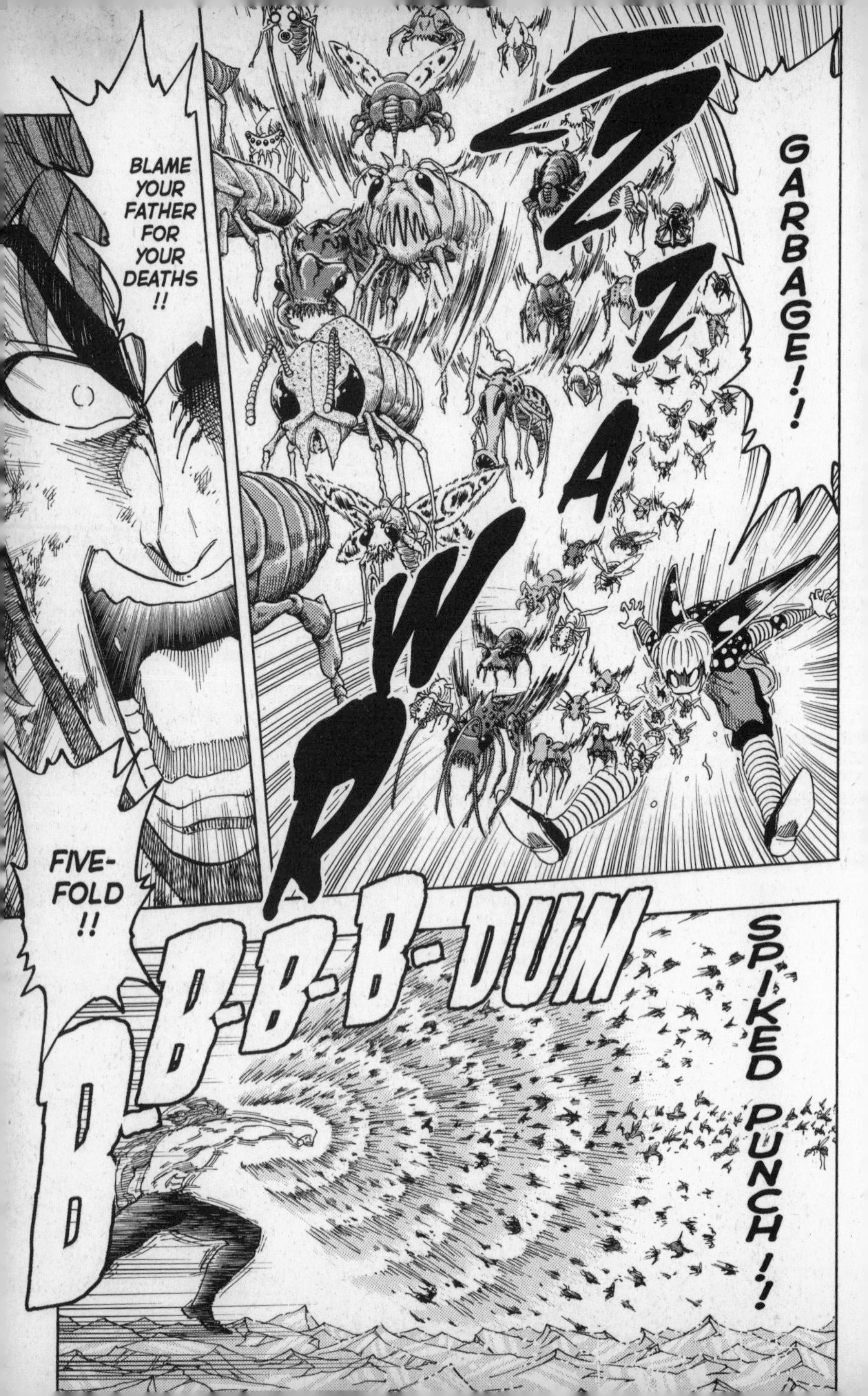
GARBAGE!!
BLAME YOUR FATHER FOR YOUR DEATHS!!
FIVE-FOLD!!
SPIKED PUNCH!!
B-B-B-B-DUM

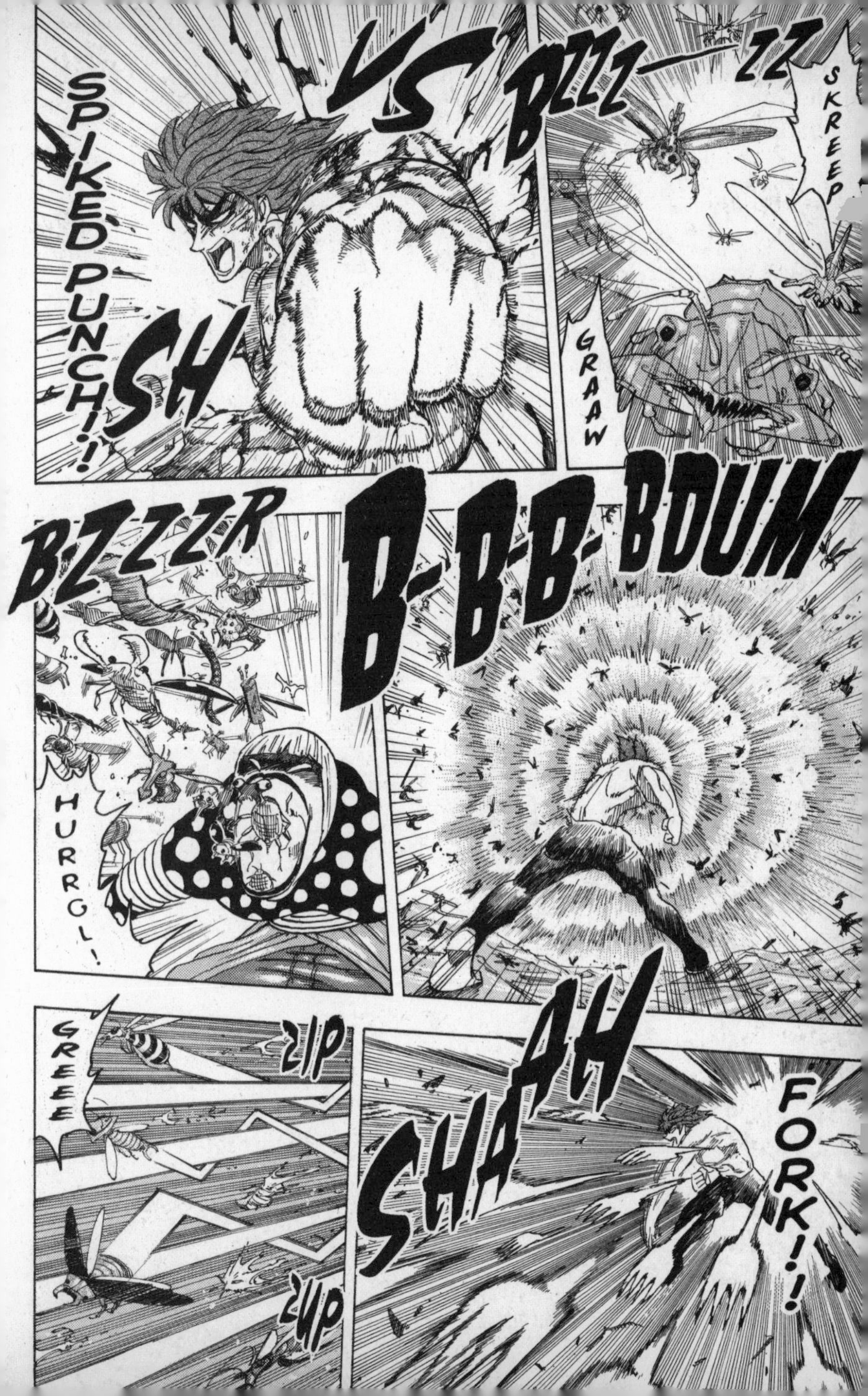

BZZZ—ZZ
SKREEP
GRAAW
VS
SPIKED PUNCH!!
SH
B-B-B-BDUM
BZZZZR
HURRGL!
FORK!!
SHAAH
ZIP
ZIP
GREEE

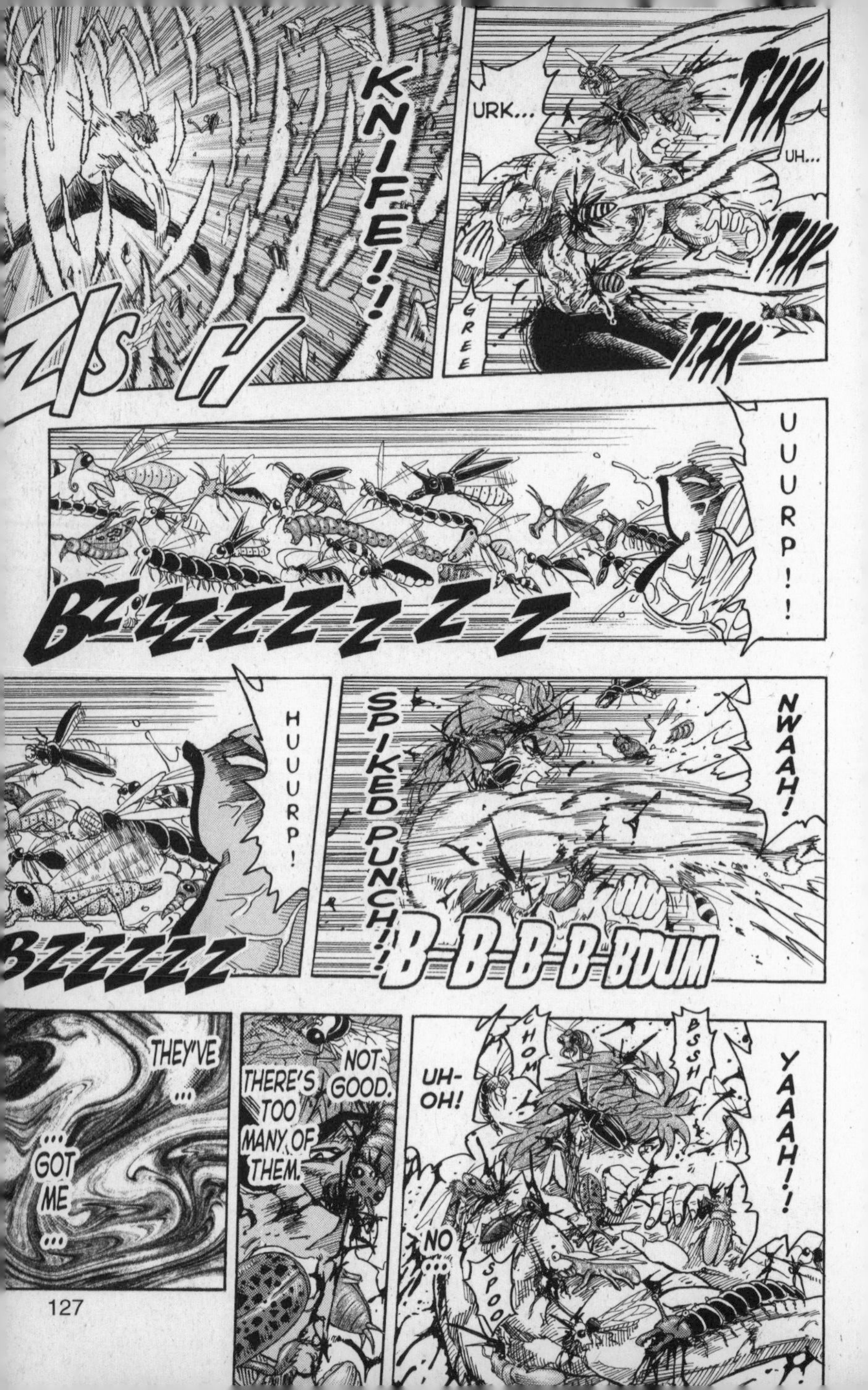
THK
UH...
URK...
THK
GREE
THK
KNIFE!!!
ZASH
UUURP!!
BZZZZZZZZZ
NWAAH!
SPIKED PUNCH!!
B-B-B-B-BDUM
HUUURP!
BZZZZZZ
YAAAH!!
BSSH
CHOM
UH-OH!
NO...
SPOO
NOT GOOD.
THERE'S TOO MANY OF THEM.
THEY'VE...
...GOT ME...

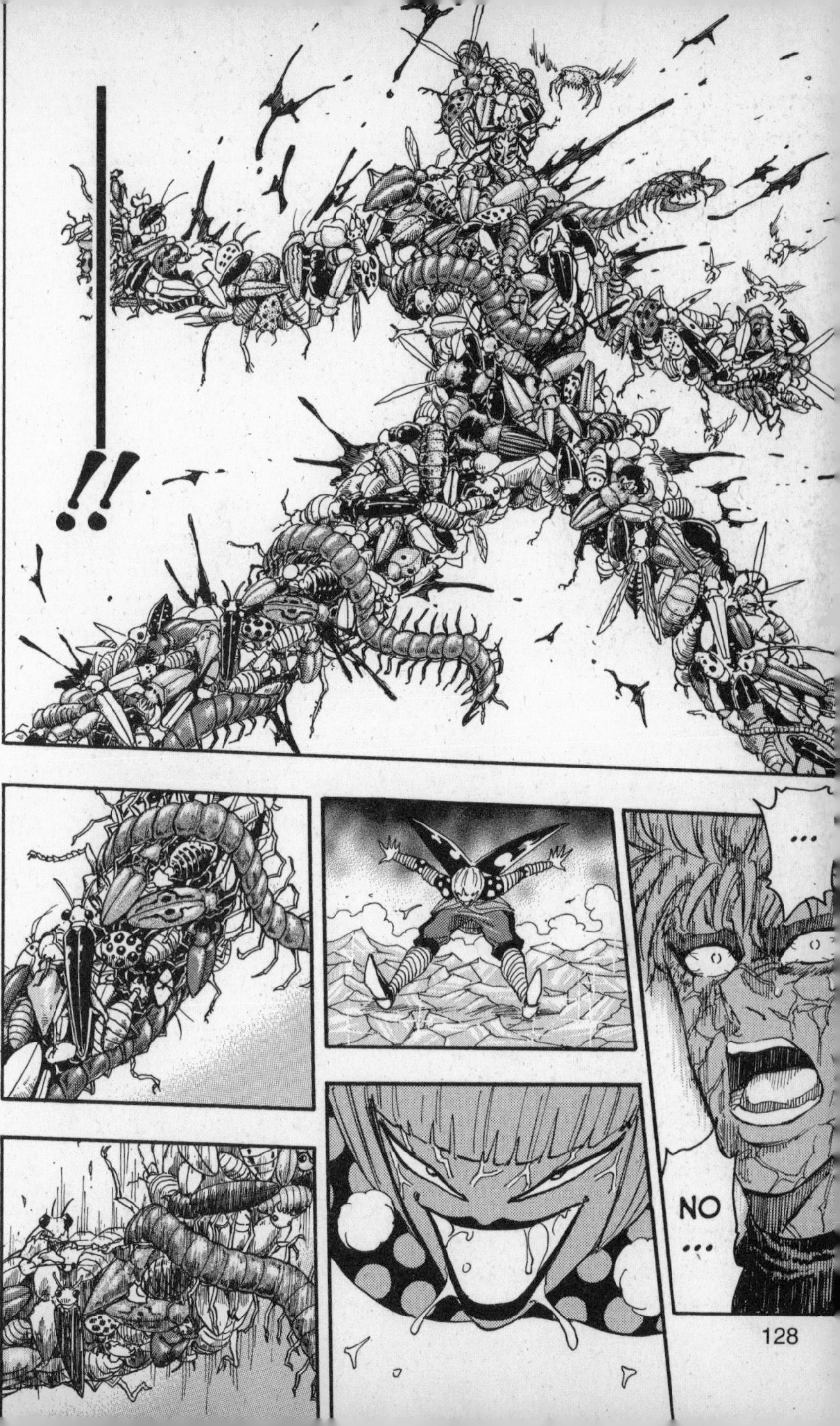
—!!
...
NO ...

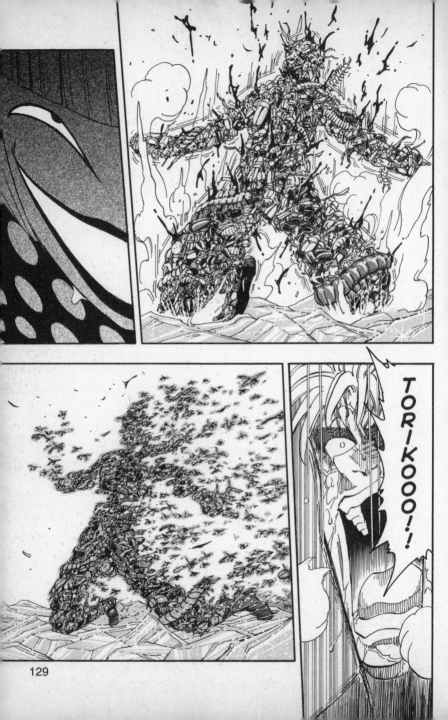

TORIKOOO!!

129

TORIKO

GOURMET CHECKLIST

Vol. 084

GARLIC CHICKEN

(BIRD)

CAPTURE LEVEL: 45

HABITAT: UNKNOWN, DUE TO CAPTURE DIFFICULTY

LENGTH: 40 CM

HEIGHT: 45 CM

WEIGHT: 3.5 KG

PRICE: 100 G / 200,000 YEN

SCALE

THE FINEST OF FINE FOODS, THIS FRAGRANT FOWL ONLY EATS WILD GARLIC. WHEN THE RICH FLAVOR OF WILD GARLIC MINGLES WITH THE CHICKEN'S FLESH, AN UNFORGETTABLE DUET IS CREATED! THE WILD GARLIC THAT IT FEEDS ON IS DIMINISHING YEAR BY YEAR, SO THE GARLIC CHICKEN POPULATION IS ALSO ON THE DECLINE AND OFTEN TURNS TO FOODS BESIDES WILD GARLIC. BECAUSE OF THEIR ENDANGERED STATUS, THEY ARE NOW BEING ARTIFICIALLY BRED, THOUGH THE FLAVOR IS NOTHING COMPARED TO THE NATURAL VARIETY.

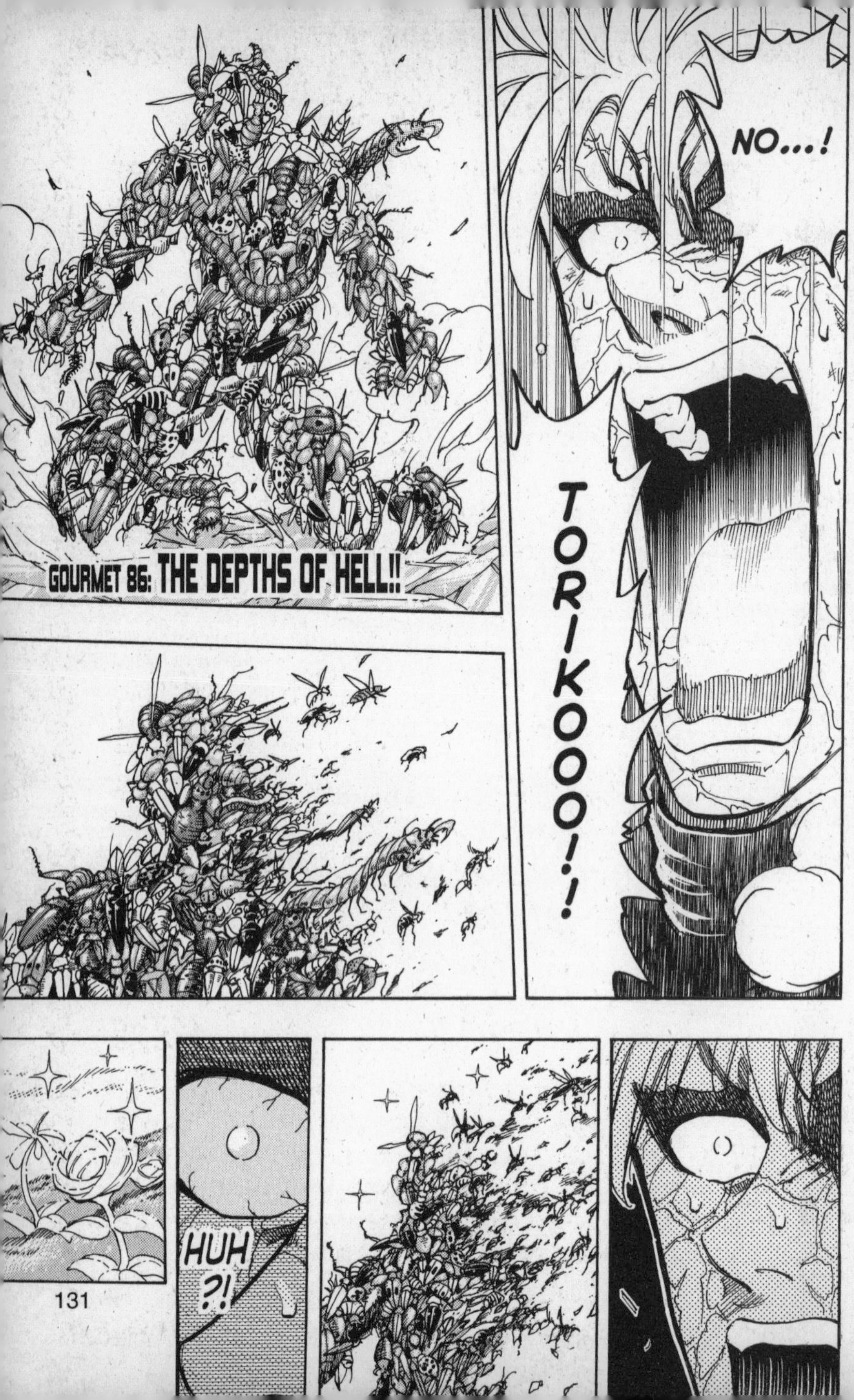
NO...!
TORIKOOOO!!
GOURMET 86: THE DEPTHS OF HELL!!
HUH ?!

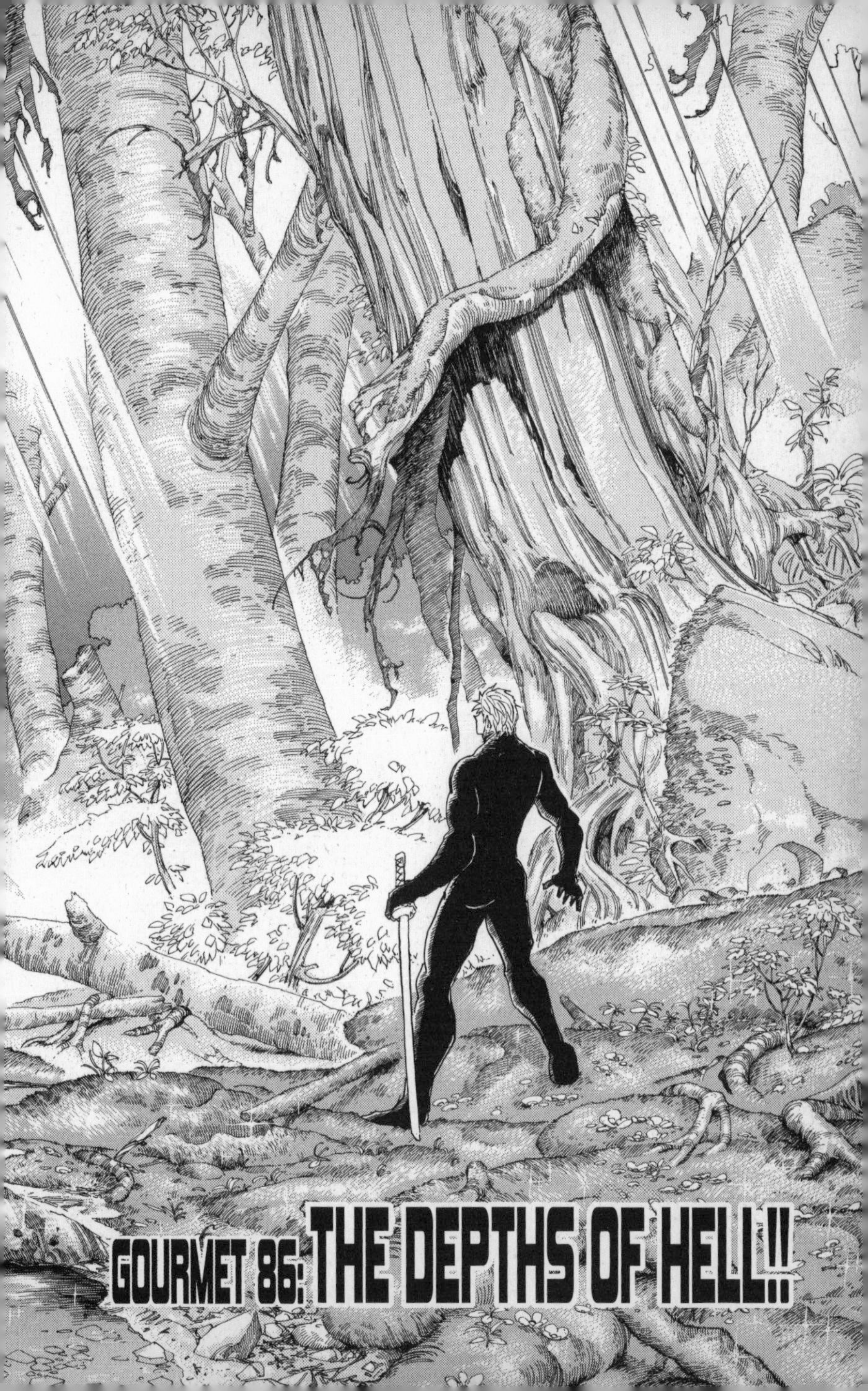
GOURMET 86: THE DEPTHS OF HELL!!

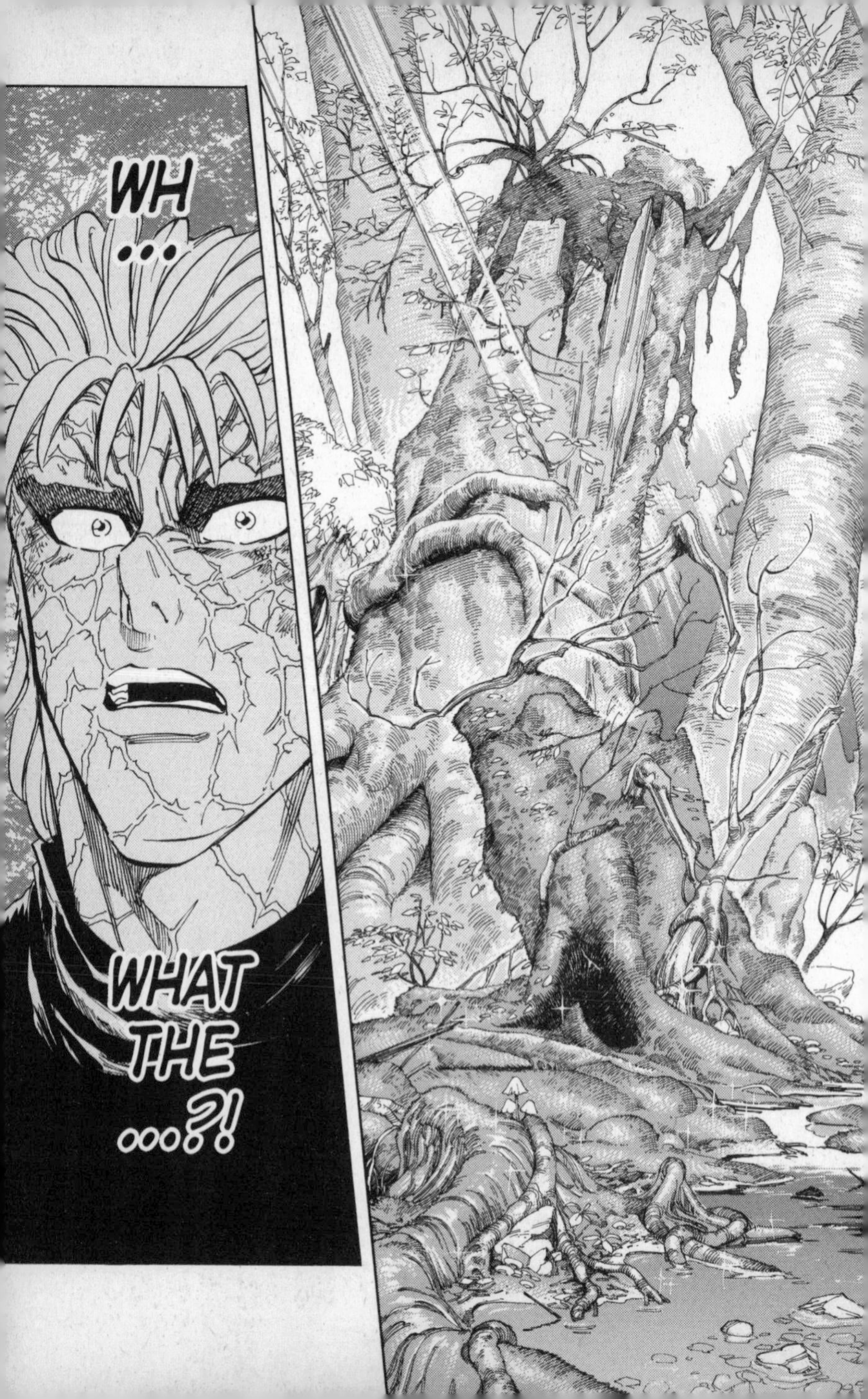
WH...
WHAT THE...?!

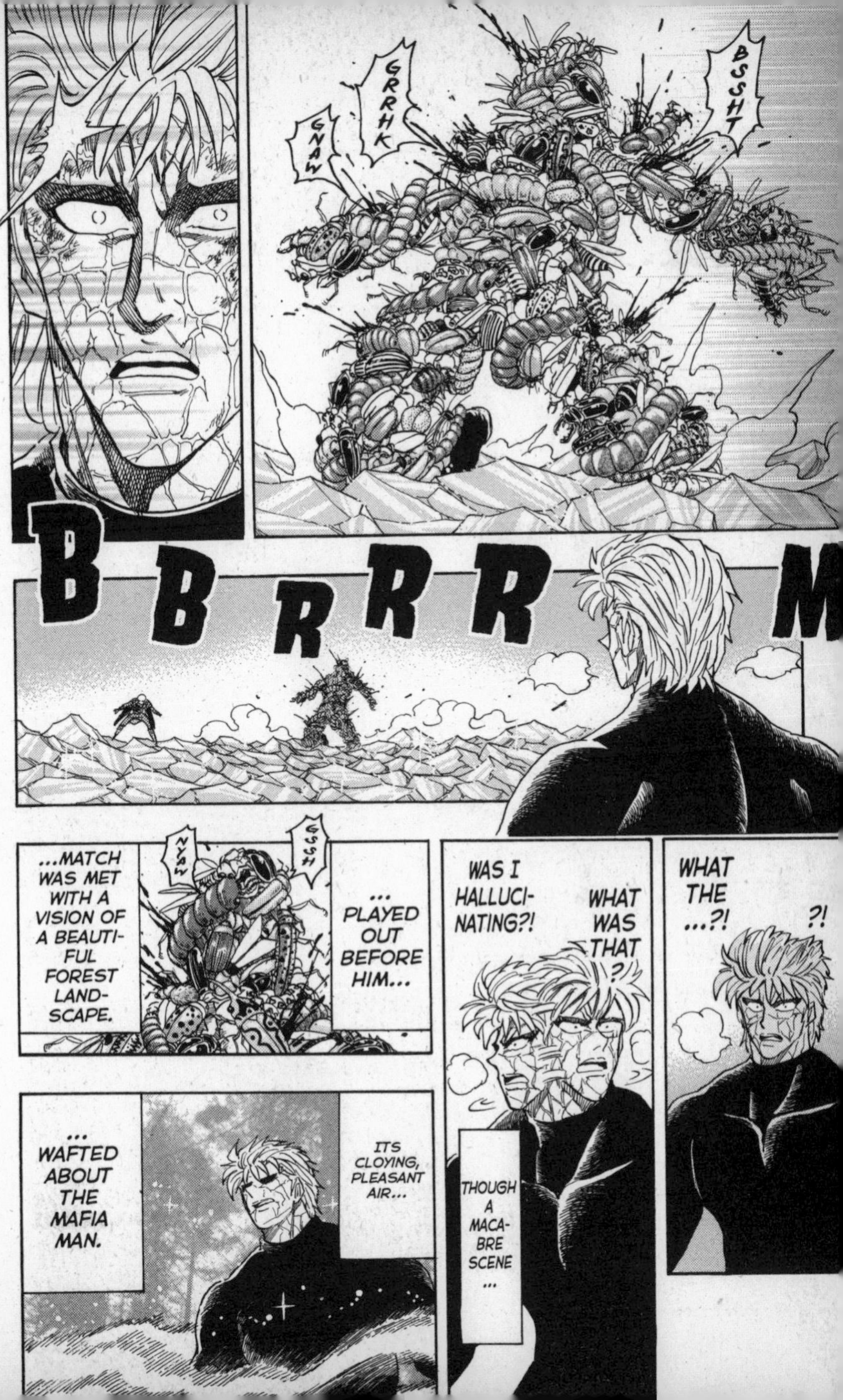
BSSHT
GRRHK
GNAW
BBRRRM
?!
WHAT THE ...?!
WHAT WAS THAT?
WAS I HALLUCINATING?!
THOUGH A MACABRE SCENE...
...PLAYED OUT BEFORE HIM...
GSSH
NYAW
...MATCH WAS MET WITH A VISION OF A BEAUTIFUL FOREST LANDSCAPE.
ITS CLOYING, PLEASANT AIR...
...WAFTED ABOUT THE MAFIA MAN.

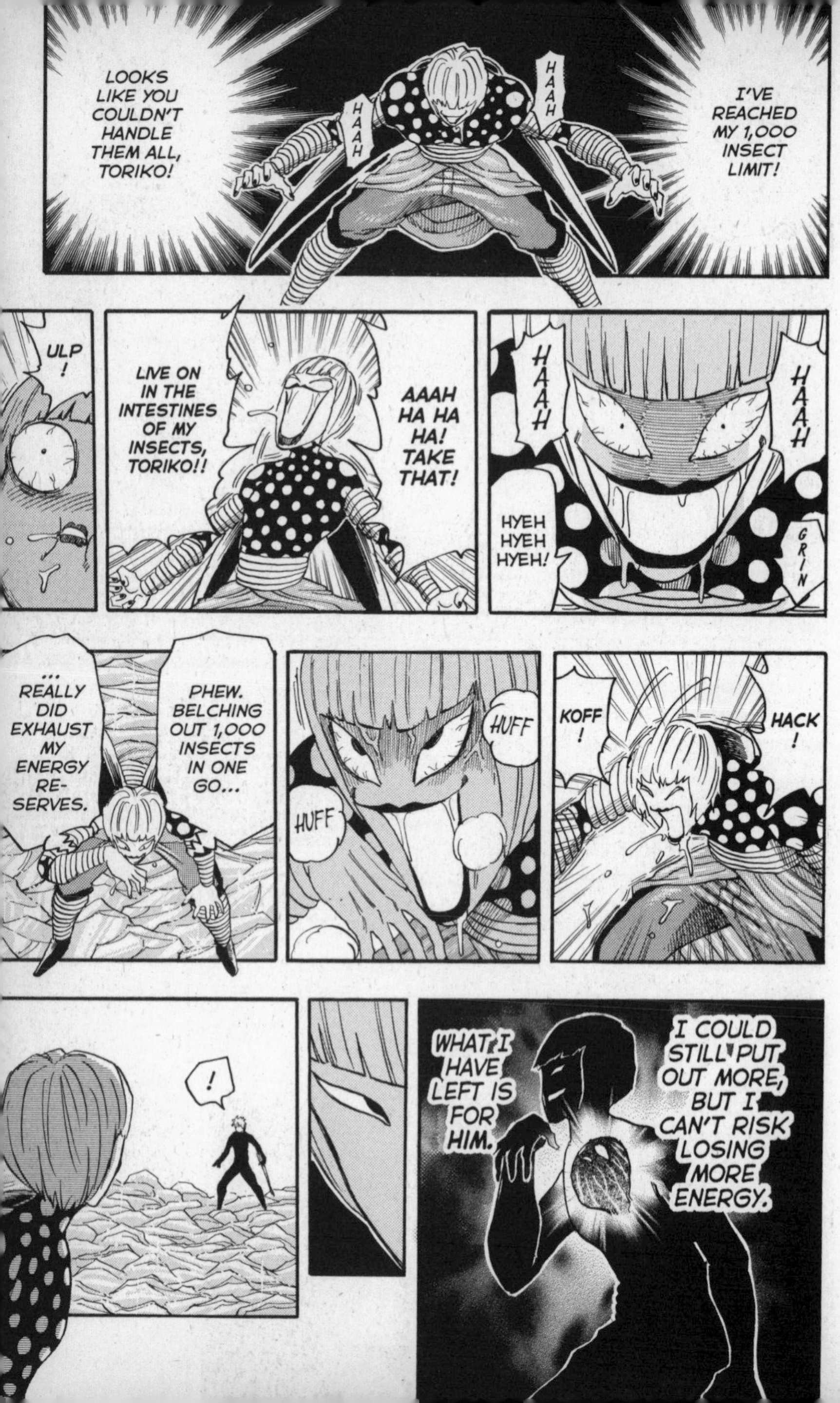
I'VE REACHED MY 1,000 INSECT LIMIT!
HAAH
HAAH
LOOKS LIKE YOU COULDN'T HANDLE THEM ALL, TORIKO!
HAAAH
GRIN
HAAH
HYEH HYEH HYEH!
AAAH HA HA HA! TAKE THAT!
LIVE ON IN THE INTESTINES OF MY INSECTS, TORIKO!!
ULP!
HACK!
KOFF!
HUFF
HUFF
PHEW. BELCHING OUT 1,000 INSECTS IN ONE GO...
...REALLY DID EXHAUST MY ENERGY RE-SERVES.
I COULD STILL PUT OUT MORE, BUT I CAN'T RISK LOSING MORE ENERGY.
WHAT I HAVE LEFT IS FOR HIM.
!

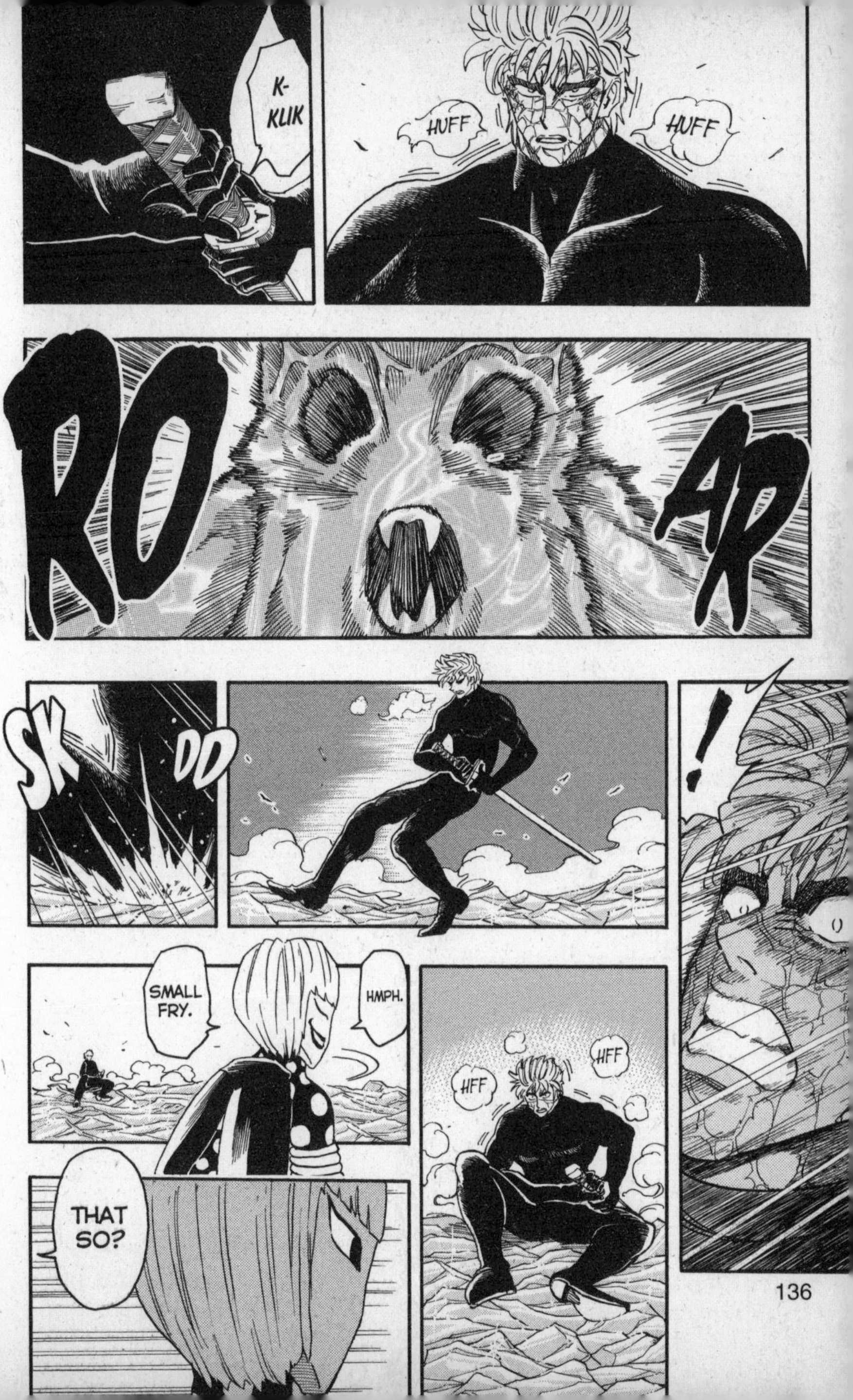
HUFF
HUFF
K-
KLIK
RO
AR
!
SK
DD
HFF
HFF
HMPH.
SMALL FRY.
THAT SO?

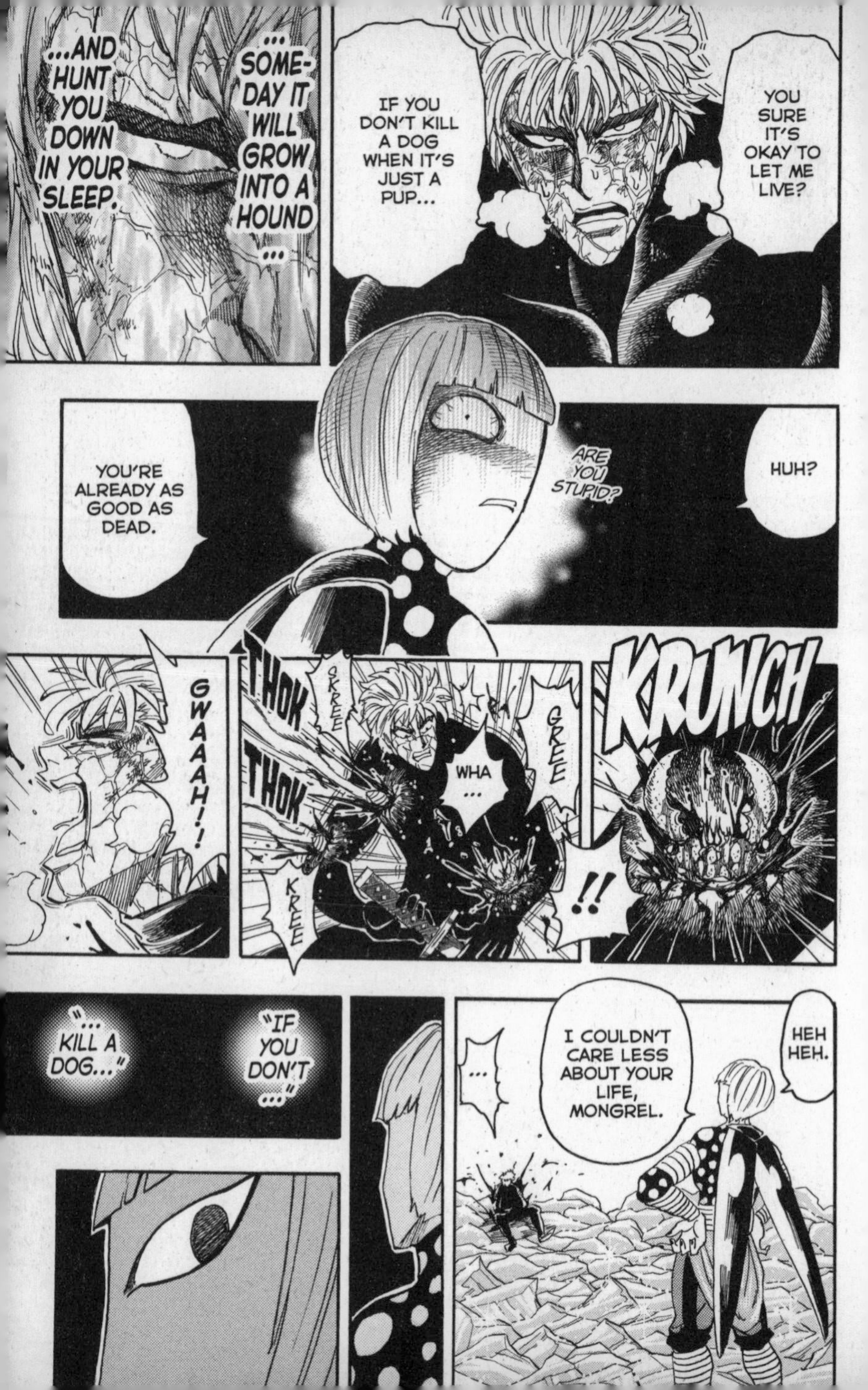
YOU SURE IT'S OKAY TO LET ME LIVE?
IF YOU DON'T KILL A DOG WHEN IT'S JUST A PUP...
...SOME-DAY IT WILL GROW INTO A HOUND...
...AND HUNT YOU DOWN IN YOUR SLEEP.
HUH?
ARE YOU STUPID?
YOU'RE ALREADY AS GOOD AS DEAD.
KRUNCH
!!
GREE
WHA...
SKREE
THOK
THOK
KREE
GWAAAAH!!
HEH HEH.
I COULDN'T CARE LESS ABOUT YOUR LIFE, MONGREL.
...
"IF YOU DON'T..."
"...KILL A DOG..."

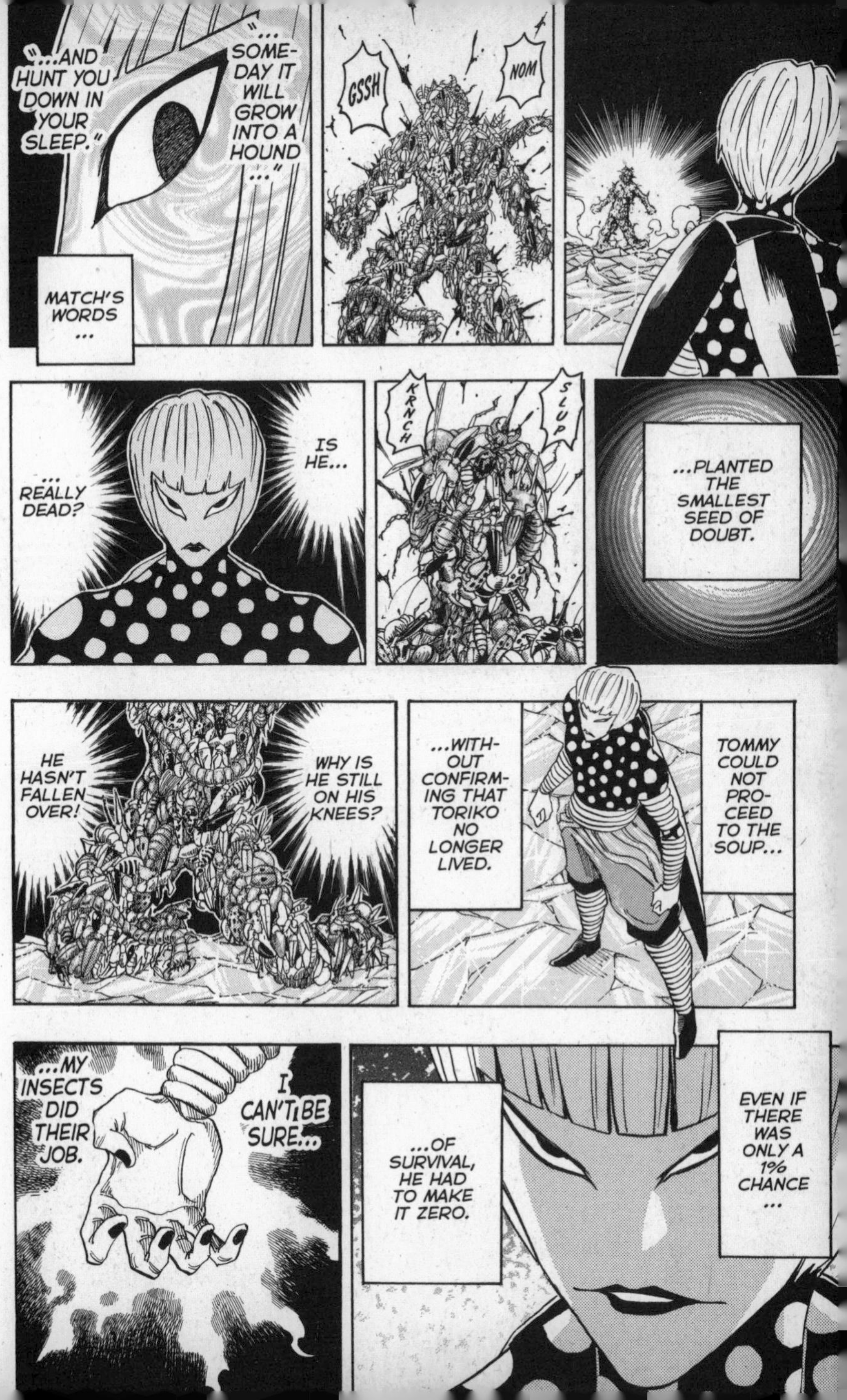
NOM
GSSH
"...SOMEDAY IT WILL GROW INTO A HOUND..."
"...AND HUNT YOU DOWN IN YOUR SLEEP."
MATCH'S WORDS...
...PLANTED THE SMALLEST SEED OF DOUBT.
SLUP
KRNCH
IS HE...
...REALLY DEAD?
TOMMY COULD NOT PROCEED TO THE SOUP...
...WITHOUT CONFIRMING THAT TORIKO NO LONGER LIVED.
WHY IS HE STILL ON HIS KNEES?
HE HASN'T FALLEN OVER!
EVEN IF THERE WAS ONLY A 1% CHANCE...
...OF SURVIVAL, HE HAD TO MAKE IT ZERO.
I CAN'T BE SURE...
...MY INSECTS DID THEIR JOB.

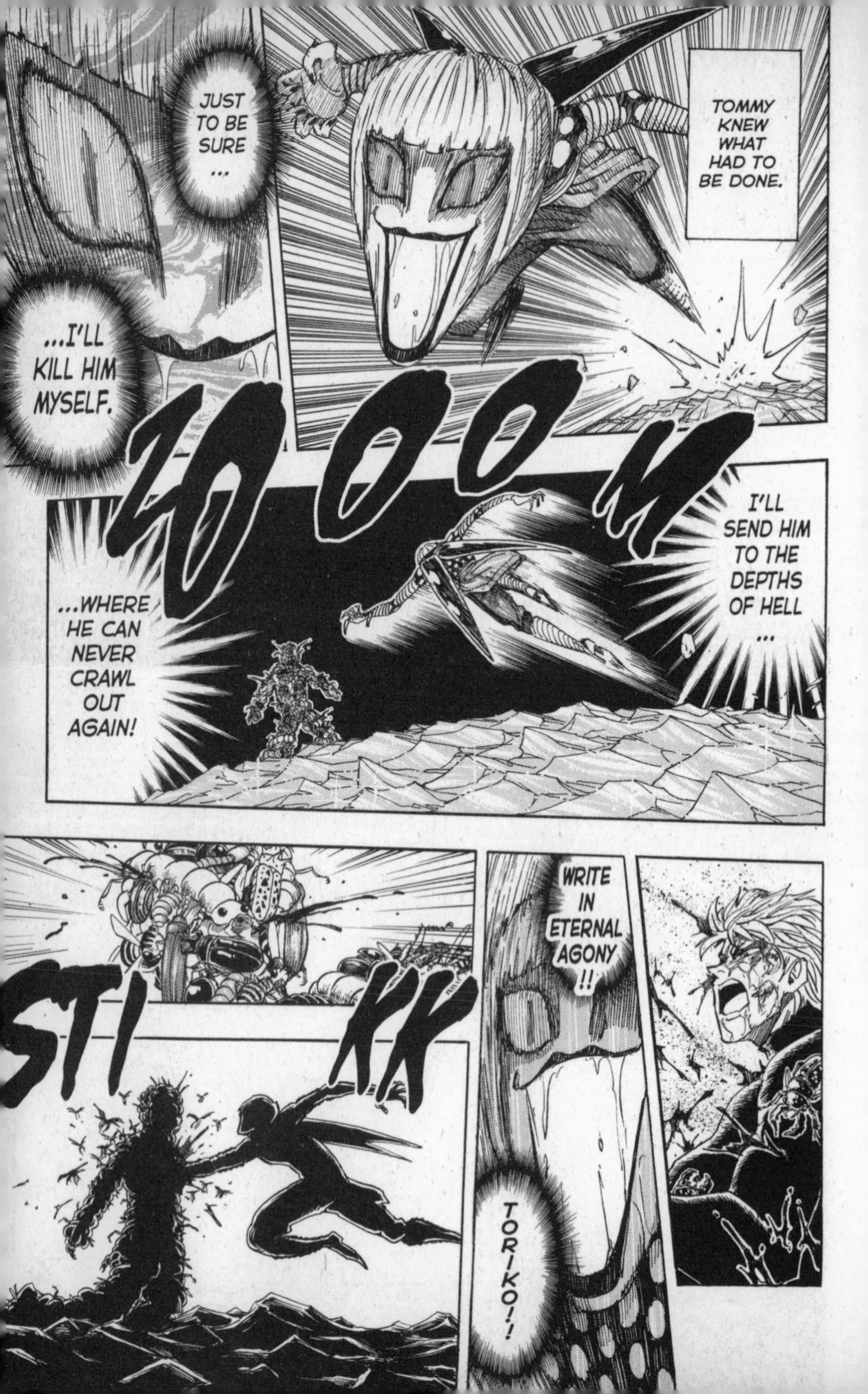
TOMMY KNEW WHAT HAD TO BE DONE.
JUST TO BE SURE...
...I'LL KILL HIM MYSELF.
ZOOOM
I'LL SEND HIM TO THE DEPTHS OF HELL...
...WHERE HE CAN NEVER CRAWL OUT AGAIN!
WRITE IN ETERNAL AGONY!!
TORIKO!!
STIKK

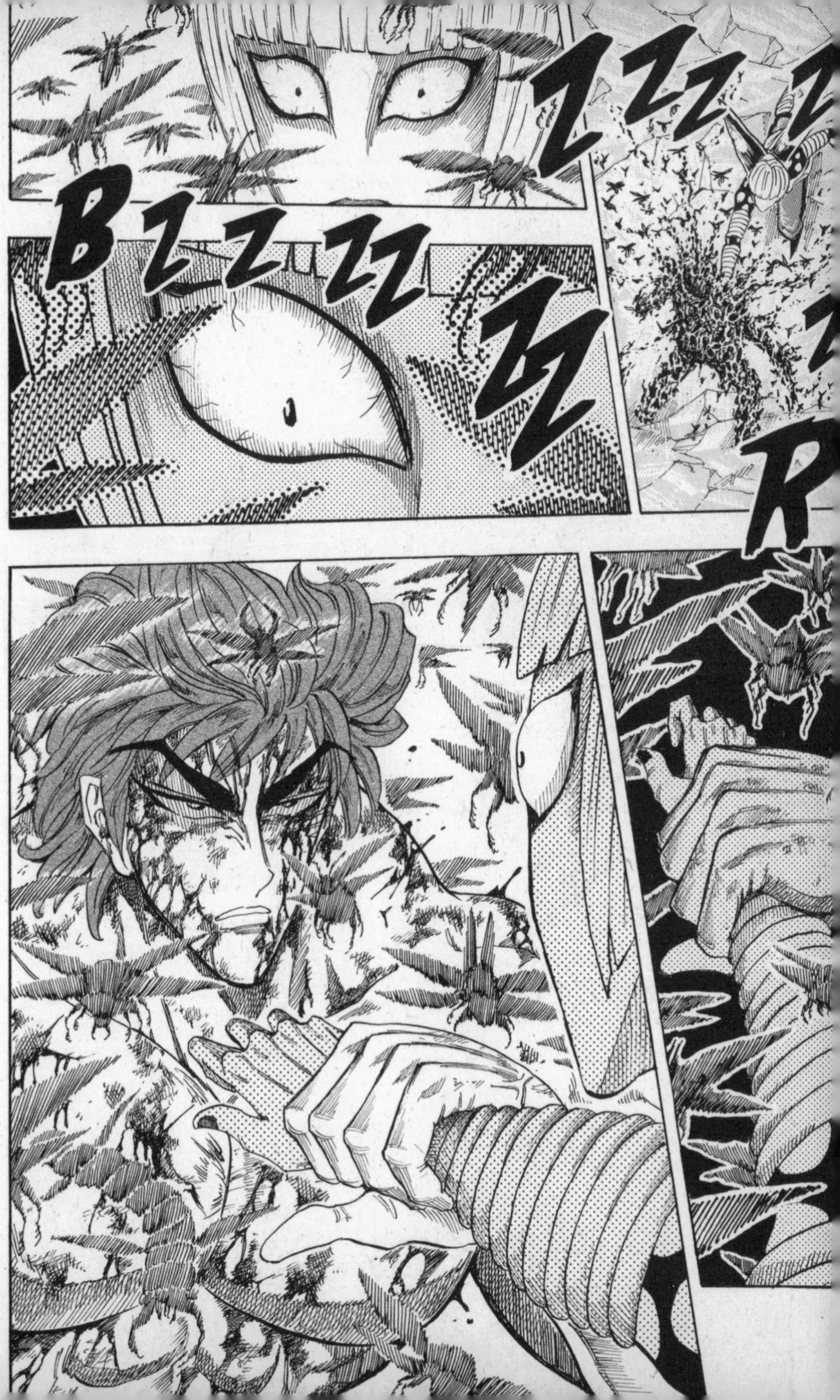
BZZZZZZ
ZZZZZ
R

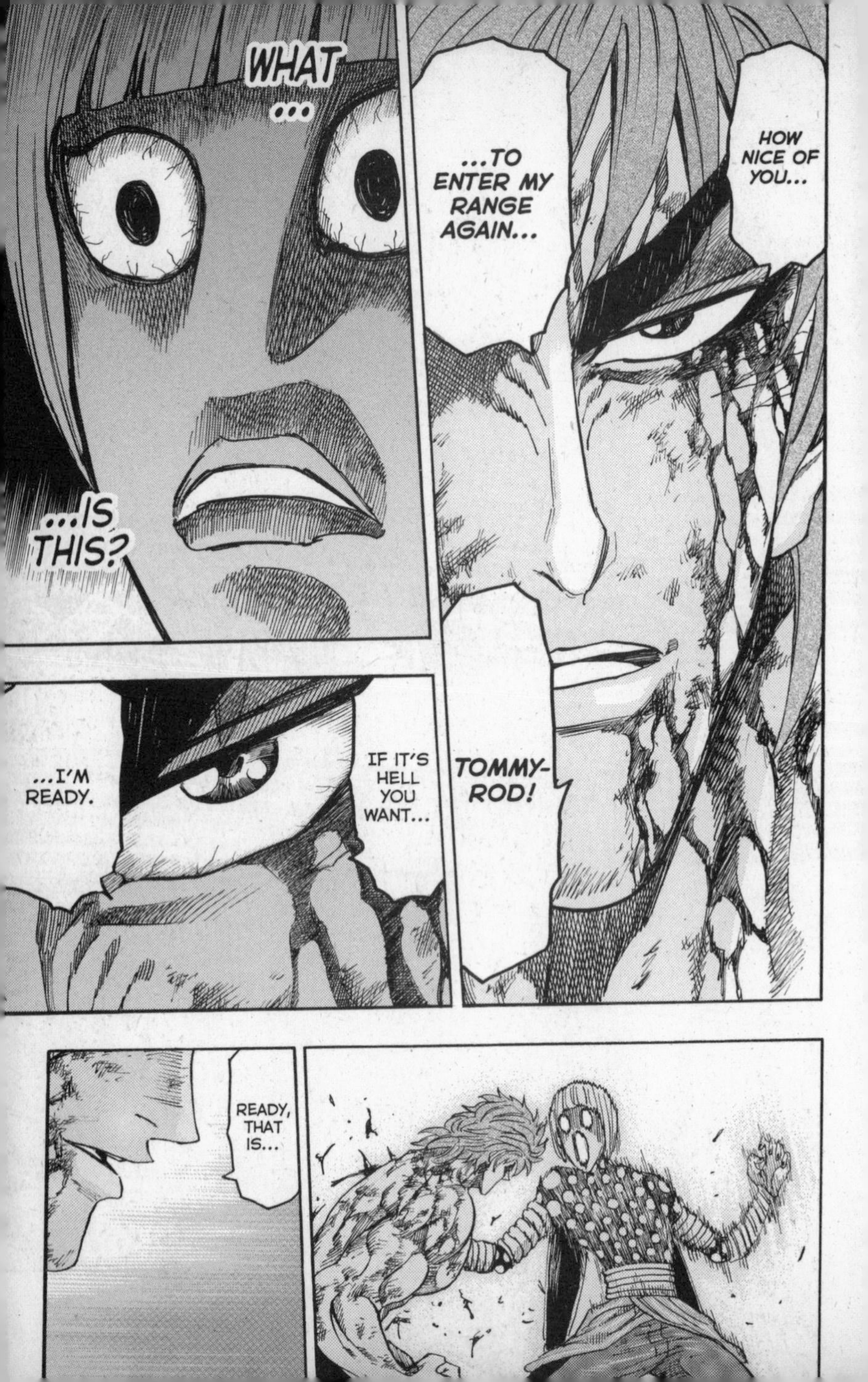
HOW NICE OF YOU...
...TO ENTER MY RANGE AGAIN...
TOMMY-ROD!
WHAT ...
...IS THIS?
IF IT'S HELL YOU WANT...
...I'M READY.
READY, THAT IS...

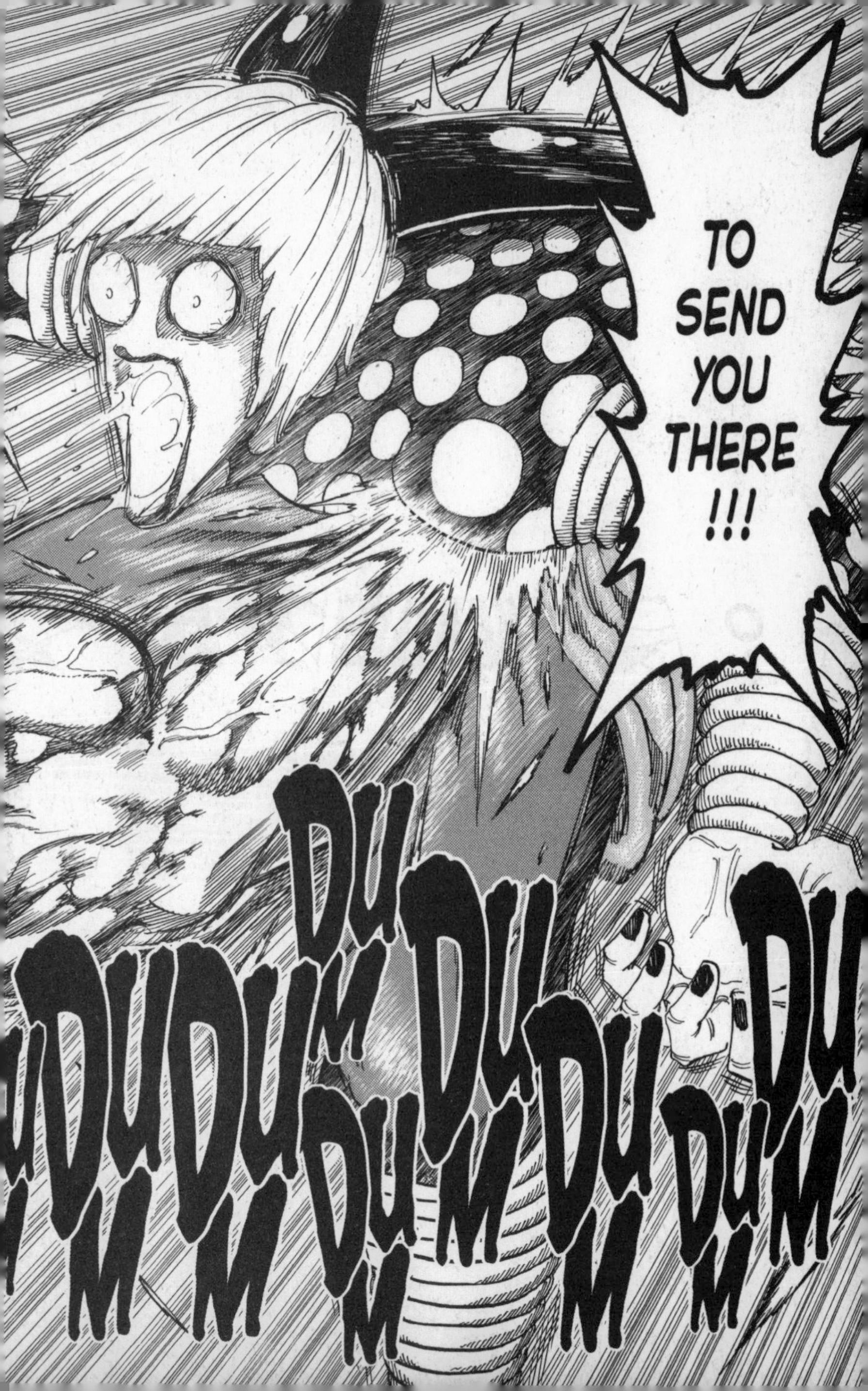
TO SEND YOU THERE !!!
DUDUM DUM DUM DUM DUM DUM DUM DUM DUM

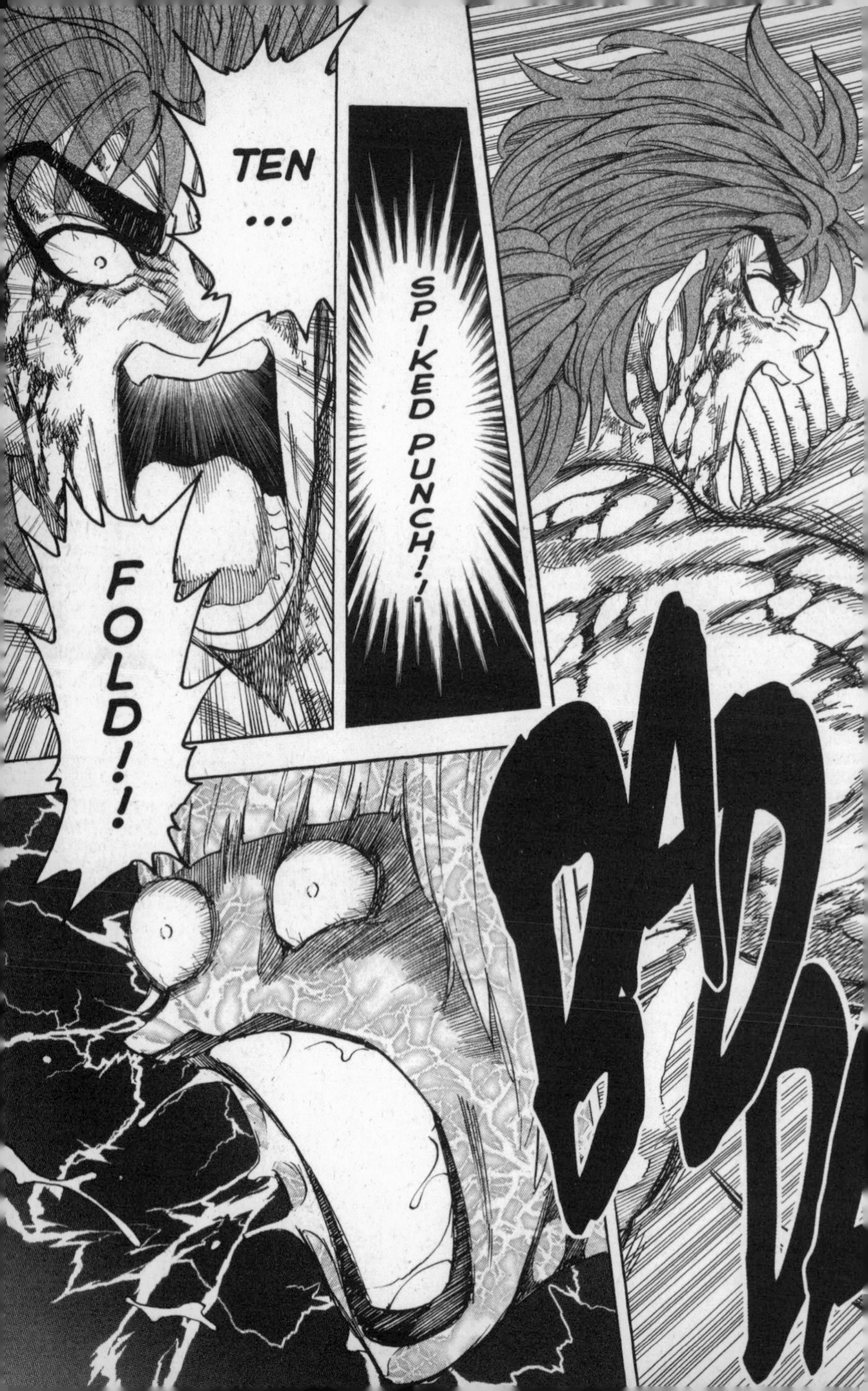
TEN... FOLD!!!
SPIKED PUNCH!!

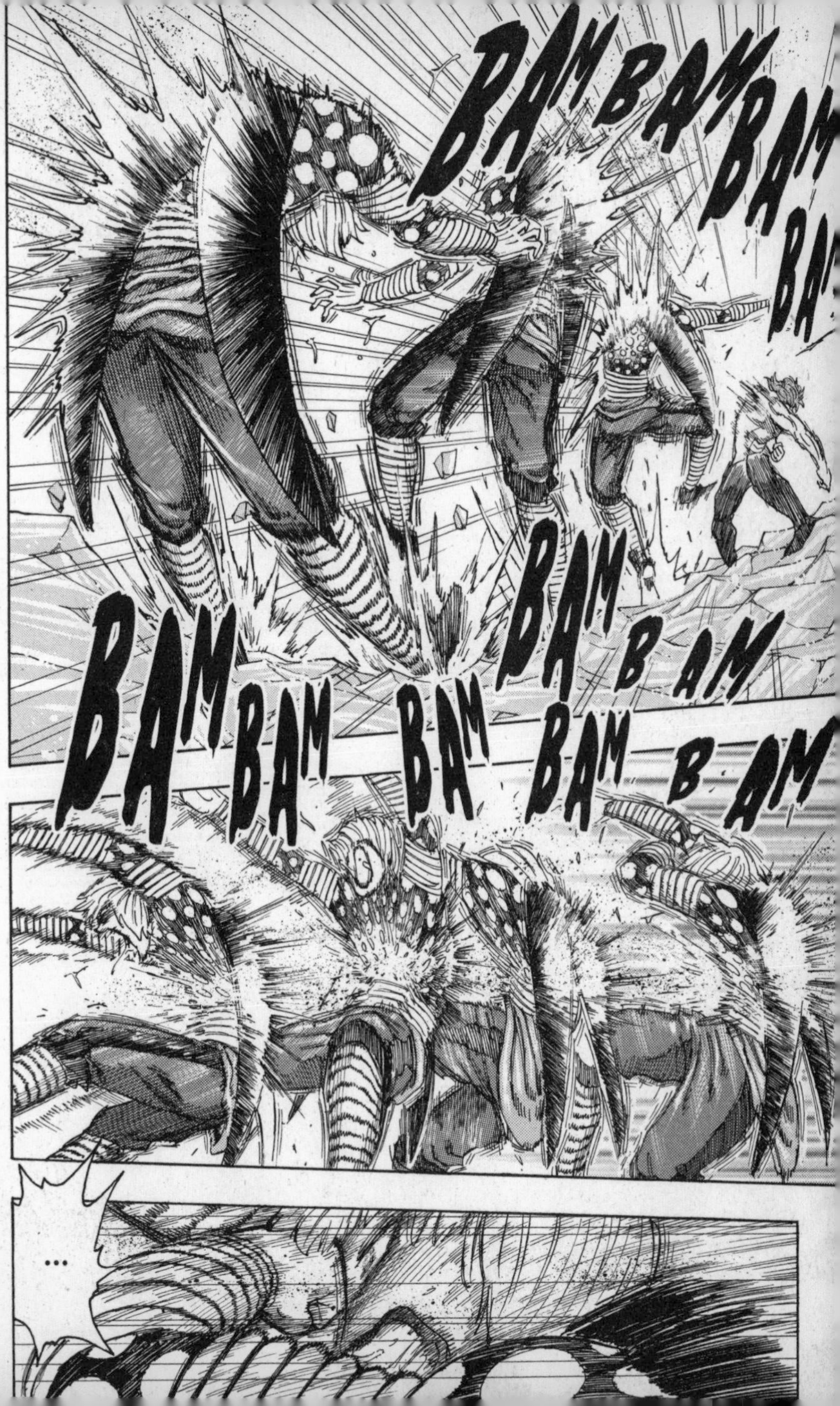
BAM BAM BAM BAM BAM
BAM BAM BAM BAM
BAM BAM BAM BAM BAM BAM
...

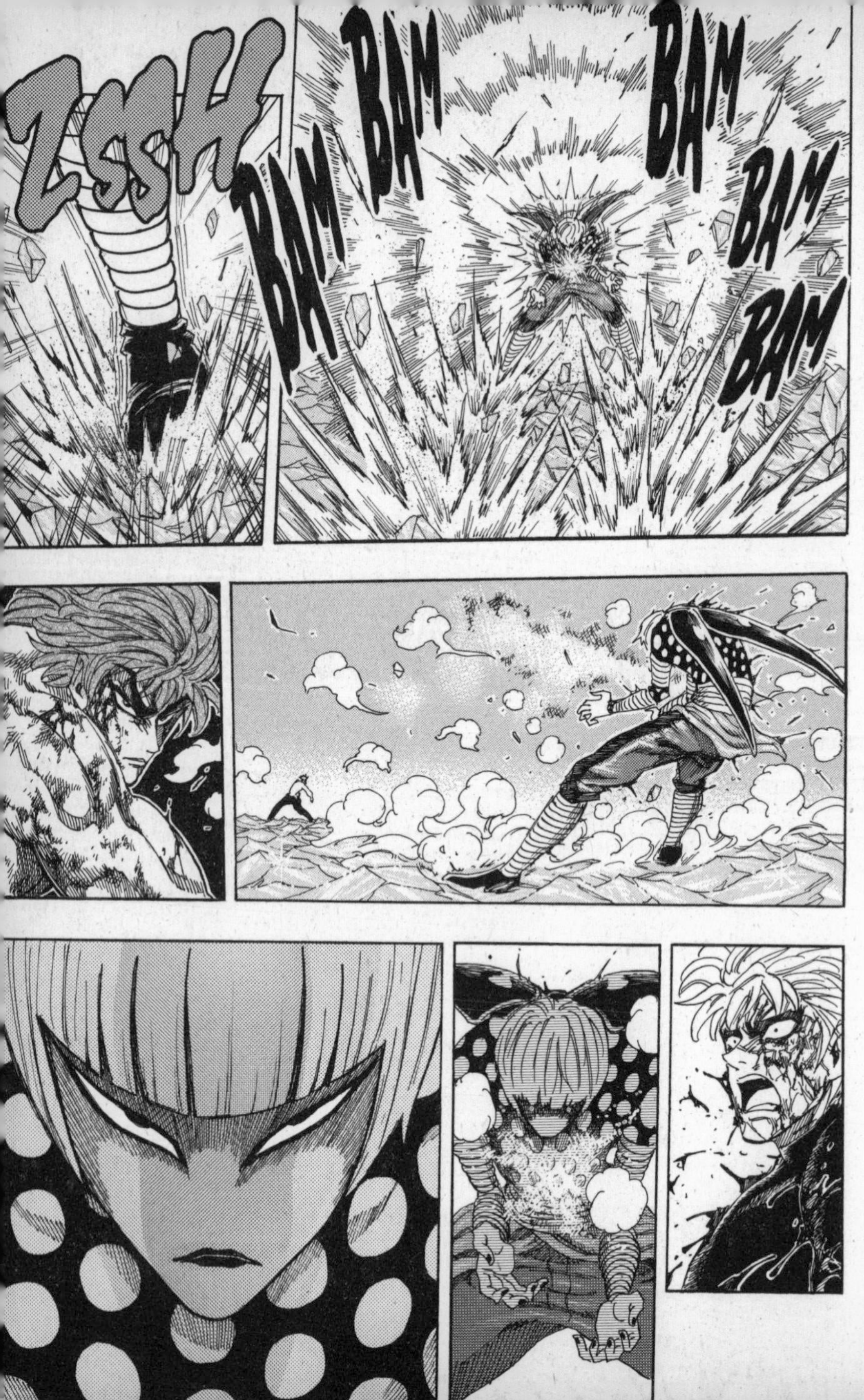
BAM
BAM
BAM
BAM
BAM
BAM
ZSSH

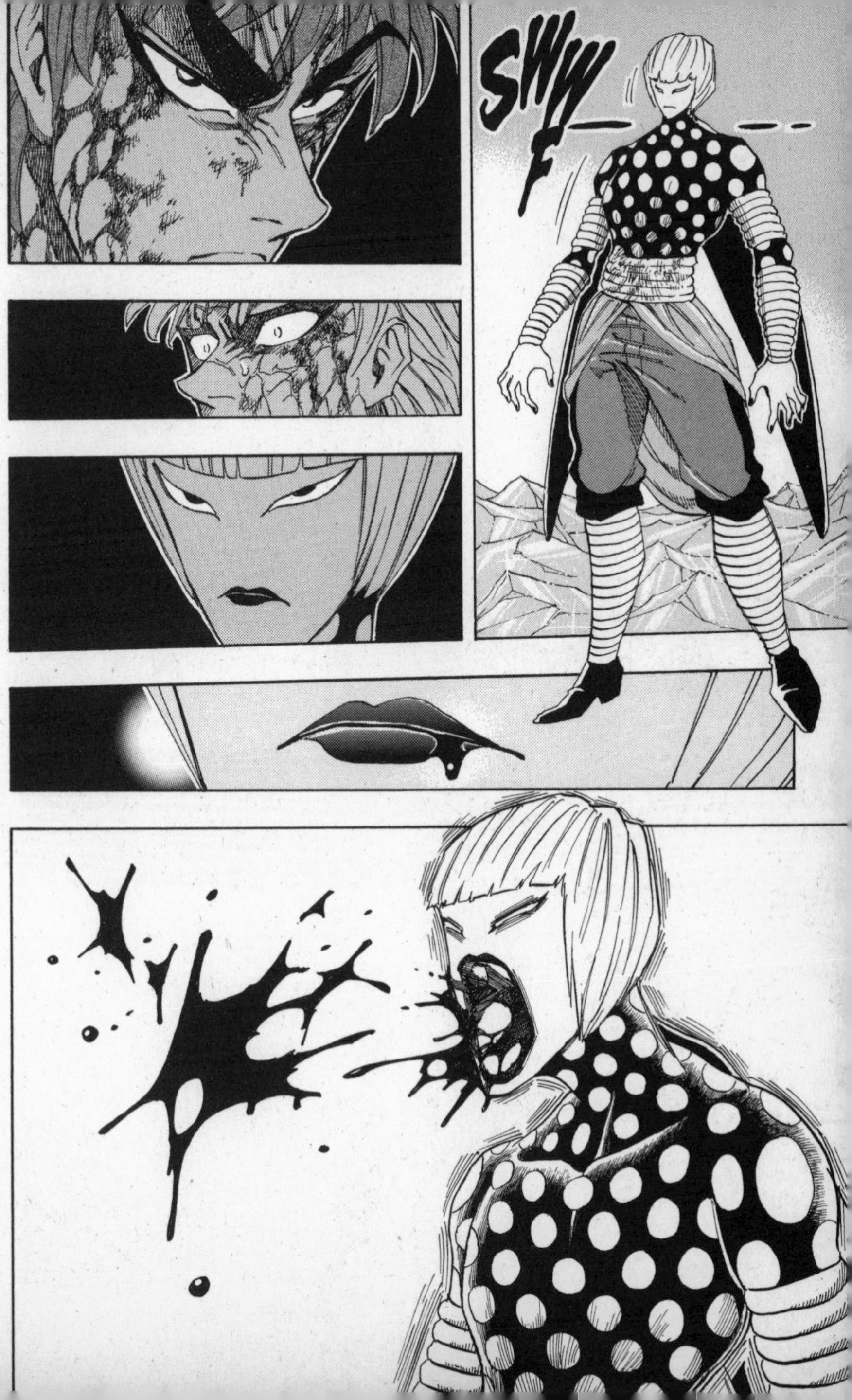
SWWF

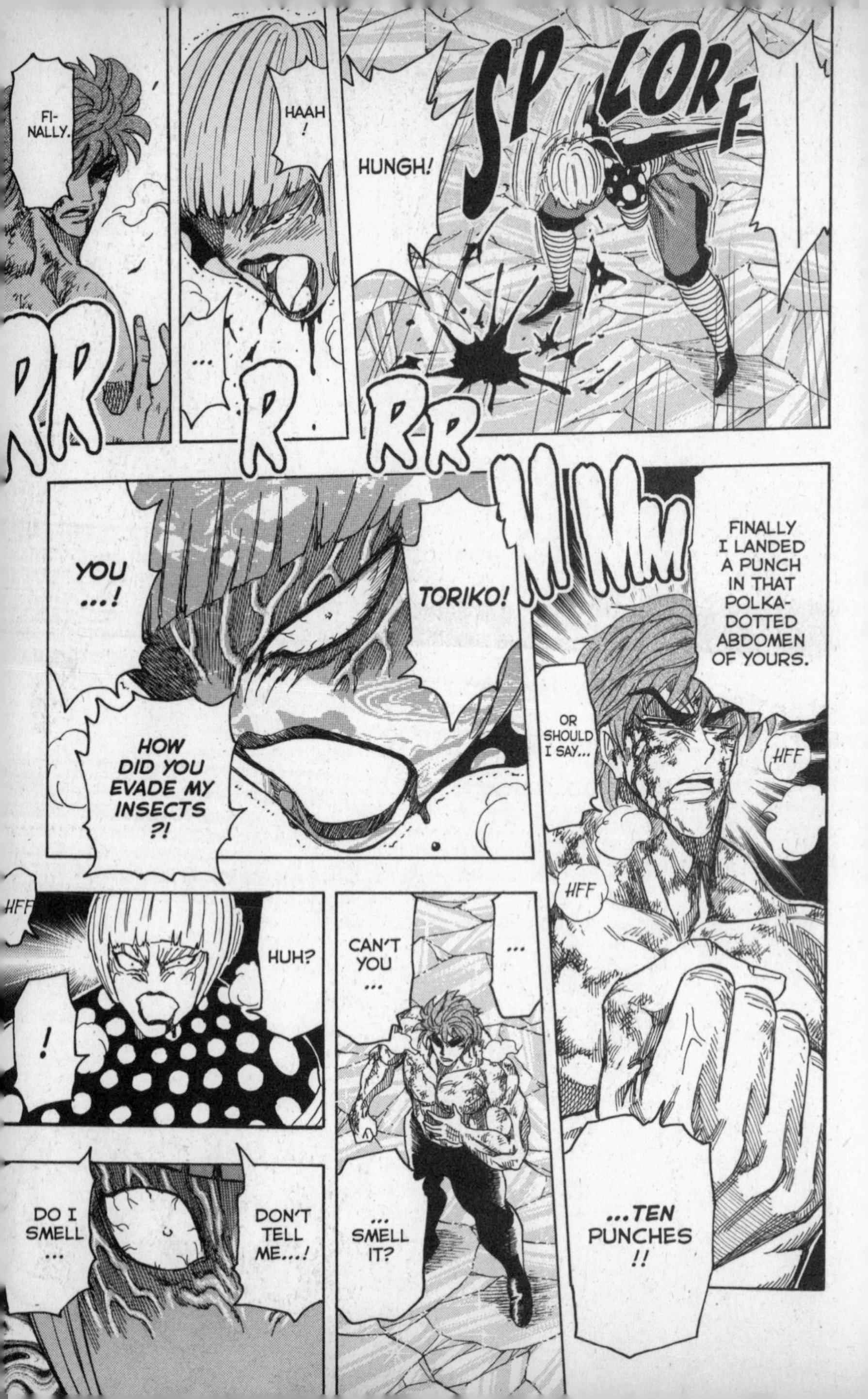
SPLORF
HUNGH!
HAAH!
...
FI-NALLY.
RR R RR
MMM
FINALLY I LANDED A PUNCH IN THAT POLKA-DOTTED ABDOMEN OF YOURS.
OR SHOULD I SAY...
HFF
HFF
...TEN PUNCHES!!
YOU...!
TORIKO!
HOW DID YOU EVADE MY INSECTS?!
...
CAN'T YOU...
...SMELL IT?
HUH?
HFF
!
DON'T TELL ME...!
DO I SMELL...

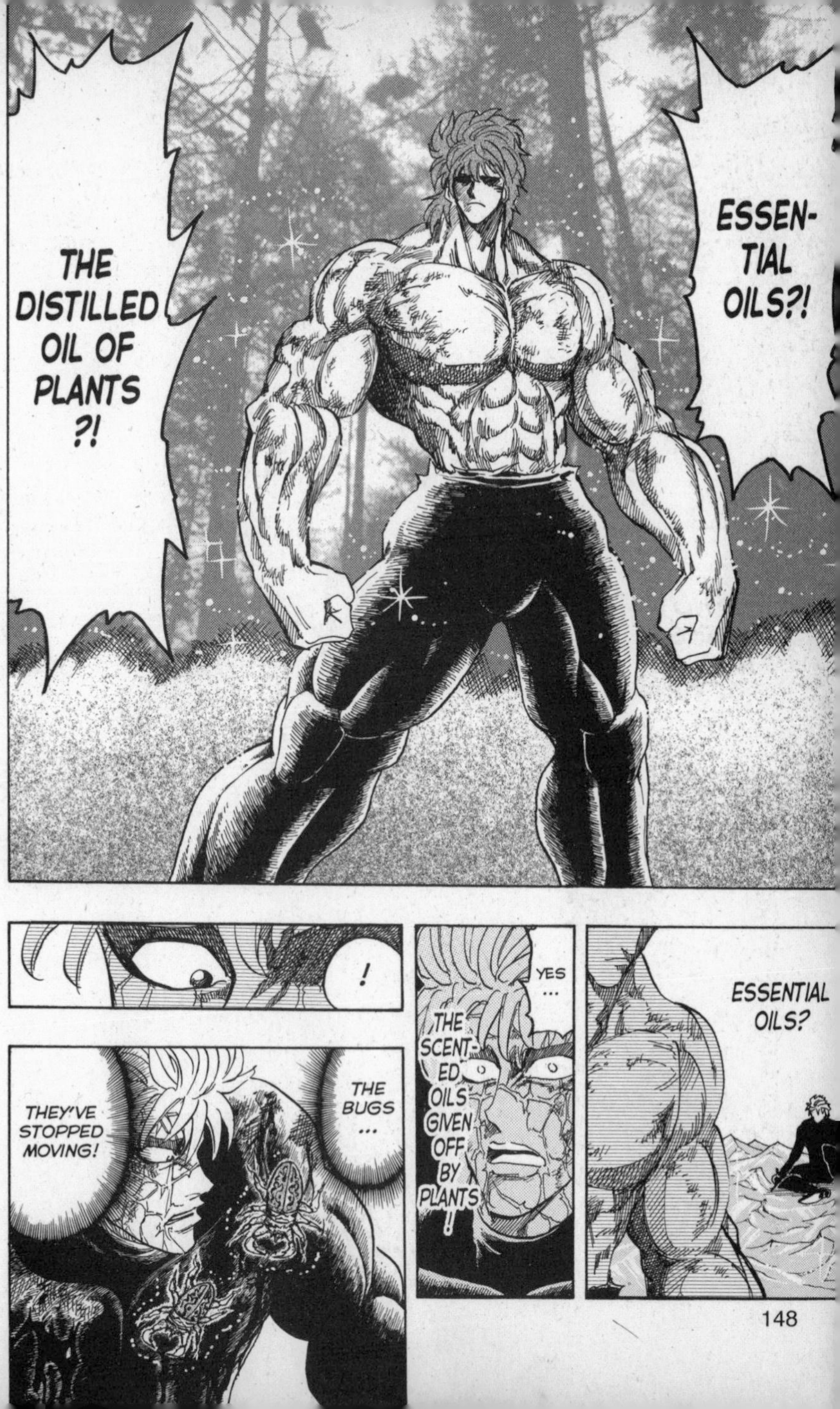
ESSEN-TIAL OILS?!
THE DISTILLED OIL OF PLANTS ?!
ESSENTIAL OILS?
YES ...
THE SCENT-ED OILS GIVEN OFF BY PLANTS !
!
THE BUGS ...
THEY'VE STOPPED MOVING!

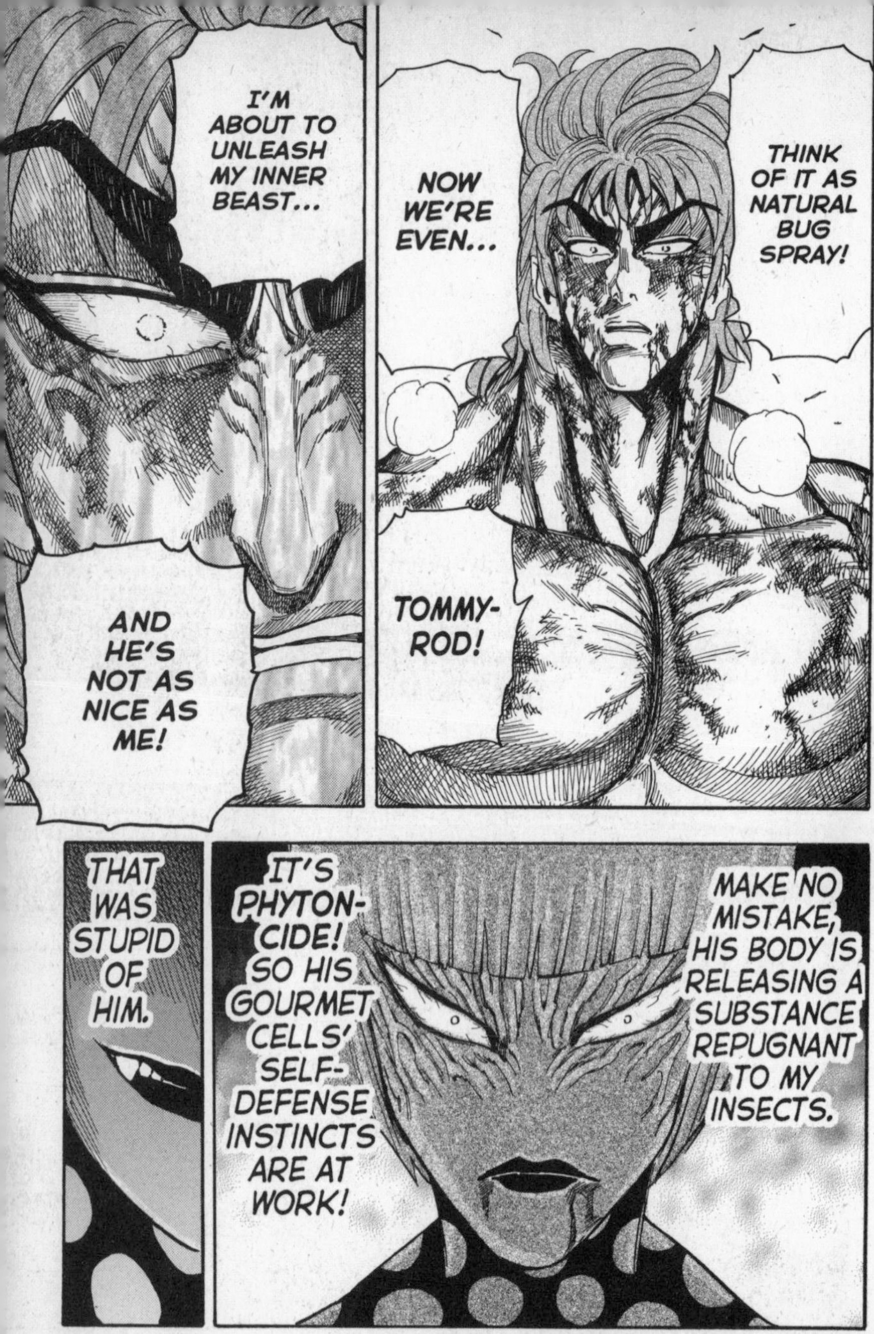
THINK OF IT AS NATURAL BUG SPRAY!
NOW WE'RE EVEN...
TOMMY-ROD!
I'M ABOUT TO UNLEASH MY INNER BEAST...
AND HE'S NOT AS NICE AS ME!
MAKE NO MISTAKE, HIS BODY IS RELEASING A SUBSTANCE REPUGNANT TO MY INSECTS.
IT'S PHYTON-CIDE! SO HIS GOURMET CELLS' SELF-DEFENSE INSTINCTS ARE AT WORK!
THAT WAS STUPID OF HIM.

TORIKO

GOURMET CHECKLIST

Vol. 085

BLISSFUL RICE
(GRAIN)

CAPTURE LEVEL: ---

HABITAT: RICH SOILS AT HIGH ALTITUDES

LENGTH: ---

HEIGHT: ---

WEIGHT: ---

PRICE: 1 KG / 3,700,000 YEN

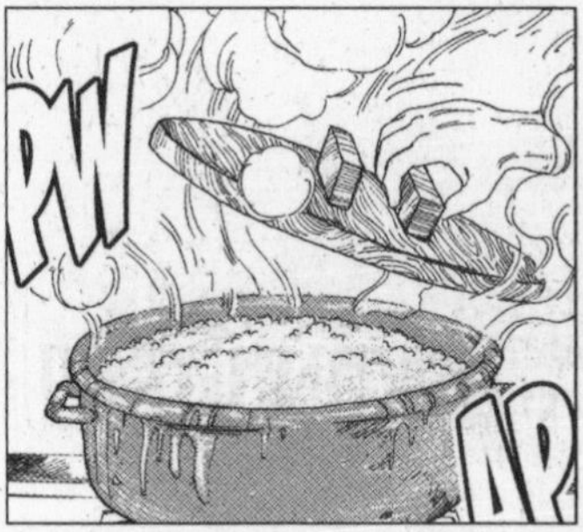
PW
AP

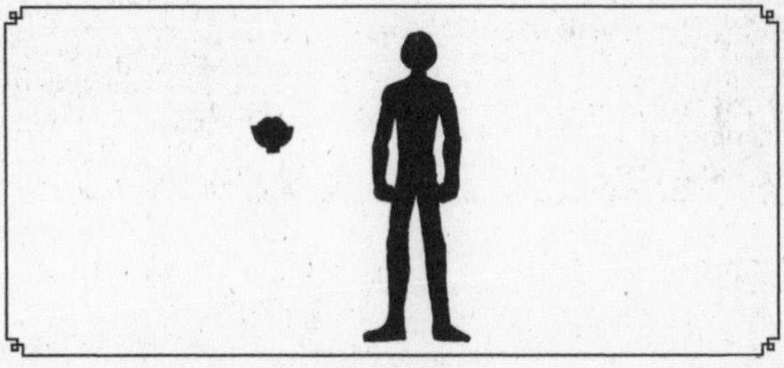

SCALE

A VERY SPECIAL RICE. FOR EACH HECTARE PLANTED, ONLY ONE STALK'S CLUSTER OF RICE GRAINS CAN BE HARVESTED. BLISSFUL RICE GETS ITS NAME FROM ITS HEAVENLY FLAVOR. A SINGLE GRAIN OF BLISSFUL RICE IS WORTH ITS WEIGHT IN GOLD!

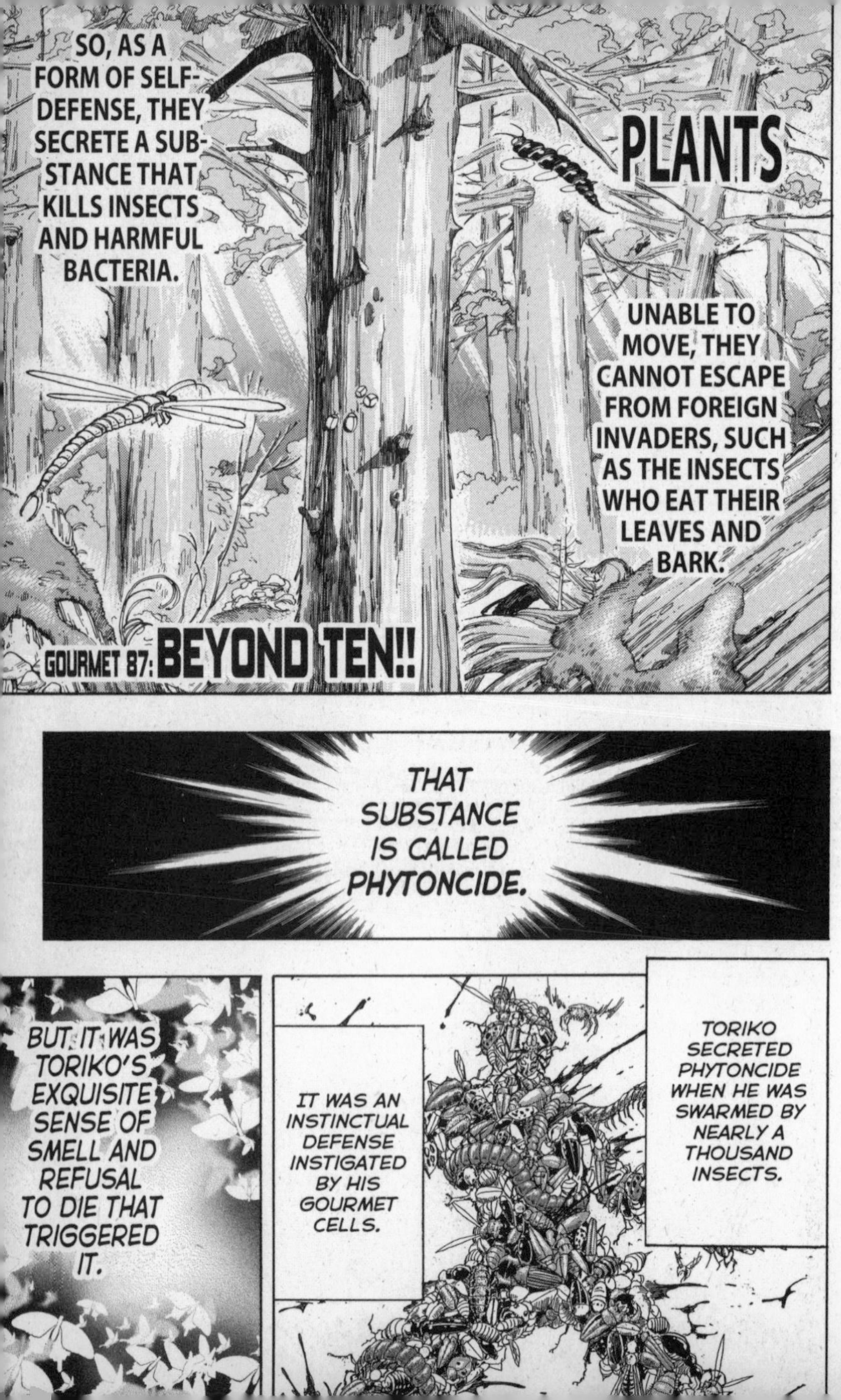
PLANTS
UNABLE TO MOVE, THEY CANNOT ESCAPE FROM FOREIGN INVADERS, SUCH AS THE INSECTS WHO EAT THEIR LEAVES AND BARK.
SO, AS A FORM OF SELF-DEFENSE, THEY SECRETE A SUBSTANCE THAT KILLS INSECTS AND HARMFUL BACTERIA.
GOURMET 87: BEYOND TEN!!
THAT SUBSTANCE IS CALLED PHYTONCIDE.
TORIKO SECRETED PHYTONCIDE WHEN HE WAS SWARMED BY NEARLY A THOUSAND INSECTS.
IT WAS AN INSTINCTUAL DEFENSE INSTIGATED BY HIS GOURMET CELLS.
BUT IT WAS TORIKO'S EXQUISITE SENSE OF SMELL AND REFUSAL TO DIE THAT TRIGGERED IT.

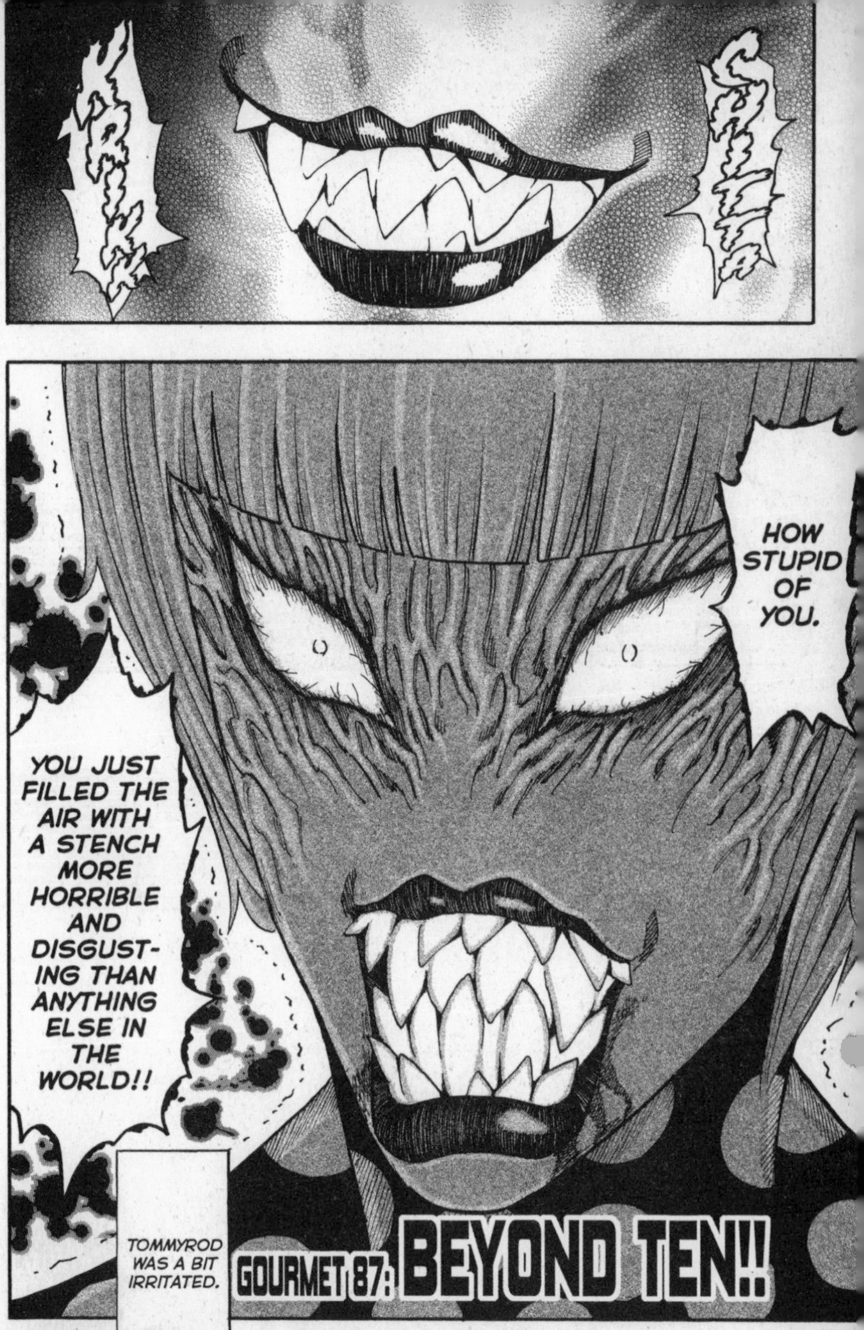
HOW STUPID OF YOU.
YOU JUST FILLED THE AIR WITH A STENCH MORE HORRIBLE AND DISGUSTING THAN ANYTHING ELSE IN THE WORLD!!
TOMMYROD WAS A BIT IRRITATED.
GOURMET 87: BEYOND TEN!!

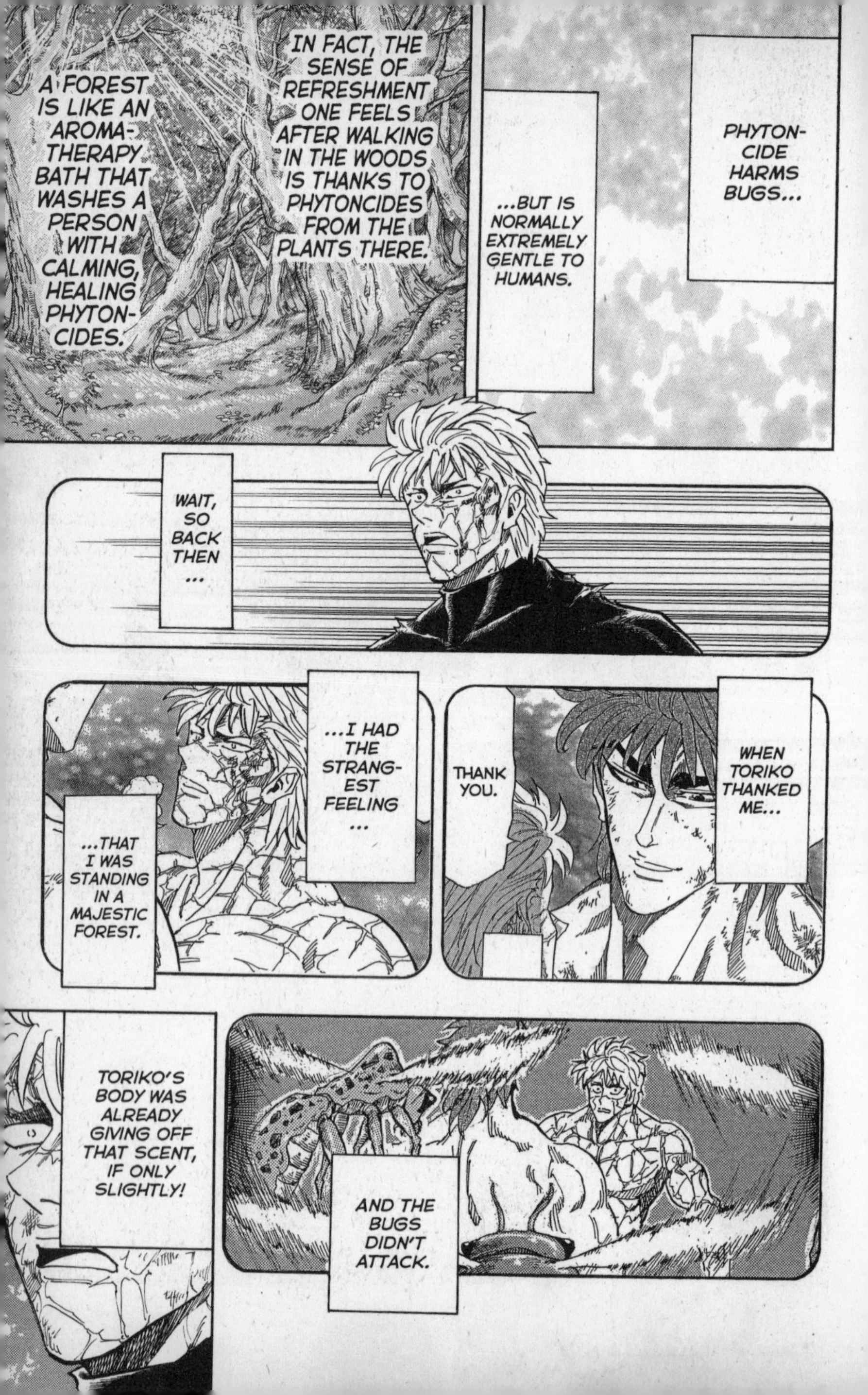
PHYTON-CIDE HARMS BUGS...
...BUT IS NORMALLY EXTREMELY GENTLE TO HUMANS.
A FOREST IS LIKE AN AROMA-THERAPY BATH THAT WASHES A PERSON WITH CALMING, HEALING PHYTON-CIDES.
IN FACT, THE SENSE OF REFRESHMENT ONE FEELS AFTER WALKING IN THE WOODS IS THANKS TO PHYTONCIDES FROM THE PLANTS THERE.
WAIT, SO BACK THEN ...
WHEN TORIKO THANKED ME...
THANK YOU.
...I HAD THE STRANG-EST FEELING ...
...THAT I WAS STANDING IN A MAJESTIC FOREST.
TORIKO'S BODY WAS ALREADY GIVING OFF THAT SCENT, IF ONLY SLIGHTLY!
AND THE BUGS DIDN'T ATTACK.

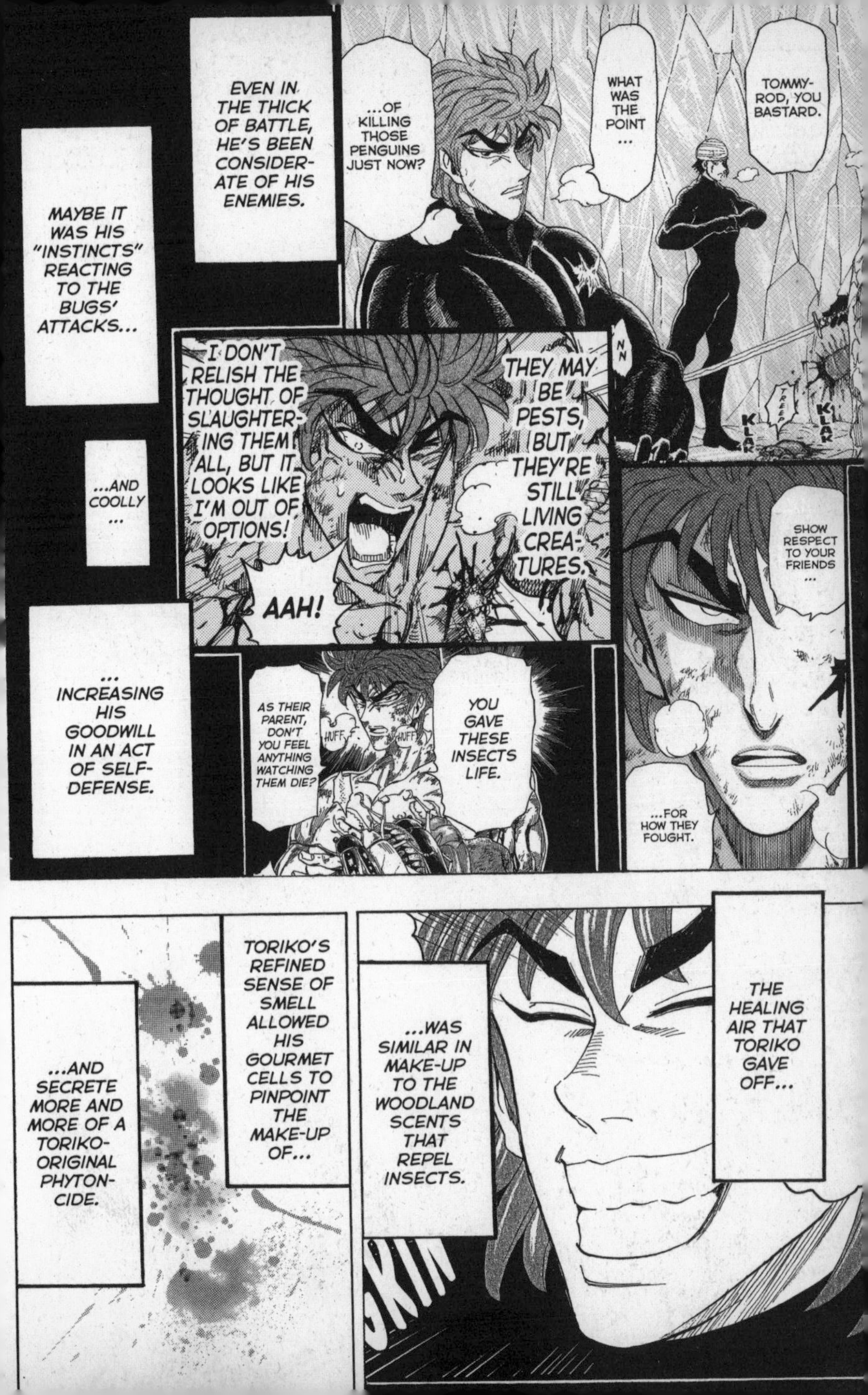
TOMMY-ROD, YOU BASTARD.
WHAT WAS THE POINT...
...OF KILLING THOSE PENGUINS JUST NOW?
EVEN IN THE THICK OF BATTLE, HE'S BEEN CONSIDERATE OF HIS ENEMIES.
MAYBE IT WAS HIS "INSTINCTS" REACTING TO THE BUGS' ATTACKS...
NN
KLAK
TREEP
KLAK
THEY MAY BE PESTS, BUT THEY'RE STILL LIVING CREATURES.
I DON'T RELISH THE THOUGHT OF SLAUGHTERING THEM ALL, BUT IT LOOKS LIKE I'M OUT OF OPTIONS!
AAH!
...AND COOLLY...
SHOW RESPECT TO YOUR FRIENDS...
...FOR HOW THEY FOUGHT.
YOU GAVE THESE INSECTS LIFE.
AS THEIR PARENT, DON'T YOU FEEL ANYTHING WATCHING THEM DIE?
HUFF
HUFF
...INCREASING HIS GOODWILL IN AN ACT OF SELF-DEFENSE.
THE HEALING AIR THAT TORIKO GAVE OFF...
...WAS SIMILAR IN MAKE-UP TO THE WOODLAND SCENTS THAT REPEL INSECTS.
TORIKO'S REFINED SENSE OF SMELL ALLOWED HIS GOURMET CELLS TO PINPOINT THE MAKE-UP OF...
...AND SECRETE MORE AND MORE OF A TORIKO-ORIGINAL PHYTONCIDE.

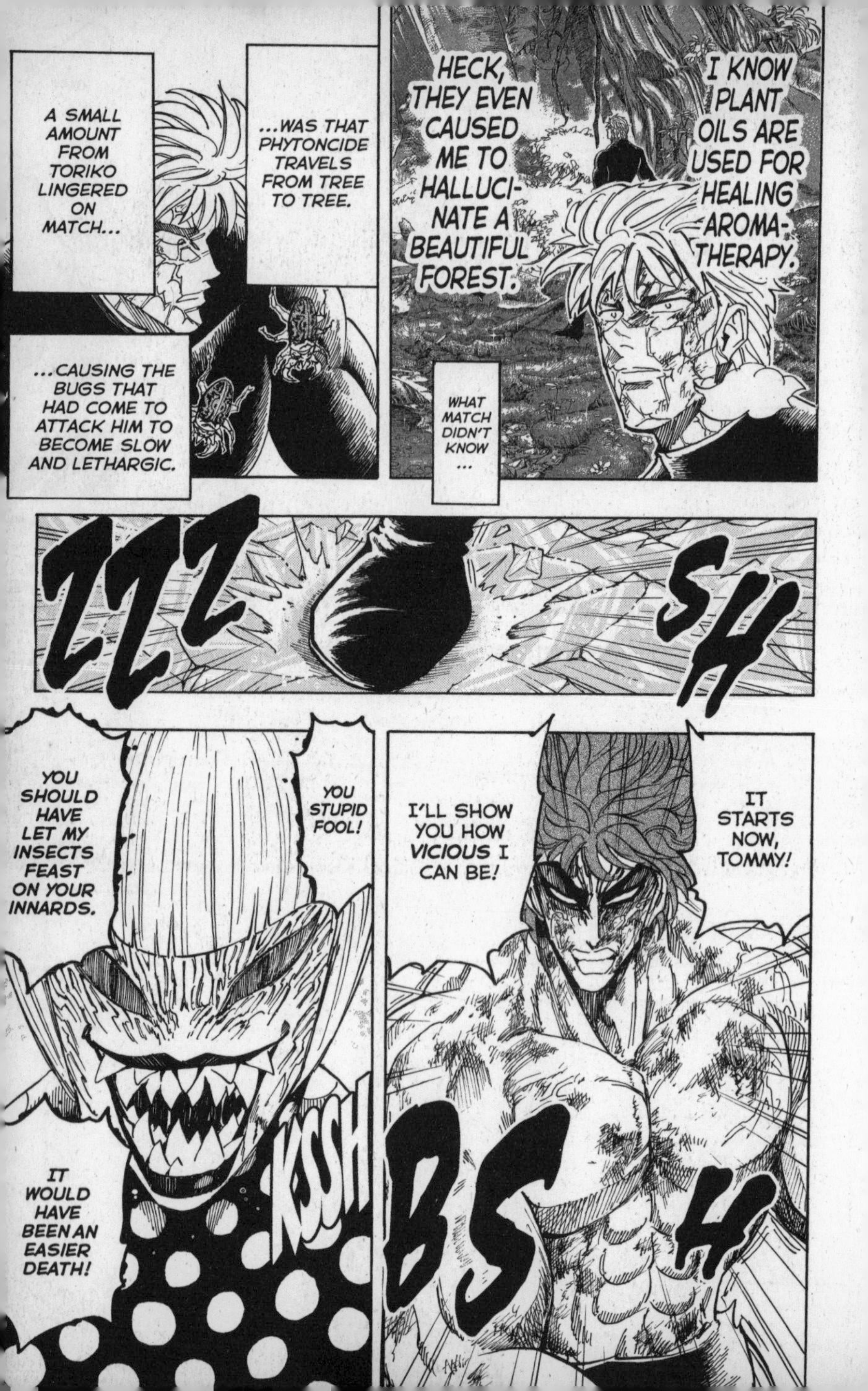
I KNOW PLANT OILS ARE USED FOR HEALING AROMA-THERAPY.
HECK, THEY EVEN CAUSED ME TO HALLUCI-NATE A BEAUTIFUL FOREST.
WHAT MATCH DIDN'T KNOW ...
...WAS THAT PHYTONCIDE TRAVELS FROM TREE TO TREE.
A SMALL AMOUNT FROM TORIKO LINGERED ON MATCH...
...CAUSING THE BUGS THAT HAD COME TO ATTACK HIM TO BECOME SLOW AND LETHARGIC.
ZZZ
SH
IT STARTS NOW, TOMMY!
I'LL SHOW YOU HOW VICIOUS I CAN BE!
BSH
YOU STUPID FOOL!
YOU SHOULD HAVE LET MY INSECTS FEAST ON YOUR INNARDS.
KSSH
IT WOULD HAVE BEEN AN EASIER DEATH!

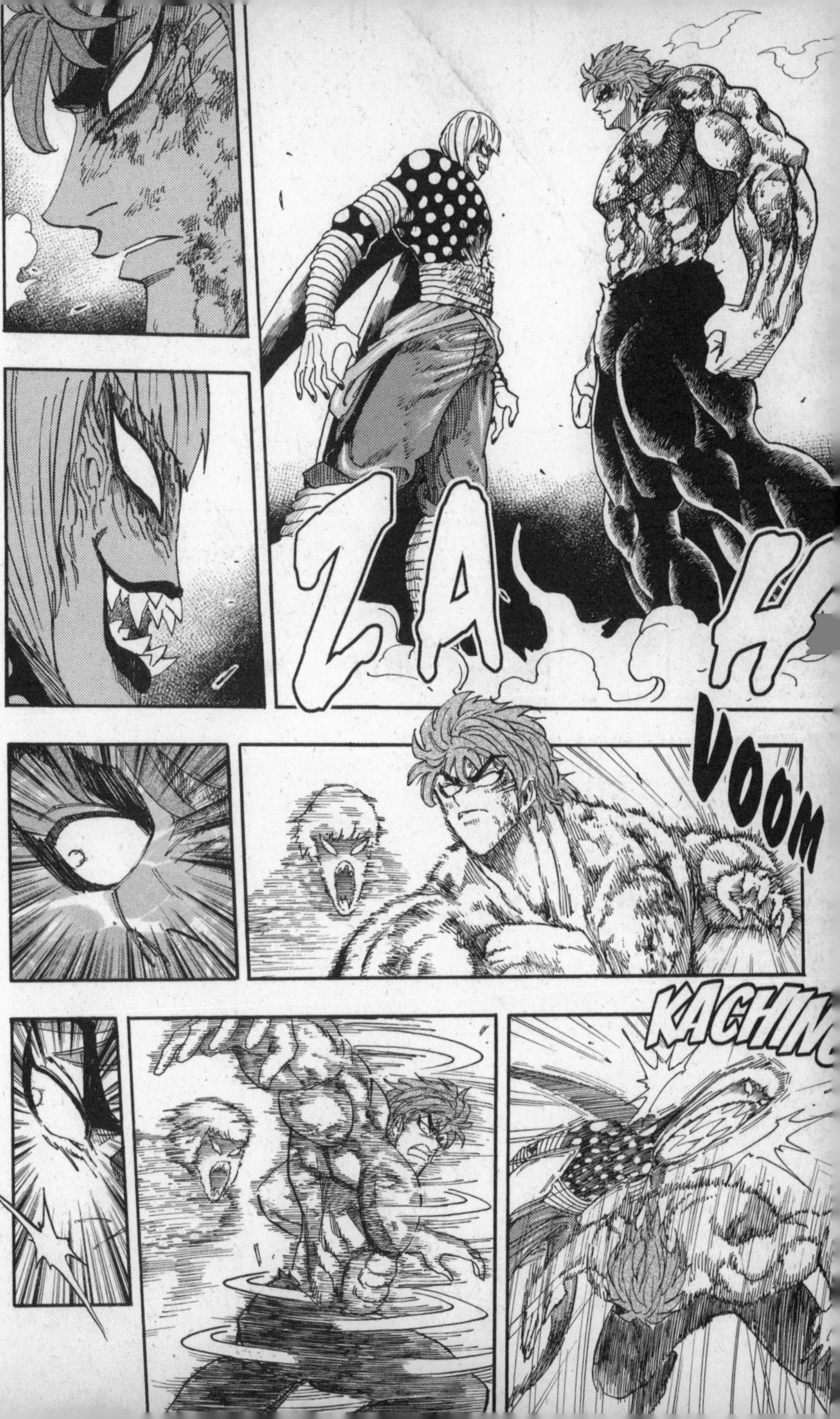
ZA
VOOM
KACHIN

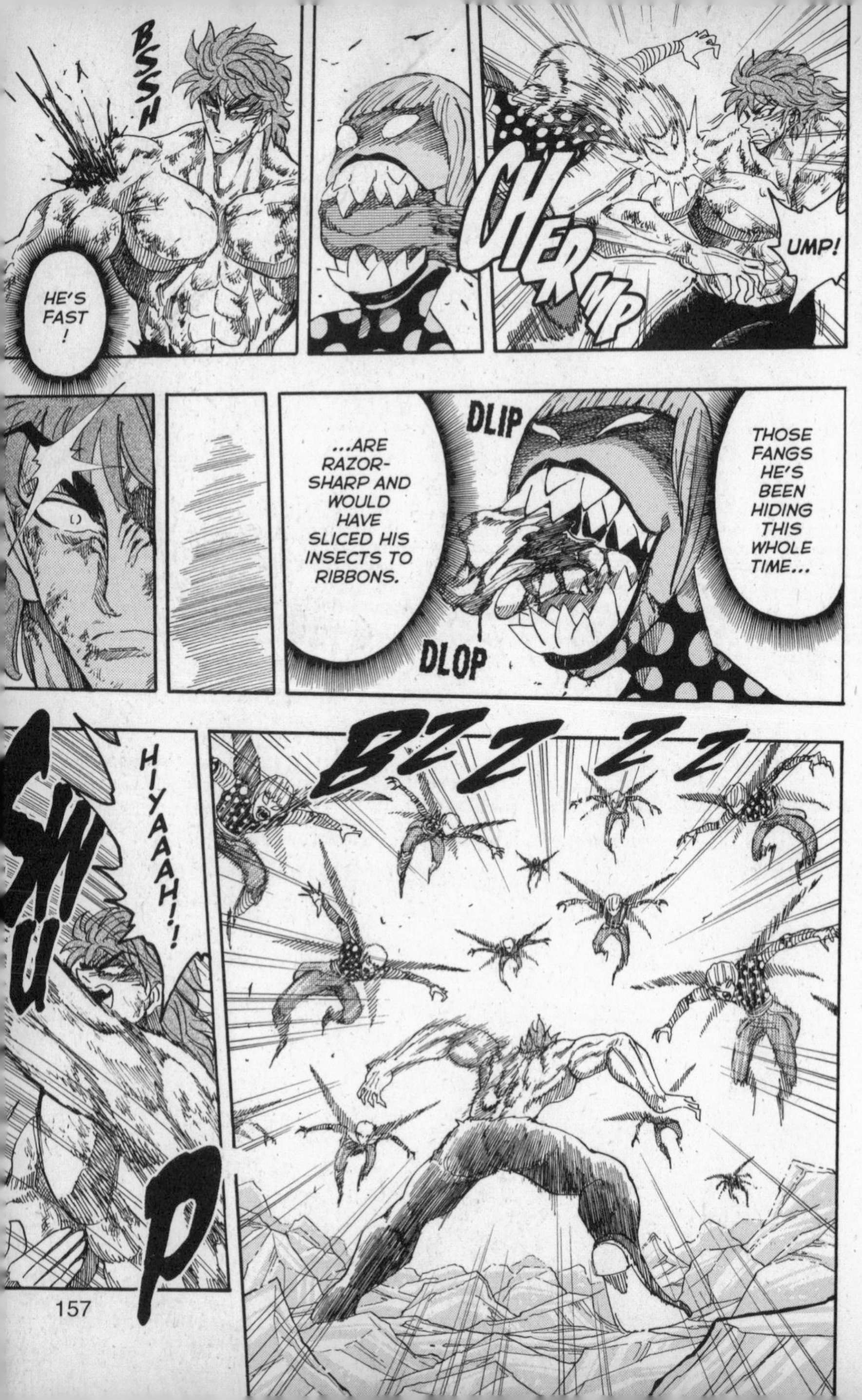
CHERMP
UMP!
BSSH
HE'S FAST!
THOSE FANGS HE'S BEEN HIDING THIS WHOLE TIME...
...ARE RAZOR-SHARP AND WOULD HAVE SLICED HIS INSECTS TO RIBBONS.
DLIP
DLOP
BZZZ ZZ
HIYAAAH!!
WUP

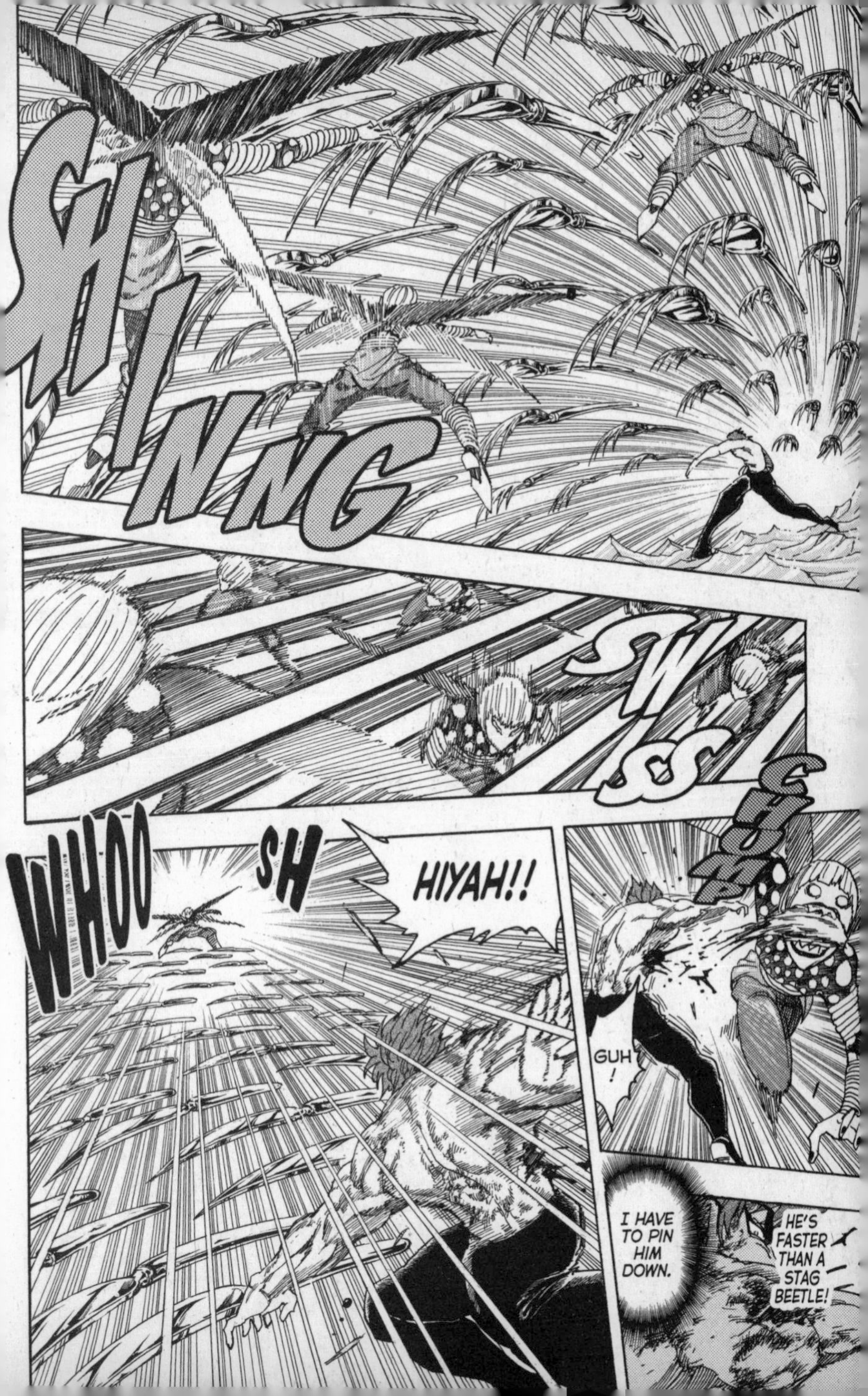
SHIINNG
SWSS
CHOMP
GUH!
HE'S FASTER THAN A STAG BEETLE!
I HAVE TO PIN HIM DOWN.
WHOOSH
HIYAH!!

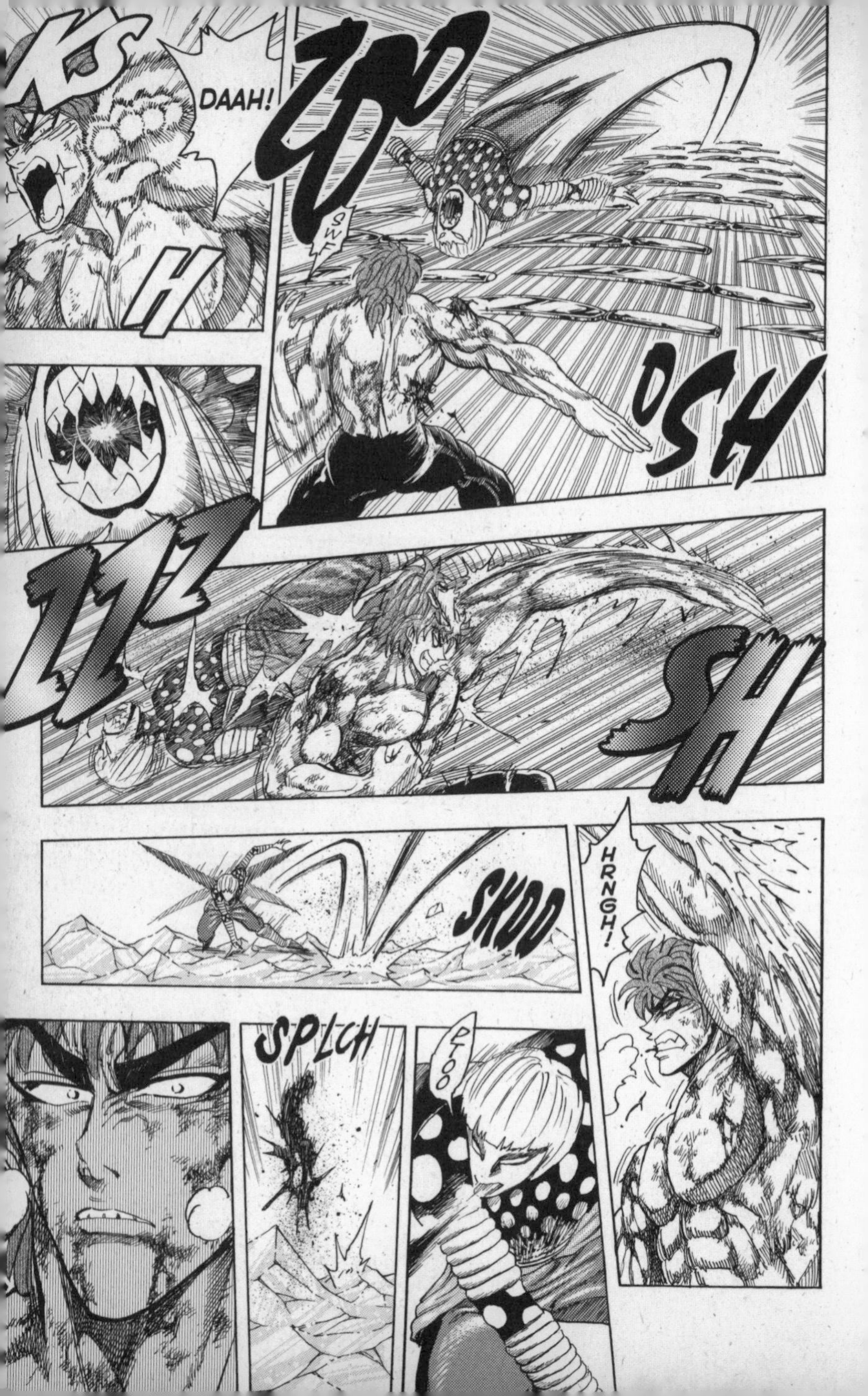
ZOOO
SWF
OSH
KS
DAAH!
H
SH
ZZZ
HRNGH!
SKOO
PTOO
SPLCH

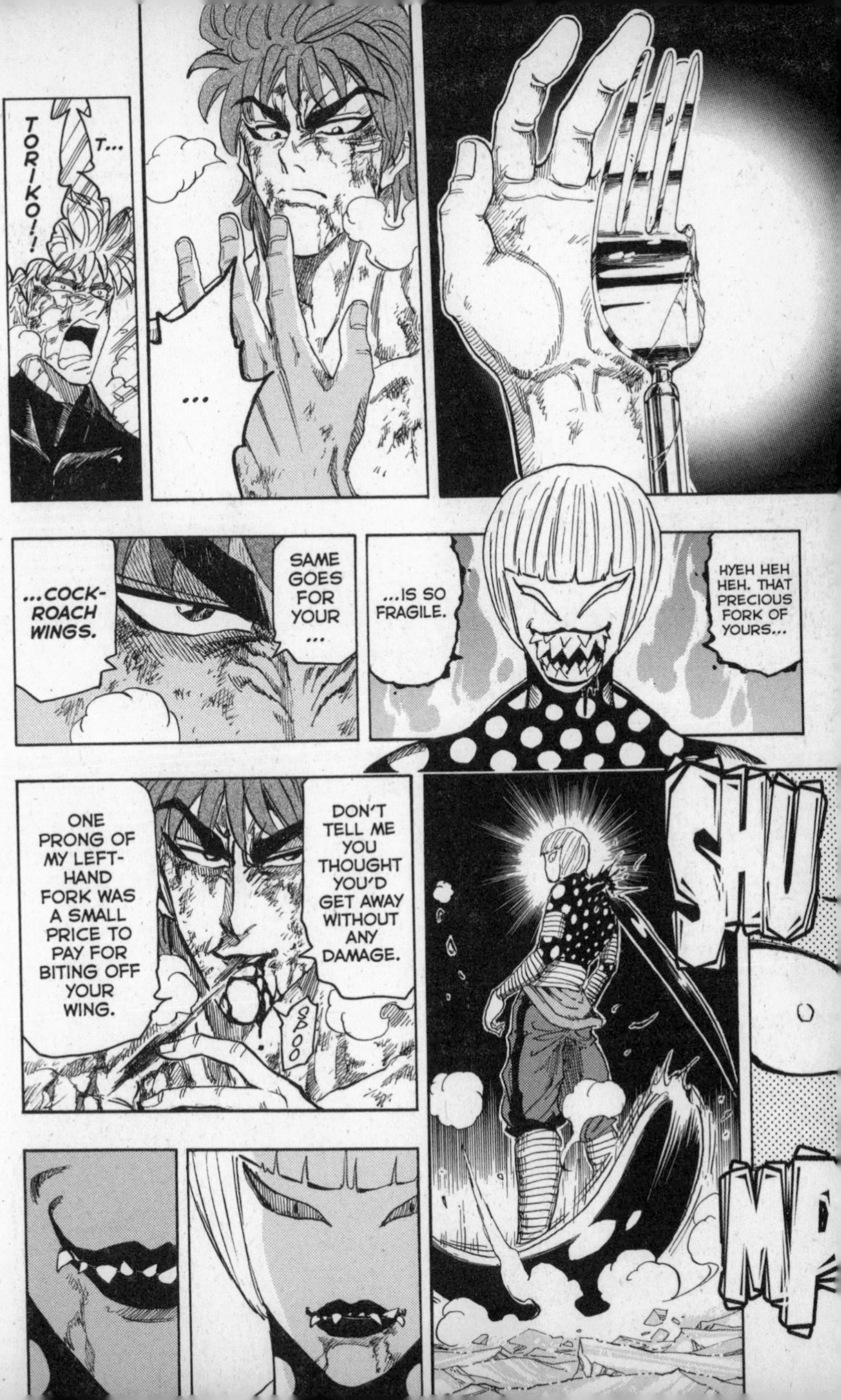
...
T...
TORIKO!!
HYEH HEH HEH. THAT PRECIOUS FORK OF YOURS...
...IS SO FRAGILE.
SAME GOES FOR YOUR ...
...COCK-ROACH WINGS.
SHU
MP
DON'T TELL ME YOU THOUGHT YOU'D GET AWAY WITHOUT ANY DAMAGE.
ONE PRONG OF MY LEFT-HAND FORK WAS A SMALL PRICE TO PAY FOR BITING OFF YOUR WING.
SPOO

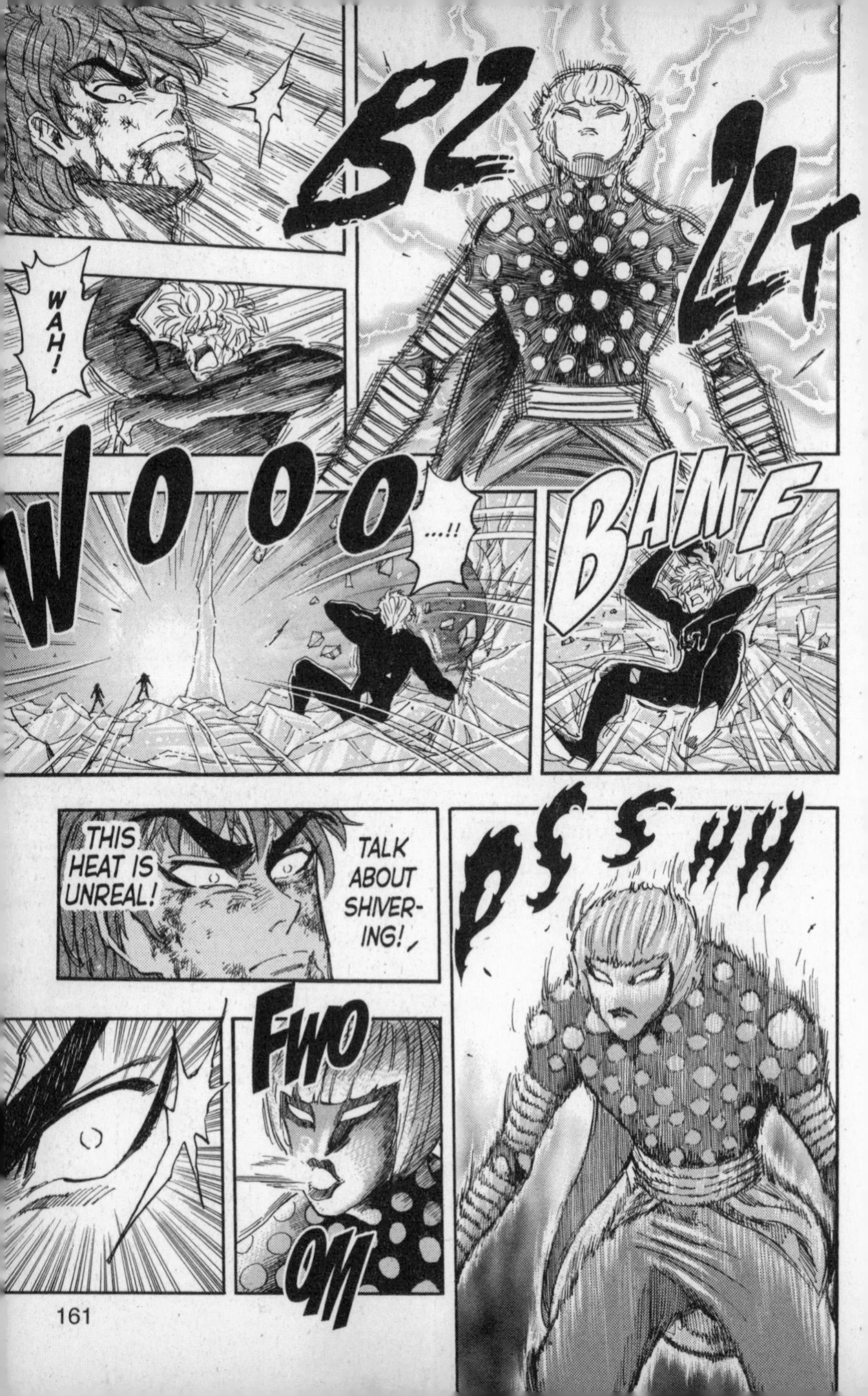
BZZZT
WAH!
BAMF
WOOO
...!!
PSSHH
TALK ABOUT SHIVER-ING!
THIS HEAT IS UNREAL!
FWOOM

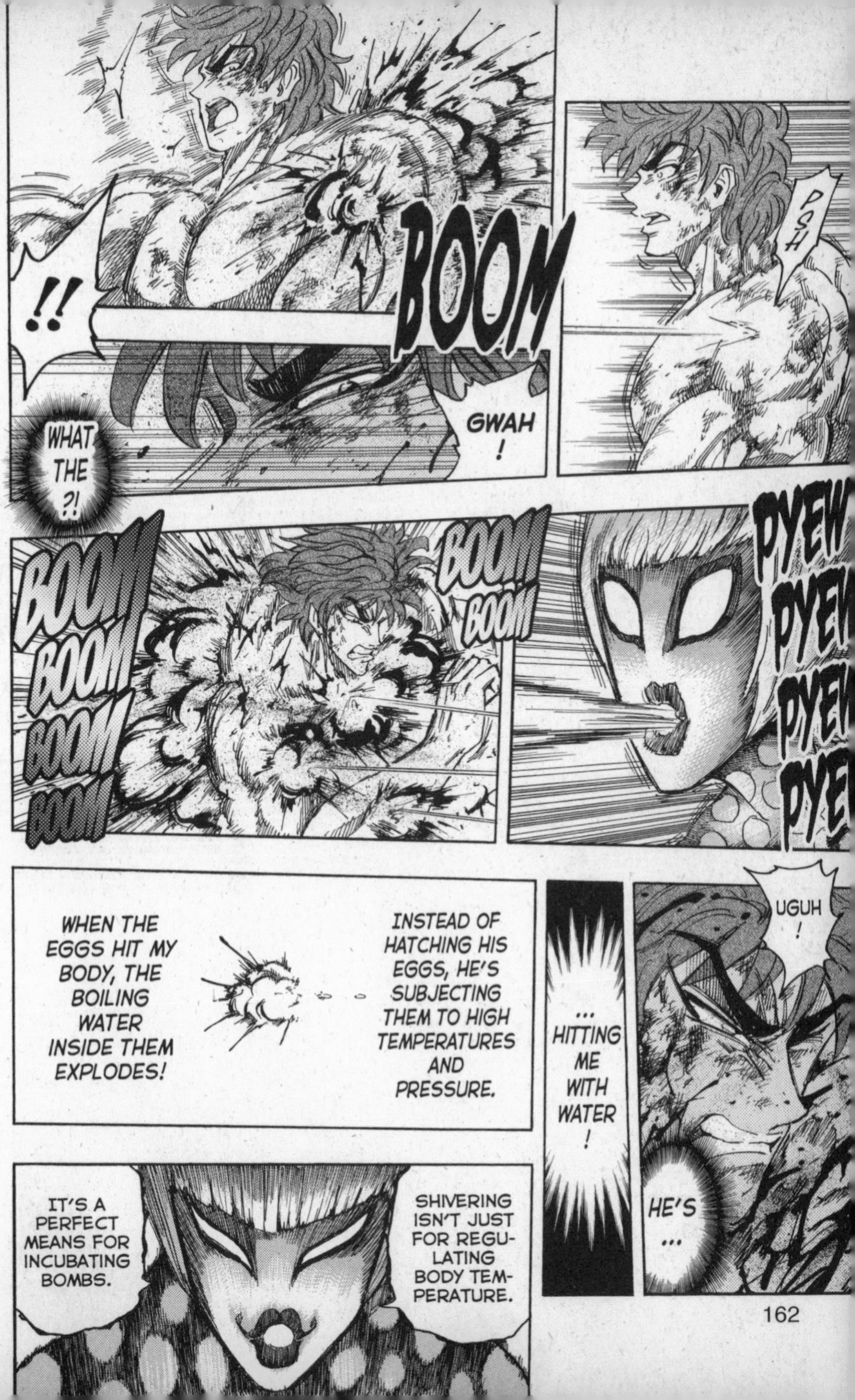
PSH
BOOM
!!
GWAH!
WHAT THE ?!
PYEW PYEW PYEW PYEW
BOOM BOOM
BOOM BOOM BOOM BOOM
UGUH!
HE'S...
... HITTING ME WITH WATER!
INSTEAD OF HATCHING HIS EGGS, HE'S SUBJECTING THEM TO HIGH TEMPERATURES AND PRESSURE.
WHEN THE EGGS HIT MY BODY, THE BOILING WATER INSIDE THEM EXPLODES!
SHIVERING ISN'T JUST FOR REGU-LATING BODY TEM-PERATURE.
IT'S A PERFECT MEANS FOR INCUBATING BOMBS.

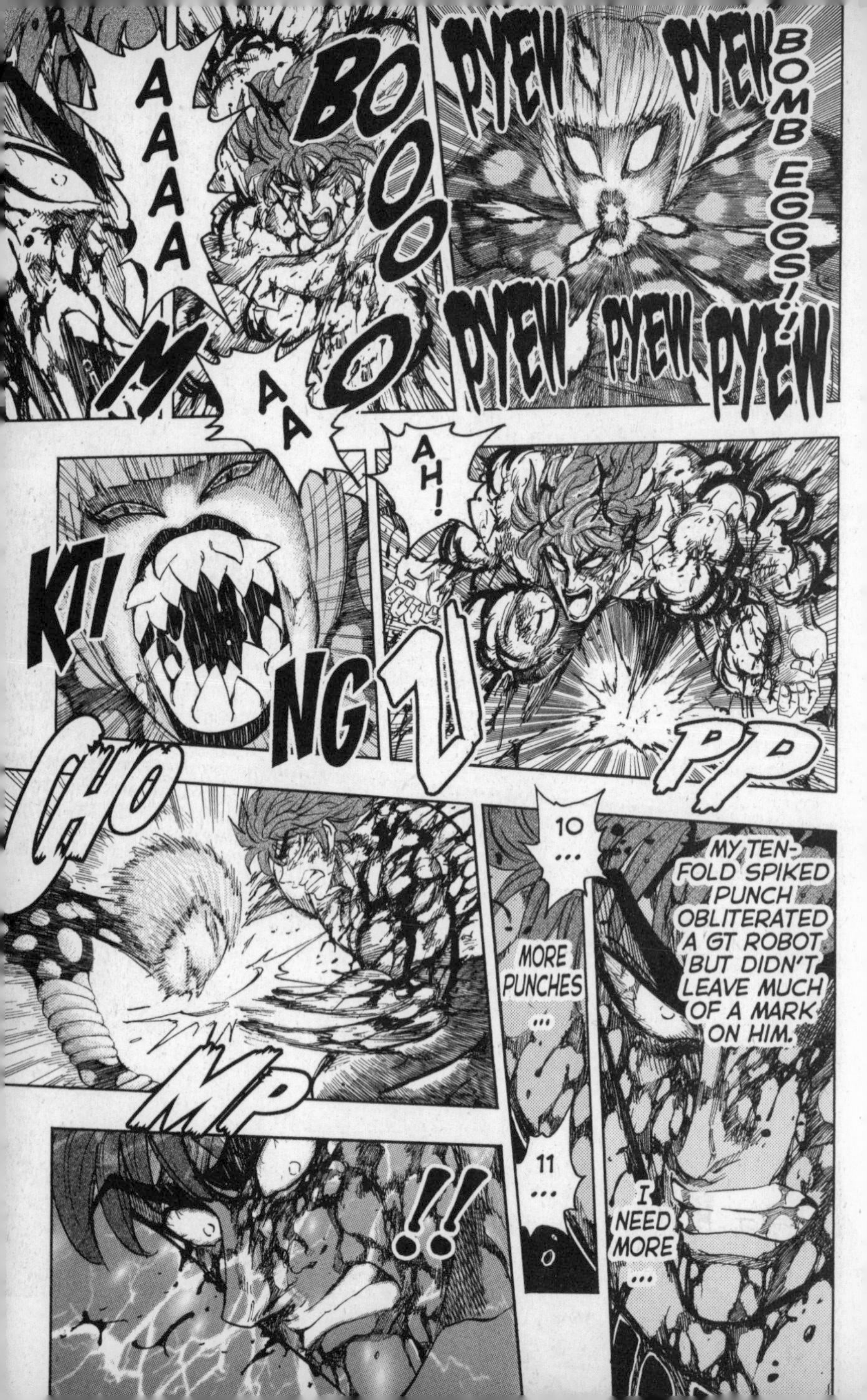
PYEW PYEW
BOMB EGGS!!
PYEW PYEW PYEW
AAAAM
BOOOO
AA
AH!
KTI
NG
ZU
PP
10...
MY TEN-FOLD SPIKED PUNCH OBLITERATED A GT ROBOT BUT DIDN'T LEAVE MUCH OF A MARK ON HIM.
MORE PUNCHES...
11...
I NEED MORE...
CHO
MP
!!

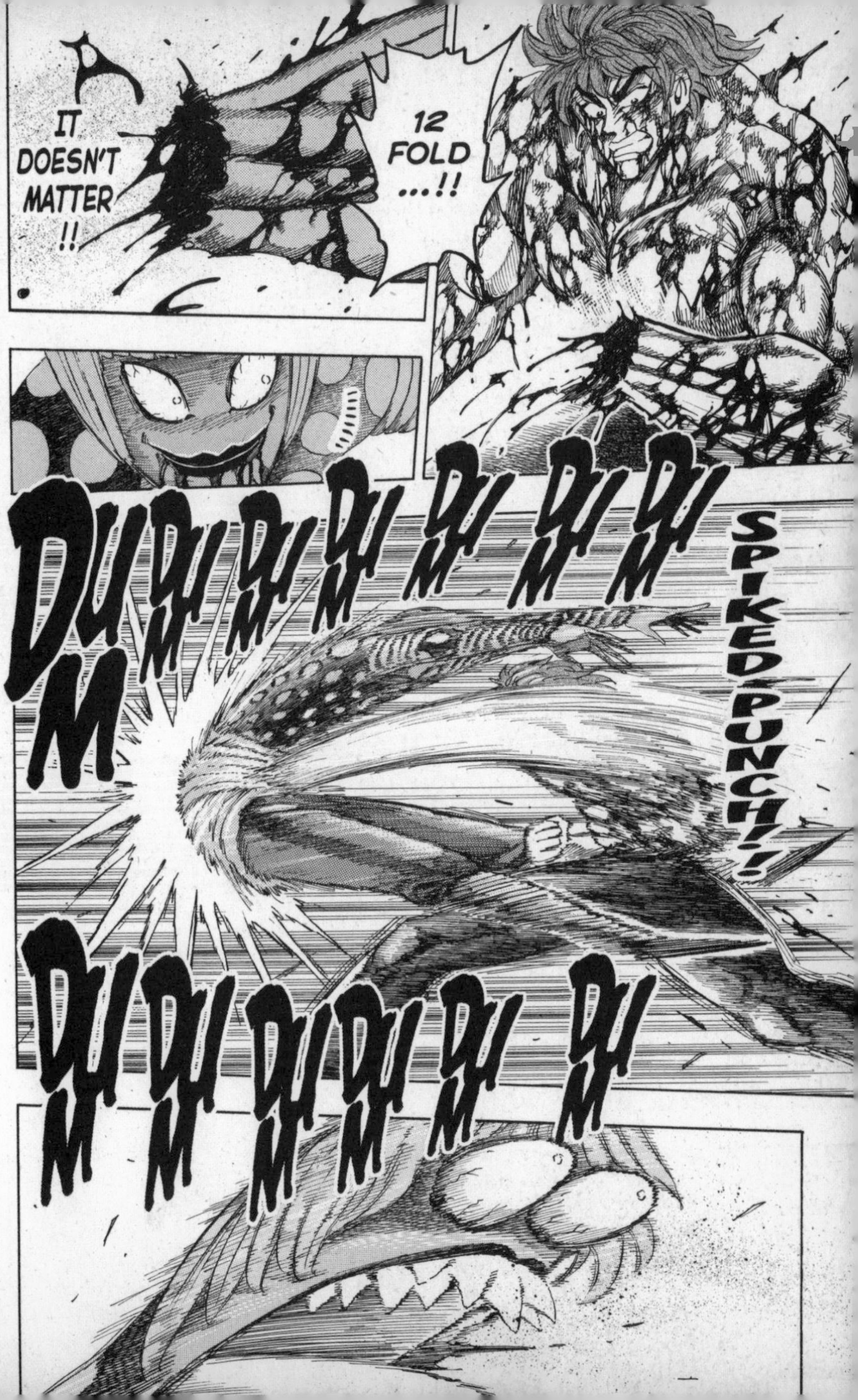
12 FOLD ...!!
IT DOESN'T MATTER!!
SPIKED PUNCH!!
DUM DUM DUM DUM DUM DUM DUM
DUM DUM DUM DUM DUM DUM

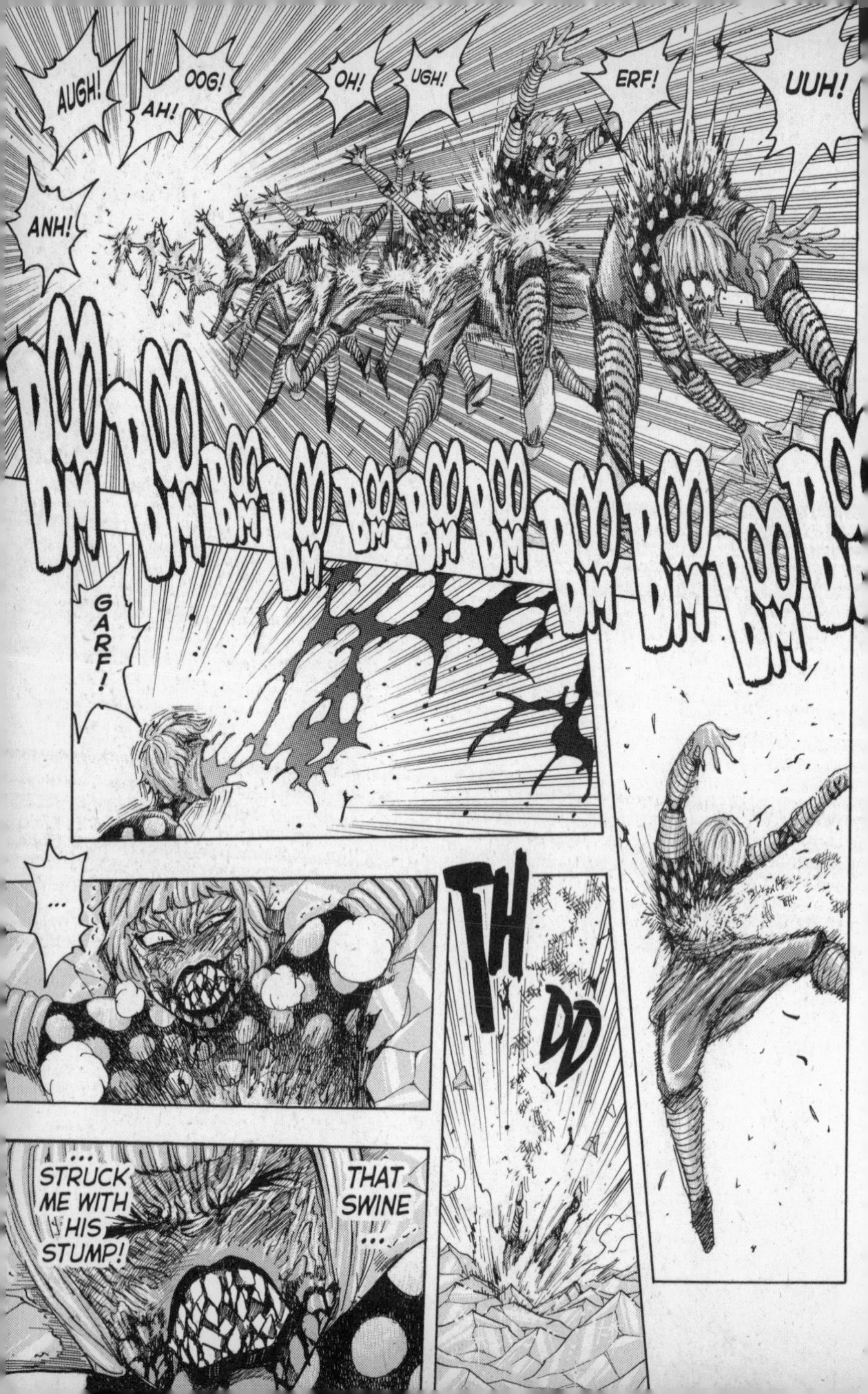
UUH!
ERF!
UGH!
OH!
OOG!
AH!
AUGH!
ANH!
BOOM BOOM BOOM BOOM BOOM BOOM BOOM BOOM BOOM BOOM BOOM
GARF!
THUDD
...
THAT SWINE...
...STRUCK ME WITH HIS STUMP!

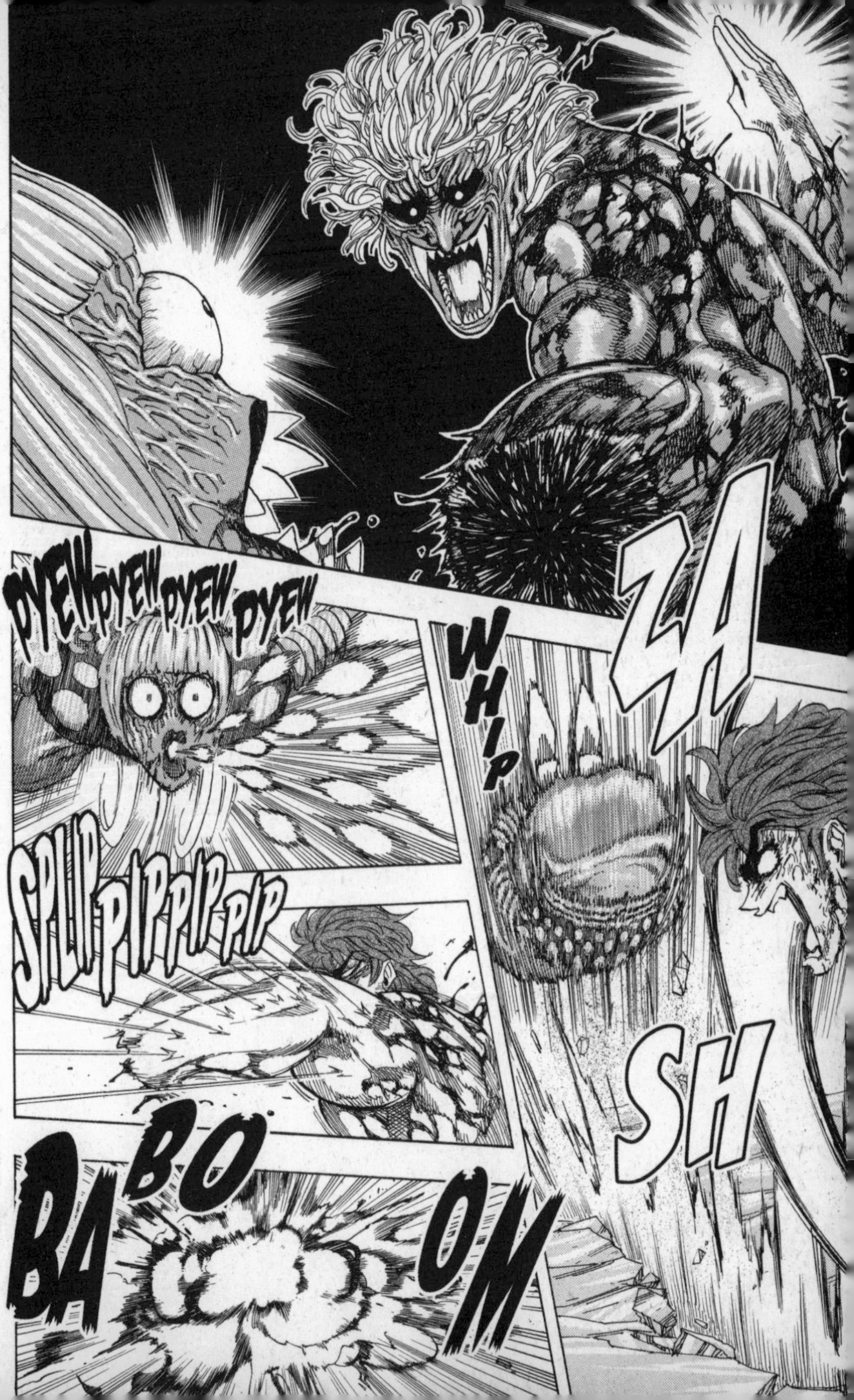
ZA
WHIP
SH
PYEW PYEW PYEW PYEW
SPLIP PIPPIP PIP
BABOOM

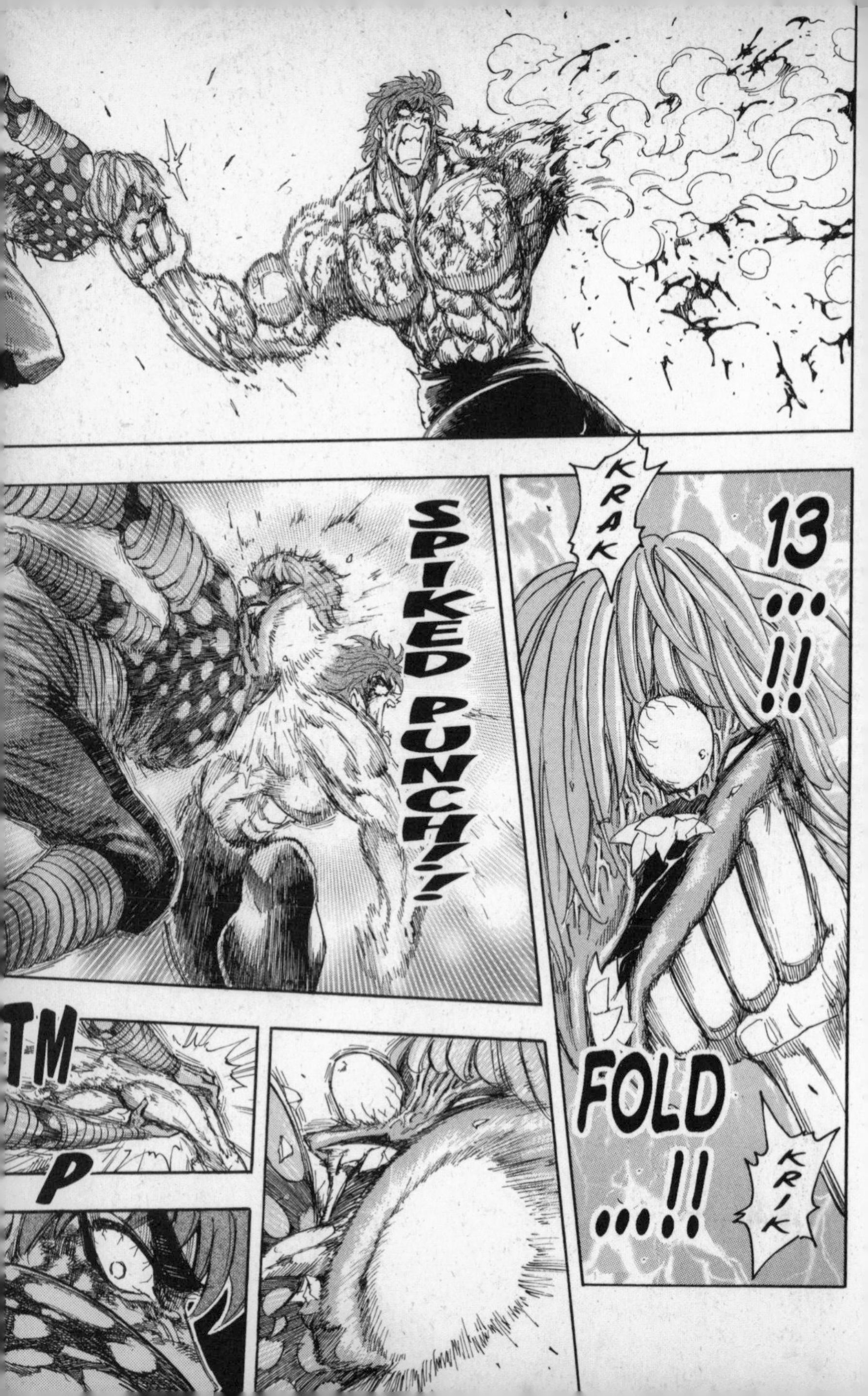
KRAK
13...!!
FOLD ...!!
KRIK
SPIKED PUNCH!!!
TM
P

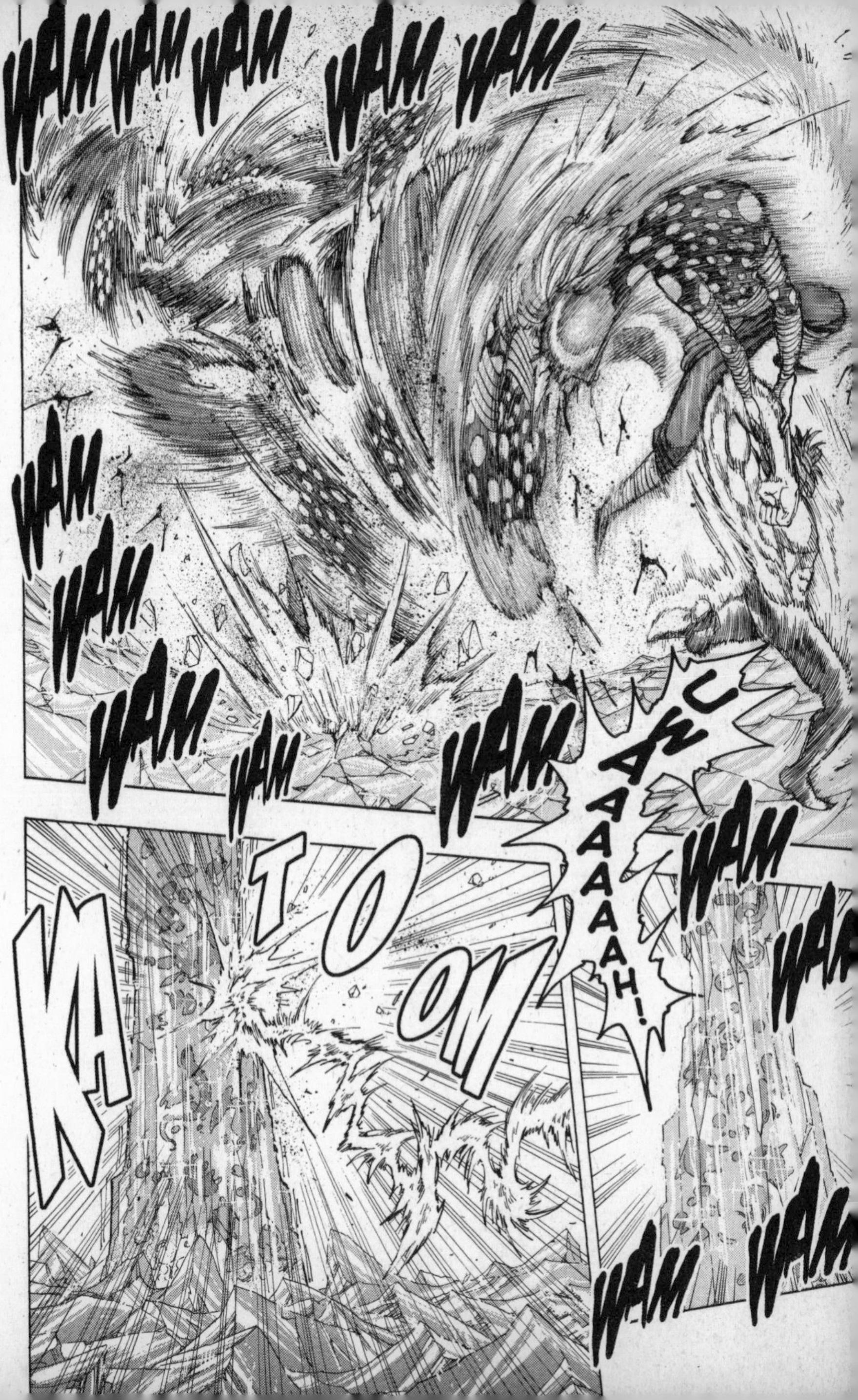
WAM WAM WAM WAM WAM
WAM WAM WAM WAM WAM
UWAAAAAAAH!
WAM WAM
KATOOM
WAM WAM

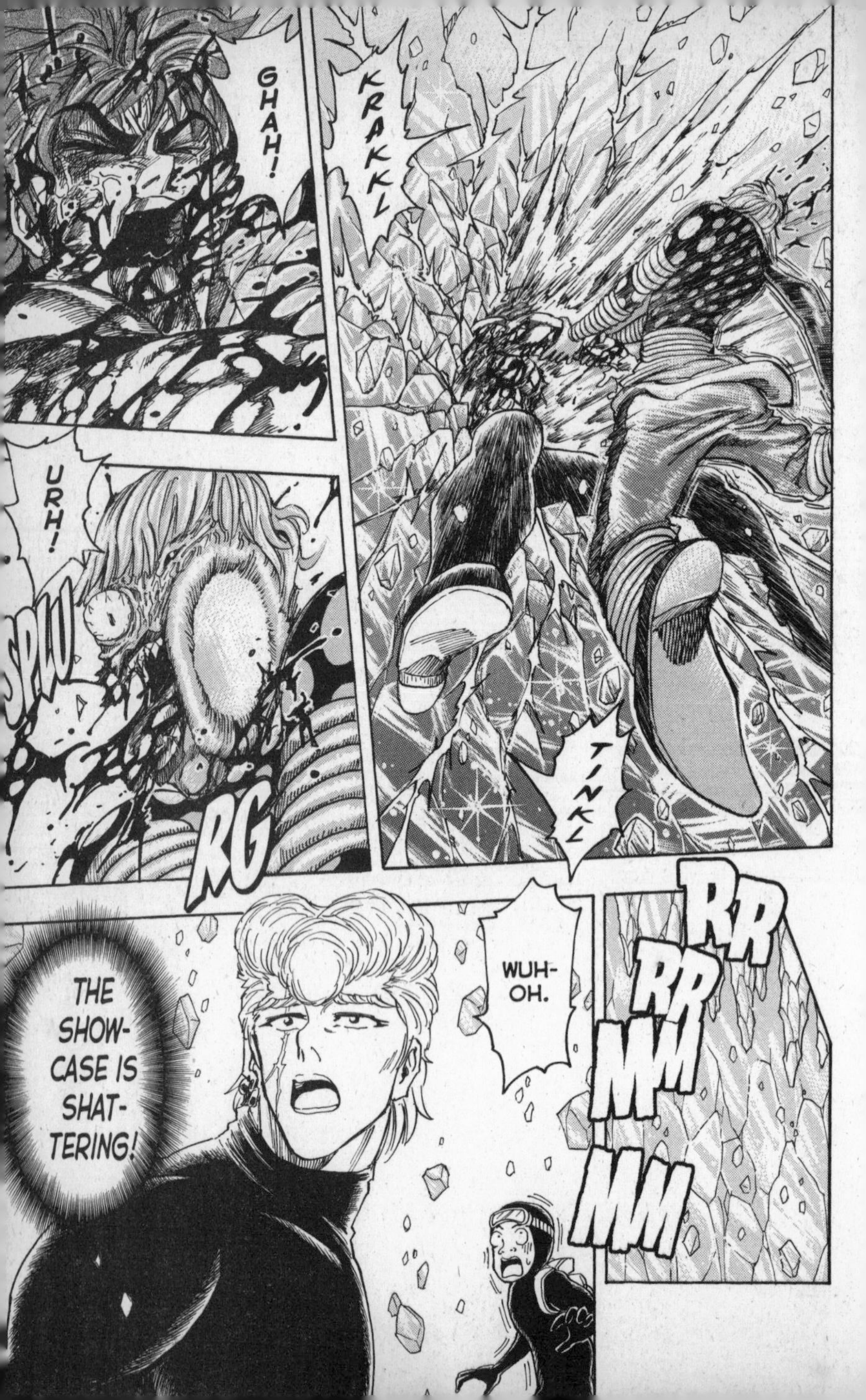
KRAKK!
TINK!
GHAH!
URH!
SPLU
RG
RRRRMMMM
WUH-OH.
THE SHOW-CASE IS SHAT-TERING!

TORIKO

GOURMET CHECKLIST

Vol. 086

SEAWEED BUG
(INSECT)

CAPTURE LEVEL: LESS THAN 1

HABITAT: WORLDWIDE

LENGTH: 15 CM

HEIGHT: ---

WEIGHT: 1 G

PRICE: 10 YEN PER BUG

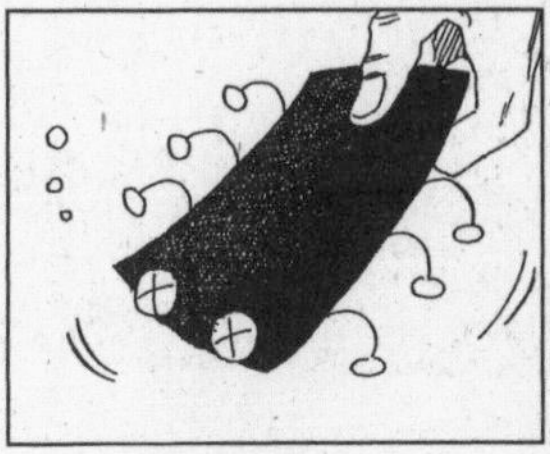

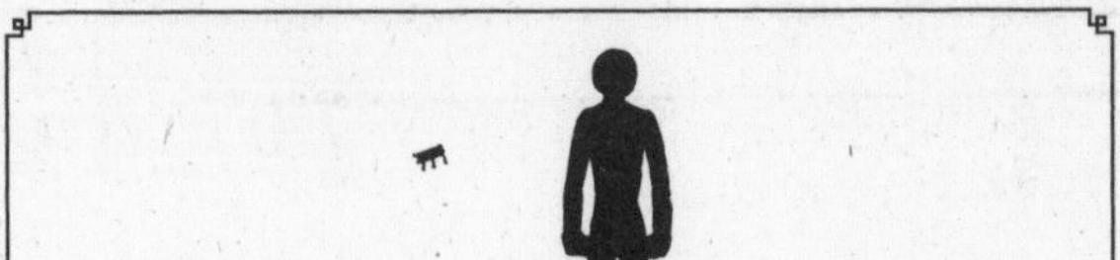

SCALE

THESE LITTLE BUGS LIVE IN SWARMS IN PRACTICALLY EVERY CORNER OF THE WORLD, WITH DIFFERENT VARIETIES TASTING LIKE SEAWEED, SEASONED SEAWEED, AND SALTY OCEAN SEAWEED. THEY GO WITH ALMOST ANY MEAL, AND THANKS TO THEIR LOW CAPTURE LEVEL, ARE A VERY POPULAR FOOD.

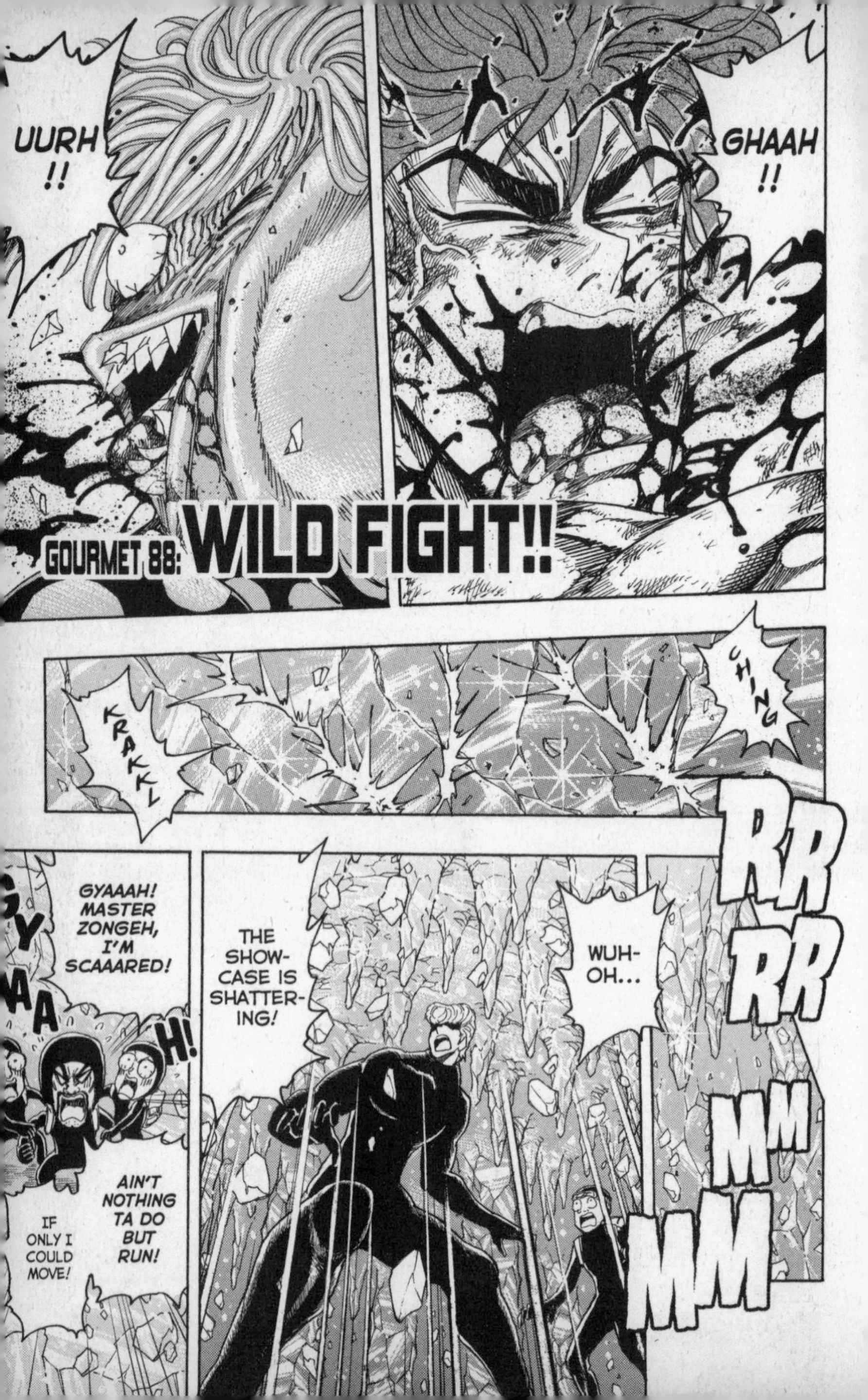
GHAAH !!
UURH !!
GOURMET 88: WILD FIGHT!!
CHING
KRAKK!
RRRR
MMMM
WUH-OH...
THE SHOWCASE IS SHATTERING!
AIN'T NOTHING TA DO BUT RUN!
GYAAAH! MASTER ZONGEH, I'M SCAAARED!
GYAAH!
IF ONLY I COULD MOVE!

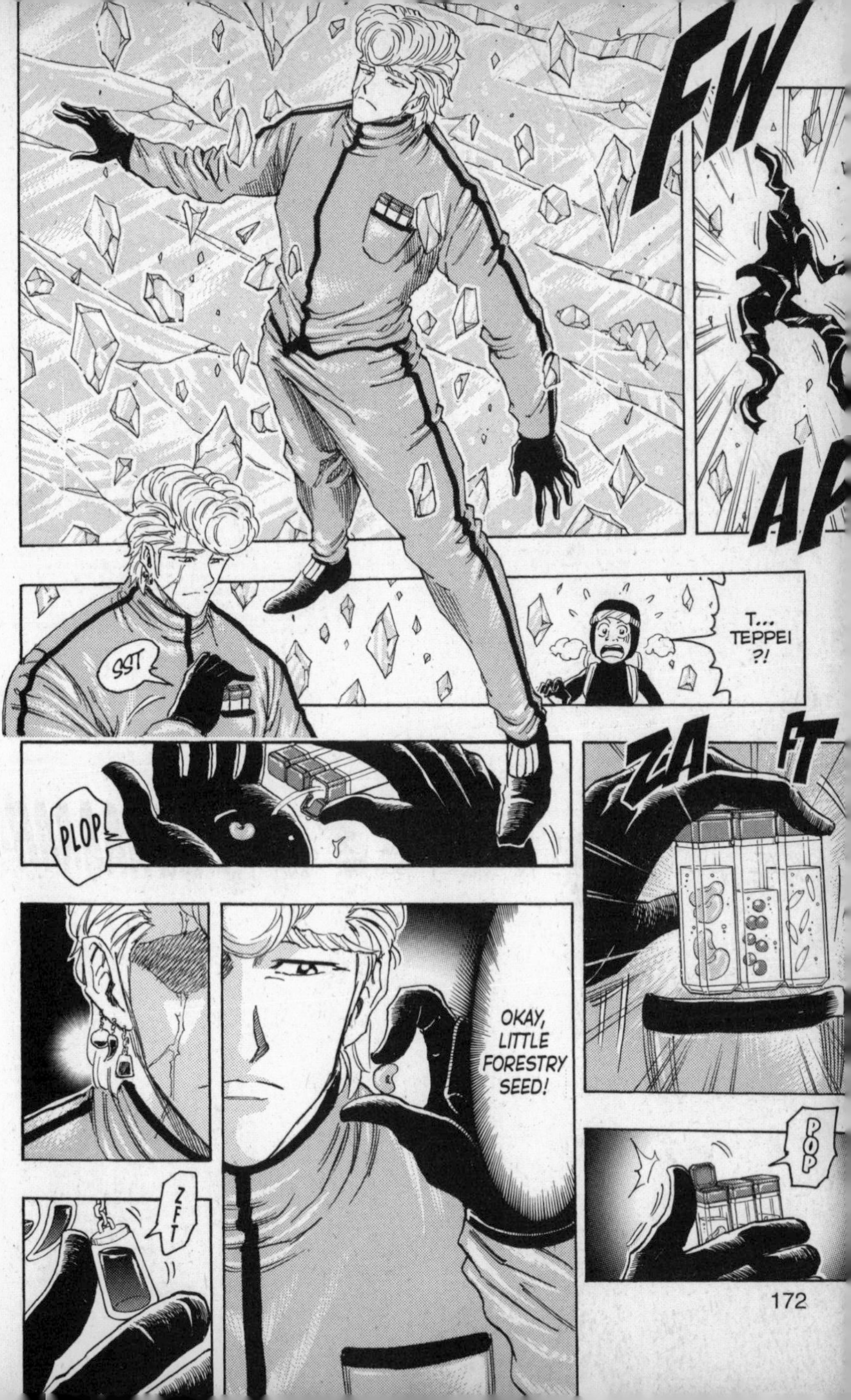
FW
A
T... TEPPEI ?!
SST
ZA FT
PLOP
POP
OKAY, LITTLE FORESTRY SEED!
ZFT

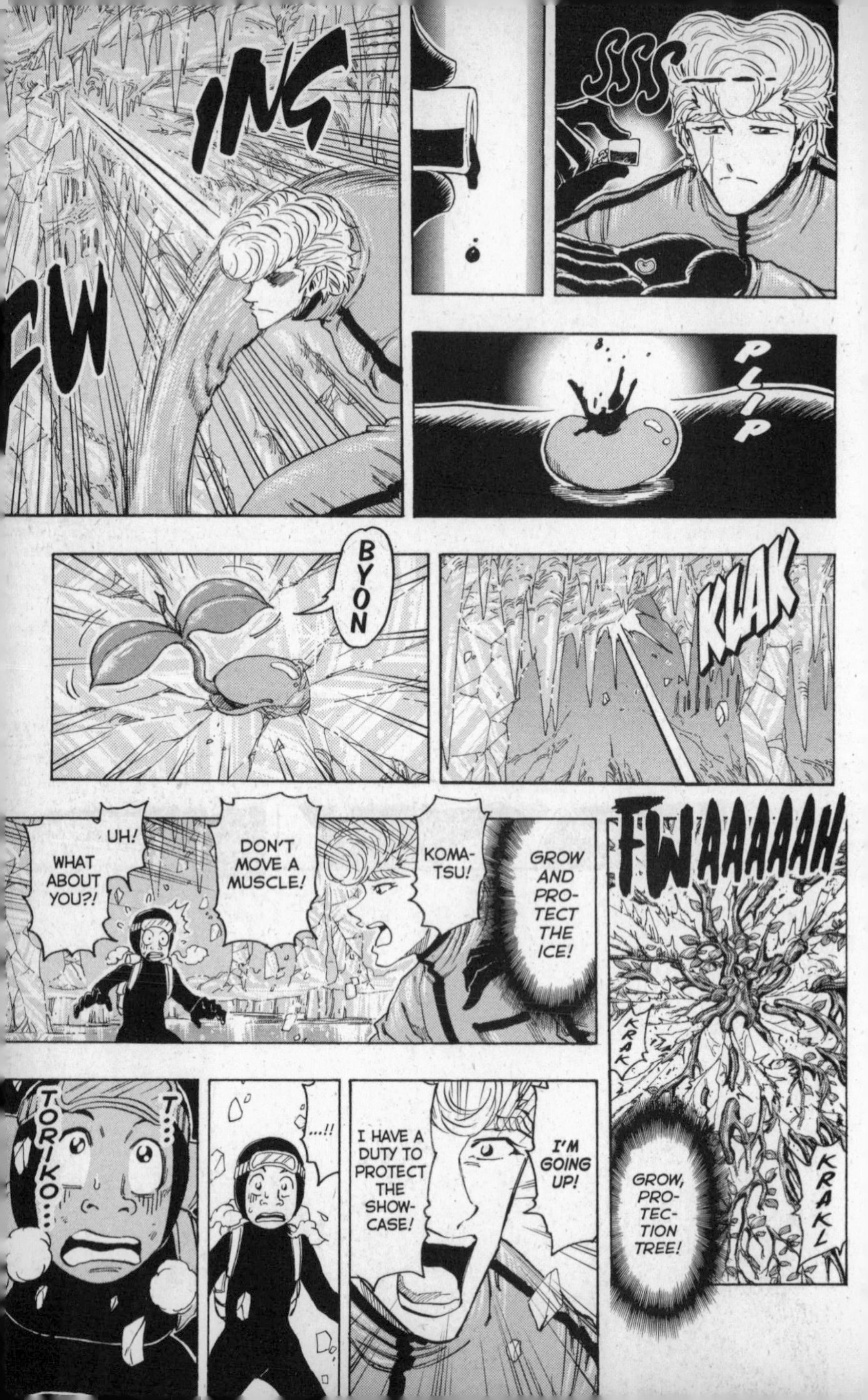
SSS
PLIP
ING
FW
KLAK
BYON
FWAAAAAH
KRAK
KRAKL
GROW, PROTECTION TREE!
GROW AND PROTECT THE ICE!
KOMATSU!
DON'T MOVE A MUSCLE!
UH! WHAT ABOUT YOU?!
I'M GOING UP!
I HAVE A DUTY TO PROTECT THE SHOWCASE!
...!!
T...TORIKO...

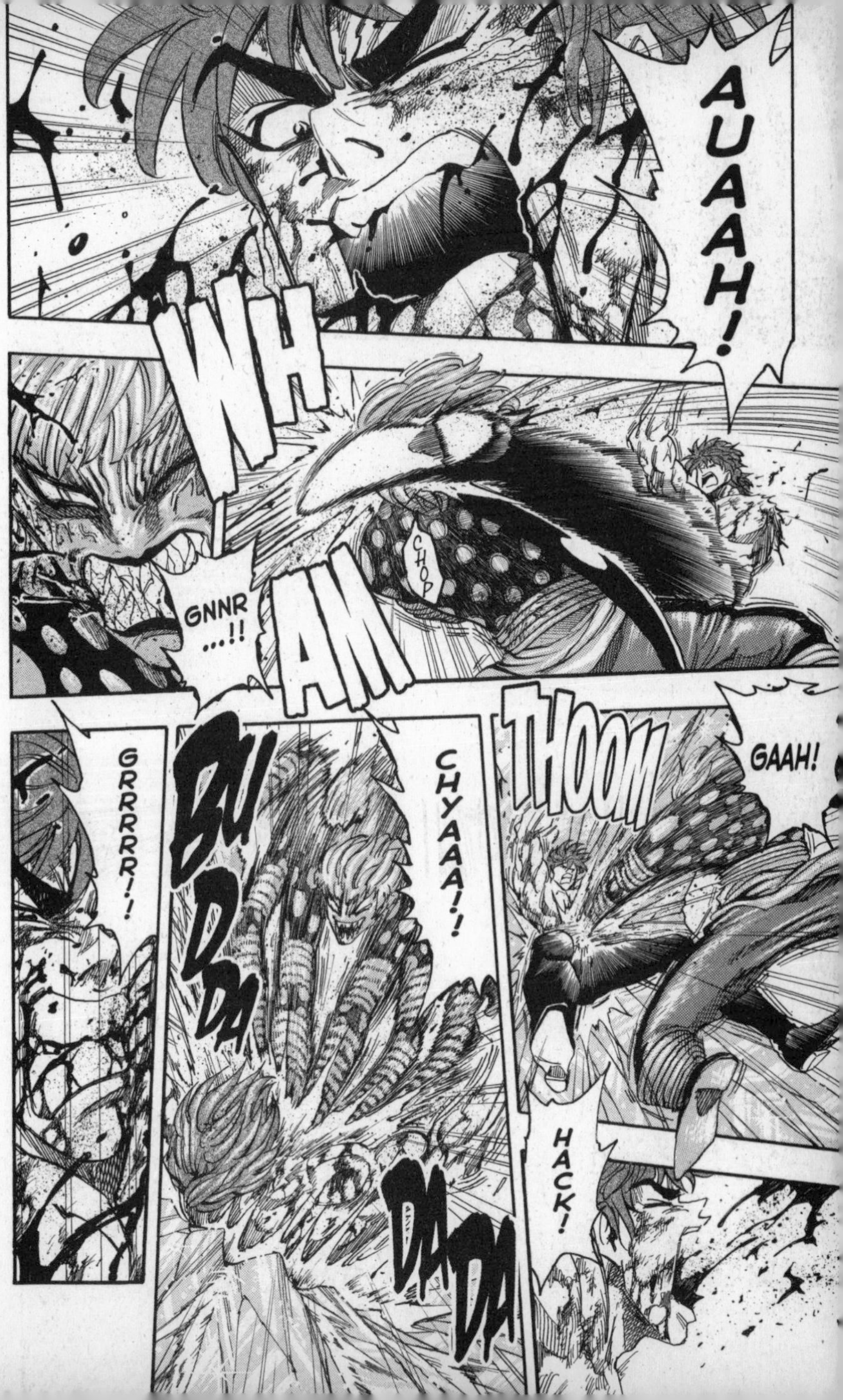
AUAAAH!
WHAM
CHOP
GNNR...!!
THOOM
GAAH!
HACK!
CHYAAAA!!
BUDADADADA
GRRRRR!!

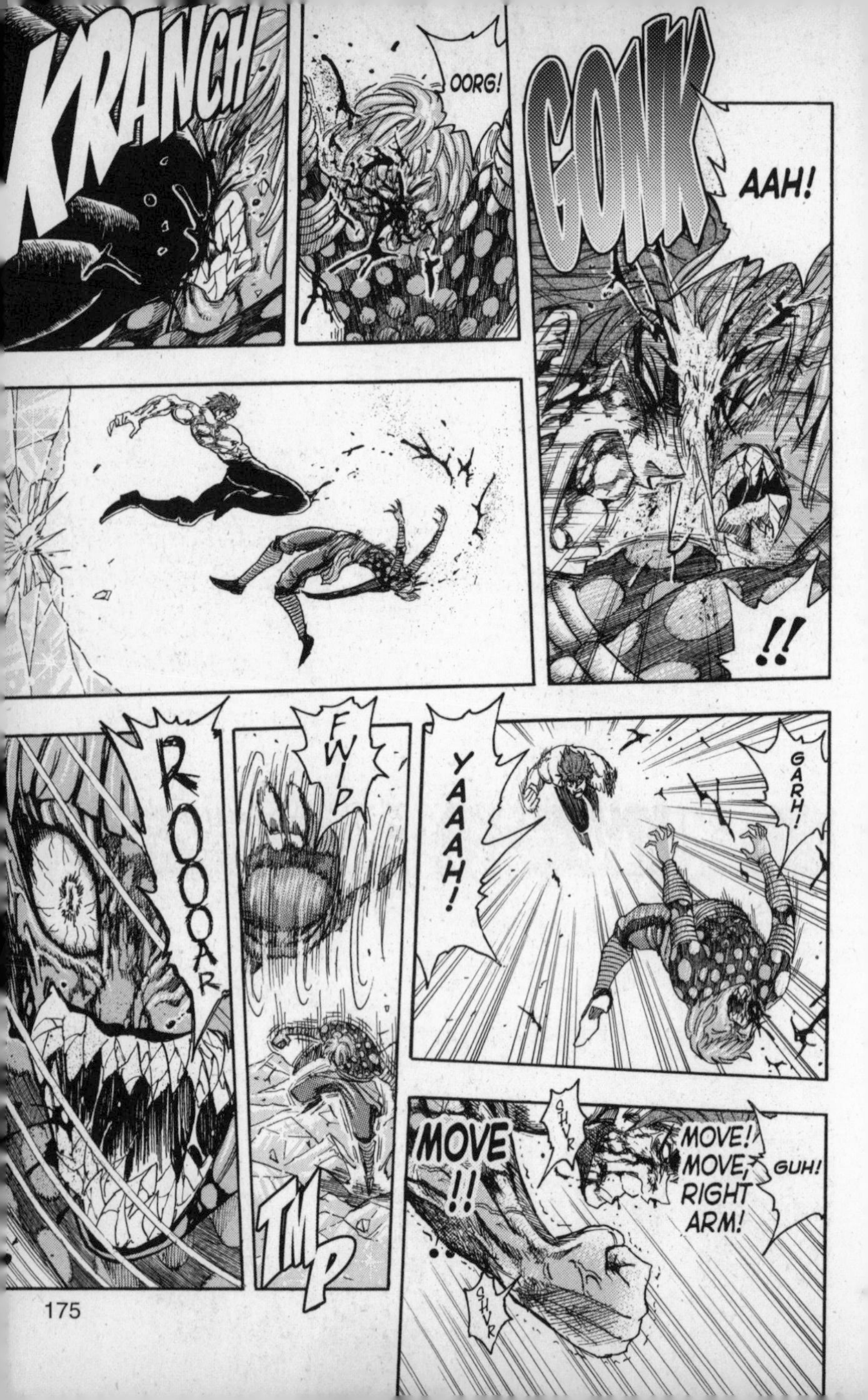
GONK
AAH!
!!
OORG!
KRANCH
YAAAAH!
GARH!
MOVE !!
SHVR
MOVE! MOVE, RIGHT ARM!
GUH!
SHVR
FWIP
TMP
ROOOAR

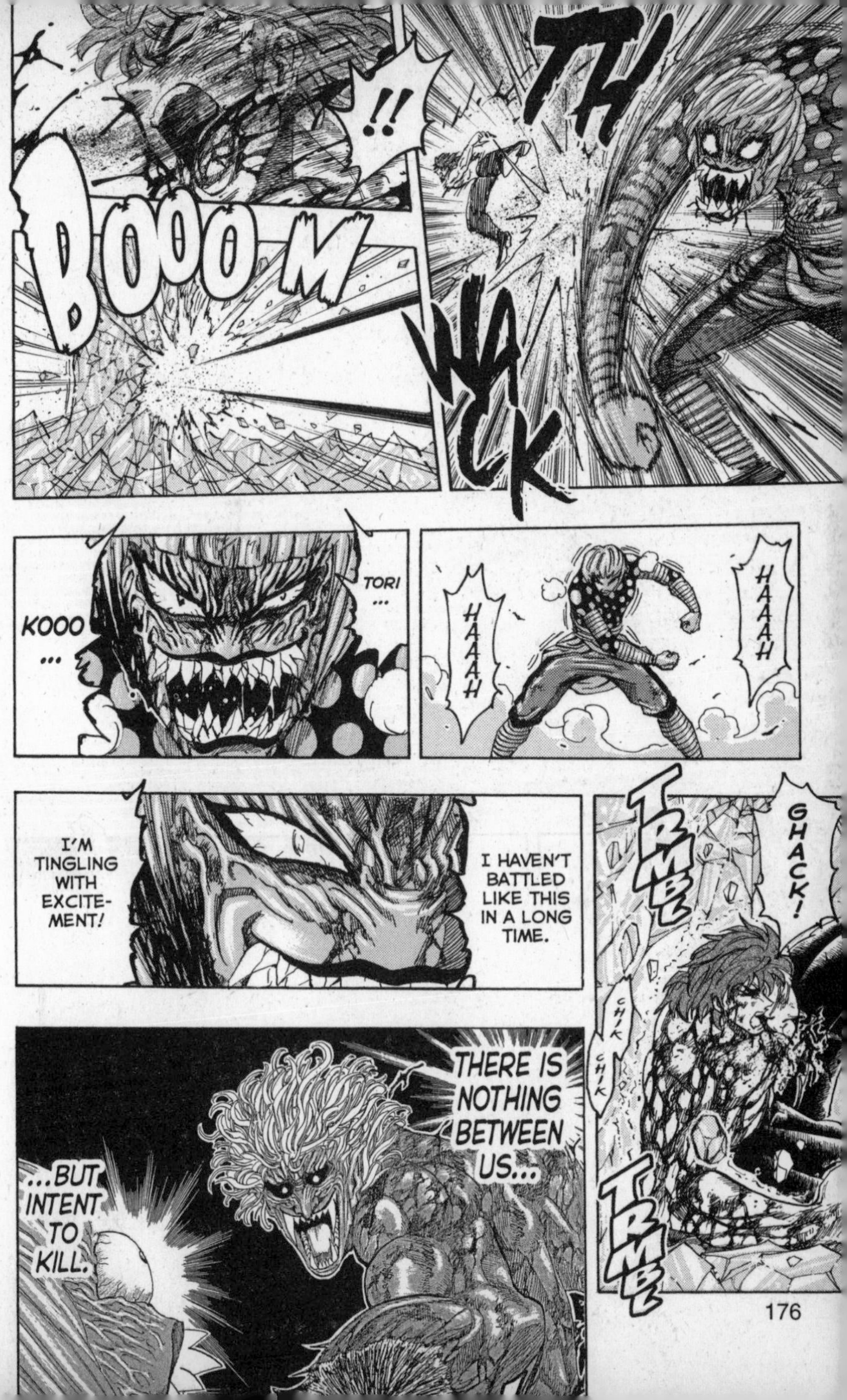
THWACK
!!
BOOOM
HAAAAH
HAAAAH
TORI ...
KOOO ...
GHACK!
TRMBL
CHIK
CHIK
TRMBL
I HAVEN'T BATTLED LIKE THIS IN A LONG TIME.
I'M TINGLING WITH EXCITE-MENT!
THERE IS NOTHING BETWEEN US...
...BUT INTENT TO KILL.

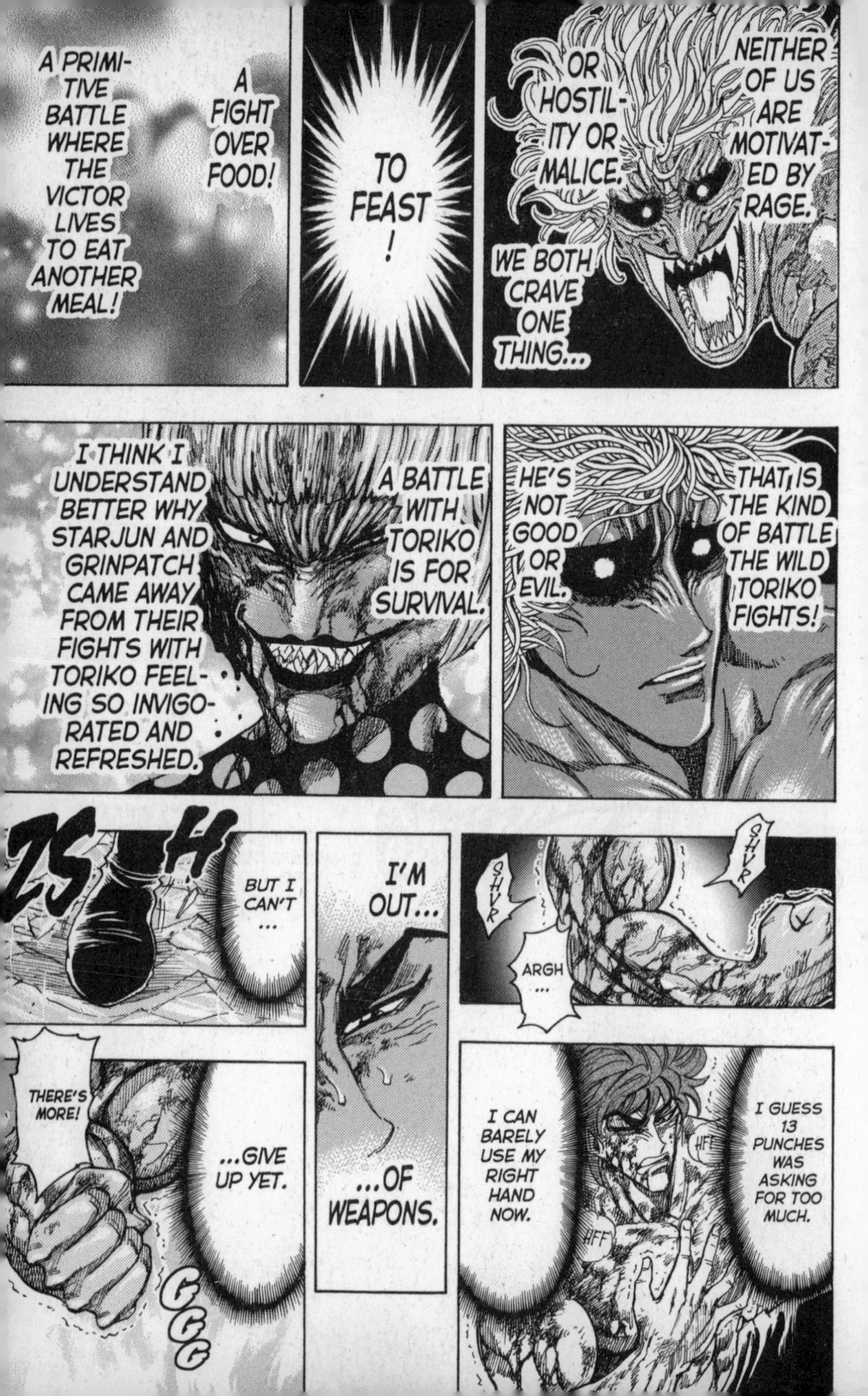
NEITHER OF US ARE MOTIVATED BY RAGE.
OR HOSTILITY OR MALICE.
WE BOTH CRAVE ONE THING...
TO FEAST!
A FIGHT OVER FOOD!
A PRIMITIVE BATTLE WHERE THE VICTOR LIVES TO EAT ANOTHER MEAL!
THAT IS THE KIND OF BATTLE THE WILD TORIKO FIGHTS!
HE'S NOT GOOD OR EVIL.
A BATTLE WITH TORIKO IS FOR SURVIVAL.
I THINK I UNDERSTAND BETTER WHY STARJUN AND GRINPATCH CAME AWAY FROM THEIR FIGHTS WITH TORIKO FEELING SO INVIGORATED AND REFRESHED.
SHVR
SHVR
ARGH...
I GUESS 13 PUNCHES WAS ASKING FOR TOO MUCH.
I CAN BARELY USE MY RIGHT HAND NOW.
HFF
HFF
I'M OUT...
...OF WEAPONS.
ZSH
BUT I CAN'T...
THERE'S MORE!
...GIVE UP YET.
GGG

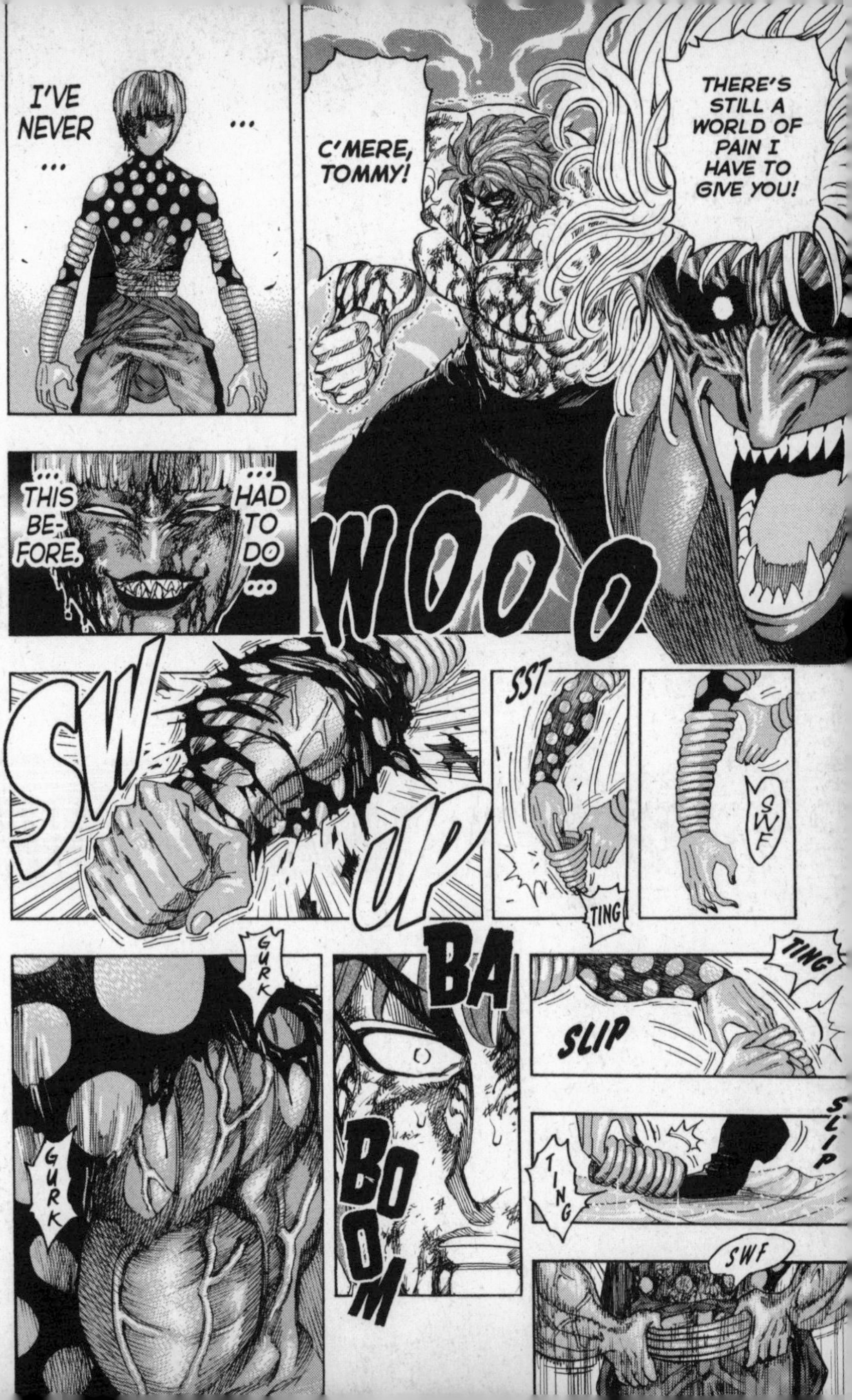
THERE'S STILL A WORLD OF PAIN I HAVE TO GIVE YOU!
C'MERE, TOMMY!
WOOO
I'VE NEVER ...
...
...HAD TO DO...
...THIS BE-FORE.
SWF
SST
TING
SW UP
TING
SLIP
SLIP
TING
SWF
BA
BOOM
GURK
GURK

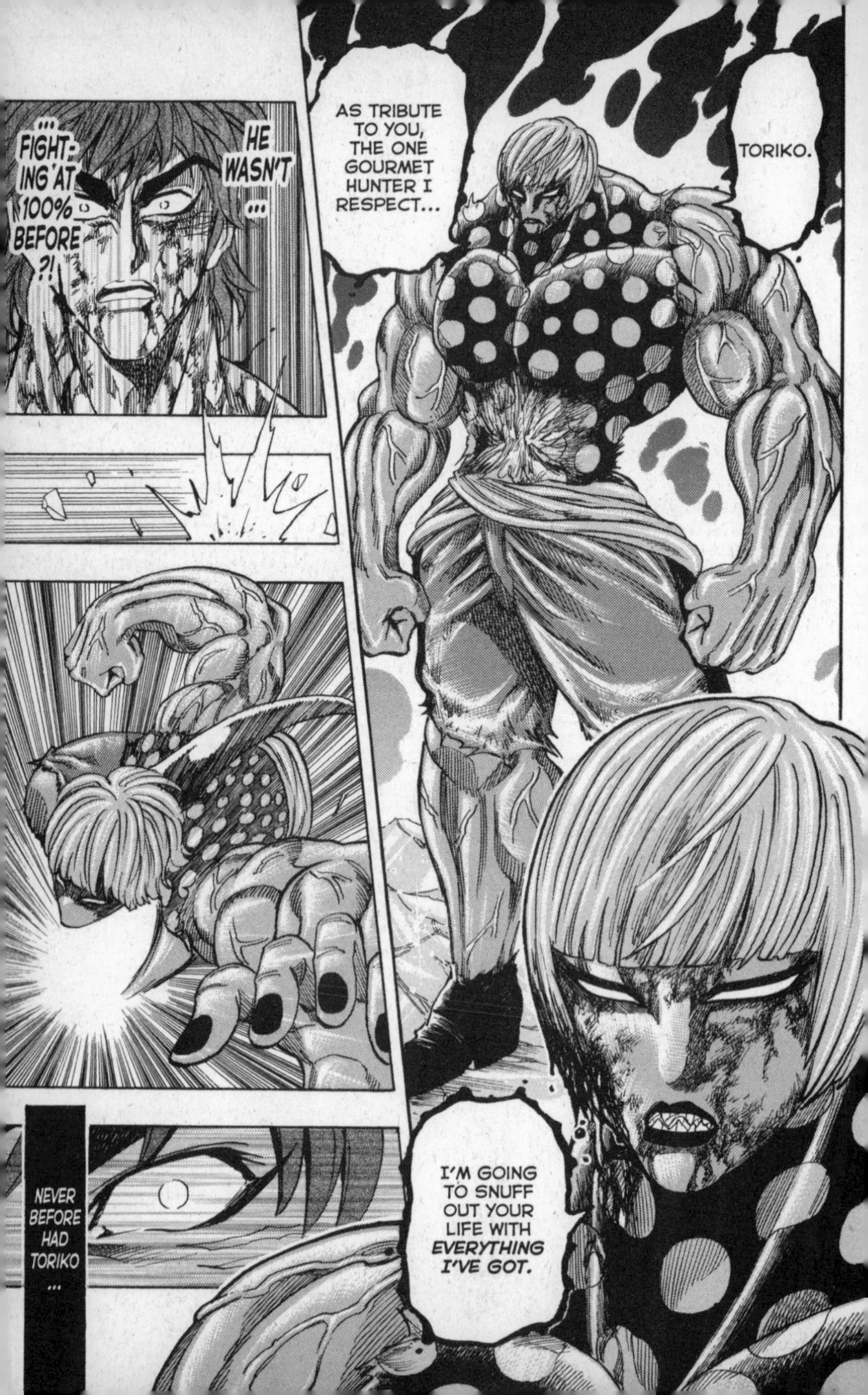
AS TRIBUTE TO YOU, THE ONE GOURMET HUNTER I RESPECT...
TORIKO.
I'M GOING TO SNUFF OUT YOUR LIFE WITH *EVERYTHING* I'VE GOT.
HE WASN'T...
...FIGHTING AT 100% BEFORE?!
NEVER BEFORE HAD TORIKO...

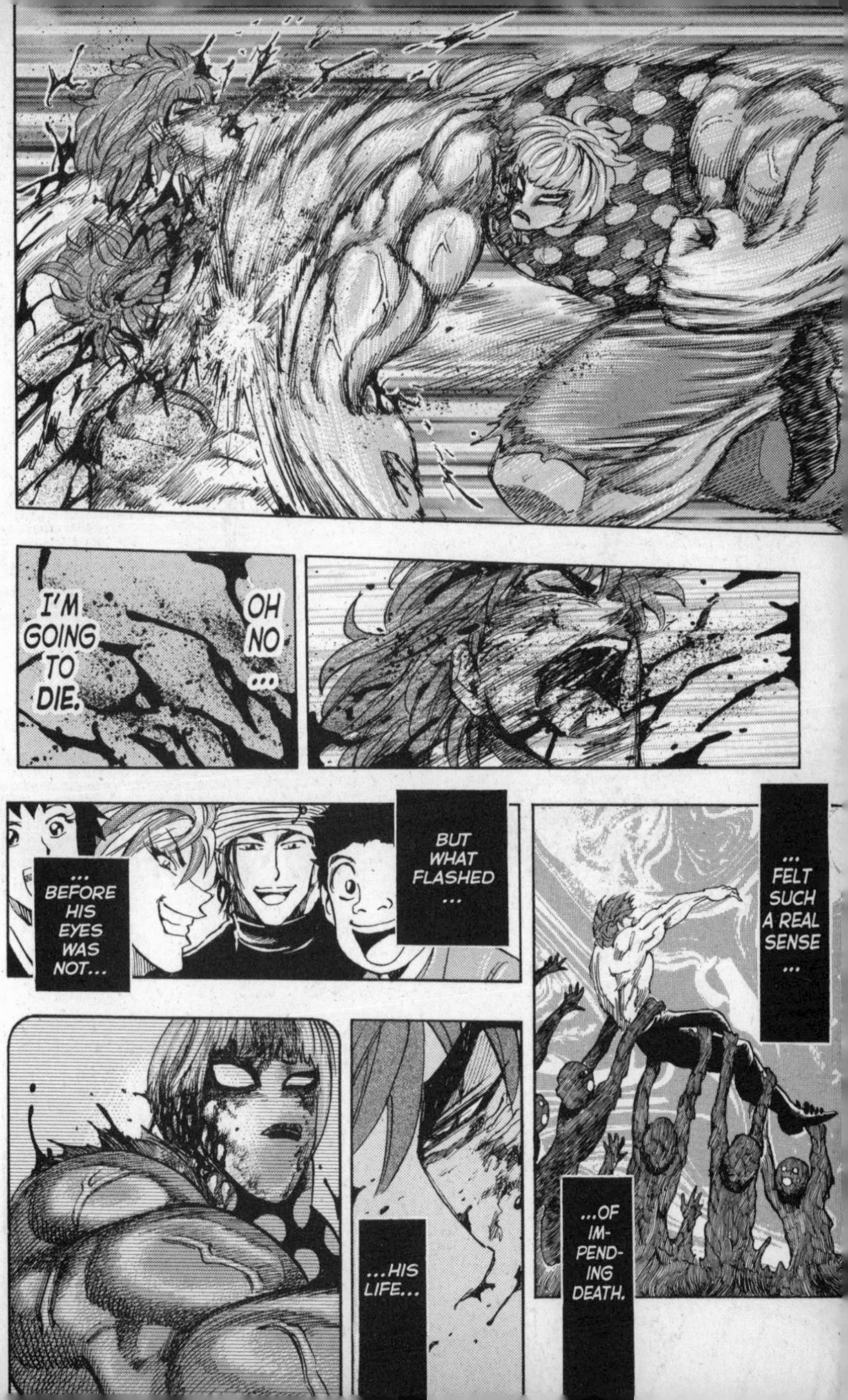
OH NO...
I'M GOING TO DIE.
...FELT SUCH A REAL SENSE...
...OF IM-PEND-ING DEATH.
BUT WHAT FLASHED...
...BEFORE HIS EYES WAS NOT...
...HIS LIFE...

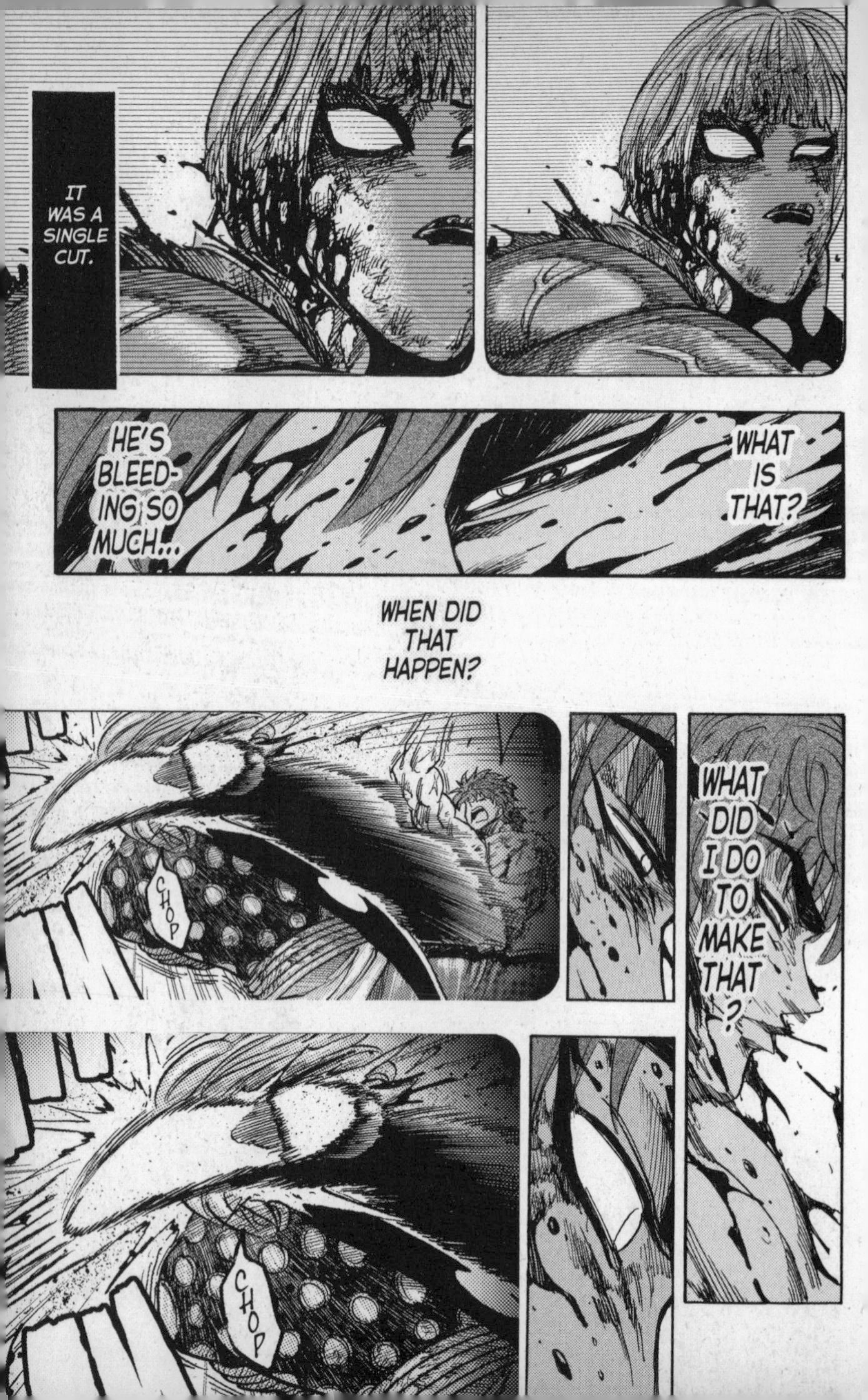
IT WAS A SINGLE CUT.
WHAT IS THAT?
HE'S BLEEDING SO MUCH...
WHEN DID THAT HAPPEN?
WHAT DID I DO TO MAKE THAT?
CHOP
CHOP

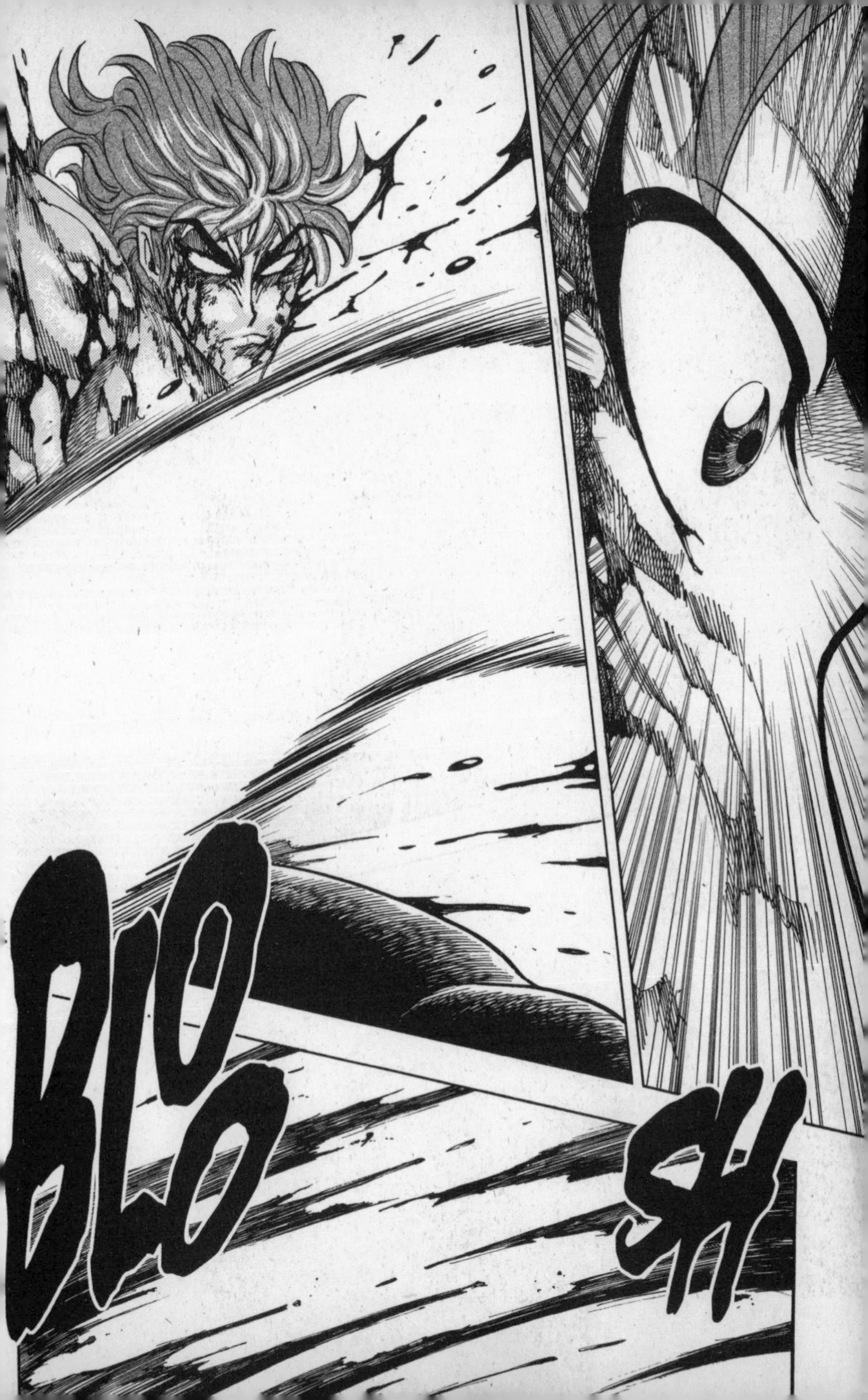
BLOOSH

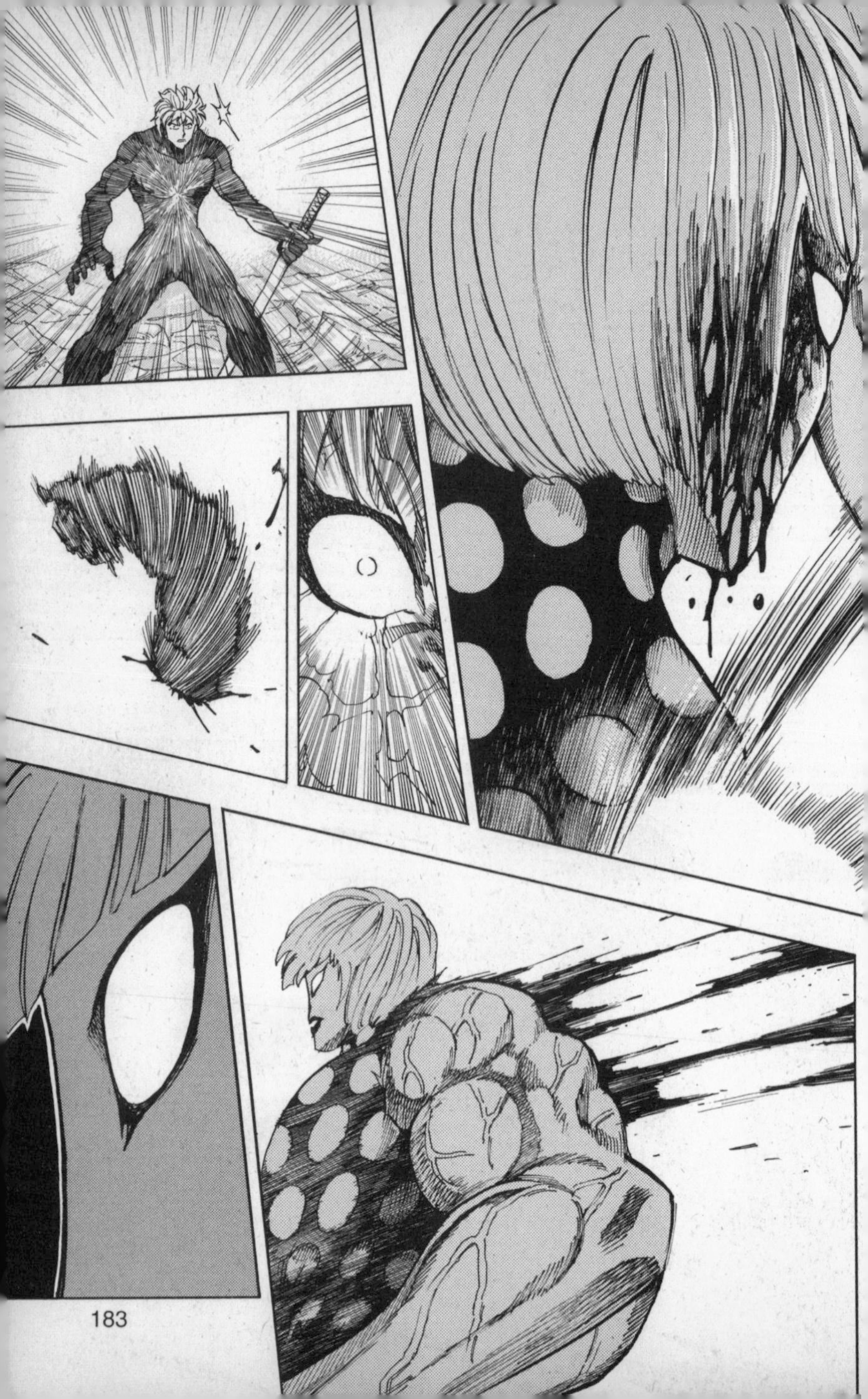

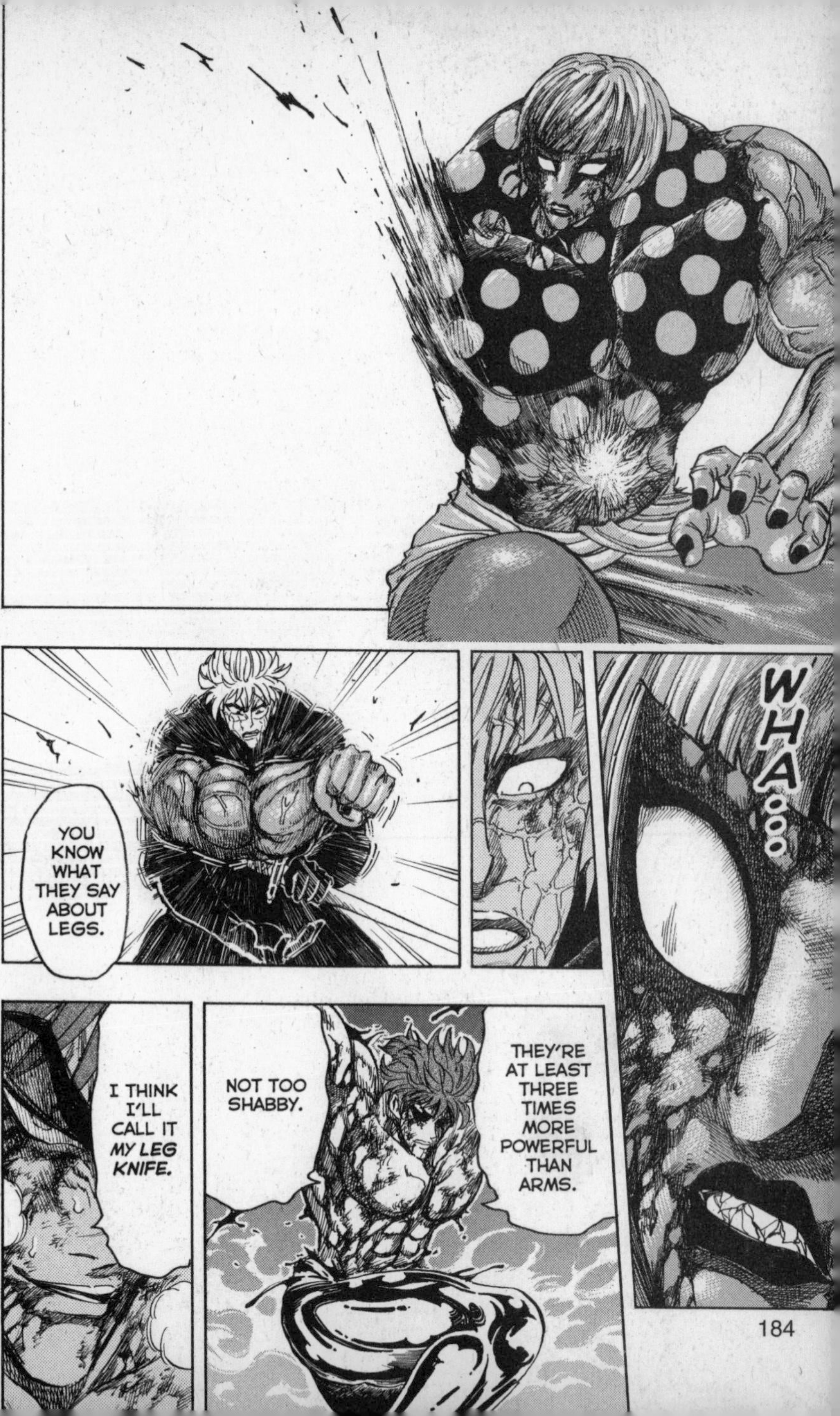
WHAooo
YOU KNOW WHAT THEY SAY ABOUT LEGS.
THEY'RE AT LEAST THREE TIMES MORE POWERFUL THAN ARMS.
NOT TOO SHABBY.
I THINK I'LL CALL IT *MY LEG KNIFE.*

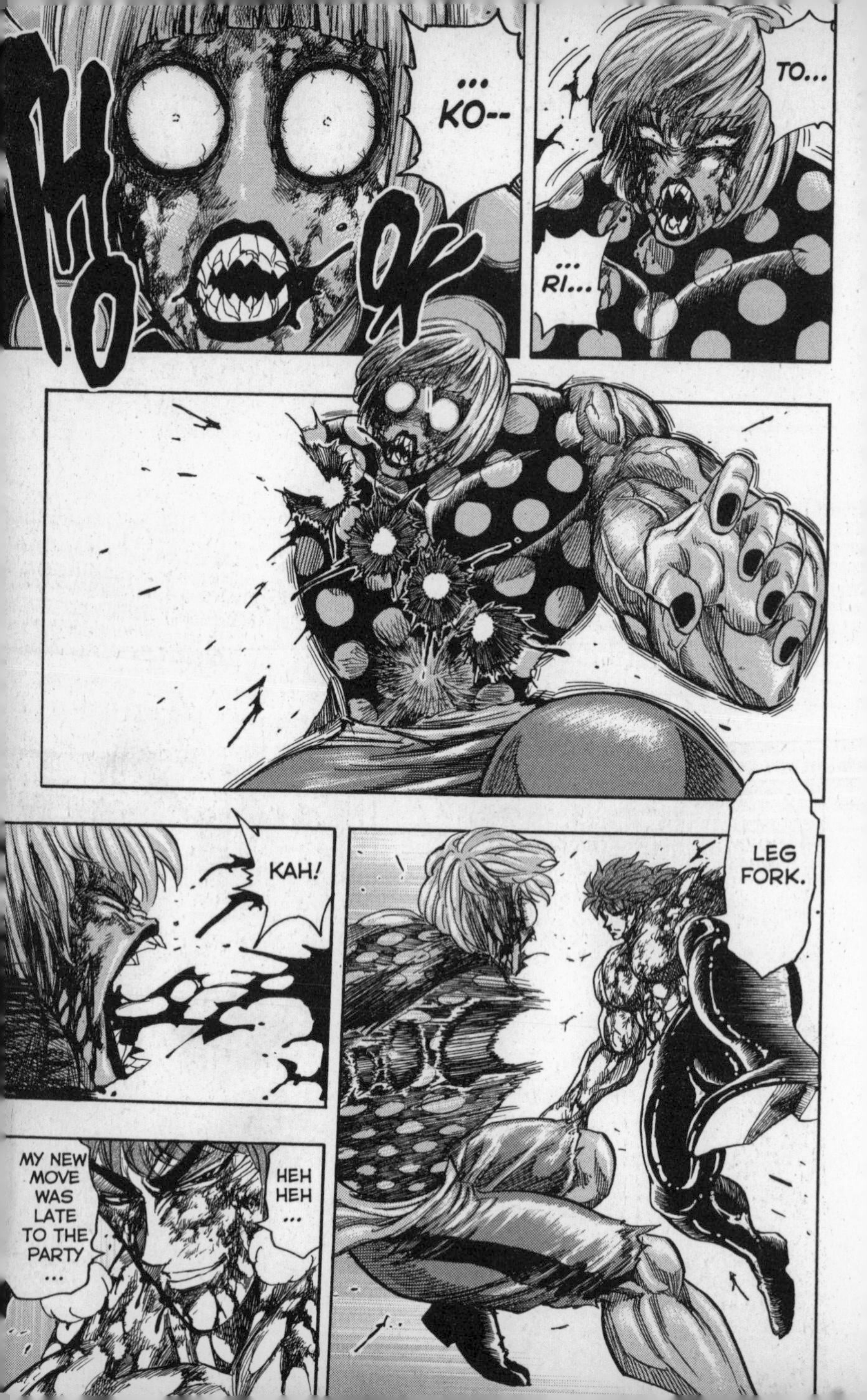
TO...
...RI...
...KO--
LEG FORK.
KAH!
HEH HEH ...
MY NEW MOVE WAS LATE TO THE PARTY ...

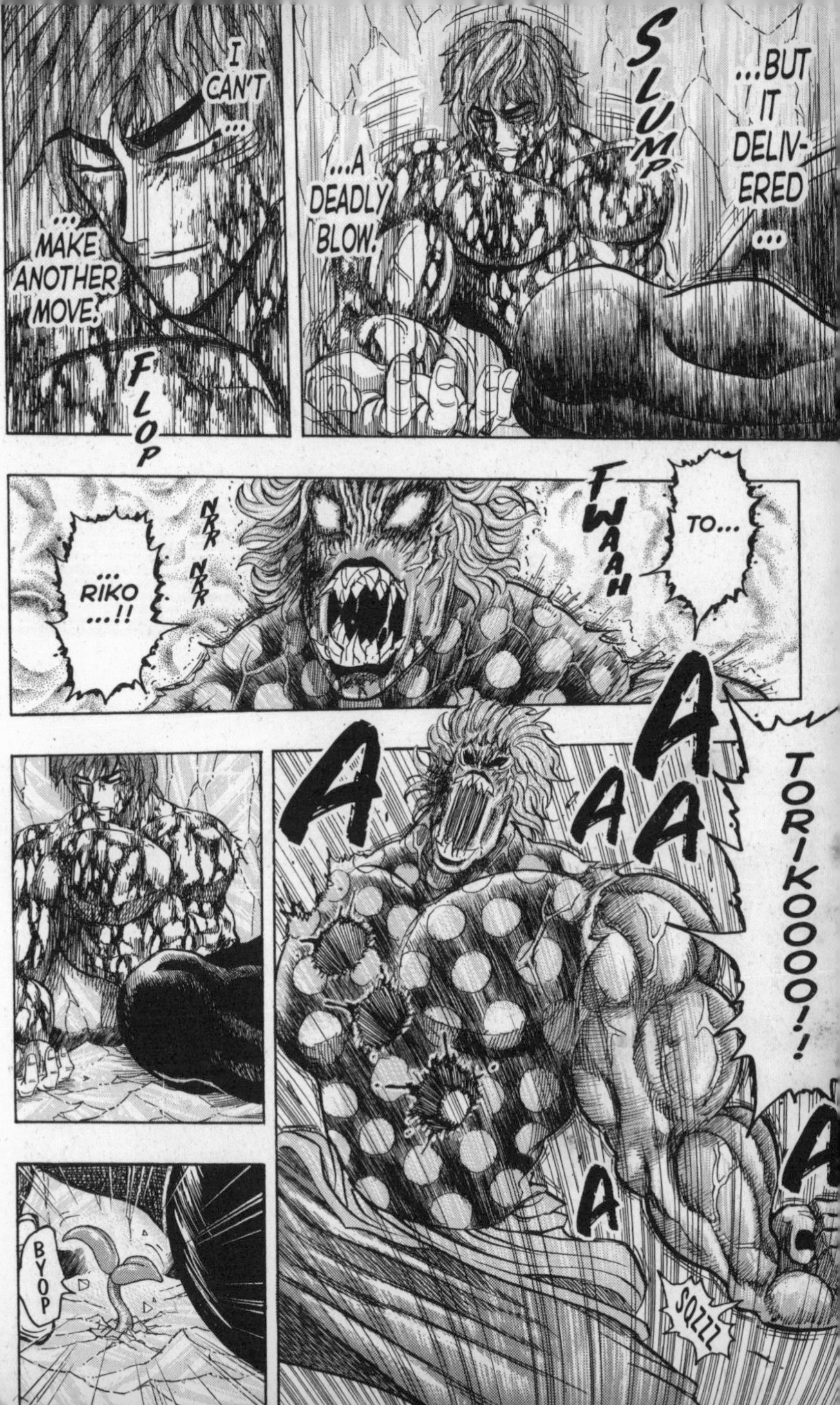
...BUT IT DELIVERED...
SLUMP
...A DEADLY BLOW.
I CAN'T...
...MAKE ANOTHER MOVE.
FLOP
TO...
FWAAAH
NRR NRR
...RIKO...!!
TORIKOOOOO!!
AAAAAAA
SQZZZ
BYOP

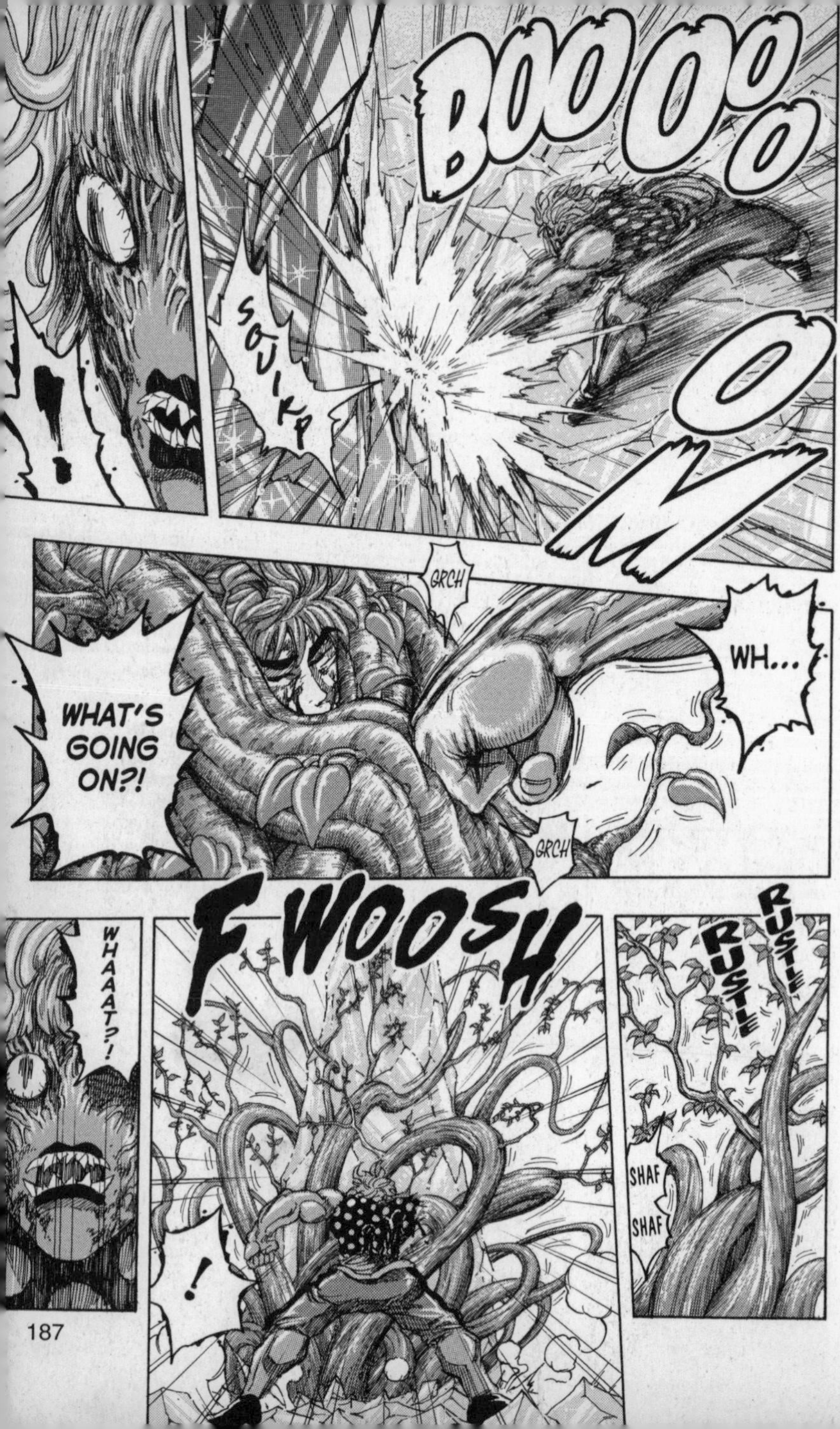
BOOOOOOON
SQUIKP
!!
GRCH
WH...
WHAT'S GOING ON?!
GRCH
RUSTLE RUSTLE
SHAF SHAF
FWOOSH
!
WHAAAT?!

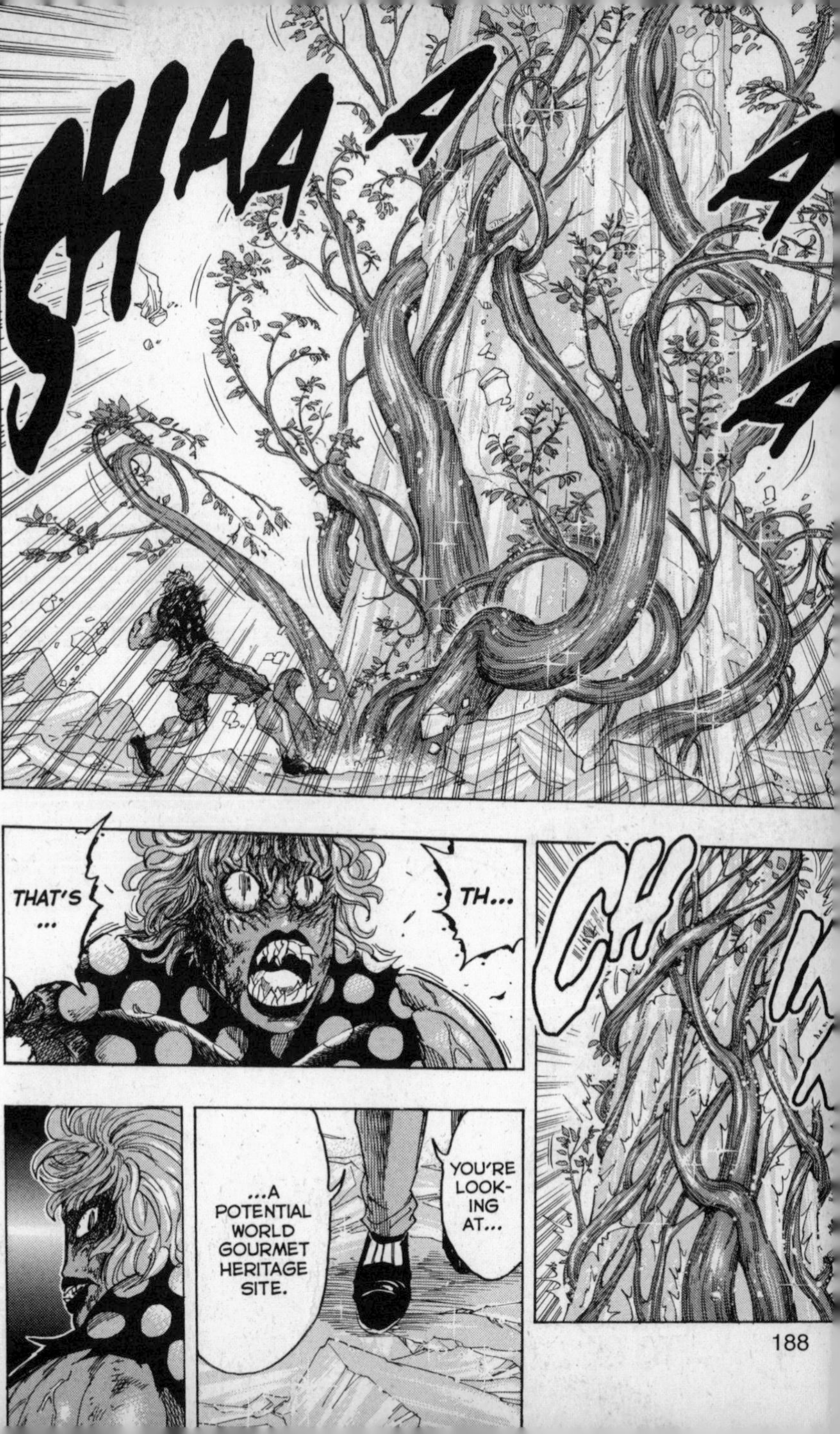
SHAAAAAA
CH
TH...
THAT'S ...
YOU'RE LOOK-ING AT...
...A POTENTIAL WORLD GOURMET HERITAGE SITE.

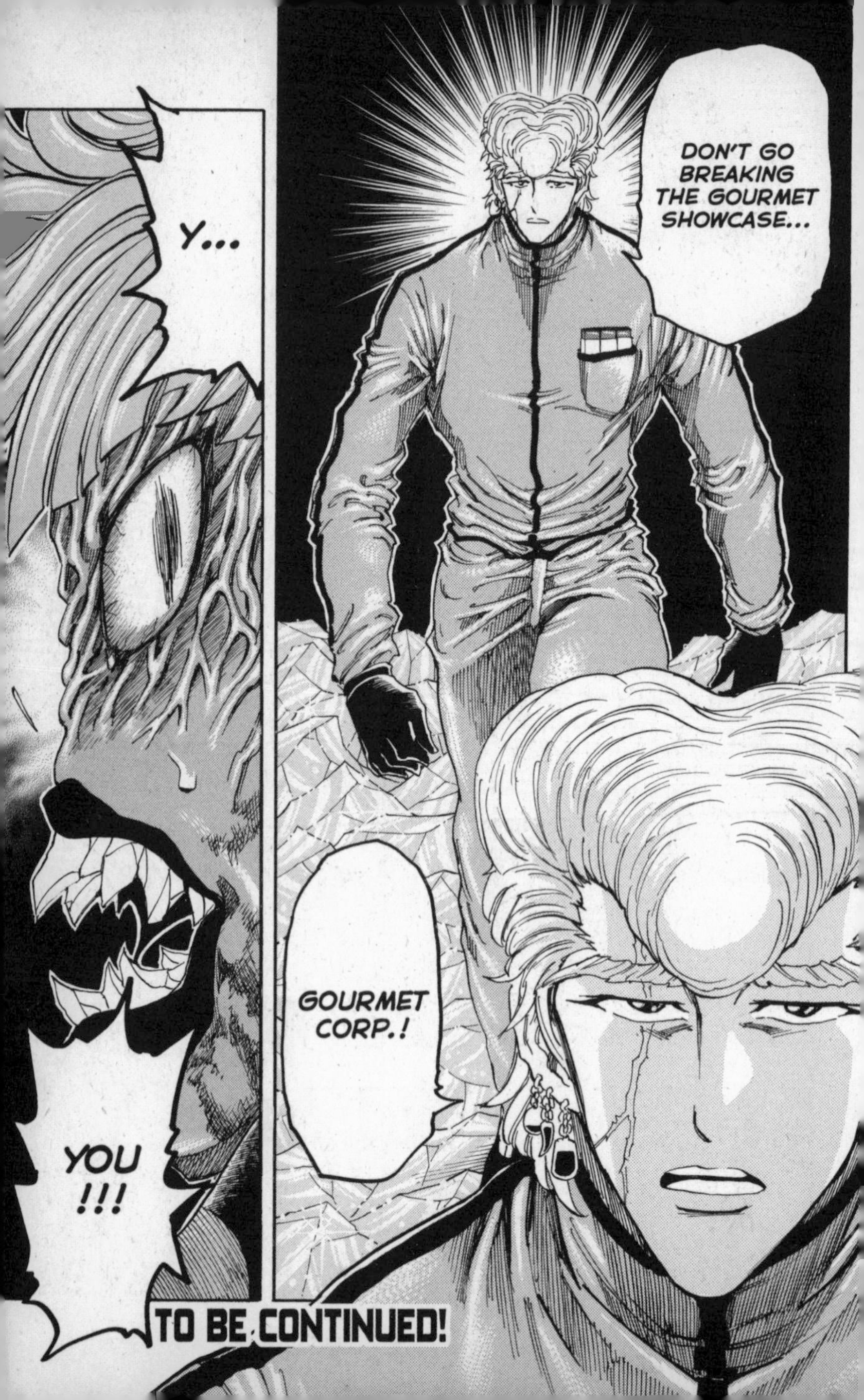
DON'T GO BREAKING THE GOURMET SHOWCASE...
GOURMET CORP.!
Y...
YOU !!!
TO BE CONTINUED!

TORIKO

GOURMET CHECKLIST

Vol. 087

TEN YOLK EGG

(EGG)

CAPTURE LEVEL: ---

HABITAT: THE NEST OF A TEN-FEATHERED GIANT CHICKEN ONCE IN A BLUE MOON

LENGTH: 9 CM

HEIGHT: ---

WEIGHT: 300 G

PRICE: 50,000 YEN PER EGG

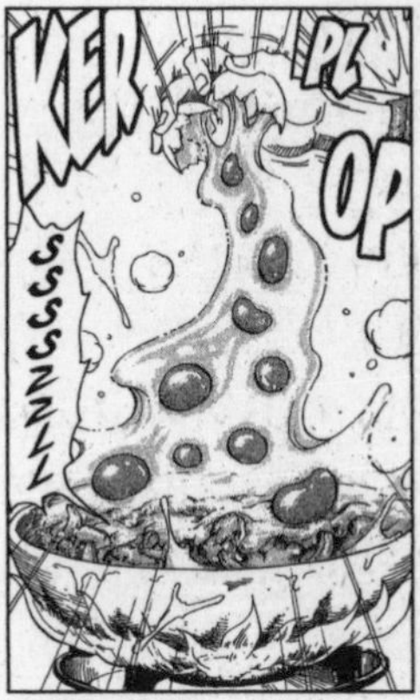
KER
PL
OP

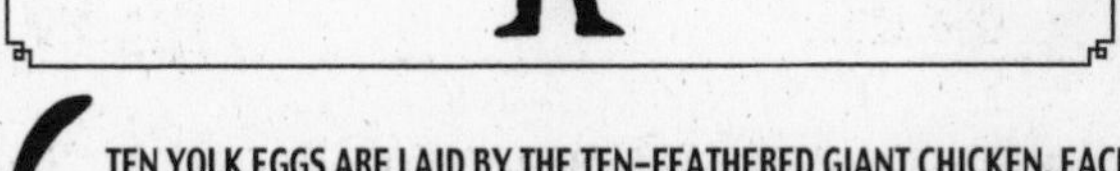

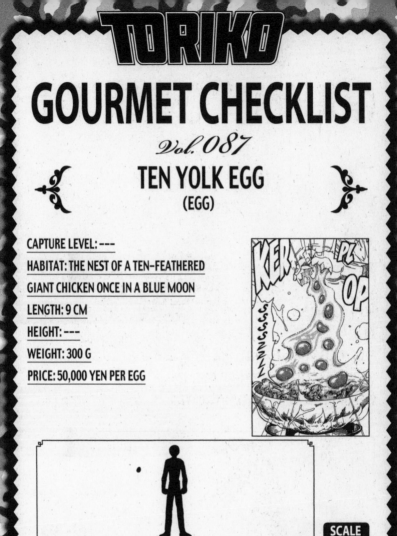

SCALE

TEN YOLK EGGS ARE LAID BY THE TEN-FEATHERED GIANT CHICKEN. EACH EGG CONTAINS TEN YOLKS. BECAUSE A TEN-FEATHERED GIANT CHICKEN ONLY LAYS ONE IN ITS ENTIRE LIFE, TEN YOLK EGGS ARE HARD TO COME BY AND VERY EXPENSIVE. THEY'RE SWEETER, MORE MELLOW, AND LOWER IN CHOLESTEROL THAN A NORMAL EGG. TURNS OUT IT'S THE EGG BEFORE THE CHICKEN IN TERMS OF PRICE--THE EGG SELLS FOR MUCH MORE THAN THE CHICKEN THAT LAID IT.

TORIKO

GOURMET CHECKLIST

Vol. 088

LONELY GRIZZLY
(MAMMAL)

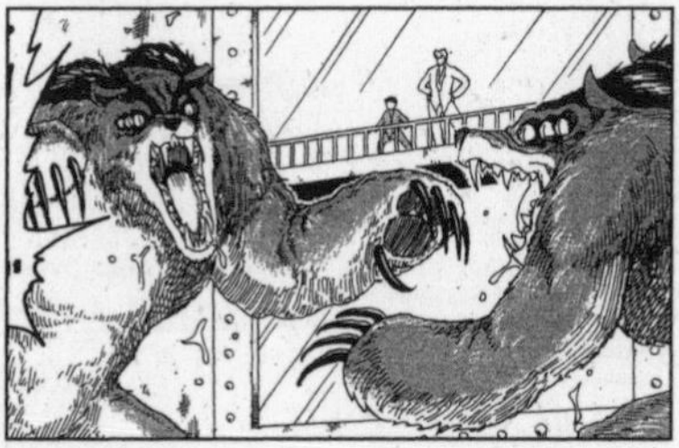

CAPTURE LEVEL: 37

HABITAT: HIGH TUNDRA

LENGTH: ---

HEIGHT: 16 METERS

WEIGHT: 12 TONS

PRICE: THEIR MEAT IS USUALLY TOO TOUGH FOR CONSUMPTION, BUT AFTER IT'S BEEN SOFTENED, 100 G GOES FOR 190,000 YEN.

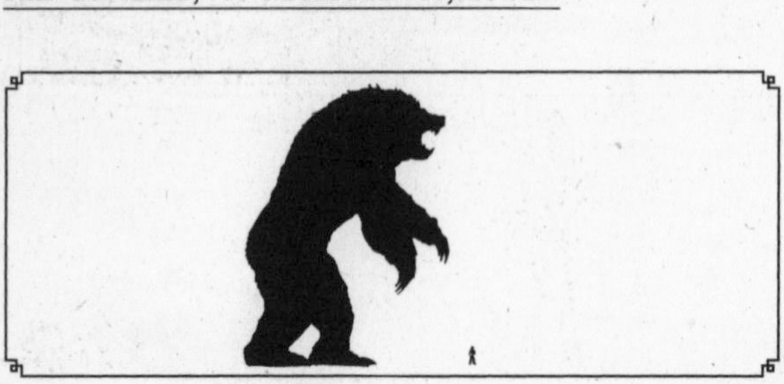

SCALE

USUALLY, THE LONELY GRIZZLY'S MEAT IS TOO TOUGH TO EAT, BUT BY KEEPING ONE IN A STATE OF BATTLE FOR LONG ENOUGH, ITS FLESH BECOMES SOFTER AND MORE DELICIOUS. TO GET THE LONELY GRIZZLY IN AN AGGRESSIVE ENOUGH STATE, IT MUST SEE ANOTHER MALE OF THE SAME SPECIES AND FIGHT IT FOR CLOSE TO A MONTH, DURING WHICH ITS MEAT INCREASES IN QUALITY. PEAK QUALITY LASTS ONLY FOR A COUPLE MINUTES, MEANING YOU HAVE MERE MINUTES TO KNOCK IT OUT AND PRESERVE THE MEAT. NO WONDER THIS FOOD HAS BEEN DESIGNATED AS NEEDING SPECIAL PREPARATION.

TORIKO

GOURMET CHECKLIST

Vol. 089

LOVE SARDINES
(FISH)

CAPTURE LEVEL: 11

HABITAT: WARM OCEAN WATERS

LENGTH: 20 CM

HEIGHT: ---

WEIGHT: 150 G

PRICE: 50,000 YEN PER FISH (250,000 YEN FOR PREGNANT FEMALES)

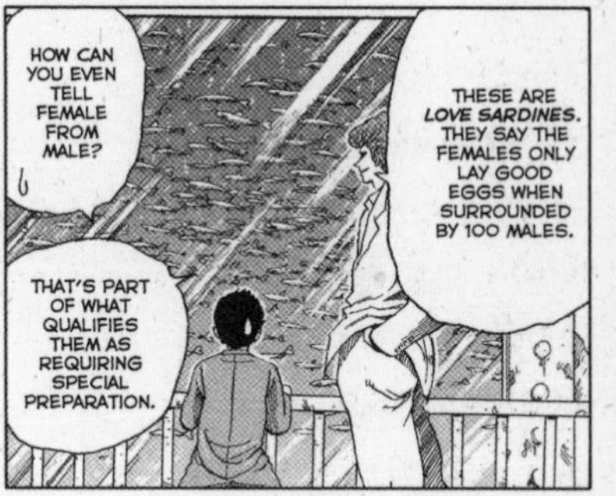
THESE ARE *LOVE SARDINES*. THEY SAY THE FEMALES ONLY LAY GOOD EGGS WHEN SURROUNDED BY 100 MALES.
HOW CAN YOU EVEN TELL FEMALE FROM MALE?
THAT'S PART OF WHAT QUALIFIES THEM AS REQUIRING SPECIAL PREPARATION.

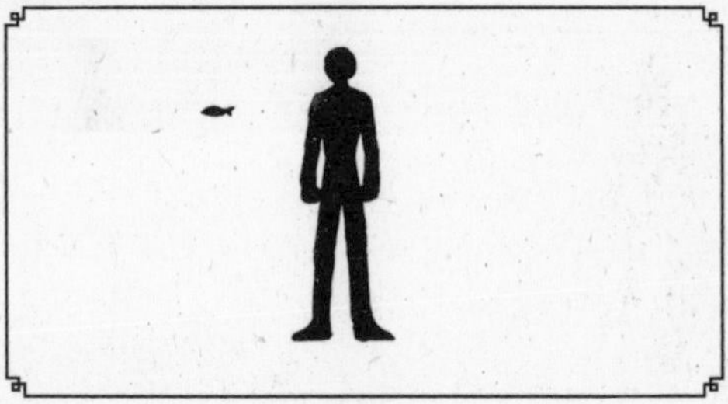

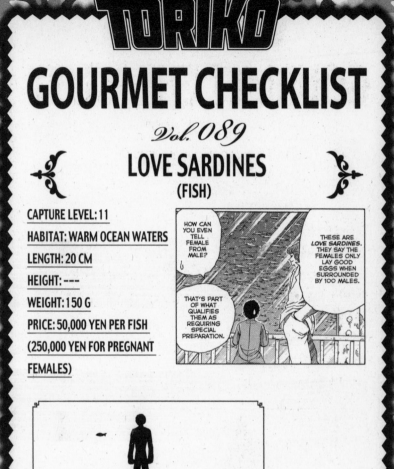

SCALE

THIS FOOD REQUIRES SPECIAL HANDLING, AS FEMALES WILL ONLY LAY HIGH-QUALITY EGGS WHEN SURROUNDED BY 100 MALES. THEY'RE NOT TOO DIFFICULT TO CATCH, BUT IT TAKES A SEASONED AND SKILLED CHEF TO BE ABLE TO DISCERN BETWEEN THE FEMALES AND THE MALES AND TO PROPERLY PREPARE THEM. IN FACT, THIS FOOD IS SO DIFFICULT TO PREPARE THAT IT WILL BRING A CHEF TO TEARS UNLESS THEY'RE DEAD SERIOUS ABOUT THE TASK.

TORIKO

GOURMET CHECKLIST

Vol. 090

PEACH POTATO
(VEGETABLE)

CAPTURE LEVEL: 2 (IN THE WILD)

HABITAT: FIELDS

(CAN ALSO BE ARTIFICIALLY CULTIVATED)

LENGTH: 10–20 CM

HEIGHT: ---

WEIGHT: 700–900 G

PRICE: 1,500 YEN PER POTATO

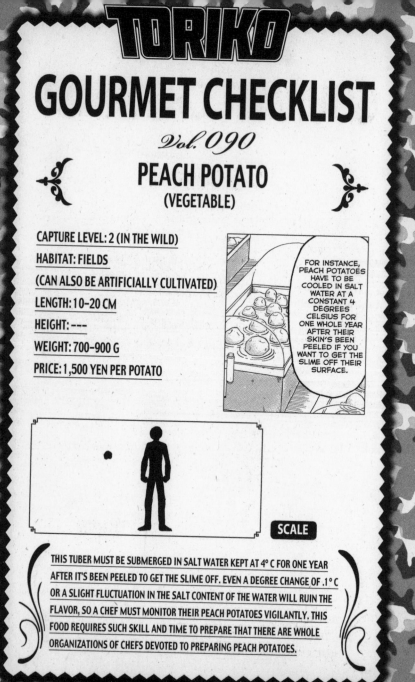

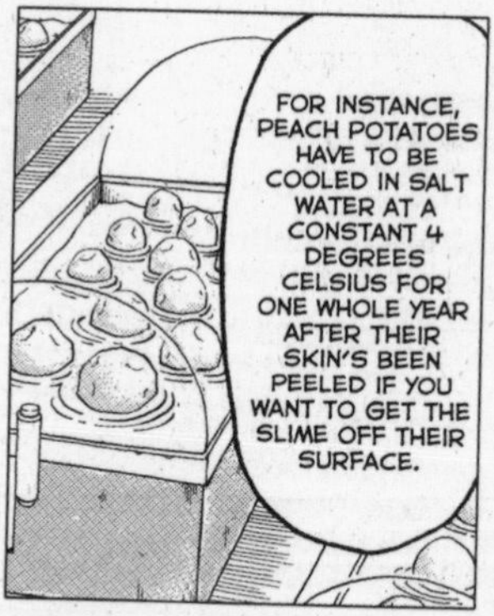
FOR INSTANCE, PEACH POTATOES HAVE TO BE COOLED IN SALT WATER AT A CONSTANT 4 DEGREES CELSIUS FOR ONE WHOLE YEAR AFTER THEIR SKIN'S BEEN PEELED IF YOU WANT TO GET THE SLIME OFF THEIR SURFACE.

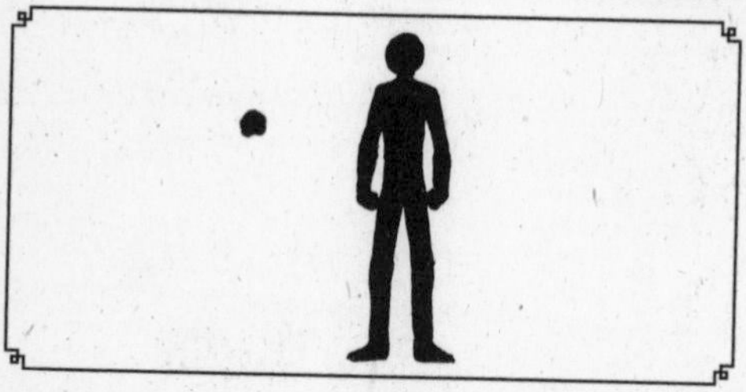

SCALE

THIS TUBER MUST BE SUBMERGED IN SALT WATER KEPT AT 4° C FOR ONE YEAR AFTER IT'S BEEN PEELED TO GET THE SLIME OFF. EVEN A DEGREE CHANGE OF .1° C OR A SLIGHT FLUCTUATION IN THE SALT CONTENT OF THE WATER WILL RUIN THE FLAVOR, SO A CHEF MUST MONITOR THEIR PEACH POTATOES VIGILANTLY. THIS FOOD REQUIRES SUCH SKILL AND TIME TO PREPARE THAT THERE ARE WHOLE ORGANIZATIONS OF CHEFS DEVOTED TO PREPARING PEACH POTATOES.

TORIKO

GOURMET CHECKLIST

Vol. 091

GORI LEEKS
(VEGETABLE)

CAPTURE LEVEL: LESS THAN 1 (IN THE WILD)

HABITAT: FIELDS (CAN ALSO BE ARTIFICIALLY CULTIVATED)

LENGTH: 50–70 CM

HEIGHT: ---

WEIGHT: 200 G PER BUNCH

PRICE: 1,000 YEN PER BUNCH

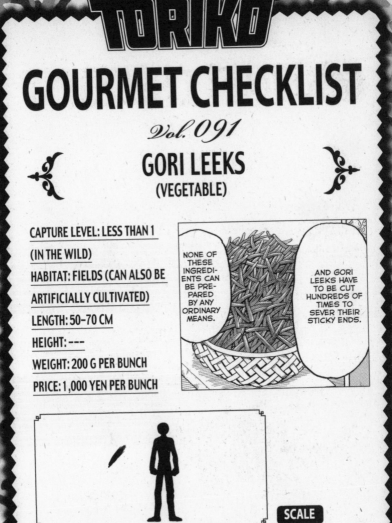

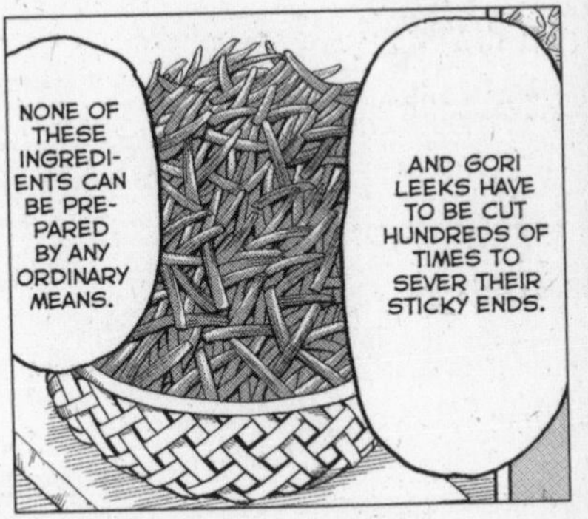
AND GORI LEEKS HAVE TO BE CUT HUNDREDS OF TIMES TO SEVER THEIR STICKY ENDS.
NONE OF THESE INGREDI-ENTS CAN BE PRE-PARED BY ANY ORDINARY MEANS.

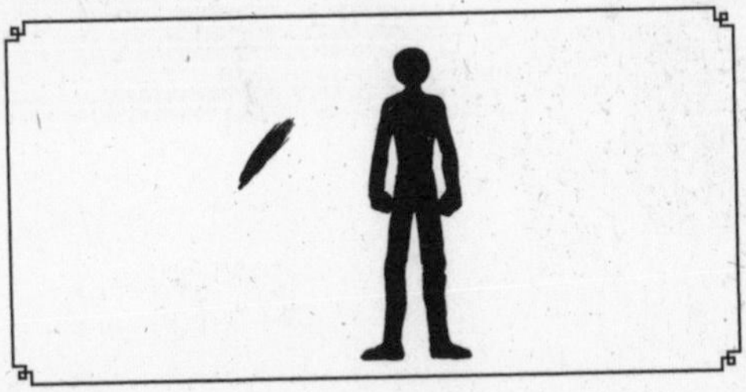

SCALE

WHEN CUT, THE SEVERED ENDS OF THIS PERENNIAL GRASS ARE SO STICKY THAT YOU HAVE TO SLICE THEM HUNDREDS OF TIMES TO TRULY SEPARATE THEM. IT'S NOT ONLY A MATTER OF STRONG SLICING, BUT PRECISION AS THE CUTS MUST BE MADE IN THE EXACT SAME SPOT. OTHERWISE, THE INJURED FIBERS BECOME BITTER AND THE FOOD IS NO LONGER FIT FOR CONSUMPTION. THIS FOOD DEMANDS THE PRECISE AND ACCURATE WIELDING OF A KNIFE.

TORIKO

GOURMET CHECKLIST

Vol. 092

GREAT LEG
(FISH)

CAPTURE LEVEL: 6

HABITAT: ICE HELL OCEANS

LENGTH: 8 METERS

HEIGHT: ---

WEIGHT: 1 TON

PRICE: 100 G / 2,100 YEN

GREAT LEG FISH CAPTURE LEVEL 6

SCALE

A SHARK CAPABLE OF LOCOMOTION ON LAND AND WATER. IT MOVES AS NIMBLY ON LAND AS IN THE SEA, BUT IT CAN ONLY STAY OUT FOR ONE HOUR. THE GREAT LEG IS RICH WITH FAT AND IT'S A FINE ADDITION TO ANY SASHIMI PLATTER. THIS FISH IS A VALUABLE SOURCE OF NUTRITION IN THE SUB-ZERO ENVIRONMENT IT CALLS HOME.

CHARACTER PROFILE

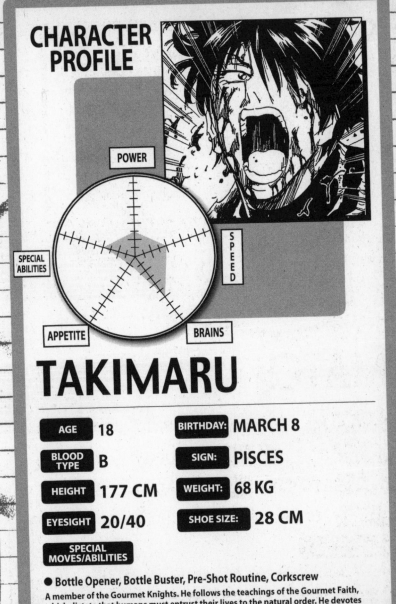

POWER

SPECIAL ABILITIES

SPEED

APPETITE

BRAINS

TAKIMARU

AGE	18	**BIRTHDAY:**	MARCH 8
BLOOD TYPE	B	**SIGN:**	PISCES
HEIGHT	177 CM	**WEIGHT:**	68 KG
EYESIGHT	20/40	**SHOE SIZE:**	28 CM

SPECIAL MOVES/ABILITIES

● Bottle Opener, Bottle Buster, Pre-Shot Routine, Corkscrew

A member of the Gourmet Knights. He follows the teachings of the Gourmet Faith, which dictate that humans must entrust their lives to the natural order. He devotes himself to eating humble fare in his daily life. He's a master of a martial art style that specializes in bone dislocation. He's still young and lacks experience, but is gifted with a pre-shot routine that could really take him places with some improvement.

CHARACTER PROFILE

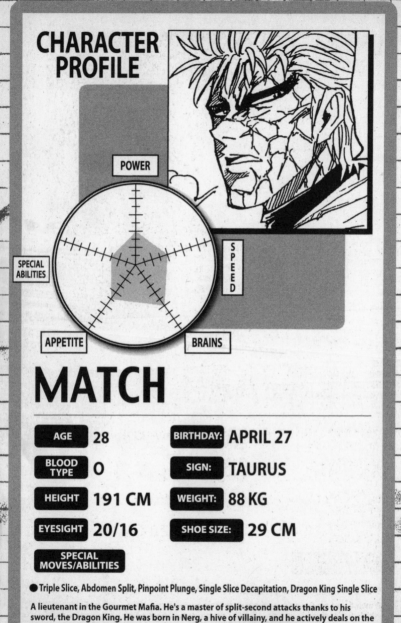

POWER

SPECIAL ABILITIES

SPEED

APPETITE

BRAINS

MATCH

AGE 28	**BIRTHDAY:** APRIL 27
BLOOD TYPE O	**SIGN:** TAURUS
HEIGHT 191 CM	**WEIGHT:** 88 KG
EYESIGHT 20/16	**SHOE SIZE:** 29 CM

SPECIAL MOVES/ABILITIES

● Triple Slice, Abdomen Split, Pinpoint Plunge, Single Slice Decapitation, Dragon King Single Slice

A lieutenant in the Gourmet Mafia. He's a master of split-second attacks thanks to his sword, the Dragon King. He was born in Nerg, a hive of villainy, and he actively deals on the black market. Still, this tough gangster is a big softie for kids, and gives food to the street children in Nerg. He's a Gourmet Robin Hood who takes from the rich to give to the poor.

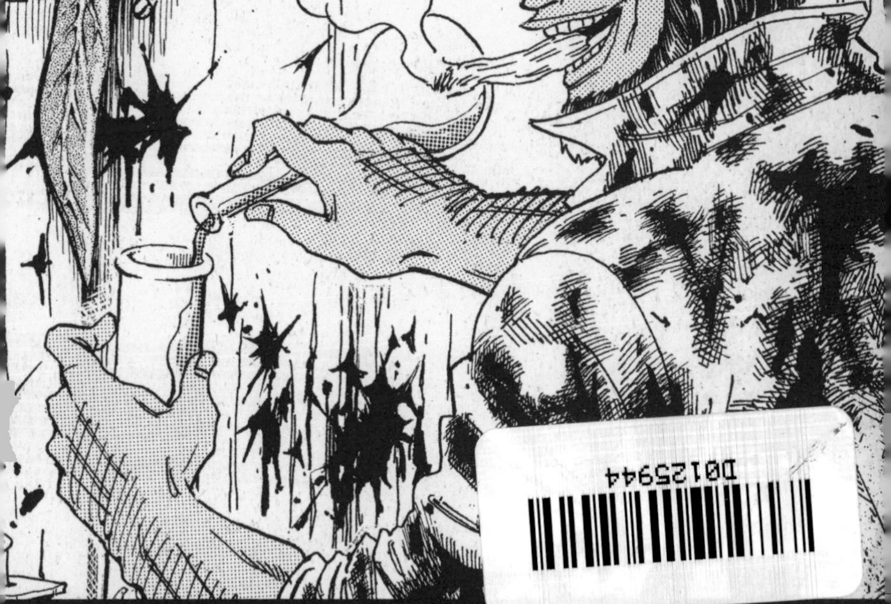

LONG ROAD TO RECOVERY

Toriko's fight with Gourmet Corp. has left him without an arm. While Komatsu continues the quest for Century Soup solo, Toriko journeys to Life, the country of healing, where getting some R&R turns into a bigger battle than anyone imagined.

AVAILABLE AUGUST 2012!